What P

˥ ....u ⊥uⵑⵦⵦ

Janet Boyer's newest take on the Tarot is sharp and saucy as F*&#. A few reasons you should strip down with Naked Tarot? 1. The correspondences are current and varied (I love interconnection!). 2. The face time given to the Minor Arcana and the Court Cards. Courts are difficult. This book lays them bare. 3. It's a fun read. Thanks to Janet's conversational flair, reading Naked Tarot is like chatting with a friend over tea. No. Make that a hot-pink Cosmo.

**Natalie Zaman,** Wandering Witch and author of *Magical Destinations of the Northeast* and *Color and Conjure*

In *Naked Tarot*, Janet Boyer leverages her significant experience with Tarot to break down each of the cards into impressive detail. While other books may tell you how each card's meaning changes with different questions and points of curiosity, *Naked Tarot* does it an utterly unique and sassy (sometimes, NSFW) way, calling up contexts and references I haven't seen in other books. From using the Tarot to explore a personality, find a career, solve a problem and deepen your spirituality—to divining the future and even discovering your Disney totem—*Naked Tarot* covers all the bases. It's a significant undertaking by someone well worthy of the task.

**Tierney Sadler,** author/Creator of *The Deck of 1000 Spreads*

*Naked Tarot* is the fresh voice of contemporary Tarot practice, leading the field toward greater accessibility. It speaks with 21st-century sensibilities. Janet Boyer tailors her book to modern culture, organized to fit seamlessly into the busy, hectic, and please-just-give-it-to-me-straight ethos of today. Yet, *Naked Tarot* deceives somewhat with its light humor: this is a serious, learned text that transfers the benefits of Ms. Boyer's depth and breadth of Tarot knowledge. The reader will digest every line—because it is just that accessible—and leave knowing more about the cards than most intermediate Tarot readers. In short, *Naked Tarot* does a phenomenal job of teaching Tarot. I love this book and had so much fun reading it. I laughed and smiled throughout.

**Benebell Wen,** author of *Holistic Tarot* (a much more boring book than *Naked Tarot*, I'm afraid to say)

Janet Boyer's writing style is blunt and lively, her knowledge of Tarot based on years of study and experience. I knew I was in for a treat when I read Naked Tarot—and her newest book did not disappoint. Janet conveys the essence of each card in a way that is easy to grasp and remember, largely because of her outrageous honesty. Even experienced readers will come away with a refreshing and novel way to view the cards To paraphrase the cinematic Mary Poppins, Janet provides us with that "spoon full of sugar" that helps the Tarot medicine go down.

**Anthony Louis,** author of Llewellyn's *Complete Book of Tarot: A Comprehensive Guide, Tarot Beyond the Basics, Tarot Plain and Simple* and other books

So much for the prettified and slightly vague Tarot books of the past. Janet Boyer takes the cards into dangerous territory in her latest book with whip-smart advice and a generous helping of humor. Forget the chanting and dewy-eyed mysticism, *Naked Tarot* speaks to you like a best friend—straight, to the point...and will help you bury the body later.

**Stacey Graham, literary agent and co-creator of** *the Zombie Tarot,* as well as author of *Haunted Stuff: Demonic Dolls, Screaming Skulls, and Other Creepy Collectibles* and *The Girls' Ghost Hunting Guide*

Janet Boyer's *Naked Tarot* is a comprehensive, straight-talking, irreverent guide to the Tarot—and then some! This isn't the same old typical Tarot book you've already read so many times before. Instead, Janet provides a fresh overview of Tarot, including insightful interpretations on the suits and cards, as well as new, thought-provoking and useful correspondences (flower essences, animal totems, spirits, Sabian symbols, crystals/stones and more) — not to mention a spread for *every* card. I know that I will actually USE this book, not just read it. Janet has outdone herself; in fact, *Naked Tarot* may be her best book yet.

**Judika Illes,** author of *Encyclopedia of 5000 Spells, Encyclopedia of Spirits, Encyclopedia of Mystics, Saints & Sages* and Other Books of Magic

Vibrant, witty, and full of wisdom, Janet Boyer's newest book, *Naked Tarot*, is a gourmet feast for those hungering for Tarot insights. Her words magically and magnetically guide us to consume her instructions and follow her astute pointers, helping us discover our core connections with each card. Because of Janet's upbeat tone, *Naked Tarot* is an easy read — yet the content is meaningfully deep and esoterically perceptive. Her reader-friendly discussions on how to use the cards are thoughtfully detailed and well organized. Positively delightful, the book assists beginning readers in developing a firm foundation for building their Tarot practice, while also providing tools enabling the advanced reader to soar to new mystical heights.

**Kooch Daniels,** author of *Tarot at a Crossroads, Tarot d'Amour, Awakening the Chakras* and Other Metaphysical Books

We loved Janet Boyer's new book — a modern, clever twist on Tarot that's chock full of irreverent wisdom. Wickedly witty, piercingly perceptive and delightfully snarky, *Naked Tarot* will have you laughing out loud. This savvy Queen of Swords cuts straight through to the truth — and oh boy, does Janet know her Tarot! She's gifted at conveying human strengths and frailties with her interpretations, correlations and spreads for each card.

**The Psychic Twins (Linda and Terry Jamison),** World Renowned Psychics and authors of *Psychic Intelligence: Tune in and Discover the Power of Your Intuition*

*Naked Tarot* is a bold, brassy, in-your-face look at the world of Tarot cards and how they relate to humanity in all its glory—including its sexuality, its faults, and its quirks—embracing the beautiful, stark reality of it all. The cards are stripped clean of a "G" rating, no punches pulled. The world of the Tarot and our nitty-gritty lives are laid bare for brutal examination. Janet Boyer's *Naked Tarot* is one of the boldest, most honest looks at Tarot interpretation yet. You'll either be laughing your ass off, nodding your head enthusiastically in agreement...or you will be left open-mouthed, newly baptized into what's commonly called "The Real World".

**Amythyst Raine,** author of *Tarot for Grownups, Tarot: A Witch's Journey* and *The Gray Witch's Grimoire*

Janet Boyer's latest work, *Naked Tarot*, is destined to be an instant classic! Truly a gift to Tarot readers everywhere, this book contains endless juicy contemporary information and associations. I see this book as Janet's Magnum Opus—and a must-have Tarot textbook. This is NOT another dry Tarot "cookbook", listing the same outdated keywords and correspondences. Whether you're a brand new Tarot reader or an old hand, *Naked Tarot* will help you connect with the Tarot like never before!

**Dax Carlisle, DD, CHt, CTM,** President of The Tarot Guild

Straightforward, different and full of useful advice for the Tarot student seeking new perspectives on the cards, *Naked Tarot* is refreshingly practical!

**Melanie Marquis,** author of *Modern Spellcaster's Tarot, The Witch's Bag of Tricks* and *A Witch's World of Magick*

This ain't yer mama's Tarot book...Janet Boyer's newest effort—*Naked Tarot*—is without a doubt one of the best "boot camp" Tarot books I've seen in a long, long time. No frills and no excess verbiage, no mystical waving about of incense or charged crystals, this is a straight up, in-your-face approach to learning the cards. The blunt cleverness of the descriptions combined with snarky, wickedly funny practical applications will bring both a smile to your face and a clear, precise image for all 78 cards.

If you have a problem with language (read: the occasional F-bomb), this likely isn't your book. If you want a dusty reference book that takes itself *way* too seriously, *Naked Tarot* is definitely not for you. If you want to have a deep understanding of the cards without having to wade through stacks of inconsequential details, you've struck pay dirt. After all, you don't need to know how to build a watch in order to tell time. I consider *Naked Tarot* a wonderful new resource and, at the risk of fan girl gushing, I can't recommend it highly enough!

**Shannon MacLeod,** author of *The Celtic Cross Spread: Cutting to the Chase* and co-creator of the *ShadowFox Tarot*

Janet Boyer's newest book *Naked Tarot* is a hard hitting, belly-laugh inducing, no-nonsense guide to Tarot. Its audience, from beginners through experienced readers, can aim for the underbelly with their clients with the help of this book. Drilling straight to the core, *Naked Tarot* enables the cards to reveal depth, hurt and hope in a contemporary language. It broadens the reader's horizons with innovative spreads and correspondences— including Australian Flower Essences. I couldn't put in down; it was like reading a racy Tarot thriller on a rollercoaster! *Naked Tarot* deserves to be a key Tarot text for those readers with a contemporary, direct style.

**Jenne Perlstein, MBBS, BSW, AASW,** Professional Member of the Australian Tarot Guild

# Naked
# Tarot

Sassy, Stripped-Down Advice

# Naked
# Tarot

## Sassy, Stripped-Down Advice

Janet Boyer

Winchester, UK
Washington, USA

First published by Dodona Books, 2018
Dodona Books is an imprint of John Hunt Publishing Ltd., No. 3 East Street,
Alresford, Hampshire SO24 9EE, UK
office1@jhpbooks.net
www.johnhuntpublishing.com
www.dodona-books.com

For distributor details and how to order please visit the 'Ordering' section on our website.

Text copyright: Janet Boyer 2017

ISBN: 978 1 78279 213 0
978 1 78279 212 3 (ebook)
Library of Congress Control Number: 2017940003

All rights reserved. Except for brief quotations in critical articles or reviews, no part of this
book may be reproduced in any manner without prior written permission from the publishers.

The rights of Janet Boyer as author have been asserted in accordance with the Copyright,
Designs and Patents Act 1988.

A CIP catalogue record for this book is available from the British Library.

Design: Stuart Davies

Printed and bound by CPI Group (UK) Ltd, Croydon, CR0 4YY, UK

We operate a distinctive and ethical publishing philosophy in
all areas of our business, from our global network of authors to
production and worldwide distribution.

# Contents

How awesome are my husband and son...let me count the ways. Bear huggers, hand holders, tear dryers, cheerleaders, counselors, best friends—my treasured, beloved Soul Group. Mere "thanks" (for all the fish) doesn't seem adequate. I guess I'll "pay you for this" with continued love and gratitude. (Noah, if you're reading this before age 30, close the book. *Now*. I mean it.)

# Eight Implications of Nakedness

1. **Nakedness implies vulnerability.** "The ability to tolerate a heightened awareness of vulnerability is crucial to resiliency and endurance." *Naked Tarot* offers durable tips for gaining confidence in the face of all the points of vulnerability that come with being a complex individual.

2. **Nakedness implies at-one-ment.** "It can be about a sense of feeling at one with one's environment." That's because nakedness "importantly removes all outward signs of rank, profession, and outward activity." By doing so, "it focuses on the ground floor of human character—the sensory, sensual, and material nature of the human body and its engagement with its environment." *Naked Tarot* begins on the ground floor but never condescends.

3. **Nakedness implies timelessness.** All solemn rites of nakedness take us back to that paradisiacal Garden of ancient lore, because "paradise implies the absence of 'clothing'—that is, of 'wear and tear' (an archetypal image of Time)." *Naked Tarot* strips away superficialities to reveal timeless wisdom.

4. **Nakedness implies the soul.** In sacred writings, the world's first couple was in a state of innocence and was naked but unashamed. *Naked Tarot* is absolutely unashamed.

5. **Nakedness implies freedom.** Unrestricted by clothes, one enjoys "a new sense of honesty, openness, and a carefree nature." *Naked Tarot* models an honest, open, carefree approach.

6. **Nakedness implies plenitude.** "It is a total presence offering itself for contemplation." *Naked Tarot* offers a

cornucopia of material to contemplate.

7. **Nakedness implies sharing.** "An emotional sharing of one's deepest self, and doing so without any need to hide." *Naked Tarot* invites you to share in a learning experience that's anything but superficial.

8. **Nakedness implies a full reveal.** Indeed, "Nakedness is a promise of a truth that abandons all the covering and sheltering layers and reveals the essence behind all things." *Naked Tarot* holds nothing back.

— **Craig Conley**, creator of the *Tarot of Portmeirion* and author of *The Young Wizard's Hexopedia: A Guide to Magical Words and Phrases*, *Magic Words: A Dictionary*, *One-Letter Words: A Dictionary* plus many other eccentric, innovative titles.

# Acknowledgements

Energetically speaking, this book took a small army to write. I'm grateful to have faithful friends, supportive fans and unseen helpers who provide love, encouragement and inspiration. Among them: Jesus (always), Ganesh (for the rough spots) and Saint Expeditus (thanks for the last-minute aid, new Friend!). On the Other Side, Sandra Seich, brilliant creator of the ANSIR personality system: much gratitude for the boost with the Court Cards. I could feel you! I miss you. Miss you, too, Neo—our beloved black cat: we know you're having fun chasing butterflies around the Rainbow Bridge. And to Mr. Rogers, my Patron Saint; thanks for being my neighbor.

Ginormous thanks to my husband, Ron, for his eagle eye proofreading—and to our son, Noah, for his help with pop culture and historical research. Love you bunches! And of course, the fur babies—Stewart and Quebie. ::head butts::

Heartfelt appreciation to the brilliant and quirky Craig Conley for the best Foreword *ever*; I'm so honored. Much love to my friend, Judika Illes, who played a big part in helping my first book, *Back in Time Tarot*, reach publication. Your books *Encyclopedia of Mystics, Saints & Sages* and *Encyclopedia of Spirits* are among my favorite tomes—and were a *huge* help for selecting the Mystical Messengers for each card. Your scholarship is such a gift to the world!

Big Thank-Yous and cyber-hugs to Facebook Friends Jamme Chantler (co-owner of *Thelonius Monkfish*) for the gift of Starbucks, this book's cover image and the queries *"When is your book with all the cussing coming out?"*; Angie Turner (geek/fan girl extraordinaire...love you, girlfriend!); Catherine Clayton; Shari Good (bless you for your encouragement!); Anne "Bagger Vance" Williamson (your thoughtful notes are such a blessing); Bea Potrony; Beth McKinney Langis. Appreciation to Theresa Reed

(The Tarot Lady) and Holly Heffelbower for their encouraging "You've *got* this!" tweets. Gratitude to Anne Newkirk Niven (publisher of *Witches&Pagans* and *Sage Woman*), for providing me a voice in her magazines and online at my *Sacred Symbols* PaganSquare blog), and to Jim Harold (of *Paranormal Podcast* and *Campfire* fame), for always giving me a platform.

Much gratitude to colleagues, authors and Tarot professionals who provided generous praise for, and about, *Naked Tarot*: Anthony Louis, Tierney Sadler, Jenne Perlstein, Dax Carlisle, Melanie Marquis, Stacey Graham, The Psychic Twins (Linda and Terry Jamison), Benebell Wen, Amythyst Raine, Shannon MacLeod, Natalie Zaman, Judika Illes and Kooch Daniels.

To all who've purchased our decks or oracles—or my books, classes, readings or workshops (::waves to Zac Flack, Willow Merrymoon, Teresa Mills, Tricia Carroll and Aja Martinez, especially::)—bless your heart: sales are one confirmation of value provided. To my Newsletter subscribers, some who've been with me for over a decade, thank you for welcoming me into your inbox. Many thanks to all the hardworking folks at John Hunt Publishing/Dodona Books for daring to publish *Naked Tarot*, and for making it beautiful. Extra gratitude to my "Boss", Maria Moloney, for her guidance, meticulousness, encouragement and good humor. And finally, appreciation to you, Dear Reader. You are brave for buying and reading this book. I trust you'll be duly compensated with illumination, inspiration and amusement; if you are, I'll consider this book a success.

RIP Terry Donaldson, who passed away during the writing of this book.

# Introduction

Greetings, adventurous seeker! If you're curious about Tarot, but want (*need?*) a down-in-the-trenches Guide who will give it to you straight—I'm the gal for you!

Unfortunately, most Tarot books gloss over the harsh realities we often live through, providing pages of dry, boring, irrelevant esoterica instead of sharing practical, relatable and understandable advice.

I've decided to remedy this by writing *Naked Tarot*—a years-long project filled with hard-won advice, down-and-dirty interpretations, modern scenarios, pop culture references...and some cussing. *Ha!*

I'm utterly thrilled that you've got your hot little hands on this book. You'll be surprised, challenged, encouraged and entertained along the way. Expect some LOLz, too!

For each card in the Tarot (all 78), I'm excited to present:

- Stripped Down Overview
- Keywords
- Personifications and Embodiments
- Quote
- Challenge
- Gift
- Occupations/Vocations
- Correspondences
  - Disney Totem
  - Animal Symbol
  - Flower Essences
  - Crystal/Stone
  - Aromatherapy
  - Body Parts/Systems and Health Issues
  - Mystical Messenger

- ⚔ Sabian Symbol
- **Writing Prompt**
- **Affirmation**
- **Naked Advice for:**
  - ⚔ Career
  - ⚔ Romance
  - ⚔ Parenting
  - ⚔ Spirituality
- **Recommended Resources**
- **Spread 'Em** (Card layout that serves double-duty as journaling prompts)

The Court Cards get extra goodies, but more about that in a bit.

In case you're wondering if I'm *really* qualified to write advice about Career, Romance, Parenting and Spirituality advice, let me give you some background on my life.

Relationship wise, I married my High School sweetheart when I was almost 19 (began dating him when I was 15). After 7 years of marriage, he succumbed to leukemia. After a year of widowhood, I met my present husband. By the time this book gets into your hands, we'll have been happily married for 20 years (that's 27 years of marriage, total).

This brings me to Career and Spirituality. For four years, I attended Valley Forge University (then, Valley Forge Christian College) near Philadelphia, Pennsylvania, majoring in Theology/Pastoral Ministry with a double minor in English and Psychology. Ever since I was very young, I had been aware of "God" — obtaining insights that was apart from my indoctrination. I had the entire King James Bible read by the time I was fourteen — and a good chunk of it (especially the New Testament) memorized. I became ordained through two organizations and co-pastored a church with my first husband, serving as a spiritual counselor and teacher. He resigned because of not feeling well — which turned out to be more than a chronic flu...

During my widowhood, I started my own interior design and decorating business, which was quite successful. I was also a Sunday School and Bible teacher. It was then that I met my present husband, Ron, who happened to be one of my students (never fear—it was a Young Adult/College-age class). We became fast friends, bonding over art and deep discussions on meaning, spirituality and navigating this world. After three weeks of becoming inseparable best friends, we knew we had found our respective soul mates. Within six weeks of meeting, we were married. Three months later, we were pregnant. Eventually, I left ministry and interior design to become a full-time mom. (Why did I leave ministry? Long story. Mostly? Rampant sexism and discrimination within the Assemblies of God and other Pentecostal/Charismatic churches who *say* they approve of women ministers but, in practice, will tell you to your face, "*I won't put you on staff because you're a woman. It's not the men from the congregation I worry about. It's the other women in the church.*" Mmmkay...)

So, the Parenting thing: our son, Noah, will be 19 by the time you read this—quite the handsome, witty, kind, polite, generous and creative young man. He was diagnosed on the Autism spectrum when he was four years old—and we had some very rough years. Through some cognitive and speech therapy—as well as my choice to refuse ABA ("dog training") in favor of following my intuition (which, I later found out was similar to the Son Rise model), our son eventually tested as NOT being on the spectrum any longer. After meeting and talking with our son, a friend of mine—a neuropsychologist from NYC—said, "*No WAY is he on the spectrum. He seeks out eye contact—and is attentive and empathetic. He may learn differently from most, but certainly isn't on the Autism/Aspergers continuum.*" In fact, Noah has starred in two musical theater productions (*Mary Poppins* and *Shrek*), written eight original piano compositions (oh, did

I mention he just "picked it up"—doing two-handed scales by his second lesson?) and designs men's clothing (look for a BINT, coming to a store near you...or maybe Etsy). I say all this not to brag on my son (although he's certainly brag-worthy!), but to establish that I've weathered some serious parental storms: we went from my son saying his ABCs and babbling words... to losing his speech right after a MMR vaccination. (Yeah, don't believe that that "Vaccinations don't cause Autism" shit; go watch the movie *Vaxxed*.) He would have inexplicable tantrums, as well as the inability to tolerate loud noises, touching or external stimulation (we used to dread going to restaurants or grocery stores). Now? He's the shiniest human I've ever encountered. Sweetness personified, truly.

Which brings me back to Career: When our son was around eight, I started another career as a writer and intuitive counselor—all while homeschooling him. In 2008, my first book, *Back in Time Tarot*, was released by Hampton Roads. In 2012, *Tarot in Reverse* came out—and my husband and I published our *Snowland Deck* (SnowlandDeck.com). In the interim, I became an Amazon.com Hall of Fame Reviewer (with over 1,200 reviews to my name—there's only about 125 of us in the world) and have had articles, features, reviews and my popular AstroTarot Forecast published in print and digital magazines like *Sedona Journal of Emergence* and *Witches&Pagans*. Since then, I've co-created the *Coffee Tarot* with my husband (Tarot.Coffee), the *Boyer Charming Oracle* and the *Animal Totem Charms Oracle* with my son (CharmingOracle.com), hosted my own radio show and guest appeared on other shows (including the national *Coast to Coast AM with George Noory* where I talked Tarot), and the popular Paranormal Podcast with Jim Harold, where I often discuss divination practices.

I've always done my own website work, graphics design, social media, querying and editing. I taught myself to write well (with the help of my English teachers and excellent how-to books)—as well as taught myself the Tarot. I handle all my financial paperwork, taxes, contracts and secretarial duties—as well as that of my family.

And I *did* mention that I've homeschooled my son since kindergarten, right?

The point being, *yes!*—I am qualified to offer you advice in the areas of Career, Romance, Parenting and Spirituality (hard won, no less)! And I felt it was important to share with you that I *was*, because nothing makes me lose respect for a teacher or author faster than discovering that they're presenting information or instruction on a topic they have *no* personal experience with— especially when they're just regurgitating what they've heard or read from someone else (who said it much better). I mean, single, childless people giving marriage and parenting advice? *Puh-leeze.*

*Whew!* With that behind us, I'm tickled pink to tell you about a section of the book I'm *especially* excited about: the Court Cards.

The Court Cards normally get short shrift in most (all?) Tarot books, so I've created juicy, fleshed-out profiles of all 16 of these babies, correlating them to modern personality systems like the Enneagram, ANSIR, MBTI/Keirsey and StrengthsFinder 2.0. I've also included extra associations like Nicknames, Love Languages, Ways to His Heart and more. When a Court Card comes up in intuitive readings or random draws for creative writing, you'll never struggle with wondering *"Who the hell is this?"* again!

So, are you ready to get naked, brave reader? Let's strip down and skinny dip into the bracing, clear, refreshing waters of Tarot clarity!

# Note from the Author

No one was hurt during the making of this book. Let's keep it that way now that *Naked Tarot* is in your hands. ::wink:: Nothing is personal unless *you* make it so. If you are prone to taking things personally, may I humbly suggest that you read *The Four Agreements* by Don Miguel Ruiz. Take some deep breaths. Then *come back* to reading *Naked Tarot*: what pricks us shows us what needs to be healed and integrated in our psyche. It's a *good* type of pain (if you want to grow).

## About Gender

In *Naked Tarot*, I use the gender pronouns "he" and "she" rather haphazardly. Please don't construe them as definitive or biased; it's just faster and easier for me to write either "he" or "she" than the oft-debated "they" — or the more modern "ze" or "zir". Sometimes, I use wo/man, to imply either a man or a woman. This book was written for *all* seekers, regardless of gender identification, sexual orientation or relationship preference.

# Ways to Use the Tarot

The striking images of the Tarot often appear mysterious, beckoning us to draw closer and learn of their secrets. While some choose to use the Tarot for predictive purposes, the metaphorical symbols can do so much more. In fact, many who work with Tarot do not use the cards for prediction at all! Here are but a few ways to enjoy and utilize the Tarot:

**Problem Solving and Self-Development** – Tarot cards provide an excellent springboard for identifying, analyzing, and working through challenging situations. Draw a card and have an imaginary conversation with it. What advice might it give you if it could "speak"? Alternatively, look through a deck and pick a card that represents how you're feeling now; then, pick another representing how you'd like to feel. How might you get from here to there? You can also use Tarot for brainstorming and planning. (Mark McElroy has written several excellent books using the cards for this purpose; *What's in the Cards for You?* is my favorite.) Tarot allows us to "freeze" different aspects of a situation, promoting objectivity, awareness, clarity and empowered choice.

**Creativity** – Are you a writer, artist or musician? The cards can inspire ideas, plots, themes and direction. For example, draw a card and write a song or create a painting based on how the image makes you feel. Or, write a short story based on three cards drawn at random: Card 1 represents one person, Card 2 represents another person, and Card 3 represents the nature of the conflict or situation involving them both. Alternatively, draw several cards and tell a story based on what you see.

**Dream Interpretation** – The rich symbolism of the Tarot can provide helpful clues to the meaning of dreams. You could choose a Tarot card for each of the elements contained within a dream, or draw several cards to specifically address the theme and its relevant message.

**Meditation and Visualization** – If your spiritual path uses rituals or altars, you can use one or more Tarot cards as a sacred tool for meditation, contemplation, and intention. For example, if you're feeling vulnerable, you could meditate on the Strength card. If you feel pulled in a hundred directions and long for time alone, you could cultivate an atmosphere of spiritual retreat and social withdrawal by meditating on the Hermit.

**Education and Intellectual Stimulation** – The Tarot can be as simple or as complex as you'd like it to be, depending on your preferences. When reading the cards you can simply "say what you see" as author Wilma Carroll encourages, or you can explore esoteric Tarot symbolism, numerology, astrology, Qabalah, western magickal traditions (such as the Order of the Golden Dawn) and much more.

**Divination and Psychic Development** – Asking questions of the Tarot and using spreads (card layouts) can help you tap into the collective unconscious, develop symbolic sight and stretch your intuitive potential. Testing the Tarot—and yourself—increases trust in innate abilities, creates personal meaning and demonstrates the power of co-creating reality.

**Communication** – If you'd like to bridge a communication gap between yourself and a child, partner, relative or friend, using the Tarot can help. Whomever you'd like to understand better, invite her to join you for lunch, tea or coffee in a private place. Ask her if she'd play a "getting to know" you game, handing her a deck of fully animated Tarot cards (that is, a Minor Arcana that shows people or figures doing something). Instruct her to go through the deck, choosing cards that reflect how she feels and what she thinks right now. Then, you do the same. Talk about the cards you chose. To "bridge" any conflicts, misunderstandings or challenges, go through the deck again and both of you choose a card (or cards) that best reflect how you may better connect with one another.

# How Does Divination Work?

Humans have practiced divination for thousands of years. The word *divination* shares the same root as the word divine, so most people have assumed that the information received through divination comes from a divine source—God, Goddess, Great Spirit, etc. Divination was often used by human oracles—shamans, prophets and religious leaders who were trained to discern and interpret omens, symbols, and messages. In many respects, the diviner served as a bridge between the Divine and everyday folks.

For some civilizations, though, divination was a normal part of living for all people. In the early Christian tradition, some people were said to have the "gift of prophecy" and delivered messages from God. However, adherents of this religion believed there were two sources for "supernatural" information: God and the devil. Therefore, it was possible for some individuals to manifest "counterfeit" psychic gifts that were demonic in nature. In fact, fortunetelling was often forbidden in the Judeo-Christian belief system, despite the fact that there are numerous accounts of divination performed by "heroes of the faith".

There are several theories about how divination works, but the foundation for *all* of the following theories is a belief in an ordered Universe—and that there is no such thing as accidents or coincidences:

**Divine Source** – This is rather straightforward: it is belief that information received through divination comes straight from a Divine Source—a spiritual Intelligence. Those who believe in an evil counterpart to the Divine, such as a devil or demons, believe that information can come from that source, as well.

**Synchronicity** – Swiss psychiatrist and psychologist Carl Gustav

Jung (1875–1961) coined the term *synchronicity* to explain that coinciding events have meaning. A student of symbol and myth, as well as the divination method of Tarot, Jung believed that nothing was random, and everything happens for a reason. When consulting a divinatory tool, the individual will receive a message pertinent to his or her concerns and questions.

**Collective Unconscious** – Jung also believed in a *collective unconscious*, which is a vast database where information about every person, object and event is stored. This collective unconscious could be accessed through archetypal recognition, hypnosis, dreaming and divination.

**Higher Self** – Some believe that the subconscious exerts an energetic force that affects divination tools. Our "Higher Self" or "spirit" already knows the information that is sought, as well as what's best for us. By using divination, we tap into this "Higher Self", bypassing the conscious, rational mind.

**Macrocosm/Microcosm** – Ancient civilizations believed that everything was connected through patterns of energy and universal laws. Divination was seen as a microcosm that reflected larger patterns of energy—the macrocosm. Modern man often assumed that these beliefs and practices were mere primitive superstitions. However, with the advent of scientific discoveries such as the theory of relativity, chaos theory, quantum physics and so on, many are realizing that science is now confirming these ancient metaphysical beliefs and practices.

**Intuition** – Believed to be a part of the brain, intuition is a "sixth sense" whereby information is directly perceived by means outside of the five senses. That is, a "knowing" not based on rational understanding or the "facts". Many believe that human intuition is in a state of evolution, especially as civilizations become more complex. We no longer need the daily "flight or fight" survival instinct that our ancestors once did, but rather, a "higher" form of knowing and understanding outside the realm of ego. Psychologist Benjamin Libert analyzed EEG results of subjects, nothing the precise moment when each decided to act *prior* to a simple behavior (like moving their fingers). Interestingly, Libert discovered that the brain responds a few milliseconds *before* the decision to act, and termed this "readiness potential". Some call this a "readiness wave", likened to a signal emitted from the frontal cortex of the brain into the surrounding area of the thinker. These signals relate to thought and experience, before the actual occurrence of those thoughts or experiences.

**Psychic Gifts** – Whether manifested through the human body (DNA/natural ability) or as a "supernatural" gift (bestowed by a divine source), some believe that certain individuals are born psychic and others are not.

**Akashic Record** – With divination methods such as clairvoyance, dream interpretation, and channeling, there is a belief in a cosmic library where every conversation and event on the earth plane is recorded in "life books". When an individual is attuned to the Holy Spirit, universal consciousness, and the "other side", he or she is able to read these books, known as the Akashic Record. Information from these books travel on light waves and are received by the diviner. Some believe that the Akashic Record is the same thing as Jung's collective unconscious.

So what happens when a Tarot reading or prediction often comes to pass? I believe that, in most cases, the diviner is reading the present energy surrounding a situation or person. Because most people are resistant to change, living their lives in the well-worn grooves of familiarity and habit, that which is discerned in the *present* comes to pass in the *future*. It's easier to determine outcomes than one might think: examining an individual's past and present is often a good determinant of where they're headed simply because of inertia. If the driver of a car never turns the steering wheel, she'll continue along the same direction that she's been traveling.

Thus, if you want to know where someone is heading, simply look at where they've been.

However, those who decide to exercise their free will with conscious choice can change the direction of their life. Your past does not equal your future, even if that's the case for most people. Thus, messages received through divination are not set in stone but, rather, are fluid in nature.

It is my belief that everyone can access their intuitive abilities, and use divination to understand their past, present and future. When we practice divination with the intent of seeking guidance for self-growth and understanding, we exercise our 6th chakra, also known as the Brow Chakra or the Third Eye.

# Anatomy of a Tarot Deck

A Tarot deck consists of 78 cards: 16 Court Cards, 40 Minor Arcana Cards and 22 Major Arcana Cards. I like to think of them as **Who**, **What/How** and **Why**.

- **Who (*Court Cards*)** – An actor in life's drama. A role being played, an approach to a situation, a significant person involved in the circumstance at hand or a character in a story or the seeker consulting the cards.

- **What and How (*Minor Arcana Cards*)** – The stage of life's drama. How everything plays out: work, relationships, thoughts, passions, conversations, career, hobbies, challenges, triumphs, disappointments, fears, learning, faith, self-esteem, decisions, beliefs, feelings, planning, celebrating, mourning, eating, drinking, spending, saving, loving, competing. This is the stuff of everyday life—and the plot points of a novel.

- **Why (*Major Arcana Cards*)** – The reasons behind all the action—usually embodied by impersonal, universal archetypes, "acts of God" (or Fate or "shit happens"). These are forces outside the direct control of the **Who** or an invisible "script" that supplies motivation (for example, familial or cultural patterns that are passed on from generation to generation via genetics, tradition or behavior). Some believe this is also the realm of past life influence, as well as the collective unconscious. Thus, it's a repository for all templates available to humans that not only causes what happens on life's stage, but also remains available to be called on when needed or wanted.

*Where the hell's the* **Where?**, you may be wondering.

Well, you can *try* to determine "where" in a reading, if you want, or for inventing a locale in a fictional story. For example, The Magician could suggest a magic shop, a magic show or a town/county/street with "Magic" or "Wizard" in the name. Or, for the abstract minded, you could theorize that The Magician card might refer to Copperfield Street, Houdini Lane, Merlin Way— or the locale of David Blaine's latest street spectacle.

Using the Minor Arcana suits only, you can also attempt to discern the **Where** of a situation. (See the section below on the Minor Arcana. Possible **Where** locales are listed at the end of each suit.)

Don't get bogged down by my **Who**, **What/How** and **Why** model, though (or sidetracked with my **Where** addendum). It's merely one way to see the function and form of Tarot. If it doesn't make sense to you or work for you, then just discard it in favor of what *does*.

**Major Arcana** – Now, the Major Arcana Tarot cards are some of the most recognizable. The Fool, The Lovers, Wheel of Fortune, Justice, Death and The Moon cards are among the Major Arcana. The Majors are the most identifiable because they are "larger than life"—those archetypal patterns that permeate every era, country and culture. These repeated themes and patterns manifest via literature, film, oral traditions and songs. Archetypal motifs also find representation through public scandal, notorious figures and pop culture phenomena. The war-mongering Emperor, the reclusive Hermit, the scales of Justice (or injustice), the drug-pushing Devil, the shit-hitting-the-fan Tower, the messianic Hanged Man—these are the foundation of our memories, shared experiences and, indeed, civilization itself.

**Minor Arcana** – The Minor Arcana cards parallel Ace through

Ten (1–10) in a regular playing card deck. However, most Tarot decks rename the Minor Arcana suits thusly: Hearts become Cups, Clubs become Wands, Diamonds become Coins and Spades become Swords. These four suits mirror the four elements of Water, Fire, Earth and Air.

- **CUPS** cards—associated with the element of **WATER**— usually govern the realm of love, aesthetics, values and moods. Its energy is feminine/receptive. Sometimes, this suit is named Emoting, Chalices or Vessels. It is considered feminine/passive in nature, especially since its symbol usually connects with a receptacle for liquids. Colors often used in CUPS cards are deep blues, aqua and, in some cases, gold (in terms of the metal, reflective qualities and implication of preciousness). CUPS connects with relationships, intuition, feelings, empathy, dreams, the unconscious/subconscious, psychic phenomena, romance, intimacy, joy, forgiveness, healing, succor and matters of the heart. Its energy is of a slower nature— steeping, stewing. In ancient Tarot de Marseilles style decks, the CUPS suit was associated with the clergy. **Symbolized by**: Wave; Droplet. **Chakra 4 (Heart)**: Love; Forgiveness; Compassion. **Astrological Signs**: Cancer, Scorpio and Pisces. **Magical Creature:** Undine. **Where**: Islands; Coastal Areas; Beaches; Marshes; Swamps; Marinas; Coffee Shops; Lakes; Rivers; Pools; Churches; Boats; Hospice Centers; Oceans; Canals; Liquor Store; Bars; Chapels; Monasteries; Cruise Ship; Fountains; Water Parks; Ponds; Yachts; Amusement Parks.

- **WANDS** cards—often associated with the element of **FIRE**—usually correlate to ambition, self-propulsion, passion, enthusiasm and vocation. Its energy is masculine/ active. Sometimes, this suit is named Energy, Staffs, Rods or Batons, with the phallic shape connecting to masculine/ active energy. Colors often used in WANDS cards are red and orange, sometimes bright yellow. WANDS connects with action, energy, enthusiasm, courage, gumption, career (as opposed to actual job), and many issues related to the "self" (as in, "self-starter", "self-esteem", "self-propelled", "self-possessed", etc.). Its energy is of a faster nature—sudden, sometimes explosive. In ancient Tarot de Marseilles style decks, the WANDS suit was associated with the peasant class. **Symbolized by**: Flame; Fire. **Chakra 3 (Solar Plexus)**: Personal power; Self-esteem. **Astrological Signs:** Aries, Leo and Sagittarius. **Magical Creature:** Salamander. **Where**: Deserts; Arid Land; Savannas; Saunas; Southern States/Countries; Weapons and Ammo Store; Firehouses; Sandboxes; Gas Stations; Oil Rigs; Volcanoes; Fireworks Vendors; Trains; Bomb Shelters; Furnaces; Chimney Sweep Shops; Gun Shows; Crematoriums; Candle Stores; Military Bases; War-Torn Areas; Steel Mills; Nuclear Reactors; Hadron Collider; Kilns.

- **COINS** cards—associated with the element of **EARTH**— usually refer to the material realm of health, body, food, resources, finances and environment. Its energy is feminine/receptive. Sometimes, this suit is named Material, Pentacles, Stones or Disks, with its rounded symbol—either coins or plates for holding food— considered feminine/passive in nature. Colors often used in COINS cards are greens (leaves, grass and money), browns (soil, wood, grains) and sometimes, gold (currency). COINS connect with the physical realm, such as material possessions, money, job, anatomy, land, home and environment. Its energy is of a slower nature— cautious, methodical. In ancient Tarot de Marseilles style decks, the COINS suit was associated with the merchant class. **Symbolized by**: Seedling; Leaf; Soil; Grain; Rocks. **Chakras 1 (Root) and 2 (Sacral)**: Survival and Tribal Connection; Power Over Others and Sexuality/Reproduction. **Astrological Signs:** Taurus, Virgo and Capricorn. **Magical Creature:** Gnome. **Where**: Land-Locked States/Countries; Deciduous Forests; Hotels; Casinos; Banks; Quarries; Mines; Campgrounds; Grocery Stores; Restaurants; Gyms; Prairies; Food Trucks; Department Stores; Malls; Parks; Farmer's Market; Caves; Repair Shops; Autopsy Rooms; Chiropractor Offices; Unemployment Centers; Jewelry Stores; Plant Nurseries; Florists; Lumber Yards; Paper Mills.

- **SWORDS** cards—often associated with the element of **AIR**—usually relate to the mental realm of decision, analysis, facts, discrimination and communication. Its energy is masculine/active. Sometimes, this suit is named Mental, Blades, Arrows or Knives. Its phallic shape connects to masculine/active energy. Colors often used in SWORDS cards are powder blue, gray, black, white and—at times—yellow (especially pale yellow). The SWORDS suit connects with the intellectual realm— thoughts, beliefs, judgments, assumptions, clarity of ideas, opinions, logic, data and so on. Many people believe that thoughts cause suffering, not situations. Thus, SWORDS is often interpreted as arguments, hostility, anxiety, injury and suffering. In ancient Tarot de Marseilles style decks, the SWORDS suit was associated with nobility. **Symbolized by:** Stylized curves as "wind"; Cloud; Feather. **Chakras 5 and 6 (Throat and Third Eye)** – Communication and Self-Expression; Vision and Symbolic Sight. **Astrological Signs:** Gemini, Libra and Aquarius. **Magical Creature:** Sylph. **Where:**

Mountains; High Elevations; Northern States/Countries; Cold Climates; Schools; Post Offices; Planes; Libraries; Museums; Courthouses; Government Buildings; TV/Radio Stations; Ski Resorts; Police Stations; Jails; Asylums; Computer Rooms; Delivery Warehouses; Ground Control; Cell Phone Towers; Air Traffic Control Centers; 911 HQ; Ambulances; Emergency Rooms; Trauma Centers; The Internet.

*So let's have some fun and see how each of the four suits and their corresponding elements might find expression in the real world:*

**Star Trek Races:**
Earth – Ferengi
Fire – Klingon
Water – Betazoid
Air – Vulcan

**Candy:**
Earth – Licorice
Fire – Fireballs
Water – Liquid Filled Wax Bottles
Air – Hard Tack Whistles

**Hogwarts Houses:**
Earth – Hufflepuff
Water – Slytherin
Fire – Gryffindor
Air – Ravenclaw

**Birds:**
Earth – Penguins
Fire – Phoenix
Water – Pelican

Air – Eagle

**Retro TV:**
Earth – *Gilligan's Island*
Fire – *A-Team*
Water – *Love Boat*
Air – *The Invisible Man*

**100 Acre Woods Denizens:**
*Earth – Winnie the Pooh*
*Fire – Tigger*
*Water – Kanga*
*Air – Owl*

**Instruments:**
Earth – Percussion
Fire – Brass
Water – Woodwinds
Air – Strings

**Football:**
Earth – Water Boys
Fire – Players
Water – Cheerleaders
Air – Coaches

**Painters:**
Earth – Andrew Wyeth
Fire – Alex Grey
Water – Claude Monet
Air – Van Gogh

**Food:**
Earth – Grains, Pasta, Tubers

Fire – Hot and Spicy Fare
Water – Lemonade, Iced Tea, Cocktails and Milkshakes
Air – Mint, Puff Pastry and Cotton Candy

**Music Genres:**
Earth – Folk; Tribal Beats; Heavy Metal; Blues
Fire – Salsa; Mambo; Zydeco; Gospel; Soul
Water – Catchy Pop; Ballads; Lullabies; New Age
Air – Electronica; Trance; Classical; Jazz; Progressive Rock

**Fiction Genres:**
Earth – Westerns and Sagas
Fire – Thrillers
Water – Romance
Air – Mystery and Science Fiction

**Seasons:**
Earth – Fall (Harvest time; Shortening Daylight; A slowing down)
Fire – Spring (New life sprouting; Fresh energy; Return of the Sun)
Water – Summer (Pool! Fountains! Margaritas!)
Air – Winter (Cold weather; Crisp Clarity; Sharpness of the wind; Barrenness)

**Jungian Functions:**
Earth – Sensing
Fire – iNtuition
Water – Feeling
Air – Thinking

**Four Humors:**
Earth – Phlegmatic
Fire – Choleric

Water – Sanguine
Air – Melancholy

*Primary Color:*
Earth – Brown (Or Green)
Fire – Red
Water – Blue
Air – Yellow

*Theme Songs:*
Earth – "Allentown" by Billy Joel
Fire – "Firework" by Katy Perry
Water – "Caribbean Blue" by Enya
Air – "Natural Science" by Rush

**Court Cards** – The Court Cards in the Tarot are Pages, Knights, Queens and Kings of all four suits—16 cards total. Sometimes, the Court Cards are also renamed in familial terms like Daughter, Son, Mother and Father. The Court Cards can indicate actual people who exhibit the hallmarks of a suit combined with literal, physical court card associations. For example, the Page of Cups could be a child under 13 who is curious and gullible (Page), as well as deeply sensitive (Cups). Often, when the Court Cards show up in a reading, they indicate a personality approach or attitude towards another person, an issue, task or life in general—regardless of age or gender. In this case, the Knight of Wands would then suggest an individual who charges ahead with enthusiasm (Knight) in vocational areas (Wands).

- Pages are usually children under the age of 13 *or* those who act childlike (or childish). In many respects, Pages are Fool-like. As an approach, Pages are walking, learning, playing and delivering.

- Knights are usually youth from ages 14-21 *or* those who act like teenagers. In many ways, Knights are Chariot-like. As an approach, Knights are running, questing, chasing, rushing and launching.

- Queens are usually adults who are maternal (regardless of gender). In many ways, Queens are Empress-like. As an approach, Queens are sitting, supporting, nurturing, teaching and connecting.

- Kings are usually adults who are paternal (regardless of gender). In many ways, Kings are Emperor-like. As an approach, Kings are standing, governing, orchestrating, ordering and designating.

Most scenarios have several components that cover more than one card or suit. However, depending on the question asked of Tarot, and amount of cards drawn, only a few may show up in a reading.

Here's an example to show you the **Who, What/How** and **Why** dynamic—and how most situations contain influences of all four elements/suits.

Let's say a 14-year-old lanky, blonde, Australian youth adores surfing. Like most days, he's out paddling on his board, looking for the perfect wave. Just as he spots an awesome wave, and stands on his board to catch it, a shark attacks him out of nowhere—biting off his lower right leg. Fortunately, he makes it to shore—and survives.

**Why** – It depends on who you ask. If surfing is a part of your culture—or something you think is "cool"—you may associate the attack (the "Why") with the shit-hitting-the-fan Tower card.

The attack is sudden, unexpected and devastating. The way nature behaves, including animals, are often attributed to "acts of God". Like the rest of the Major Arcana, there may be no rhyme or reason—the situation seems like a force acting beyond human prediction or comprehension. If you consider risky activities like surfing in shark-infested waters "stupid" or "naïve", then you may attribute The Fool to the attack.

**What/How** – The attack takes place in the ocean—water, water everywhere (Cups). Not only that, the emotional impact of such an attack (also Cups) will likely be felt for decades. It's the passion of the youth (Wands) that drives him to surf. The sharp teeth of the shark (Swords) tore into the youth's flesh (Coins). He required surgery (Swords) to repair his body and save his life (Coins).

**Who** – He's a youth, so he could either be a Page or a Knight. Because he charges into the ocean despite obvious risks, I'd associate him with a Knight—specifically, the adventurous Knight of Wands. Some of you may wonder, *"Why not Knight of Cups?"* Well, plunging (Knight) into the sea (Cups) *could* work— but as you'll discover in the Court Cards Overview section, Cups individuals are usually more dreamy and risk-adverse compared to action-oriented Wands types. However, if such a person had a "love affair" with the ocean or surfing—feeling a deep connection that borders on a transcendent, spiritual experience—he may very well be a Knight of Cups.

# Methods for Reading the Tarot

There are various methods for decoding and reading Tarot cards. I've devised two methods to help you suck as much information from each card as you possibly can. The first technique, the **BIT** (Back in Time) **Method**, is the basis of my first title *The Back in Time Tarot Book*. It teaches Tarot "backwards", in that you begin with your *own* memories—then work towards the Tarot for associations and meaning. The other method, my **7 Clue Tarot Method**, takes into account various educational learning styles. While many of us have one or two dominant learning styles, the 7 Clues forces us to examine a Tarot card through *each* of the seven lenses—giving us valuable, and often surprising, information that would not have surfaced otherwise.

## BIT Tarot Method

At first glance, my **BIT** (Back in Time) **Tarot Method** may seem deceptively simple. While easy to perform, the benefits can be monumental—especially for those attempting to learn Tarot and/or bond with a particular deck. This is because associations created from your own personal "database"—your observations, impressions, assumptions, correlations, sensory memories—come from *you*, not some outside source like a Tarot book or expert. As you well know from experiencing (and reliving) certain memories, the past—and our personal associations and assumptions—are never far from us. So when we merge the personal and the immediate with a particular Tarot card, we will likely remember it well for readings.

In a nutshell, my **BIT Tarot Method** goes like this:

1.   Think of any incident from the past, whether it's one second

ago or millennia ago. It can be a memory, an overheard discussion, a news story, world event, biographical profile, historical milestone, movie, TV, book, song, fairytale— anything.

2.  After you have one particular memory in mind, take a moment to break down that memory into a few components. (Or, if you're adventurous or Tarot-savvy, as many components as you'd like.)

3.  Look through any Tarot deck, images up, with an illustrated Minor Arcana (that is, a deck that shows people and situations on cards Ace through Ten). Choose a card (or cards) that best represent each component of your memory from number two. Your choices can be based on attire, visage, posture, colors, environment, card name, numbers, symbols, animals, objects, people, emotions evoked when you see it, "gut feeling", etc. It's impossible to do my BIT Method "wrong". Anything that causes you to connect a card (or cards) with a component is correct for you, according to your own reasons.

4.  I encourage you to journal your associations and reasons in a notebook, word processing program or personal blog— whatever works best for you—so your association becomes further cemented in your mind. By associating memories with various cards, you are, in a sense, "imprinting" on a particular card. You know how some parents imprint their toddler's hands in clay, and then bake the impression for posterity? Or how a baby duck "imprints" on the first life form it sees? Well, my BIT Method is similar, except you're "imprinting" the Tarot card/s and deck/s of your choice with your own personal associations—making any deck that resonates at first blush truly "yours".

5. Congratulations! You've just completed a BIT Method Snapshot.

My shark attack story at the end of the **Anatomy of a Tarot Deck** section? That was a form of my BIT Tarot Method: I took a scenario and then associated the components with cards (or suits, as was the case). Instead of elements/suits, I could be even more specific and connect an actual card with each aspect, such as, the expansive, potentially dangerous ocean (Moon), the torn flesh (10 of Swords), his ability to keep his wits while paddling to shore injured (Strength), his recovery (4 of Swords) and his gratitude for survival (The Star).

## 7 Clue Tarot Method

The 7 Clue Method is a system I devised for exploring Tarot and oracle cards. If you apply the 7 Clue Method to any deck, I assure you that not only will your imagination broaden, but so will your intuitive skills. In addition, you will finally be able to bond with decks that have been elusive or mute to your attempts at understanding and using them. Here are the **7 Clues**:

**1st Clue: *Visual.*** Look at the card closely. What do you notice?

**2nd Clue: *Auditory.*** Imagine that the card is broadcasting sounds. Do you hear music? Conversation? Animal noises? Wind blowing?

**3rd Clue: *Kinesthetic.*** Pretend that the card's border enlarges. It's so big, you can walk through it, as a door. What do your surroundings feel like? Touch what's around you. What is the temperature?

**4th Clue: *Emotional.*** How does this card make you feel? What mood does it evoke? What are the figures in the card feeling?

**5th Clue:** *Conversational.* Imagine that you are able to converse with any person, animal or figure in the card. What do you say? What do they say? Someone or something has a message for you from this card. What is it?

**6th Clue:** *Memory.* As you're interacting with this card, do any personal memories come to mind that seem similar? What about books, stories, myths, TV shows, songs or movies? Perhaps a current event or historical situation seems parallel to what you're experiencing with this card, or even a recent conversation you witnessed. What is it?

**7th Clue:** *Analytical.* Now it's time to play esoteric detective and analytical sleuth. How did the figure come to be in this card? What happened right before you "stepped in"? What will happen next? Notice any symbols, colors or unusual placements. How might they connect with other systems, such as astrology, numerology, color theory or the Kabbalah?

Here's an example of my **7 Clue Tarot Method** using the Beginnings (Fool) card from the *Snowland Deck* (SnowlandDeck. com).

**The Image:** His foot on an old-fashioned wooden sled (with an "0" painted on the front), a young boy stands on top of a steep, snowy hill. A Boston terrier tugs at the rope attached to the sled. A cardinal sits in a snowy bush behind him and a blue jay perches on a twig below. Out of view, a rock juts out of the side of the hill. It is a bright, clear winter day, with the sun shining in the sky.

*Visual Clue* – As you gaze at Beginnings, what do you notice about the colors, the placements, the objects, the postures?

*Auditory Clue* – Imagine that this card is broadcasting sound, almost like an archetypal radio. What types of sounds emanate from Beginnings?

*Kinesthetic Clue* – You are able to enter this card. What is the temperature of your surroundings? Notice any smells wafting toward you. Walk around. How does the ground feel under your feet? Notice each figure and animal in the card. How do they act? Touch the sled. How does it feel?

*Emotional Clue* – As you gaze at Beginnings, how do you feel? What is the mood evoked by this card? What predominant emotions is the child feeling? The dog? The birds?

*Conversational Clue* – Strike up a conversation with either the child, the dog or one of the birds. Whom do you select first? Who speaks first—you or a figure from the card? The child has a message to pass onto you. What is it? The Boston terrier, too, has a message for you. What is it?

*Memory Clue* – As you're interacting with Beginnings, what story, fairytale or movie comes to mind? What about a personal memory? Is there someone you know that is similar to the child or the dog? What famous person or event comes to mind as you ponder this card? What book, movie or song seems to capture Beginnings based on your interactions with the cards?

*Analytical Clue* – An animal companion accompanies the boy in the Beginnings card. Why might this be so? Where, when and how did the boy acquire the sled? Whose property is he sledding on? What might the rock symbolize? The birds? What about the "0" on the sled?

# Telling Time with Tarot

Some ~~control freaks~~ Tarotists and clients want to know *everything* about life, including timing. *"When will Jill get pregnant?"*, *"When will my soul mate sweep me off my feet?"*, *"When will all these pimples clear up?"*, *"When will I win the lottery?"*, *"When did I contract this STD?"* —these are questions asked by fortunetellers, not Tarot coaches or counselors (who care more about ascertaining roots of problems and encouraging clients to take personal responsibility for their lives).

Lest you think I'm biased against you fortunetellers, O Madame Midnight Dragonfly or Wildman Pan a' Tootin, here's a way to use Tarot cards to tell time (although I wouldn't do it if I were you):

## Major Arcana

The situation is out of your hands *or* dependent on the mastery/ healing/or integration of pervasive life lesson indicated by the card. For example, if you draw The Hermit while trying to discern timing, it either indicates there ain't a thing you can do about the situation *or* that the client (or you) must learn to be comfortable in solitude and without constant social stimulation before the outcome will come to pass or fruition. If you drew Strength, this would indicate that you or the client needs to master self-control, courage and grace under pressure before the answer arrives. Oh, hell, let me just give you a list. When a Major Arcana card shows up for timing, it means that the individual must learn, heal or integrate issues concerning the following:

*Fool* – Playfulness, innocence and willingness to take chances
*Magician* – Applying all the talents and tools at hand

*High Priestess* – Accessing and heeding personal counsel/ intuition

*Empress* – Nurturing life, growth and creativity

*Emperor* – Setting boundaries, organization and ruling your own life

*Hierophant* – Adopting or discarding tradition, religious beliefs or cultural expectations

*Lovers* – Ability to discern the best course and commit to the path or person

*Chariot* – Forward movement despite distractions and obstructions

*Strength* – Self-control, courage and grace under pressure

*Hermit* – Ease with solitude and lack of social stimulation

*Wheel of Fortune* – Adaptability during flux; remaining centered among vicissitude

*Justice* – Fairness, injustice and earthly/human laws

*Hanged Man* – Patience among stasis and immobility

*Death* – Transitions and impermanence

*Temperance* – Ability to mix, blend and include; holding incongruent ideas

*Devil* – Addiction, self-destructive tendencies, materialism and abuse

*Tower* – Catastrophe, sudden loss and destruction

*Star* – Optimism, hope and faith

*Moon* – Deception; feminine cycles/hormones; dealing with the unknown

*Sun* – Vitality; holistic health; relating to children

*Judgment* – Karma; reaping what's been sown; making amends; admission of wrong; honoring a call

*World* – Completion; unfinished business; last piece of the puzzle; tying it up in a bow

## Minor Suits

*Swords – Winter – Days* (Number indicates how many)
*Wands – Spring – Weeks* (Number indicates how many)
*Cups – Summer – Months* (Number indicates how many)
*Coins – Autumn – Years* (Number indicates how many)

In the Northern Hemisphere:

**Winter** = December, January, February
**Spring** = March, April, May
**Summer** = June, July, August
**Autumn** = September, October, November

Southern Hemisphere peeps, adjust accordingly.

If you live in the Northern Hemisphere and draw the 3 of Swords, it would suggest either the third day of one of the Winter months (e.g., December 3, January 3 or February 3) *or* three days from the time the cards were drawn and the question asked. If you draw the 10 of Coins, you're screwed, since it looks like at *least* a decade for your situation to resolve or your fondest wish to come to pass (*if ever*). Or, it could just mean the 10th of September, October or November. Use your intuition to figure out which. (You don't expect me to give you *everything*, do you?)

So what about the Court Cards for timing questions? Drawing one of those characters either indicates that there's a person connected to the situation that directly affects the outcome (read: out of your hands) *or* that you must adopt the persona and strengths of that Court Card for clarity to descend or for you to get what you're after.

# Reversals

It is my belief that no card in Tarot is wholly "good" or "bad". In fact, one of the first lessons I taught my students in my online Tarot Classroom is the Light/Shadow Continuum. I present the idea that the meaning and energy of each of the 78 cards of Tarot are stretched along a continuum, from worst-case scenario to best-case scenario—from beneficial to detrimental—in import, application and result.

Thus, cards deemed "negative" by some Tarotists—most of the Swords suit, Death, The Devil and The Tower, for example— can find redemption and profundity through reversed meanings. Likewise, those cards noted for being "happy" or "positive"— The Empress, The Star, The Sun, The World, most of the Cups suit, the Ten of Pentacles and so on—can indicate stressful, suffocating, delusional or even abusive energy when reversed.

From my experience as a Tarot author and reviewer, as well as a professional Tarot reader with a worldwide clientele (not to mention the hours of trial and error I invested in the cards when trying to learn Tarot, especially reversals!), I have found that upside down cards can mean:

- *No or Not* – Although this sounds simplistic, when a reversal comes up in a reading, it can be as easy as putting a "no" or "not" in front of the upright meaning of the card.

- *Inward/Inside* – Sometimes a card's upright energy is directed inwardly or manifesting its energy "behind the eyes" (or within the heart). Thus, the energy of a reversal may be more psychological or spiritual in nature, rather than overt or material.

- *Outward/Projected* – At times, a card's upright energy is aimed outward in the form of blame or projection. Some truths or behavior patterns are too painful for the person to recognize and admit. These can be negative traits such as lying or condescension, or positive traits such as intelligence or eloquence. If the querent's psyche has been damaged from childhood abuse, for example, he or she may not be able to "own" negative behavior *or* positive behavior (largely because of low self-esteem).

- *Desired, But Not for the Best or Not to Be Attained* – A reversal can often indicate what a client really wants, but is not (or will not be) getting.

- *Extreme or Unhealthy Manifestation of Energy* – What happens when the upright energy of a card is taken to an extreme? Sometimes, reversals indicate extremism and its repercussions.

- *Hidden* – A reversal may reveal an energy that has been completely unseen or overlooked by the client.

- *Needed, but not Utilized* – A tool only serves the user when it's actually picked up and utilized. Reversals can highlight an area or energy that is sorely lacking or needed in a person's life, but is absent or unused.

- *Fear of* – Fear of whatever the upright card would suggest often manifests in a reversal. For example, *fear of having children* can be indicated by The Empress reversed, while The Hermit reversed can suggest *fear of being alone*.

- *Blocked* – At times, an upside-down card can point to "molasses energy"—a slowness that is hampering the full expression of the upright meaning. Or, the reversal can signify an actual blockage that prevents the energy of the card from moving, flowing or manifesting in the material world.

- *Emerging or Lessening* – A reversed card can indicate that the upright energy is present, but is just now entering the situation or is on its way out.

- *Play on Image* – Sometimes, the Tarot seems to have a sense of humor—suggesting an offbeat (but accurate) interpretation based on card imagery or even the title. This is why the Ace of Cups reversed can indicate a leaky faucet or overflowing toilet...or how the Wheel of Fortune reversed can suggest "spinning your wheels" or the Ace of Pentacles reversed can refer to playing basketball! (Take a look at the Ace of Pentacles reversed later in this book; doesn't the hand appear as if it's about to dribble a ball, with the flowering arch serving as a hoop?)

- *Esoteric connection* – When a card ends up reversed, it may very well indicate that an esoteric connection needs to be considered in the reading. This could be correlations with astrology, Hebrew letters, Kabbalistic paths on the Tree of Life, esoteric functions, numerology, Golden Dawn attribution, Crowley's writings and so on.

I've also discovered that the prefixes un-, dis-, mis-, in-, ir-, pre-, non-, ex-, re-, over-, under- and de- often apply to reversed card meanings. For example, words like refusing, rejecting, reliving, repressing, returning, recovering, relief, reexamining, redoing, recognizing, resenting, repairing, resurrection [of] and recurring may apply to reversed Tarot card meanings, as can words such as disturbed [by], disgusted [by], disappointed [by], discontent [concerning], dissolution [of], defying, disappearance [of], inability [to], misunderstanding [of], misplaced, disintegration [of], underestimating, inadequate, undiagnosed, premature, preoccupation [with] and so on.

For more information on upside-down cards, get your hands on a copy of my full-color, gloriously glossy book *Tarot in Reverse*. It includes extensive reverse keywords for all 78 cards, an example from pop culture showing how a card's reversal plays out "in real life" and 1,560 affirmations to help you deal with life's "reversals" (which can be blessings in disguise).

# Choosing a Deck

Determining the ways you'd like to work with the Tarot can help you decide on which deck or decks to work with. Tarot decks span hundreds of themes—from baseball to dragons, saints to fairies, cats to coffee. Selecting a deck can be an overwhelming task in light of such a vast array!

The internet is a great portal for discovering and purchasing decks, especially when you get to see many of the cards. *The Encyclopedia of Tarot Volume IV* by Stuart Kaplan features artwork from 850 tarot decks and reproductions of more than 11,000 different tarot cards from the 20th century. Because most decks cost between $20 and $30, a book such as this one can help you save money in the end by learning more about various decks. However, Kaplan's book was published in 2005, and there have been hundreds of decks published since that time.

Another great source to scope out decks—especially vibrant, unusual artisan decks—is Etsy.com. Just put "Tarot" or "Tarot Decks" in the search there.

So which deck should you ultimately choose? Even some long-time Tarotists are still on the quest for the "perfect deck"! Purpose, attractiveness, and theme are the three main considerations when looking for a deck. For example, if your primary purpose for using the Tarot was storytelling or creative writing, you would want a deck with illustrated Minors. It's much easier to tell a story about an individual standing on one foot and holding (juggling?) two coins than trying to glean meaning from an image of two static coins.

Attractiveness is also an important consideration. If you like the theme of a deck but abhor the illustrations or coloring, then working with it won't be enjoyable. Choose a deck that appeals to your sense of touch (including size). Some New Age and occult bookstores display sample cards for you to examine.

In addition, read reviews of decks (such as those on my site JanetBoyer.com) and scrutinize the images. How do the pictures make you feel? Do you like the artistic style? Can you picture yourself interacting with the characters—or easily identify with the depicted situations?

Theme is another element to consider. If you don't resonate with the Christian symbolism of a Rider-Waite-Smith (RWS) deck, then you may prefer Tarot decks with pagan imagery, such as those with Wiccan or Druidic themes. If you practice feminine spirituality, you may choose a deck reflecting goddess themes. If you're looking for a colorful, positive deck that can be used with, or in the presence of, children—and you're delighted by all things snow and winter—consider the **Snowland Deck** (SnowlandDeck.com). My husband, Ron Boyer, did the art—and our son (and I!) posed for a few of the cards. In fact, in his book *Llewellyn's Complete Book of Tarot,* author Anthony Louis named our *Snowland Deck* one of two decks that are perfect for reading for children (along with his advice for ethical considerations while doing so). And what about coffee? Are you an addict like my son and I? Well guess what? Ron and I have a coffee-themed deck, as well (Tarot.Coffee)—the **Coffee Tarot**! So as you can see, whatever your passions and interests, there's probably a related deck out there—so allow them to guide you as you choose an appropriate set of cards.

One of the fascinating elements about Tarot is there is no "wrong" way to read the cards. Each person brings his/her unique life experience and frame of reference to the cards. For example, although most individuals interpret the 3 of Swords as heartache or grief, others may see the three swords piercing the bright red heart in Rider-Waite-Smith style decks as symbolic of "the three musketeers"—three friends joined by the bonds of love, enduring the challenges and heartaches of life together.

Whether you use the cards for journaling, self-discovery, creativity, brain storming, or spiritual practice, the Tarot provides a vast array of symbols and metaphors for inspiration, clarity and insight.

If you're in the market for a deck, here's a list of 20 fine sets of cards. Decks with an asterisk before them are more complex or abstract—and may not be best for those brand new to Tarot:

*The Green Witch Tarot* by Ann Moura

*Madam Clara Sees All Tarot* by Madam Clara

*\*MidCenturian Tarot* by Madam Clara

*DruidCraft Tarot* by Philip and Stephanie Carr-Gomm; art by Will Worthington

*Golden Tarot* by Kat Black

*\*Mythical Goddess Tarot* by Sage Holloway and Katherine Skaggs

*Pictorial Key Tarot* by Davide Corsi

*\*Mystical Cats Tarot* by Lunaea Weatherstone and Mickie Mueller

*Halloween Tarot* by Kipling West and Karin Lee

*\*Celestial Stick People* by Brian Crick

*Tarot of Vampyres* by Ian Daniels

*\*Monstarot* by Joanna Nelson

*Zombie Tarot* by Stacey Graham

*The Victorian Fairy Tarot* by Lunaea Weatherstone and Gary A. Lippincott

*Faulkner Tarot* by Rhiannon Faulkner

*\*Shadow of Oz Tarot* by Illogical Associates (Various Artists)

*Tarot of the Water* by Kayti Welsh and the 78 Tarot Dream Team (Various Artists)

*Tarot Carnival* by by Kayti Welsh and the 78 Tarot Dream Team (Various Artists)

*\*OSHO Zen Tarot* by OSHO and Deva Padma

*\*Steampunk Tarot* by John Matthews and Wil Kinghan

You may be wondering, "*Yeah, but which decks do **you** use most* *of the time? For yourself or those you read for?"* Honestly? For clients, I use our *Snowland Deck* 99 percent of the time. It's my absolute favorite. Clients—and other people who own it—report amazing accuracy and insight when using our deck. (As of this writing, our *Coffee Tarot: Grande Edition* isn't completed yet—but *will* be by the time you read this. I'm sure I'll be using that one frequently once it's published!) When I perform readings for myself, I really dig the *Green Witch Tarot*.

# About the Correspondences

Why bother with correspondences, especially when Tarot, alone, is a complex, complete system? I believe author Lupa Greenwolf (*New Paths to Animal Totems*) sums up the value of correspondences quite nicely:

> *We are meaning-making creatures. A set of correspondences tells a story, and provides a framework we can use to better understand different concepts... Ultimately, correspondences are about multiple levels of symbolism used to better understand the world and the patterns in it. Therefore, it's better to adopt symbols that resonate with you, even if they aren't historically 'correct'. As long as you aren't claiming that your new system is something ancient, and the system works for you, then go with it!*

Every correspondence associated with a Tarot card amplifies its meaning. In the case of flower essences, aromatherapy and crystals, correspondences connect healing modalities with every Tarot card. This practical connection expands the ways we can empower ourselves and our clients.

And frankly? Correspondences provide kick-ass fun! You can take just about any system, look at its components and ask yourself, "*What Tarot card would I associate with this symbol or item? Why?*" For example, I thought about associating each Tarot card with an I Ching hexagram, Rune or Astrological glyph or planetary placement—but other authors have done that. Even though my associations would likely differ from theirs, the *last* thing I want to do in *Naked Tarot* is re-hash what many have already done!

If some of my correspondences don't seem like a good fit for any reason, feel free to cross it out and replace it with your own. Although I spent many, many hours researching and contemplating each system and the various qualities of its components — and how each connects with the energy, symbolism and archetypal import of its corresponding Tarot card — you may find a better fit based on your unique personality, experience or worldview. As Lupa also says in her book, *"While there are many historical and well-established correspondences, don't be afraid if your own observations differ from them."*

**Disney Totem** – I love all-things Disney, especially their animated movies. I've never come across Disney Totems connected with Tarot cards, so I thought this would be a fun exercise coming up with associations. If you're familiar with Disney movies, then you can contemplate how certain characters seem to reflect the traits, qualities, symbols or archetypal motifs of a particular Tarot card. You'll never look at Disney characters — or Tarot cards — quite the same when you view them through the lens of each other! (P.S. The Tarot card that most embodies the vision and energy of Walt Disney — and the Disney experience in general? The Star!)

**Animal Symbol** – Animal symbolism and totemism is a deeply satisfying part of my own personal journey. From my observation, most people interested in Tarot also happen to love animals. Even if you *don't* happen to like critters (*WTF?*), myth, nursery rhymes, songs, legends, poems, TV shows, fables, cultural celebrations, art, fairytales, movies and news bulletins are filled with winged, finned, furred, scaled or multi-legged creatures. They are recognizable, accessible and universal. As such, the unique qualities of each — appearance, habitat, enemies, mating behavior, preferred food, calls, defense mechanisms, protective traits — may sensibly correlate with a particular Tarot card. By learning more about each animal correspondence (which is beyond the scope of this book, but I highly recommend *Animal Speak* by Ted Andrews), you'll not only add to your totemic tool kit, but also expand your understanding of its corresponding

Tarot card.

**Flower Essences** – Flower Essences are an energetic elixir made from floating or steeping a flower within pure water (although some practitioners use brandy as a preservative). Each flower correlates with specific emotional, psychological or spiritual challenges or traumas. Although Edward Bach pioneered the use of Flower Essences, other healers began to intuit that their local flora *also* contained healing properties—energies "extracted" when steeped in pure water, then ingested. It's *not* a concentrated herbal remedy, whereby petals, leafs and roots *themselves* are ingested. Rather the steeped flower "transfers" its healing properties to water, which, when consumed, gently realigns imbalanced emotional or psychological states—working on an energetic, or etheric, level. I've included the two systems I'm most familiar with: the Bach Remedies, and the Australian Bush Flower Remedies. These bottled elixirs can be found in your local health food store or online. Or, if a particular flower blooms in your backyard, you can make your own. Just be sure to learn how to correctly identify a particular plant or flower, as well as how to safely make your own Flower Essences. By connecting a Flower Essence/s with a Tarot card, you can amplify its healing focus and energy with this visual, tactile talisman. The card can then be fashioned into a piece of jewelry, displayed prominently where you can see it often, tucked in your wallet, affixed to your bathroom mirror and so on—magnifying the healing properties of the Flower Essence/s you are using.

**Crystal/Stone** – I don't know about you, but I'm a rock lover! There's something magical and soothing about a smooth river stone, a bright purple amethyst or a delightful spotted snowflake obsidian. Some individuals use crystals and stones for healing, empowerment and attraction. Whether the healing benefits result from physical traits like piezoelectricity or psychosomatic ones, many people have reported feeling more balanced when holding or meditating with crystals. Paired with a Tarot card, this healing modality packs a "double whammy" of intention.

**Aromatherapy** – In her book *Aromatherapy for the Soul*, author Valerie Ann Worwood notes:

> *From a vibrational, electromagnetic, and energetic point of view, essential oils are in harmony with life...On a molecular level, natural plant aroma molecules touch receptors on cells with the lightest of contact, then retreat, their job of instigating a series of reactions having been done. With an etheric quality, essential oils active the receptors of love, compassion, and empathy. They are an informational network, carrying messages and crossing boundaries, operating on many different levels.*

Combining aromatherapy with Tarot cards helps magnify and anchor the healing properties of a particular scent with a visual reminder of a desired result.

**Body Parts/Systems and Health Issues** – Unless you're a qualified health practitioner, it's illegal to diagnose medical issues—plain and simple. However, I'm including body parts/ systems, diseases and health issues for two reasons: One, in case you happened to be a licensed medical professional who's also a Tarot reader and two, if you happen to be a fiction writer who uses Tarot for character and plot ideas. Please only use as directed. I've created these associations based on my own intuitive experience.

**Mystical Messenger**–Gods, goddesses, demigods, saints, angels, etheric beings — whatever you call these assistants from "the other Side", their qualities and trademark "power packs" have been documented in sacred and channeled texts for centuries.

Because these Mystical Messengers are so "big", so "other", we humans sometimes find difficulty in connecting with such potent Beings on our own. By connecting a Divine Messenger with a Tarot card, we create a tangible reminder of a particular skill set, gift or energy imparted from these heavenly helpers. After much study, research and meditation, I felt that each of my correlations "called out" to be associated with a particular card — many, surprising. For example, logic would have me pick Jesus or Odin for The Hanged Man, but Argentinean "Guacho Saint" Gaucho Gil made himself known and volunteered his service — much like he sacrificed himself in true Hanged Man fashion. If you feel resistance at any of my associations, I encourage you to first research the Mystical Messenger; you may find that he/she/they will touch you and illuminate your understanding in unexpected ways. But feel free to substitute the saint, mystic, god, goddess or divine helper of your choice if you estimate mine aren't a good fit.

**Sabian Symbol** – Australian astrologer Lynda Hill introduced me to Sabian Symbols via her seminal book *360 Degrees of Wisdom: Charting Your Destiny with the Sabian Oracle*. There are other books about the Sabians — a set of 360 channeled messages correlated to every degree of the zodiac — but none as revealing, accessible and soulful as Lynda's. I've pored over her book and connected a Sabian Symbol to every Tarot card. Of course, there are only 78 cards in Tarot — and 360 Sabian Symbols — but I chose the most uncanny and appropriate correspondences for inclusion in *Naked Tarot*. The Sabians are powerful on their own. Combined with Tarot? We're talking some super-charged revelation and illumination!

# Time to Strip Down!

And now, fearless reader, it's time to get "down and dirty" with the cards! We'll begin our nitty-gritty exploration with the sixteen **Who** cards (the Court Cards), then make our way through the forty **What/How** cards (the Minor Arcana), then finish our in-depth foray with the twenty-two **Why** cards (the Major Arcana). The majority of Tarot books begin with the Major Arcana, but I've decided to put them last. Most (if not all) Tarot authors put the Majors first and spill the most ink on them, as if they're somehow more important than the other 56 cards— something I disagree with, and seek to remedy with *Naked Tarot*. And, unfortunately, the Minors and Courts usually receive little attention in Tarot books. In fact, some books only list a few keywords or sentences for the Minors—and mere regurgitated esoteric physical descriptions for the Courts. *Gah!* Rest assured this will *not* be the case with *Naked Tarot*: The Court Cards and Minor Arcana *finally* get their well-deserved due.

# The Court Cards

Arguably, the most difficult cards of the Tarot to understand, interpret and apply in a reading are the 16 Court Cards (most commonly named Page, Knight, Queen and King). The good news is that I've created original profiles of all 16 cards based on my many years of studying various personality systems, conducting professional readings, teaching students and considering Rank/ Suit associations.

When interpreting Court Cards, you need to discard the whole notion of gender. Each of the Court Cards is an *approach* to a situation, relationship or life itself, which includes strengths and drawbacks. In a Tarot reading, it is possible that a Court Card *can* refer to an actual person that resembles the image on the card or reflects the gender, but from my experience as a non-fortunetelling reader, the 16 character cards refer more to ways of being, seeing and reacting to circumstances, challenges and other people.

And, while it is *possible* that the Court Cards can also reflect actual age (e.g., Pages under 13, Knights 14–21, etc.), more than likely, the character indicates mindsets, attitudes and vitality (e.g., naïve, energetic, mature).

I've spent lots of time thinking about the Court Cards and crafting comprehensive, fleshed-out personality profiles for you. Not only can these be used for actual Tarot readings, but also for creative writing and artistic inspiration. If you've lived on the Earth longer than fifteen years and your eyes were open the whole time (*er*, at least *most* of the time), you've realized that human beings are insanely complex. They are prone to change on a dime, do the unexpected or surpass our expectations—all before the strike of noon!

Think of these varying quirks, complexities, habits, tendencies, strengths and weaknesses in terms of percentages or ingredients

51

that make up a human.

For example, when I'm baking something and need to add liquid ingredients for a recipe, I use a glass pouring cup with a handle that has measurements printed right on it. In fact, I can measure according to Cups, Millimeters or Ounces.

Now, if a single Court Card profile is one "ingredient" to the humanity mix, hardly any of us would be, say, 100 percent Queen of Wands or Page of Cups. Perhaps we act and react *mostly* like the Queen of Wands—maybe 60 percent—but we also exhibit 30 percent Knight of Coins and 10 percent Queen of Cups (during our period, *natch*—right girls?).

So while all 16 profiles I've created accurately reflect specific personality styles and recognizable traits (to the point where you'll probably be laughing your ass off, saying, "*OMG, she nailed Aunt Betty as a Queen of Coins!*" or "*Ouch. I'm mostly like the Page of Swords—and I'm a nosy pain in the ass, just like she said!*"), remember that *no* set of Court Card interpretations can capture the scope of an *entire* person with all their glorious talents and aggravating predispositions.

Although I sure as hell tried, let me tell you!

In *Creative You: Using Your Personality Type to Thrive* by David B. Goldstein and Otto Kroeger, the authors sum up not only how *they* feel about Myers-Briggs (MBTI) and Keirsey correlations, but also how *I* view the Court Cards:

**Psychological type theory doesn't explain every aspect of personality, as there is a large degree of latitude in individual behavior within each of the sixteen types.**

You're going to get extra goodies in this chapter, as I mentioned in the beginning: Beneficial Traits, Detrimental Traits, Nickname, Conflict Orientation (Knights), Love Language (Queens), Way to His Heart (Kings) and more.

**Please note**: These profiles were built from the ground up via 20 plus years studying personality theory, psychological texts, personal reading/counseling experience and my knowledge of the four elements and ranks—*not* other Tarot books. It's taken me *months* just to write this chapter on the Court Cards. The Nicknames, including MBTI/Keirsey monikers (e.g., The Aristocrat and Tycoon Tony), were originated by yours truly. So, if you decide you want to refer to the Court Cards using my nicknames, keywords or profile descriptions—on your blog, in your book, at a Tarot MeetUp, in your class, in your Newsletter, in a Facebook group, via social media or during your conference presentation—give credit where it's due by citing the original source (i.e., me, and *Naked Tarot*), OK? Please?

Let's begin!

# PAGES

## Page of Wands – Spitfire

**Stripped Down Overview:** It's no surprise many of these excitable, energetic spitfires sport a form of red hair—carrot, tomato, cinnamon—since their flaming *joie de vivre* lights up any room. Impetuous, insanely curious and often rebellious, these Pages thirst to know how things work and what makes people tick (as evidenced by their harebrained schemes and endless online posting of personality tests). Although they tend to be quick-tempered, the firestorm blows over quickly with little collateral. Some are bookish (with bulging shelves to prove it), and exhibit literary, musical or illustrative aptitude. Others can reverse engineer any gadget or software program, not to mention jumping off cliffs and building a hang glider on the way down. Still others are unabashed exhibitionists, often twerking and boob flashing across the stage. They love taking exams (seriously) and entering competitions (spelling bee, anyone?), for testing their mettle makes them feel alive. However, their *"put me in, coach!"* exuberance lends itself to hasty, ill-considered promises—so if they offer to help paint the clubhouse, bake cookies for the charity sale or promote your new book, you may be standing empty-handed in the wake of their retreating plume.

**Keywords:** Student of Self-Help; Youthful Exuberance; Naïve Experimentation; Exploring Self-Reliance; Curious About Identity; Emerging Self-Esteem; Ambitious Beginner; Seeking Excitement; Immature Zeal; Learning Poise; Childish Daring; Searching for Innovation; Wondering About Vocation; Messages About Profession; Premature Aggression; Undeveloped Enthusiasm; Seeking Originality

**Personifications and Embodiments:** Anne Shirley (*Anne of*

*Green Gables*); Sister Steve (*Father Dowling Mysteries*); Pippi Longstocking; Eep (The *Croods*); Tigger; Lewis Robinson (*Meet the Robinsons*); Nancy Drew; Maria Von Trapp (*Sound of Music*); Mystery, Inc.; Raven (*That's So Raven*); Huck Finn; *Hannah Montana*; Miley Cyrus; Lady Rose (Downton Abbey)

**Quote:** *We keep moving forward, opening new doors; and doing new things, because we're curious and curiosity keeps leading us down new paths.* – Walt Disney

**Nickname:** Exuberant Emma

**Challenge:** Dilettantism

**Gift:** Gumption

**Occupations/Vocations:** Illustrator; CGI Animator; Comic Book Writer; Voice Actor; Children's Book Author; Team Mascot; Amateur Sleuth; Teen Idol

**Disney Totem:** Jessie (*Toy Story 2*)

**Animal Symbol:** Hummingbird

**Flower Essences:** Scleranthus (Bach); Jacaranda (Australian Bush)

**Crystal/Stone:** Fire Opal – Promotes zest for life. Encourages impulsiveness. Helps with overcoming inhibitions. Aids in enjoyment of sexuality. Awakens enthusiasm for interesting ideas. Enhances energy and performance.

**Aromatherapy:** Coriander

**Body Parts/Systems and Health Issues:** ADD; Oppositional Defiant Disorder; Splinters; Skin Infections

**Mystical Messenger:** Saint Lucy

**Sabian Symbol:** Pisces 10 – An aviator in the clouds.

**Writing Prompt:** A curious, redheaded girl's hair changes color when...

**Affirmation:** I instigate new adventures!

**StrengthsFinder 2.0:** Ideation; Learner

**Cattell's 16PF:** Liveliness

**Enneagram:** Type 7w6; Type 2w3; Type 6w7 (Phobic)

**ANSIR:** Scintillator; Visionary; Healer; Empath; Philosopher

**MBTI/Keirsey:** ENFP – "The Motivator"

- **Beneficial Traits**
  - Excitable, spontaneous and lively—usually with a wild streak
  - Very funny with a great sense of humor
  - Independent and intense, refusing to be controlled or labeled
  - Extraordinary intuitive perceptions about people and situations

- **Detrimental Traits**
  - Often lacks follow through on all the new envisioned projects

A Disinterested in mundane or detail-related tasks

A Usually plagued by anxiety or worry

A Preoccupation with *what could be*, sometimes missing *what is*

## Naked Advice for the Page of Wands

*Career:* Guidance counseling, strengths finding, Enneagram coaching, personality test giving, motivation assessment—any job that unlocks and fuels your desire to know self and others better are a great fit for you. Whether mystery writing, book selling, problem solving or armchair detecting, every day needs to feel like a new adventure (or Pandora's Box) for you to experience true vocational fulfillment.

*Romance:* If you're looking for a playful, inventive lover, look no further. This eager beaver has the stamina of the Energizer bunny, and will likely outlast anyone fortunate to fall into her bed. She'll keep it fresh and intoxicating, but don't expect callbacks the next day (or any day), for she's likely moved on to a new playmate (that is, unless you've matched her fervor and piqued her interest). It's nothing personal, mind you, so if you're easily hurt, you may want to reach for a vibrator, instead.

*Parenting:* Society loves to cram children into little labeled boxes, throwing around terms like "ADHD" and "Oppositional Defiance Disorder". Forty years ago, this was called "being kids". Inquisitiveness needs to be encouraged, and impatient excuses for answers like *"because I said so"* don't pass muster as good explanations for valid questions. If your child seems hyper (and sugar rushes have been ruled out), she may be bored, so ensure that plenty of puzzles, word challenges and trivia-packed books are on hand. If more than one child is in your brood, make sure this one is honored as an *individual*—or else she'll feel forced to "prove" it by standing out (not always in a socially acceptable manner).

*Spirituality:* So many walk this earth in a daze, wondering what their life purpose may be. Here's a secret: uncover what stimulates, enlivens and intrigues you. Pretend you're a kid, just gifted with a magic wand that will paint your ideal reality. What does it look like? What are you doing? Where are you at? Who are you with? Point your imagination in the direction of your excitement to find out Why You Are Here.

**Recommended Resources:** *Anne of Green Gables* (miniseries); *Wet Paint* by Normal Rockwell; *Shiner* by Normal Rockwell; *Flame Leaper* (Sculpture) by Ferdinand Preiss

**Page of Wands Card Layout:** *Mysterious Magic Wand of Wonder* Spread

1. What is keeping me from exciting discoveries?
2. What mystery needs exploring?
3. What subject/topic needs opening to me?
4. Where should I next point my imagination wand?
5. What area holds a surprise for me?

## Page of Swords – Stoolpigeon

**Stripped Down Overview:** *"Why?" "How come?" "Are you sure?"* Whether voiced by precocious kids, suspicious youth or cynical citizens, the Page of Swords expects explanations, proof and damn good reasons to swallow your story or do what you want. Usually smart mouth, know-it-all tattletales, these pain-in-the-ass sentinels watch everyone like a hawk—making sure Joe follows the rules, Jenny completes her homework and Charlie Brown misses yet another football kick. Ideas of humor often includes sarcasm, mockery and malevolent pranks—anything that catches prey off-guard, skewers foibles or scares the living shit out of them. Although mentally sharp and exquisitely observant, these ones refuse to get their manicured hands dirty via actual accomplishment, preferring to expose perceived failures, poke at system weakness, hack "impenetrable" defenses or chip away pedestals—often signing their work "Anonymous".

**Keywords:** Learning to Think; Immature Decisions; Childish Communication; Naïve Theories; Anxieties with Studying; Preparing for Separation; Exploring Restrictions; Testing Limits; Asking for Thoughts; Rush to Judgment; Searching Beliefs; Experimenting with Words; Developing Logic; Planting Doubt; Curious About the Mental Realm; Undeveloped Viewpoint; Beginning to Talk; Budding Intellectual; Message of Severance; Inexperienced Transmission; Seeking Information; Bringing Judgments; Premature Assumptions; Requesting Facts; Playful with Words; Jumping to Conclusions; Watching for Mistakes; Student of Engineering

**Personifications and Embodiments:** Dr. Zachary Smith (*Lost in Space*); Candace Flynn (*Phineas and Ferb*); Lucy Van Pelt (*Peanuts*); Snoops; Talebearers; Stoolpigeons; IRS; Tattletales; Informants; Tabloids; Perez Hilton; TMZ; *Punk'd*; *Candid Camera*; Internal Affairs; Watchdog Groups; "Dirty Laundry" (Song); Mrs. Rachel Lynde (*Anne of Green Gables*)

**Quote:** *Curiosity is lying in wait for every secret.* – Ralph Waldo Emerson

**Nickname:** Nosy Norah

**Challenge:** Suspicion

**Gift:** Vigilance

**Occupations/Vocations:** Summons Server; Hacker; Informant; Gossip Columnist; Paparazzi; Information Specialist

**Disney Totem:** Randall (*Monsters, Inc.*)

**Animal Symbol:** Mockingbird

**Flower Essences:** Holly (Bach); Impatiens (Bach)

**Crystal/Stone:** Tree Agate (Chalcedony) – Helps with irritation, restlessness and displeasure. Helps one communicate directly and argue rationally. Stimulates mental energy and improves memory. Supports self-esteem.

**Aromatherapy:** Oregano

**Body Parts/Systems and Health Issues:** Tourette's Syndrome; Speech Disorders

**Mystical Messenger** – Saint Bartholomew

**Sabian Symbol:** Scorpio 19 – A parrot listening and then talking, repeats a conversation he has overheard.

**Writing Prompt:** A young boy misinterprets what he sees.

**Affirmation:** I learn new words and allow myself to experiment with language.

**StrengthsFinder 2.0:** Focus; Input

**Cattell's 16PF:** Vigilance

**Enneagram:** Type 6 (counterphobic); Type 5w6; Type 1

**ANSIR:** Sentinel; Diligent; Philosopher (Unhealthy)

**MBTI/Keirsey:** ISTP – "The Instigator"

- **Beneficial Traits**
  - ⚔ Staunch believers in equality and fair treatment
  - ⚔ Quick thinking and decision making
  - ⚔ Technical proficiency
  - ⚔ Skilled fact checkers and researchers

- **Detrimental Traits**
  - ⚔ Secretive; aggressively defends privacy and personal space
  - ⚔ Incites conflict when bored
  - ⚔ Tendency towards sarcasm and ridicule
  - ⚔ Emotionally distant; inability to articulate feelings

## Naked Advice for the Page of Swords

*Career:* If you need an unparalleled fact checker, detail ferret, dirt gatherer or undeterred paparazzi, this Page is your man (or woman). Adept at keeping files (and tabs) on everyone at the office, no damaging deed will escape notice. From pink slips to downsizing, random drug tests to unfavorable evaluations, if bad news needs dispensing, these are the ones for the job. More like the Anti-Human Resource Department, they specialize in big data over warm data, so if kid gloves, EQ or Zappos-esque customer service is called for, find someone else to fill those shoes.

*Romance:* Often petty, insecure and empathetically crippled, these ones not only find it difficult to form and maintain close relationships, but tend to be most likely to sport a fake Facebook profile. Hovering around the single digits on the Emotional Intelligence scale, they think nothing of using false names, bogus status updates or photoshopped selfies (or ones from 30 years ago—when they were 18). Feelings rarely enter interpersonal equations, so if they engage you in an online game of 20 Questions, the motive is information gathering... not romantic interest. So how do you know if the person on the other side of the computer monitor or smart phone screen is the real deal? Heed red flags like evasion and "too good to be true" stories (including the "unmarried" relationship status), as well as contradictions and a persecution complex.

*Parenting*: You wouldn't like it if someone snooped into your private affairs, right? So unless you want to plant seeds of mistrust that may one day bloom to full-blown disgust, leave the diary lock *alone*. However, when it comes to the internet, the virtual playground looks more like a minefield, so restrict your children's social media contacts and do set the password (despite possible protests). There are too many misanthropic trolls online gnashing their teeth in friendless isolation, just waiting for young minds to ensnare and exploit.

*Spirituality:* We both know that mentally nitpicking at the moral faults of others (and, sometimes, strategically divulging them) masks your own feelings of defectiveness and unworthiness. In the Greek, the word for "sin" is an archery term meaning, "missing the mark". Guess what? *Everyone* misses the mark (whether set by a sacred text, religious leader, teacher, parent or coach), which is what makes us delightfully human. Confront your own brokenness and begin to glue your shattered soul together with gentleness, patience and understanding. Because *you* have changed, the world will mirror the same.

**Recommended Resources:** "Four O'clock" (*Twilight Zone*); *Travel Experience* by Normal Rockwell; *Boy Reading His Sister's Diary* by Normal Rockwell

**Page of Swords Card Layout:** *I Spy With My Little Eye* Spread

1. What am I paying too much attention to right now?
2. What *really* needs my focus?
3. How do I view flaws in others?
4. How do I view flaws in myself?
5. How can I best avoid giving "stink eye" towards others and myself?

# Page of Coins – Be Prepared

**Stripped Down Overview:** Trustworthy, studious and serious, these always-prepared Boy Scouts do their homework, clean their room and help out with chores—all without being told. Sharpened pencils in pockets, alphabetized books on shelves and color-coded clothes in closet, these Pages tend to have a narrow range of preferences—making them picky about food, fabrics and temperature. Chapped hands testify to their avid use of anti-bacterial products, while their check/re-check loop borders on OCD. Early enterprises like lemonade stands, babysitting gigs and snow shoveling services hint that they may very well grow up to be Big Business Kings of Coins—especially since they're savers, not spenders. Their cautious "rather-be-safe-than-sorry" nature contributes to labels like "stick-in-the-mud" or "party pooper". Usually quiet and polite to a fault, you'll not find a better friend—or someone to take the blame.

**Keywords:** Student of Finances; Developing Property; Learning About Wealth; Curious About the Body; Exploring the Environment; Naïve About Spending; Immature with

Responsibility; Learning to be Grounded; Kinesthetic Development; Delivering Possessions; Preparing to Exercise; Searching for Money; Wondering About Resources; Asking for an Allowance; Requesting Resources; Immature Development; Vulnerable to Illness; Studying Anatomy; Experimenting with Food; Vulnerable with Loyalty; Playing with Investments; Searching for Security; Childlike Caution; Messages from/about the Body

**Personifications and Embodiments:** Mary Ingalls (*Little House in the Prairie*); Cinderella; Dudley Do-Right; Rowley Jefferson (*Diary of a Wimpy Kid* Series); Ken Jennings; Eagle Scouts; Girl Scouts; Howard Sprague (*Mayberry RFD*); Eeyore; Mr. Snuffalupagus; Mr. French (*Family Affair*)

**Quote:** *If I had eight hours to chop down a tree, I'd spend six sharpening my axe.* – Abraham Lincoln

**Nickname:** Dutiful Danielle

**Challenge:** Variation

**Gift:** Consistency

**Occupations/Vocations:** Eagle Scout; Student; Butler; Crossing Guard; Sports Medicine; Health Teacher; Food Taster; Tour Guide; Accountant; Bank Teller; Grant Writer

**Disney Totem:** Russell (*Up*)

**Animal Symbol:** Squirrel

**Flower Essences:** Crab Apple (Bach); Sturt Desert Rose (Australian Bush)

**Crystal/Stone:** Goshenite (Colorless Beryl) – Promotes efficiency, perseverance and discipline. Makes one goal-oriented. Aids intensive learning. Encourages a careful, systematic approach.

**Aromatherapy:** Patchouli

**Body Parts/Systems and Health Issues:** Developmental Delays; Learning Disorders; PDD-NOS

**Mystical Messenger** – Gabriel of the Sorrowful Mother

**Sabian Symbol:** Aries 20 – A young girl feeding birds in winter.

**Writing Prompt:** The Boy Scouts create a new, controversial badge.

**Affirmation:** I am careful with my possessions and resources.

**Strengthsfinder 2.0:** Consistency; Includer; Responsibility

**Cattell's 16PF:** Rule-Consciousness

**Enneagram:** Type 1; Type 3; Type 6w5 (Phobic); Type 9w1

**ANSIR:** Diligent; Sage; Kinsmen

**MBTI/Keirsey:** ISTJ – "The Dependable"

- **Beneficial Traits**
  - ⋏ Dutiful, loyal and trustworthy
  - ⋏ Upholders of laws and traditions
  - ⋏ Model citizens involved with the community
  - ⋏ Cautious, careful and consistent

- **Detrimental Traits**
  - ⋏ Stingy with both money and praise for others
  - ⋏ Unquestioned compliance and conformity to authority or rules
  - ⋏ Disapproving of those without high principles or convictions
  - ⋏ Studious and serious to the point of eschewing fun or frivolity

## Naked Advice for the Page of Coins

*Career:* Going back to school, enrolling in an online program, studying texts from your field or taking classes—one or more of these are indicated when the Page of Coins shows up. The difference between a promotion or whole new career trajectory depends on your willingness to learn and expand your skill set.

*Romance:* Often shy and reserved, this delicate dandy needs taking by the hand and shown the ways of romance and seduction. A careful, considerate lover, he may need told what to do and where you like it, so be patient and gentle. Once he knows his way around tit and twat, you'll thank your lucky stars that you took him under your titillating tutelage.

*Parenting*: Helping old ladies across the street, serving as an altar boy, achieving Eagle Scout, earning a scholarship—in many ways, you have the model child. However, because he's not one to make waves, check in with him to ensure he's not being bullied by peers or burdened by the expectations of others. When quite young, stay regular with his annual checkups so any developmental delays, learning disabilities or hearing problems can be diagnosed early.

*Spirituality:* You may have stopped to smell the roses—but have you taken the time to consider the flower's message to *you*? Pay attention to notes from the Universe in the form of trees, animals, stones, leaves, metals, herbs and soil-dwelling creatures. Look closely, listen carefully, and ask the spirits of nature to reveal their mysteries.

**Recommended Resources:** *The Remains of the Day* (Movie); *Master Hilary – The Tracer* by William Holman Hunt; *Home from Camp* by Normal Rockwell; *The Student* by Normal Rockwell

**Page of Coins Card Layout:** *Wanting What I Have* Spread

1. What am I not appreciating (or am taking for granted) right now?
2. What material or physical blessing needs closer inspection?
3. How can I increase my gratitude towards this blessing?

## Page of Cups – Head in the Clouds

**Stripped Down Overview:** Head in the clouds and feet off the ground, these whimsical dreamers envision Technicolor lands over the rainbow, sunny tomorrows and silver linings on every cloud. Often attracted to worlds more beautiful, surprising and gentle than our own, these Pages frolic with unabashed joy and open hearts. As kids, they love to play dress up, tell stories and stage plays for anyone within earshot. When they grow up, this penchant morphs into Steampunk cosplay, ComiCon geekfests and online fanfic. The more eccentric strain fancies themselves as "unique" and "different" — sometimes replacing their given name with an enigmatic symbol (Prince) or masterminding contests from cloistered chocolate factories. Or, they feel part of a "special" club — including Whovians and Whedonites. The other type is more Sesame Street than Elm Street — lovers of "Just Be Glad" games, red balloons, careening kites and playful rhymes. Because these ones tend to reside in the Land of Make-Believe (or Disney), many people don't take them seriously...or find their sugary sweetness bordering on a diabetic coma.

**Keywords:** Exploring Dreams; Searching for the Divine; Studying Healing; Seeking Forgiveness; Developing Values; Preparing for Love; Vulnerable with Emotions; Delivering Uplifting Messages; Immature About Sharing; Inexperienced with Empathy; Naïve About Relationships; Student of Aesthetics; Childish Values; Learning About Compassion; Messages of Affection; Bringing Optimism; Planting Wonderment; Underdeveloped Feelings; Premature Idealization; Studying Moods

**Personifications and Embodiments:** Willie Wonka; Dr. Seuss; Jim Henson; Polyanna; Dorothy Gale; Sarah (*The Little Princess*); Annie Warbucks; Spongebob SquarePants; *Harold and the Purple Crayon*; Strawberry Shortcake; Fanboys/Girls; Backyardigans; Barney; Sebastian (*Never Ending Story*); Disney's Imagineers; Shirley Temple; Pamela Colman Smith

**Quote:** *There are some who live in a dream world, and there are some who face reality; and then there are those who turn one into the other.* – Douglas Everett

**Nickname:** Dreamy Dawn

**Challenge:** Escapism

**Gift:** Imagination

**Occupations/Vocations:** Deliverer of Flowers, Balloons or Singing Telegrams; Greeting Card Writer; Family Entertainer; Puppeteer; Foley Artist; Sound Effect Engineer

**Disney Totem:** Ariel (*The Little Mermaid*)

**Animal Symbol:** Goose

**Flower Essences:** Clematis (Bach); Red Lily (Australian Bush)

**Crystal/Stone:** Tourmaline Cat's Eye – Stimulates drawing on a rich inner world of images. Brings new perspectives. Reflects and enhances the beauty in everything. Augments perception.

**Aromatherapy:** Helichrysum (Imortelle)

**Body Parts/Systems and Health Issues:** Seafood Poisoning; Shellfish Allergy; Sense of Smell; Nose

**Mystical Messenger** – Hyacinthus

**Sabian Symbol:** Cancer 9 – A small naked girl bends over a sparkling pond trying to catch a fish.

**Writing Prompt:** A stray kitten brings magic to a rural town.

**Affirmation:** I will play, laugh and dream like a child.

**Strengthsfinder 2.0:** Adaptability; Positivity

**Cattell's 16PF:** Abstractedness

**Enneagram:** Type 2; Type 4; Type 7; Type 9

**ANSIR:** Scintillator; Evokateur; Healer; Empath; Kinsmen

**MBTI/Keirsey:** ISFP – "The Imaginator"

- **Beneficial Traits**
  - ⅄ Sensitive, gentle, quiet and reserved
  - ⅄ Highly attuned to the five senses, as well as form and function
  - ⅄ Values beauty, nature and animals
  - ⅄ Live in accordance with strong personal values

- **Detrimental Traits**
  - ⅄ Difficulty with long-term planning and goal setting
  - ⅄ May come across as sluggish or dim-witted
  - ⅄ Optimism glosses over potential problems or hazards
  - ⅄ Very self-critical, especially after real or perceived mistakes

## Naked Advice for the Page of Cups

*Career:* Game developers, toy makers, costume designers, puppeteers, happy clowns, analog special effect creators, comic bookstore owners and Foley artists—any career where you can play for pay will suit your exquisite tastes. Although you create fantastical experiences for the rest of us to enjoy, you work best alone—especially when in the throes of world building, character development and reality bending.

*Romance:* With your fertile imagination, beware of projecting your ideal date, mate or escapade upon someone else. The virtual theater between your ears unfurls with kaleidoscopic sight and sound—but the flesh and bone in front of you (or in your bed) can never match the impressionistic brushstrokes of your manufactured bliss.

*Parenting:* The tender shoots of "what if?" and "once upon a time" need nurturing, not clipped or uprooted with admonitions to "grow up" or "face facts". The time will come soon enough when kiddo is faced with a reality ladder where he'll either climb to retrieve his pie in the sky—bringing his dreams from cloud to table—or settle for the *same-o, same-o* gruel as the status quo.

*Spirituality:* It's time for you to discover the Pearl of Great Price, but you may be amazed (and dismayed) to realize that, like its oyster counterpart, this spiritual gem is created by grit and irritation. Imitation pearls are pretty, easy to obtain and can fool most people, but true wisdom is found in dark wetness between hard shells—not hanging from the neck of a plastic mannequin.

**Recommended Resources:** *Just Around the Corner* (Movie); *A Lute Player* by Hendrick Terbrugghen; "Over the Rainbow" by Harold Arlen

**Page of Cups Card Layout:** *Dream On* Spread

1. What am I pretending about?
2. What costume am I wearing?
3. What "special effects" does my life need?
4. Where am I being "too practical"?
5. How do I find my Pearl of Great Price?

# KNIGHTS

## Knight of Wands – Ready, Fire, Aim

**Stripped Down Overview:** *I feel a need...a need for speed.* Girded by fearless audacity, the Knight of Wands' internal engine is fueled by one of three things: adrenaline, religious fervor or a "cause". For the adrenaline junkies, pushing envelopes, taking unusual risks and playing chicken with the Grim Reaper makes them feel *alive*. Sensation seekers and mortality challengers, they populate the ranks of explorers and pioneers. Without them, shark-infested waters, wild frontiers and darkest space would be *terra incognita*—untouched and undocumented for the rest of us to behold and understand. For those seized with religious fervor, "spreading the gospel", proselytizing and fiery evangelism stems from extreme unction that often even *they* cannot explain. Lastly, those with a "cause" exhibit the same zeal and conviction as their religious counterparts, but their target may have nothing to do with spirituality. Instead, an invisible fire—usually catalyzed by witnessing tragedy or experiencing devastating loss—spurs these ones to crusade against social injustice, battle deadly diseases, fight poverty, combat child abuse or expose corruption. Charismatic, charming and persuasive, each permutation lives spectacularly, dares greatly and seduces absolutely—rarely giving a rat's ass what anyone thinks about their exploits or tactics.

**Keywords:** Chasing Exhilaration; Pursuing Self-Exploration; Crossing Boundaries; Zealous Ambition; Daring Innovation; Crusading for Individualism; Running After an Exciting Mission; Acting Aggressively; Pushing for Self-Reliance; Questing for Initiation; Awakening Catalyst; Message Bolstering Self-Esteem; Attacking Inflammation; Escalating Expansiveness; Fast Acquisition; Launching Self-Help Projects; Adventurous Self-

Starter; Burgeoning Vocational Pursuits; Exuberant Passions

**Personifications and Embodiments:** Captain Kirk (*Star Trek*); Evel Knievel; Demolition Experts; Buzz Lightyear (*Toy Story*); Lion Tamers; Stuntmen; Evangelists; Daredevils; Car Chases; Fire-and-Brimstone Preachers; Erin Brockovich; Firefighters; Charismatic Gurus; Tightrope Walkers; Extreme Sports; Steve-O; Skydivers; Bomb Squad; Base Jumpers; Escape Artists; *Jackass*; Pentecostalism; Test Pilots; Activists; Jimmy Swaggart; Search and Rescue; The Wallendas

**Quote:** *When you discover your mission, you will feel its demand. It will fill you with enthusiasm and a burning desire to work on it.* – W. Clement Stone

**Nickname:** Zealous Zeke

**Conflict:** Man versus Nature

**Challenge:** Fanaticism

**Gift:** Conviction

**Occupations/Vocations:** Fire Fighter; Extreme Sports Athlete; Coach; Fire-and-Brimstone Preacher; Vulcanologist; Stunt Driver; Daredevil; Wild Animal Handler

**Disney Totem:** Lightning McQueen (*Cars*)

**Animal Symbol:** Ram

**Flower Essences:** Elm (Bach); Vervain (Bach) [Especially as Crusader]

**Crystal/Stone:** Carnelian Agate (Banded Agate) – Helps with overcoming challenges and defending a cause. Stimulates and motivates. Enhances receptivity.

**Aromatherapy:** Frankincense

**Body Parts/Systems and Health Issues:** High Blood Pressure

**Mystical Messenger** – Saint Francis of Paola

**Sabian Symbol:** Leo 8 – An activist is stirring up discontent by spreading his revolutionary ideals.

**Writing Prompt:** A famous daredevil performs an unexpected act on live TV.

**Affirmation:** I am wild, free and bold!

**Strengthsfinder 2.0:** Activator; Self-Assurance

**Cattell's 16PF** – Dominance

**Enneagram:** Type 1 (As Crusader); Type 6 (Counterphobic); Type 7; Type 8

**ANSIR:** Extremist; Realist; Sentinel (As Crusader)

**MBTI/Keirsey:** ENTP – "The Warrior"

- **Beneficial Traits**
  - ∧ Excellent debaters
  - ∧ Incredibly resourceful problem solvers and improvisers
  - ∧ Sizes up situations, environment and people quickly and accurately

A Forthright communicators

- **Detrimental Traits**
  - A Penchant for verbal sparring may provoke heated arguments
  - A Pushing limits of body, nature and machine may turn dangerous
  - A Zeal can turn into cult-like fanaticism
  - A Adverse to romantic commitments

## Naked Advice for the Knight of Wands

*Career:* You have an uncanny ability to predict the behaviors and outcomes of animal, man and machine—so any career (especially freelance) that allows your one-step-ahead brilliance to shine would fit your restless disposition. Working at dizzying heights and face-flattening speeds appeals to you, so high-rise window washer, mountaineer, circus performer, race car driver, heavy equipment operator, stunt pilot or wild animal trainer would thrill you to no end. After all, you mostly work to afford your expensive—and dangerous—recreational pursuits, right? I'm sure you hear this all the time, but *be careful*...especially on commutes. Getting tickets for speeding in your little red corvette or for recklessly driving your motorcycle is one thing; being pronounced DOA, wrapped around a telephone pole, is quite another.

*Romance:* When this Knight blazes into your orbit, expect sex for sport, tireless lovemaking and exciting role playing burned onto the bedroom's menu. Conquering physical challenges— including marathon fuckfests—sustains their addiction to natural highs. Although the best choice for lover, they're the worst one for a long-term mate. Generally commitment-phobic, these doubly fiery *just-passing-through* peacocks refuse to be responsible for others. Impossible to tame or train, the domestic life repels them; remaining free to pursue their death-defying hobbies or advance their *cause du jour* ranks as highest priority. Forthright communicators, there's never a question what's on their minds—so doubletalk, fabricated bullshit or passive-aggressive behavior are blessedly absent from their interpersonal repertoire.

*Parenting*: Climbing on dressers, jumping from the top stair, dangling from tree branches—it's enough to give you a heart attack! If kiddo just can't seem to stop testing limits of time and space—and largely remains unharmed—you may well have to accept the idea that dancing with danger is DNA encoded. Some are just *born* to prance the jagged edge of risk. If your progeny comes home with a bee in her bonnet about some cause or project, support her zeal for righting wrongs, adopting animals or raising money for the homeless. After all, she may evolve into an extraordinary humanitarian, philanthropist or (*gasp*) conscious politician.

*Spirituality:* You're not one to navel gaze, preferring to ask *when* and *how*, rather than the existential *why*. "The Universe, "God" or "The Divine" — the "bigger than Self" vastness mostly gets those titles from *others*. You, however, name it "mountain", "ocean", "jungle" or "sky" —a terrestrial expanse to explore and conquer. *Hazard is next to godliness* could be your motto, for coursing adrenaline mimics your idea of "spiritual". Your perilous self-determined priorities leave little (or no) room for mate or child, so if/when disease, accident or age comes knocking, realize you'll likely answer that door *alone*. Remember this: you don't *have* to wait for the unwelcome visit of misfortune or midlife before forging meaningful relationships and soul connections.

**Recommended Resources:** *The Apostle* (movie); "Speed"

(Radiator Cap 1925) by The Gorham Company; *Tattoo Artist* by Normal Rockwell

**Knight of Wands Card Layout:** *Risky Business* Spread

1. In what area am I most willing to take a risk?
2. In what area do I *refuse* to take a risk?
3. What do I need to risk for my soul's growth right now?
4. Who or what will help me take this risk?
5. What is the worst that could happen?
6. Best case scenario.

# Knight of Swords – Running with Scissors

**Stripped Down Overview:** The domain of rogues, juvenile delinquents and career criminals, the worst of this bunch lines the seedy underbelly of both sides of the law. From crooked cops to vigilantes, clever serial killers to smooth talking tyrants, the Knight of Swords is arguably the most dangerous person in the Tarot—not the least because of his preference for sharp objects. He's often in the middle of conflict somehow, somewhere—usually the *man versus man* or *man versus society* variety. Fleet of foot, thought and tongue, these ones relentlessly pursue their idea of "justice", tribalism or even anarchy. The first rumblings of revolution begin with these Knights, who take to spray cans, crowbars and machetes to drive their point home. In the wake of riots, looting and destruction, the responsibility for restoring order falls to the uneasy bedfellows of Justice and The Emperor—and their generals, the Tarot Kings.

**Keywords:** Questing for Beliefs; Attacking Restrictions; Rebelling Against the Law; Acting to Sever; Pursuing Separation; Rushing Strategy; Conquering Principles; Launching Discrimination; Modifying Language; Running with Knives; Pushing Against

Narrowness; Crusading for Judgment; Harvesting Assumptions; Daring Sharp Communication

**Personifications and Embodiments:** Javert (*Les Miserables*); Rorschach *(Watchmen)*; *Lord of the Flies*; *The Outsiders*; KKK; The Black Panthers; Khan (*Into Darkness*); *Training Day*; *The Shield*; *West Side Story*; BTK; Gangsters; Militant Extremists; Vikings; Mongols; Charles Manson; Avengers; Repeat Offenders; Hate Groups; Fred Phelps (Westboro Baptist Church); Hell's Angels; Mobs; Idi Amin; Skinheads; "Bad to the Bone" (Song)

**Quote:** *He who lives by the sword dies by the sword.* – Matthew 26:52

**Nickname:** Dangerous Derrick

**Conflict:** Man versus Society/Laws; Man versus Man

**Challenge:** Restraint

**Gift:** Instinctiveness

**Occupations/Vocations:** Transplant Surgeon; Helicopter Pilot; Paramedic; Ambulance Driver; ER Doctor; Roller Coaster Designer; Cop; Outlaw

**Disney Totem:** Sid (*Toy Story*)

**Animal Symbol:** Kingfisher

**Flower Essences:** Cherry Plum (Bach); Mountain Devil (Australian Bush); Red Helmet Orchid (Australian Bush)

**Crystal/Stone:** Volcano Jasper – Enhances sixth sense for danger. Promotes calm and speed in critical situations. Encourages alertness and caution.

**Aromatherapy:** Tuberose

**Body Parts/Systems and Health Issues:** Assault; Abuse; Self-Harm/Cutting

**Mystical Messenger** – Sarita Colonia

**Sabian Symbol:** Gemini 8 – Aroused strikers surround a factory.

**Writing Prompt:** Mob rules in a futuristic America.

**Affirmation:** My reactions are quick and precise.

**Strengthsfinder 2.0:** Competition; Context

**Cattell's 16PF:** Social Boldness

**Enneagram:** Type 6 (Counterphobic); Type 8w7; Type 7w8

**ANSIR:** Extremist; Realist; Sentinel

**MBTI/Keirsey:** ESTP – "The Deviant"

- **Beneficial Traits**
  - ⋏ Cool-headed in emergencies
  - ⋏ Excellent at crisis management
  - ⋏ Undaunted by conflict or criticism
  - ⋏ Active, quick and effective

- **Detrimental Traits**
  - ⋏ Bullies; may be abusive
  - ⋏ Unscrupulous

⊼ Insensitive and boorish

⊼ Easily bored; seeks out taboo diversions

## Naked Advice for the Knight of Swords

*Career:* Handy with knives, axes, needles or rifles? Comfortable with the sight of blood, broken bones and exposed organs? If you tend to go where angels fear to tread (or wouldn't be caught dead) consider a job as a first responder—paramedic, ambulance driver, battlefield physician, SWAT and related emergency careers. When shit hits the fan, your nerves of steel, quick reflexes and cool decisiveness can turn the tide in matters of life and death.

*Romance:* Several years ago, a woman in her 50s came to me asking if she should move in with her boyfriend (both were grandparents). The Knight of Swords came up, and I inferred a domestic situation fraught with sharp words, a violent temper and reckless behavior. About a year later at a bar, the boyfriend tried to cheat a guy in a game of pool, got into a drunken altercation, went out to his car, retrieved a gun, and went back *into* the bar. He followed the guy into the bathroom, shot himself in the hand (*d'oh!*) and fled the scene. When he was due to go to trial, none of the witnesses showed up (intimidation was suspected). He got away with attempted murder—and continues to be a menace (e.g., poisoning animals, harassing neighbors and driving drunk). Despite his criminal acts, the woman eventually married the guy. With the Tarot, forewarned is forearmed—but free will being what it is, there's no guarantee that querents (or perhaps you?) will make the wisest choice based on revealed information.

*Parenting:* Do kids turn out according to nature or nurture? Some anecdotal evidence suggests stable homes with loving caretakers spawning monstrous miscreants. Other stories describe despicable parenting and crushing maltreatment—yet the child grows up to be a productive member of society (David Pelzer, *A Child Called "It"*, comes to mind). If any children are under your charge or influence, do your best to shield them from violence (including video games, TV and movies), harsh words and hostility. Spend as much quality time with them as you can so they feel seen, heard and understood. Also, try boosting their self-esteem with encouragement and recognition.

*Spirituality:* In the Bible's Old Testament, King David sent his faithful soldier, Uriah, to the frontlines of the battlefield knowing he'd be killed—just so His Majesty could bury his weasel in Bathsheba's bush. In the New Testament, Paul—once named Saul—was responsible for persecuting and killing Christians, including the stoning of Stephen. No matter what you've done wrong (or think you've done wrong), grace and redemption is possible. The first step requires forgiving yourself. The second one involves making amends and providing restitution (only if your actions would not cause further harm or grief). Now that you know better, you'll have the opportunity to *do* better. Don't screw it up.

**Recommended Resources:** *Watchmen* (Movie); *Judith Slaying Holofernes* by Artemisia Gentileschi

**Knight of Sword Card Layout:** *WTF?* Spread

1. What the hell was I thinking?
2. What is the root of my actions?
3. How can I deal with the root?
4. What is the unforeseen collateral damage?
5. How will my actions affect my life in the next year?
6. How will my actions affect my life in the long run?

7. How do I make it right?
8. How do I forgive myself?
9. How can I do better?

## Knight of Coins – Slow and Steady Wins the Race

**Stripped Down Overview:** Mosey up to the jukebox, pardner, and cue up "Eye of the Tiger", for this slow and steady cowboy can outrun and outwork just about any varmint in the Tarot. Whether clad in plaid or swathed in spandex—and usually soaked in sweat, dirt or grease—these hands-on Knights tend to be more brawn than brains. Lassoed to measurements, productivity and predictability, these dependable tortoises often beat the hares to the finish line with their relentless work ethic. From endless reps at the gym to furrowing hardened soil, any conflicts entered usually remain confined to *man versus nature* or *man versus himself.* Steady, useful and affable as a rule, this *in-it-for-the-long-haul* workhorse doesn't know the meaning of the word *quit*—even when he's galloping down the wrong road.

**Keywords:** Pursuing Physicality; Tracking Health; Chasing Money; Questing for Material Goods; Moving Soil; Harvesting Crops; Burgeoning Agriculture; Promoting Caution; Acting Slowly; Awakening Senses; Hunting Animals; Acquiring Possessions; Conquering Nature; Going After Security; Subjugating the Body

**Personifications and Embodiments:** John Wayne; Cowboys; Farmers; Isometrics; Self-flagellation; Personal Trainers; Bodybuilders; Hanz and Franz (*Saturday Night Live* skit); Rodeos; Plowing; Bear Grylls; Mr. Fixit; Handyman Negri (*Mr. Rogers' Neighborhood*); Arnold Schwarzenegger; The Rock (Dwayne Johnson); Construction Workers; Health Nuts; Fitness Gurus; "To Build a Fire" (Jack London); *Old Man and the Sea* (Ernest

Hemingway); Survivalists; Physical Therapists; *Handy Manny*; Tomboys; *Dukes of Hazzard*; Good Ol' Boys; Rednecks

**Quote:** *Hard work spotlights the character of people: some turn up their sleeves, some turn up their noses, and some don't turn up at all.*
– Sam Ewing

**Nickname:** Workhorse Wayne

**Conflict:** Man versus Nature; Man versus Himself

**Challenge:** Obstinacy

**Gift:** Steadfastness

**Occupations/Vocations:** Farmer; Mover; Handyman; Department of Agriculture Employee; Truck Driver; Garbage Collector

**Disney Totem:** Wall*E (*Wall*E)

**Animal Symbol:** Ox

**Flower Essences:** Oak (Bach); Old Man Banksia (Australian Bush)

**Crystal/Stone:** Garnet Mica Schist – Boosts fitness and performance. Promotes vigor to carry out duties. Broadens capacity to work. Gives strength to master great difficulties.

**Aromatherapy:** Ginger

**Body Parts/Systems and Health Issues:** Nail Fungus; Corns; Calluses

**Sabian Symbol:** Taurus 29 – Two cobblers working side by side at a table.

**Mystical Messenger** – Saint Isidore the Laborer

**Writing Prompt:** A farmer who plants only red flowers, vegetables and fruit.

**Affirmation:** I work hard in my chosen field.

**Strengthsfinder 2.0:** Deliberative; Discipline

**Cattell's 16PF:** Tension

**Enneagram:** Type 6; Type 9; Type 3w2;

**ANSIR:** Realist; Diligent; Sentinel; Kinsmen; Healer

**MBTI/Keirsey:** ESFP – "The Demonstrator"

- **Beneficial Traits**
  - Great with the hands; talented builders and renovators
  - Excellent work ethic; not afraid to sweat
  - Consummate team players; gets along well with others
  - Committed partners and parents

- **Detrimental Traits**
  - Comfort with repetition and familiarity may limit potential
  - Takes criticism personally
  - Fears taking risks or doing things differently
  - Detests "quitters"; reluctant to "surrender" or "give up"

## Naked Advice for the Knight of Coins

*Career:* Any job that requires stamina, reliability and long hours will suit your blue-collar bent just fine. You're not afraid of manual labor, strenuous activity or pushing your body to its limits, so if feelings of frustration or restlessness abound, check to see if you're being challenged in the right areas. What suits preppy Paul or glad-handing Gary will likely bore you silly, especially if you're stuck behind a desk or chained to a computer. If you're the type that loves to build or repair, take that taste for tinkering and transform it into an income stream.

*Romance:* A perfect attendance record, reluctance to miss a day (even when sick), volunteered overtime or extra credit—if you desire a responsible partner that goes the extra mile (or two), this is the Knight to snag. However, don't expect romantic gestures like flowers, candy or candlelit dinners; instead, count on gestures of affection along the lines of changing your flat tire, mowing the lawn, insulating the attic, walking the dog or bringing home pizza for supper after work/school. Just remember, though, that this brand of dedication extends to extracurricular pursuits and hobbies, as well—so softball games, gym workouts, mountain biking, skiing and marathon training may bump you off the schedule.

*Parenting*: Instead of pampering your progeny, try instilling a "no pain, no gain" perspective. In this microwave *gotta-have-it-now* milieu, kids need to realize that building a stable life involves dedication, repetition and patience. Pass on the value of delayed gratification, persistent effort and sweat equity and, one day, they may apply this worthwhile wisdom to their education, goals, relationships and dreams. Start by creating a visual checklist assigning daily chores and ensuring they get done—at the risk of losing social and entertainment extras if they *don't*.

*Spirituality:* Deacon, greeter, Sunday School teacher—you're the epitome of religious faithfulness once you find a fitting house of worship. If gathering with others enriches your soul, do look for a place to serve others and commune with God. However, if solitude soothes your spirit, dedicate yourself to crafting or enacting daily rituals to connect with the Divine—maintaining a personal altar, practicing meditations, saying prayers with mala beads or a rosary, chanting, sacred singing or working with crystals/stones.

**Recommended Resources:** *Men at Work* by Vincent Van Gogh; *Bob the Builder* (TV Show); *Farmer and the Bird* by Normal Rockwell; *Gold Morning in California* by Grafton Tyler Brown

**Knight of Coins Card Layout:** *Pumping Iron* Spread

1. Where am I the weakest?
2. How do I best strengthen this area?
3. Where am I overdoing it?
4. How do I ease up in this area?
5. What area could bear more weight?
6. Right now, where am I strongest?

## Knight of Cups – In Love with Love

**Stripped Down Overview:** A young woman holds the door for you, a teenager gives a rose to a first date, an elderly gentleman holds an umbrella over the head of a mother pushing a stroller in a rainstorm—chivalry in action, this courteous cavalier personifies the *let-me-throw-my-cloak-over-the-mud-puddle-so-you-don't-have-to-get-your-feet-wet* gallantry rarely seen these days. Like all Tarot Knights, the Knight of Cups is "after" something: in this case, a romantic ideal, Utopia, aesthetic or otherworldly experience. In fact, he epitomizes almost everything we associate with the Knight archetype—sans bravery, which may not be a part of his constitution, given his aversion to conflict and danger. Ardent, sensual, mysterious and generous, he rides a torrent of emotion, although his oft-unruffled exterior belies the depth of his tumultuous feelings. Symbolic actions and poetic speech lace his comportment, rousing misjudgments as effete at best and insincere at worst. Often artistic by nature, he may be a theater geek—pining for the stage as a dancer, singer or choreographer—but possibly settling for prop guy, scenery painter or light operator for lack of confidence. When plagued with unfulfilled desires, money burns a hole through pocket or purse as this one attempts to assuage gnawing pangs of "want". At times, he'll divert his longings into "people projects", attempting to rescue damsels or turn bad apples into palatable pies.

**Keywords:** Questing After Romance; Conquering Mystery; Chasing Love; Running After Ghosts; Acting Upon Dreams; Pursuing Spiritual Communion; Moving to Mend; Running Towards Relationships; Daring Idealism; Running with Imagination; Rushing Feelings; Crusading for Aesthetics; Rescuing Preciousness; Passion for the Divine; Enamored with the Paranormal; Practicing Healing

**Personifications and Embodiments:** Troubadours; Pepé Le Pew; Gomez Addams (*The Addams Family*); "Song of Solomon"; Mystics; Quest for the Holy Grail; "Cyrano De Bergerac"; Don Juan; Valentine's Day; Ghost Hunters; Paris; He Loves Me, He Loves Me Not; Sir Galahad; Elaborate Romantic Gestures; Rumi; Leopold (*Kate and Leopold*); Love Letters; Parsifal/Percival; Flowers and Candy; Saint Teresa of Avila; *Song of Solomon*; Don Quixote; Marriage Proposal on the Jumbotron; Knight in Shining Armor; White Knight; Knights of the Round Table; Paranormal Researchers; "Every Breath You Take" (The Police); Delilah (Radio Host); Public Displays of Affection

**Quote:** *Romance is the glamour which turns the dust of everyday life into a golden haze.* – Elinor Glyn

**Nickname:** Quixotic Quincy

**Conflict:** Man versus Himself

**Challenge:** Obsequiousness

**Gift:** Devotion

**Occupations/Vocations:** Poet; Romance Novelist; Love Songs DJ; Folk Singer; Composer; Dancer; Choreographer

**Disney Totem:** El Chupacabra (*Planes*)

**Animal Symbol:** Puffin

**Flower Essences:** Centaury (Bach); Clematis (Bach); Honeysuckle (Bach)

**Crystal/Stone:** Ammolite (Korite) – Promotes seductive charm and charisma. Magnifies beauty. Awakens interest in mysteries. Releases mental obsessions. Fortifies the heart.

**Aromatherapy:** Rose Maroc

**Body Parts/Systems and Health Issues:** Needing to Take Medicine Regularly and Consistently

**Mystical Messenger** – Saint Sebastian

**Sabian Symbol:** Taurus 26 – A Spaniard serenading his senorita.

**Writing Prompt:** A mysterious valentine is sent to a Catholic priest.

**Affirmation:** I pursue love, beauty and courtesy.

**Strengthsfinder 2.0:** Harmony; Relator

**Cattell's 16PF:** Apprehension

**Enneagram:** Type 2; Type 4; Type 9

**ANSIR:** Empath; Healer; Scintillator; Evokateur

**MBTI/Keirsey:** INFP – "The Romantic"

- **Beneficial Traits**
  - Emotionally expressive and highly intuitive
  - On a quest to discover love and find meaning
  - Poetic; gifted at expressing themselves through writing
  - Chivalrous and mannerly; makes people feel at ease

- **Detrimental Traits**
  - Given to emotional outbursts when stressed
  - Prone to co-dependence and staying in unhealthy relationships
  - Struggles with insecurity; flatters as overcompensation
  - May become obsessive with objects of affection

## Naked Advice for the Knight of Cups

*Career:* Ass kissing, brown-nosing, boot licking—whatever you want to call your pink-petaled, ingratiating flattery, it still smells like *eau du flatulence*. Twisting Darwin's "survival of the fittest" into "survival of the *fitters*" may get you special privileges, pay raises and promotions, but deep down, you'll know that you're nothing but a sycophantic poseur. You may ascend the corporate ladder faster than a slimeball with a hungry piranha up his bunghole, but the rungs are greased with yes-man bullshit... and you're all out of goodwill parachutes. (Don't despair: your innate talent for massaging words for a desired effect makes you a perfect candidate as a phone sex operator.)

*Romance:* Infatuation, thy name is Knight of Cups. Long-stem roses, boxes of chocolates, gourmet picnic lunches, dates at the opera—when this charmer comes a calling, upswept feet, intoxicating giddiness and hyperventilation may occur. These Knights, though, are more in love with the *idea* of love—so attempts to prolong the "honeymoon" stage may escalate to bizarre, convoluted efforts. Many of these paladins are prone to jealousy and co-dependence, taking high-maintenance to skyscraping heights. It's quite possible your paramour is as delicious as he appears. If so, *SCORE!* However, if his ardor devolves into incessant texts, hourly Facebook pokes and daily demands for your whereabouts between 6 AM and 11 PM— congratulations: you just won a ticket to StalkerMania.

*Parenting:* *Crunch. Crunch. Crunch.* That's a song called "Walking on Eggshells", a difficult tune you'll need to master around hypersensitive children. Often feeling misunderstood and fearing abandonment, these tykes crave acknowledgement for their uniqueness. It's imperative to engage with them emotionally, honoring their need to connect, delicate feelings and soul-searching questions. Logical or practical adults may find their intensity confusing or even intimidating—especially when these youngsters cycle through bouts of envy, sadness, dreamy longing and self-criticism. Loud noises scare them, and harsh, angry words fill them with shame—but they are comforted by undivided attention, sympathy and focused perception. Rather than labeling them "hysterical", recognize that their internal river flows broader and faster than most. Receptive to subtle energy, these kids may display an aptitude for sensing disease or distress, as well as healing gifts manifesting via therapeutic touch or prayer. They can often "see" or "hear" family members that have passed on, are the ones most likely to remember past lives and frequently tend towards an unusual connection with God, Saints, Angels or other Divine Manifestations.

### Spirituality:

*Strange fits of passion have I known;*
*And I will dare to tell,*
*But in the Lover's ear alone,*
*What once to me befell.*
– William Wordsworth

Rumi's ecstatic poetry, Shakespeare's sonnets, Saint Teresa of Avila's autobiography, the biblical *Song of Solomon*, power ballads from the 80s—such sublime verse gives shape, form and voice to myriad longings. Some call it love in all its permutations: *Eros* (sexual), *Phileo* (brotherly affection) and *Agape* (unconditional positive regard for humanity). No matter the tendril, the root is the same: yearning for connection, communion and consummation—a joining with an Other larger than the Self, to be swallowed up in Wholeness. What is wooing you right now, enticing your soul to "biggerness"? When all else fails, remember this: service ameliorates brooding.

**Recommended Resources:** *The Secret Life of Walter Mitty*; *Starstruck* by Normal Rockwell; *St. Bernard Dogs* by Sir Edwin Landseer

**Knight of Cups Card Layout:** *Deepest Desires* Spread

1. What is my deepest unconscious desire?
2. What is my deepest conscious desire?
3. What is the best way to fulfill or remedy my deepest unconscious desire?
4. What is the best way to fulfill or remedy my deepest conscious desire?
5. Final Advice/Blessing

# QUEENS

## Queen of Wands – Superwoman

**Stripped Down Overview:** *Bitch*. While the feminine Queens of Tarot (Coins and Cups) bristle when called a bitch (yet, have no qualms lobbing the moniker towards other women in fits of jealousy), the spirited Queen of Wands wears the "B" word as a badge of honor. For her, BITCH is an acronym for **B**abe **I**n **T**otal **C**ontrol of **H**erself, because she actively nurtures her passions, stokes the fires of individualism and fans the flame of innovation. When she's in the room, there's never a question where you stand with her. With dizzying versatility, she easily changes hats—shifting from mom to wife to visionary to businesswoman to advisor to achiever to volunteer, all without a hitch—adeptly embodying each role as if it were the "real" her. Generous and supportive, she has a knack for bringing out excellence in others, spurring them to live their "best life" or give their "best performance". Whatever piques her interest, she quickly masters—then teaches to others (if she feels like it). Mesmerizing to watch, she holds people's attention like a *Cirque du Soleil* performance, with just as much color, flexibility and uniqueness as those acrobatic phenoms. Often the catalyst and always an influencer, she affects "the field" with an almost otherworldly power—regardless of whether she gets official credit for her original contributions. Although money isn't the carrot that leads her to bigger and better things (that particular vegetable is novelty, originality and pioneering), she has superb good business sense; in fact, no other can sniff out a bargain like her...nor turn it around, sell it and make a tidy profit. The ultimate feminine Warrior, she tends to protect animals, children and the disadvantaged. (The charity that collects fashionable business clothes for low-income women so they'd be properly attired for a job interview? That's a classic Queen of Wands endeavor.) As a permutation of The Empress, she "mothers" projects, books, fashion, art, visionary ventures, pioneering endeavors, strong women and fellow creatives. If an enterprise needs pizzazz, she brings it. Her love language is *Quality Time* because she won't waste yours...and you sure as hell better not waste *hers*.

**Keywords:** Advocating Self-Reliance; Producing Originality; Valuing Vocation; Catalyzing Through Connection; Promoting Personal Expression; Protecting Individuality; Supporting Self-Starters; Encouraging Enthusiasm; Networking Passions; Coordinating Innovation; Teaching Entrepreneurship; Influencing Style; Cultivating Zest; Persuading with Flair; Nurturing Adaptability

**Personifications and Embodiments:** Mae West; Kathleen McGowan; Hypatia; Wonder Woman; Danielle LaPorte; Lady Gaga

**Quote:** *My passions were all gathered together like fingers that made a fist. Drive is considered aggression today; I knew it then as purpose.* – Bette Davis

**Nickname:** Versatile Vivian

**Challenge:** Overextension

**Gift:** Influence

**Occupations/Vocations:** Entrepreneur; Publicist; Workshop Presenter; Image Consultant; Lobbyist; Social Worker

**Disney Totem:** Princess Tiana (*The Princess and the Frog*)

**Animal Symbol:** Heron

**Flower Essences:** Holly (Bach); Black-Eyed Susan (Australian Bush)

**Crystal/Stone:** Lace Agate – Supports elegance. Enhances dynamism, liveliness and mental agility. Promotes flexibility in thinking and action.

**Aromatherapy:** Basil

**Body Parts/Systems and Health Issues:** Cat, Dog or Other Pet Allergy; Nut or Seed Allergy

**Mystical Messenger** – Brigid

**Sabian Symbol:** Capricorn 25 – An Oriental rug dealer in a store filled with precious ornamental rugs.

**Writing Prompt:** A makeover artist sets up shop, causing unexpected changes.

**Affirmation:** I rely on my originality to make waves and achieve greatness.

**StrengthsFinder 2.0:** Communication; Maximizer

**Cattell's 16PF:** Warmth

**Love Language:** Quality Time

**Enneagram:** Type 7w8; Type 8w9; Type 3w2

**ANSIR:** Visionary; Healer; Philosopher

**MBTI/Keirsey:** ENFJ – "The Versatile"

- **Beneficial Traits**
  - Intuits the thoughts and motivations of others
  - Multitasker extraordinaire
  - Generous with knowledge; uses influence to help colleagues
  - Entertaining and effective teachers

- **Detrimental Traits**
  - Disdain for sycophants; inability to "hear" praise from others
  - Overprotective and highly defensive of loved ones and projects
  - Contempt for the lazy, the derivative and the conventional
  - Gregarious energy may cross into brash and tactless interactions

## Naked Advice for the Queen of Wands

*Career:* Lead, follow or get the hell out of the way. Choose one, because twiddling your thumbs and saying *"ummm"* isn't on the agenda. If you're not fired up about your job, career path or profession, get thee to a competent life coach ASAP. A passionate vocational life isn't found by imitation, comparison or envy, but in pursuing a self-made path fueled by curiosity, courage, creativity and conviction. Satisfying careers for this fiery Queen include design (fashion, jewelry, art), decorating (spaces or cakes), event planning, writing (Self-Help or mainstream fiction) and public relations.

*Romance:* Is your partner's libido a mere candle to your conflagration? Does your idea of a "good time" involve art, music, design or fashion? Or maybe your girlfriend doesn't know Van Gogh from Van Halen, or your boyfriend thinks "Rush" refers to blowhard Limbaugh instead of the Canadian prog-rock trio? Such disparities can be overlooked to a point, but are you willing to sink a shitload of energy into building compatibility bridges to take your relationship from *"aw, shit"* to *"awesome!"*?

*Parenting*: Forcing Danny to play baseball (when he obviously hates it) or Denise to sing in chorus (when it's wilting her spirit) makes for miserable children. It's one thing if your kids have an aptitude for sports or a passion for music, but quite another if you're (**a**) trying to live vicariously through them (newsflash: time machines make for sucky parenting choices) or (**b**) trying to keep up with the Joneses' progeny. Remember: one day, your children will choose your nursing home, so don't piss them off by forcing their square pegs into round holes.

*Spirituality:* You feel most alive when you're devoted to a deity, pantheon, cause or creative endeavor. With zeal matched only by your "can do" attitude, you move mountains when you finally decide to go "all in". In this case, commitment will cause you to burn brighter—not extinguish your resourcefulness and enthusiasm (as you sometimes fear). Get mind, body and spirit into alignment, chart your course and sail forth in a blaze of brilliance!

**Recommended Resources:** *Big Magic* by Elizabeth Gilbert; *Discover Your Authentic Self* by Sherrie Dillard

**Queen of Wands Card Layout:** *Where's the Fire?* Spread

1. *Kindling*: What are the tools, resources or attitudes that I need?
2. *Match*: What will start the process or spark a creative

blaze?

3. *Gas*: What will fan the flames?
4. *Oxygen*: What needs space to breathe?
5. *Water*: What douses my motivation or progress?
6. *In Case of Emergency*: What will keep the fire constructive?

## Queen of Swords – Battle Axe

**Stripped Down Overview:** Here, we have the *other* Bitch of Tarot, except her acronym would be **B**allsy **I**conoclast **T**otally **C**leaning **H**ouse. Whether through tongue or ink, this no-nonsense Queen wields a lethal sword of truth, often slaying sacred cows and serving them up as juicy cheeseburgers (do you want a pickle with that?). Not one to suffer fools gladly, she refuses to enter a battle of wits with unarmed boobs. In fact, her steel-trap mind captures the unaware like a drunken hunter stepping into a bear snare. She battles corruption, fights injustice, exposes lies and unmasks poseurs. Her unparalleled bullshit detector knows no bounds, so if you're a liar, thief, toady or fraud, you best avoid her penetrating gaze. If you're an author or deck creator pumping out shoddy work or shallow prose, you'd better *hope* this Queen isn't on duty as the dreaded *Reviewer from Hell*. As a permutation of The Empress, she "mothers" accuracy, honesty, clarity and knowledge. Her love language is *Words of Affirmation*, so if she happens to toss a compliment your way, consider yourself lucky to have earned her approval.

**Keywords:** Promoting Critical Thought; Nurturing the Intellect; Advocating Discernment; Supporting Rationalism; Encouraging Curiosity; Valuing an Open Mind; Influencing Academics; Catalyzing Complex Ideas; Mending Disparity; Cultivating Inquiry; Preserving Principles; Teaching High Standards; Coordinating Communication; Persuading Scholasticism; Endorsing Analysis

**Personifications and Embodiments:** Margaret Thatcher; Ayn Rand; Helen Mirren; Simon Cowell; Judge Judy; Anton Ego (*Ratatouille*); Caroline Myss; Siskel and Ebert; George Carlin; Critics; Reviewers; Marilla Cuthbert (*Anne of Green Gables* series); Hetty King (*Tales of Avonlea* series); Grammar Police; School Marm; Stern Headmistress; Eyes in the Back of the Head; Ann Coulter; Bill Maher; Penn Gillette; Lewis Black

**Quote:** *Criticism may not be agreeable, but it is necessary. It fulfills the same function as pain in the human body. It calls attention to an unhealthy state of things.* – Winston Churchill

**Nickname:** Evaluating Esther

**Challenge:** Perfectionism

**Gift:** Discernment

**Occupations/Vocations:** Archivist; Researcher; Critic/Reviewer; News Reporter; Criminal Profiler; School Principal; Scholar

**Disney Totem:** Dean Abigail Hardscrabble (*Monsters University*)

**Animal Symbol:** Crane

**Flower Essences:** Pine (Bach); Rock Water (Bach); Yellow Cowslip Orchid (Australian Bush)

**Crystal/Stone:** Diamond – Supports an indomitable spirit. Promotes strength of character, ethics and faithfulness to oneself. Encourages responsibility and objectivity. Aids in stroke recovery.

**Aromatherapy:** Cypruss

**Body Parts/Systems and Health Issues:** Dementia; Memory Loss; Alzheimer's

**Mystical Messenger** – Hypatia

**Sabian Symbol:** Taurus 21 – A moving finger points to significant passages.

**Writing Prompt:** A tough but fair-minded reviewer gets blackballed and slandered.

**Affirmation:** I demand excellence from myself and others.

**StrengthsFinder 2.0:** Command; Intellection

**Cattell's 16PF:** Perfectionism

**Love Language:** Words of Affirmation

**Enneagram:** Type 1w9; Type 8; Type 6 (Counterphobic)

**ANSIR:** Diligent; Sentinel; Idealist (*Thinking Realm Only*); Visionary; Philosopher

**MBTI/Keirsey:** INTJ – "The Critic"

- **Beneficial Traits**
  - Knowledgeable, competent and honest
  - Promotes excellence and insists on clarity
  - Knack for knowing what will improve almost anything or anyone
  - Open-minded, big-picture philosophers

- **Detrimental Traits**
  - ⚔ Often misunderstood; blames others for misinterpretation
  - ⚔ Sharp tongues; oblivious to the feelings of others
  - ⚔ Quick to judge and vocalize admonition
  - ⚔ May come across as arrogant or elitist when frustrated

## Naked Advice for the Queen of Swords

*Career:* Uncovering discrepancies, evaluating employees, clarifying fuzzy math, checking performance, penning reviews, balancing the books, writing technical manuals—any job or career path that requires excellence and sky-high standards (or the enforcement of such) offers you a snug fit. If Ivory Towers beckon, look towards literary criticism, scientific research and social psychology for rarified air.

*Romance:* Not many can handle your brand of "take it or leave it" when it comes to intimacy. You'd rather be hated for who you *truly* are than loved for what you are *not* (the exact opposite of how most relationships—indeed, society itself—operates). Those with a natal Sun and/or Moon in Scorpio, Aquarius or Sagittarius will appreciate your authenticity the most—so you may want to ask for the day, time and place of birth on the first date. However, you of all people know it's better to be alone than paired with a self-delusional idiot.

*Parenting:* Make sure the kiddos are completing their homework and understanding their assignments. Should little Laura have a teacher phoning in her lectures, you may have to pick up the slack with supplemental instruction—private tutoring, engaging DVDs (e.g., *The Great Courses*), edutainment materials and so on. Better yet, if you have the time and means to homeschool, your temperament is unmatched for such an endeavor.

*Spirituality:* Desiring to please a deity, perfect a ritual or follow the letter of a religious law *just so* often robs you of spiritual fulfillment. Don't miss the point of sacred practice: connecting with the Ground of Being, integrating life lessons and honoring your Soul.

**Recommended Resources**: *Ayn Rand and the World She Made* by Anne C. Heller; *The Iron Lady* (movie); *The Inventor and The Judge* by Normal Rockwell

**Queen of Swords Card Layout:** *Recovery from Perfectionism* Spread

1. Why do I strive for perfection?
2. How can I cut myself some slack?
3. How can I cut *others* some slack?
4. What's more important than perfection right now?
5. Deliberate "mess up" advice?

## Queen of Coins – Tree Hugging

**Stripped Down Overview:** Hang on to your Birkenstocks, because the granola chompin', PETA lovin' Earth mother is on the *scene!* Wearing eco-friendly clothes and sporting cosmetic-free faces, these plain Janes favor pedaling bicycles, buying electric cars, taking public transit or driving horse-drawn buggies. One expression of the Queen of Coins leans so far left, she's practically horizontal. The other leans so far right, you can scrub the floor with her puritanical bun. Often political, many of these Queens populate the Moral Majority or NOW, picketing both sides of the abortion clinic fence. Knitters, basket weavers, seamstresses and crafters, these crones love working with their callused hands. If you want to raise money, barns or awareness, these are the gals to call (they don't take "*I gave at the office*" for an answer). Often obsessed with health, nutrition or cleanliness, they tend to keep the natural remedy industry in business—although many line medical waiting rooms with hypochondriacal complaints. As a permutation of The Empress, this Queen "mothers" flora, fauna, soil, water and the body. Their love language is *Gifts*, so expect double your pleasure from the community co-op or drumming circle exchange.

**Keywords:** Nurturing the Environment; Advocating Sustainability; Supporting Shared Resources; Tending Gardens; Valuing Community; Encouraging Conservation; Promoting Health; Reflecting Simplicity; Networking Artisans; Catalyzing Political Groups; Cultivating Cleanliness; Teaching Crafts; Maintaining Usefulness; Fostering Animals; Preserving Food

**Personifications and Embodiments:** Mrs. Patmore (Downton Abbey); Jane Goodall; Julia Butterfly Hill; Rachel Carson; Pagan Spirituality; Aunt Bee (*The Andy Griffith Show*); The Amish; Mennonites; Communes; Vegans; Freegans; Peace Protesters; Grass-Roots Activists; *The Beverly Hillbillies;* Red Tent Movement; Co-ops; Medicine Women

**Quote:** *Nature favors those organisms which leave the environment in better shape for their progeny to survive.* – James Lovelock

**Nickname:** Earthy Edith

**Challenge:** Dullness

**Gift:** Practicality

**Occupations/Vocations:** Veterinarian; Massage Therapist; Textile Artist; House Cleaner/Maid; Cook; Basket Weaver; Environmentalist; Greene Peace Activist; Community Garden

Director; Animal Foster Family; Red Cross Volunteer

**Disney Totem:** Edna Mode (*The Incredibles*)

**Animal Symbol:** Turtle

**Flower Essences:** Cerato (Bach); Larch (Bach)

**Crystal/Stone:** Bustamite – Deepens connection with the Earth. Helps focus thoughts to turn them into deeds. Brings inner composure. Promotes ability to relax. Aids environmental efforts.

**Aromatherapy:** Vetiver

**Body Parts/Systems and Health Issues:** Esophagus; Acid Reflex; Stomach; Ulcers; Colon; IBD; Crohn's; Colitis; Gall Bladder; Sense of Touch

**Mystical Messenger** – Saint Paraskeva

**Sabian Symbol:** Aries 17 – Two prim spinsters sitting together in silence.

**Writing Prompt:** Three women who make clothes for their village.

**Affirmation:** I embrace a simple, useful life.

**StrengthsFinder 2.0:** Arranger; Connectedness

**Cattell's 16PF:** Openness to Change

**Love Language:** Gifts

**Enneagram:** Type 1w9; Type 6w5; Type 9w1

**ANSIR:** Realist; Diligent; Kinsmen

**MBTI/Keirsey:** ISFJ – "The Rustic"

- **Beneficial Traits**
  - ⚔ Deep respect for human rights
  - ⚔ Gladly contributes time and resources for environmental issues
  - ⚔ Uncanny ability for upcycling and repurposing "cast offs"
  - ⚔ Talented at creating rituals, herbal remedies and spells

- **Detrimental Traits**
  - ⚔ Stays in the box
  - ⚔ Usually have a hard time saying "no"
  - ⚔ "Clannish"; suspicious of those who don't share their ways
  - ⚔ Desire for harmony prevents them from acknowledging differences

## Naked Advice for the Queen of Coins

*Career:* Never mind dishpan hands, barking feet or a stiff back: it's time to roll up your 100 percent cotton sleeves and get to work. Pitch in for the practical stuff that needs doing—scrubbing, sweeping, dusting, polishing, washing, mopping, painting, pulling weeds—and you'll prove your worth to present or potential employers. Your forte includes beneficial contributions to environmental, civic and agricultural efforts. If anyone can be referred to as "indispensable", it's you.

*Romance:* If you're in the market for a potential mate, look for common ground and shared values among material, financial and environmental concerns. Otherwise, you'll end up bitching about her huge carbon footprint, wasteful practices and spending habits. If you dress for comfort, eschew makeup or consider a plain ponytail the epitome of a good hair day, make sure potential partners aren't gunning for a fashionista; you couldn't do "arm candy" if you tried.

*Parenting*: Do your offspring share an affinity for handmade presents or practical tokens of affection? Don't underestimate the power of a well-timed (and much-needed) gift. Ask your kids if they need shampoo, toothpaste, shoes, jeans or other necessities—and let them choose their own.

*Spirituality:* Of all the Tarot dames, the Queen of Coins is most comfortable with goddess spirituality. What does the Divine Feminine mean to *you*? How does spirituality intersect with the material world? If you were Gaia's hands, feet and mouth, how would you conduct yourself on this Earth?

**Recommended Resources:** *The Legacy of Luna: The Story of a Tree, a Woman and the Struggle to Save the Redwoods* by Julia Butterfly Hill; *Census Taker* by Normal Rockwell; *La Cardeuse* by Jean-Francois Millet

**Queen of Coins Card Layout:** *Inner Hippie* Spread

1. How can I help my community?
2. How can I help the environment?
3. How can I best conserve resources/energy?
4. How can I best use my hands right now?
5. Advice from my Inner Hippie.

# Queen of Cups – Putting Out

**Stripped Down Overview:** Strollers, aprons and boobies—
*oh my*! Of all the Queens, this pleaser enjoys caretaking—and
motherhood—the most. Dripping with honey and tripping with
guilt, this goody-two-shoe minds her manners, priding herself
on playing nice. Highly intuitive and deeply sensitive, she
gushes, weeps or sleeps her way through casting couches, beauty
pageants, bake sales, cocktail parties and church potlucks. If you
need a sympathetic ear, this true friend is the one to call—as
long as you don't mind a heaping side dish of gossip. She knows
what you want and what you need before *you* do earning her the
reputation "Black Magic Woman". In extreme cases, she may kill
with kindness—so hide the elderberry wine and beware dog-
eared copies of *Final Exit*. As a permutation of The Empress, the
Queen of Cups "mothers" people through preparing food, giving
hugs, running errands, nursing illness and offering prayer. Her
love languages are *Physical Touch* and *Acts of Service*, so expect
lots of hand holding—and reminders of *"all I've done for you"*.

**Keywords:** Valuing Relationships; Encouraging Compassion;
Mirroring Emotions; Nourishing Intuition; Mending Hearts;
Cultivating Connection; Preserving Harmony; Tending
Domesticity; Nurturing Dreams; Reflecting the Subconscious;
Alleviating Suffering; Promoting Empathy; Protecting Intimacy

**Personifications and Embodiments:** Kathie Lee Gifford;
Matchmakers; Drama Queens; Dolly Levi; June Cleaver; Anna
Nicole Smith; Elizabeth Taylor; Southern Belles; Kuan Yin; Tammy
Faye Bakker; Marilyn Monroe; Jan Crouch; Laura Petrie (*The
Dick Van Dyke Show*); Beauty Pageants; Femme Fatales; Florence
Nightingale; *Arsenic and Old Lace*; Charm School; Beauty Salons;
Cosmetics Counters; *Cosmopolitan*; Ginger (*Gilligan's Island*); "Do
*You Really Want to Hurt Me?*" (Culture Club); Vaseline Lens

**Quote:** *Do not give in too much to feelings. An overly sensitive heart is an unhappy possession on this shaky earth.* – Johann Wolfgang Von Goethe

**Nickname:** Sympathetic Sally

**Challenge:** Martyrdom

**Gift:** Empathy

**Occupations/Vocations:** Nurse; Healer; Hairdresser; Charm School Instructor; Beauty Pageant Candidate; Makeup Artist; Morning TV Personality; Matchmakers; Red Cross Volunteer

**Disney Totem:** Bianca (*The Rescuers*)

**Animal Symbol:** Dove

**Flower Essences:** Chicory (Bach); Heather (Bach); Red Chestnut (Bach)

**Crystal/Stone:** Anthophyllite – Helps with creating and maintaining space for personal interests. Releases stress and self-imposed pressure of "doing everything". Boosts self-esteem and acknowledgement of one's worth.

**Aromatherapy:** Jasmine

**Body Parts/Systems and Health Issues:** Blood Disorders/ Infections

**Mystical Messenger** – Yemaya

**Sabian Symbol:** Cancer 21 – A *prima donna* singing.

**Writing Prompt:** A diva opera singer gives unexpected comfort.

**Affirmation:** Whenever possible, I provide solace and compassion.

**StrengthsFinder 2.0:** Empathy; Woo

**Cattell's 16PF:** Emotional Stability

**Love Languages:** *Physical Touch* and *Acts of Service*

**Enneagram:** Type 2; Type 3; Type 6 (Phobic)

**ANSIR:** Empath; Kinsmen

**MBTI/Keirsey:** ESFJ – "The Accommodator"

- **Beneficial Traits**
  - Instinctive desire to help others and take care of them
  - Enjoys planning celebrations and events; consummate hostess
  - Upbeat, conversational and friendly
  - Well-groomed and "put together"; makes great first impression

- **Detrimental Traits**
  - Attention-seeking Drama Queen; will create "situations"
  - Manipulative and passive-aggressive; often plays "the victim"
  - Lacks strong personal moral compass; adopts code from a "tribe"
  - Insatiable need to be liked provokes insecurity and jealousy

# Naked Advice for the Queen of Cups

*Career:* It's time to oil the wheels of industry with flattery, deference and a megawatt smile. Flash those bleachy whites, press the flesh, work the room and land the sale. So what if you're skating on your looks, pedigree or connections? Be nice, play nice, dress nice and smell nice (but if you can't tell *Tabu* from *Obsession*, it's better to go scentless). Remember your boss's birthday, pass around a get-well card for an ailing colleague and bring donuts to the office for everyone to share. After all, people may not remember your achievements, but they'll definitely remember how you made them feel.

*Romance:* Although it's tempting to jump into bed on the first date, you know the old saying: Why buy the cow when you can get the milk for *free*? Respect yourself so that others will do the same. Get off the crazy-making merry-go-round and sell your "Trainwreck" T-shirt: it's time to use your emotional intelligence to attract, and maintain, a stable relationship.

*Parenting*: It's so very kind of you to mend Jerry's boo-boos by baking cookies—and enrolling Jenny in basketball, dance, Girl Scouts, piano and cheerleading—but are you *sure* that's what your kids really need from you right now? Rolling yourself out like a welcome mat every morning may leave you frayed, faded and worn thin. Before you grow to resent them or experience a meltdown, take time to roll out the red carpet for *yourself* once in a while.

*Spirituality:* Giving without expecting anything in return may be difficult for you, but remember: if your acts of kindness come with strings, you become energetically entangled with the object of your affection. This renders you, essentially, an emotional puppet. Your feelings get pulled one way, and then yanked another—causing you to dance to the tunes of "Wanting Thanks", "Yearning for Praise" and "Desiring Appreciation" rather than "I Did It Because I Care" or "My Nature Is Love". Get back in touch with the melody of your heart, allowing its notes to melt the threads of expectation.

**Recommended Resources:** *Hello, Dolly!* (Musical); *Woman at Vanity* by Normal Rockwell; *Caring* by Alex Grey

**Queen of Cups Card Layout:** *Sittin' Pretty* Spread

1. *Curling Iron* – Where am I wound up?
2. *Hairspray* – What needs to be stabilized or set in place?
3. *Eye Shadow* – What am I blind to?
4. *Eyeliner* – What do I need to see?
5. *Mascara* – What am I exaggerating?
6. *Concealer* – What am I covering up or whitewashing?
7. *Earrings* – What am I hearing?
8. *Lipstick* – What do I need to say?
9. *Mirror*: What is the key to true beauty?

# The Queens as Healers

Technically, any card in a Tarot deck can contribute to healing. However, I associate the Queens of Tarot with nurturing and supporting, so I view them as forms of Healers.

Each heals differently, and no one is more effective or preferred than the others. Yet, because two of them are feminine Queens (the Cups and Coins), those are often the most recognizable and lauded.

But the two masculine Queens, the Wands and the Swords, are just as powerful and needed.

How are they different?

The **Queen of Wands** heals through passion, advocacy, inspiration, creativity and energy. She cultivates authenticity through shaking up the status quo, defending the underdog, encouraging self-reliance, adding flair, revealing patterns, promoting strength, accessing intuition, going within, understanding myth and coloring with abandon. Warrior, Pioneer, Visionary, Entrepreneur, Creator/Destroyer, Networker, Rebel, Advocate, Liberator, Mystic, Artist, Storyteller and Alchemist are archetypes associated with this queen.

*Examples:* Lady Gaga; Madonna; Annie Besant; SARK; Mary Anne Radmacher; Colette Baron-Reid; Clarissa Pinkola-Estes; Marion Woodman; Karla McLaren; Brene Brown; Cyndi Dale; Anodea Judith; Danielle LaPorte; Terry and Linda Jamison (The Psychic Twins)

*Theme:* To thine own Self be true.

The **Queen of Swords** confronts and exposes disempowering thoughts, stuck patterns, poor choices and ignorance. She heals through exposing shadows, piercing illusions, expanding perspectives, deconstructing fabrications, and applying reason. This queen can be impersonal, objective and analytical. Archetypes like Judge, Prophet, Teacher, Scholar, Sage, Detective, Exorcist, Trickster, Wordsmith and Provocateur are connected with this queen. She is like a laser or scalpel, honing in on disease that needs to be cut out lest it spread and kill.

*Examples:* Hillary Clinton; Elizabeth Warren; Caroline Myss; Louise Hay; Pema Chodron; Karen Armstrong; Joyce Meyer; Debbie Ford; Don Miguel Ruiz; Ken Wilber; Bryon Katie; Helena Blatavatsky; Dr. Phil

*Theme: The truth will set you free.*

The **Queen of Coins** heals through attending to the body, protecting the environment, advocating good nutrition and promoting prosperity, as well as encouraging stress relief, sexual expression, ancestral veneration, rootwork, rituals and connecting with animals. Archetypes connected with the Queen of Coins include Coach, Craftsperson, Crone, Witch, Bon Vivant, Mentor, Shaman, Environmentalist, Yogini, Animal Whisperer, Gardener, Companion, Medicine Woman. She is like a warm blanket, hot bowl of soup, vigorous work out or helpful prescription.

*Examples:* Michelle Obama; Dr. Christiane Northrup; Crystal Andrus; Dr. Andrew Weil; Peggy McColl; Dr. Ruth; Nicki Scully; Margot Adler; Caitlin Matthews; Angeles Arrien; Stephanie Rose Bird; Judika Illes; Dr. Lissa Rankin; Dawn Brunke; Kooch Daniels; Anne Newkirk Niven

*Theme: The body is the temple of Spirit.*

The **Queen of Cups** nurtures emotions. Archetypes like the Caregiver, Mother, Lover, Angel, Samaritan, Servant, Martyr and Rescuer are connected with this queen. Ways of healing include soothing emotions, promoting peace, entertainment, holding hands, running errands, talking on the phone, revealing past lives, connecting humanity, Reiki, crystals, swimming with dolphins, therapeutic touch, channeling spirits and energy healing. These types can cross the line from hand up to hand out. When of the New Age persuasion, they can be spiritual space cadets. If Buddhist, cultivators of loving-kindness practice. The Queen of Cups as healer is akin to a momma kissing boo boos to make the ouchies go away.

*Examples:* Amma (The Hugging Saint); Mother Theresa; Elizabeth Clare Prophet; Doreen Virtue; Sonia Choquette;

Marianne Williamson; Denise Linn; Lucy Cavendish; Dr. Judith Orloff; Sharon Salzberg; Jack Kornfield; Guy Kawasaki

**Theme:** *All you need is love.*

See how each of these queens are powerful healers in their own right?

# KINGS

## King of Wands – Ahead of the Pack

**Stripped Down Overview:** Prophets, pioneers and passionate leaders—you either love (admire) or hate (envy) these powerful visionaries. Exuding irresistible charm and displaying myriad talents, the King of Wands' charisma and confidence draws others like moths to a flame: those who get close find warm and inspiring dynamos—but thin-skinned, easily offended groupies who prefer idols with feet of diamond feel the burn. Milquetoasts expecting mollycoddling, too, pull away from the fire—for these Kings refuse to clean up messes or wipe ossified asses. Frustrated by reticence, appalled by dishonesty and enraged by incompetence, they are compelled to accomplish something significant and meaningful with their lives—hence their characteristic impatience with the reserved, the deceitful, the inept. If/when surrounded by village idiots, this King's motto kicks into high gear: *If you want something done well and done quickly, do it yourself.* Thriving on challenges and embracing necessary conflicts, they handle stress like no other. Because they follow a strong, self-defined set of reasons for being and doing, they can't be bought—so no lure (solid gold or not) will steer them off their chosen path. They risk boldly and screw up spectacularly, redefining "failure" or "mistake" as "proactive experimentation" and "valuable experience". On their deathbed, they'll not feel regret at what they've done or said—but may self-recriminate for what they've left *un*done.

**Keywords:** Leading Self-Exploration; Governing Proactivity; Monitoring Self-Reliance; Determining Potential; External Mastery of Innovation; Organizing Ambition; Decisive Catalyst; Regulating Expansion; Authority on Personal Growth; Guiding Life Purpose; Managing Self-Starters; Arranging Creative

Passion; Strategizing Originality; Directing Excitement; Developing Self-Esteem; Commanding Optimism; Controlling Initiation; Orchestrating Individualism; Designing Projects

**Personifications and Embodiments:** Tony Stark (*Iron Man*); Oprah Winfrey; Viggo Mortensen; Publications Dedicated to Creativity; Self-Help Magazines; Tony Robbins; Bruce Dickinson; Richard Branson; Jeff Bezos; Leonardo da Vinci; Amazon.com; Steve Jobs

**Quote:** *Innovation distinguishes between a leader and a follower.* – Steve Jobs

**Nickname:** Visionary Vance

**Way to His Heart:** Passionate Purpose, Self-Knowledge and Candidness

**Challenge:** Asperity

**Gift:** Prescience

**Occupations/Vocations:** Pioneer; Innovator; Daring Inventor; Life Coach; Head Hunter; Self-Help Author; Motivational Speaker

**Disney Totem:** Jack Skellington (*The Nightmare Before Christmas*)

**Animal Symbol:** Cardinal

**Flower Essence:** Red Helmet Orchid (Australian Bush)

**Crystal/Stone:** Richterite – Promotes wisdom, foresight and a sense of right timing and sequence. Broadens horizons. Helps recognize and assess trends.

**Aromatherapy:** Thyme Linalol

**Body Parts/Systems and Health Issues:** Elbows; Forearms; Muscle Atrophy

**Mystical Messenger** – Saint Isidore of Seville

**Sabian Symbol:** Aries 17 – Through imagination, a lost opportunity is regained.

**Writing Prompt:** Amazon.com begins selling something no one thought possible.

**Affirmation:** Self-growth is important to me, so I look for ways to progress.

**Strengthsfinder 2.0:** Belief; Strategic

**Cattell's 16PF:** Self-Reliance

**Enneagram:** Type 7; Type 3; Type 8

**ANSIR:** Visionary; Idealist; Philosopher

**MBTI/Keirsey:** ENTJ – "The Visionary"

- **Beneficial Traits**
  - ⋏ Highly interested in self-growth and personal advancement
  - ⋏ Fascinated by the ideas, inventions and achievements of others
  - ⋏ Dares to try new ways of thinking, being and doing

⋏ Values constructive and instructive criticism; uses it to progress

- **Detrimental Traits**
  - ⋏ Often feels like they're not "doing enough" thanks to internal clock
  - ⋏ Seems to have an "edge"; enjoys collaboration, but tends to offend
  - ⋏ Control freak; natural born leaders, they want to be in charge 24/7
  - ⋏ Highly critical of inefficiency, sloppiness and careless errors

## Naked Advice for the King of Wands

*Career:* Seeking meaningful work, you may change jobs often—especially if you're a Renaissance Soul with too many passions to pick "just one". This doesn't mean you can't "stick to anything" or are unable to "settle down"; it just means that you're a hexagonal peg that couldn't fit into a round hole even if you tried. You're a quintessential leader (sometimes, reluctant), so freelancing or flexible management roles catering to your out-of-the-box innovation and multiple interests would serve you well. Once you step off society's plodding treadmill (usually after graduating from the "school of hard knocks") and begin to live as born and meant, you're the one most likely to become that "overnight success". You believe that if you can envision something, it *must* be possible—so seek a vocational outlet where your far-reaching foresight is supported.

*Romance:* Both in bed and in committed relationships, the "like attracts like" maxim holds most true with fire signs. Upon first meeting, an electric spark crackles—almost as if meeting a soul cut from the same sizzling existential cloth. Expect exciting adventures and whirlwind romances when the King of Wands strides into your life. When others fall apart under pressure, this one excels—so when he's in your corner, expect him to stare hardships, setbacks and disappointments right in the eye. Somehow, he'll make things better (even if things don't turn out exactly as desired). He values openness as much as finding (and living) a meaningful existence, so don't hold back on your thoughts or feelings. Your relationship hinges on forthright communication and authenticity.

*Parenting*: When your child blurts out what he thinks or bosses other kids around, don't assume he's being a sass-mouthed brat—even when his *"gets along well with others"* score receives the perennial "N" (for "needs improvement") in school. Born leaders, they refuse to bleat *"baaaaa"*, simply because "follower" isn't part of their genetic code. If the hand holding the singular baton in the Ace of Wands is human, you can be sure it belongs to the King of Wands. Will you offer *your* progeny the gift of non-conformity and individualism—the seeds to his greatness?

*Spirituality:* With balls of brass and spine of steel forged in the crucible of suffering, you've seen your share of abuse, adversity and disillusionment. But like the majestic Phoenix, you rise from the ashes every time—emerging bigger, badder and bolder. Your resilience is a testament to something transcendent, an invisible force pulling you upward and onward through the incessant, mocking *tick-tock* reverberating *"why am I here?"* and *"for what was I born?"*. Once you discover your "who" and "why", everything will click into place—and the internal purpose clock (and nagging self-doubt) will torment you no more.

**Recommended Resources:** *Steve Jobs* by Walter Isaacson; *The Impact Equation* by Chris Brogan and Julien Smith

**King of Wands Layout:** *Making It Happen* Spread

1. What needs to happen in my life?
2. How can I make that happen?
3. In what area do I need to grow?
4. How do I make that happen?
5. What does "success" look like to me right now?
6. How can I make that happen?
7. When naysayers, pessimists or doubts arise, what will help me most?
8. How can I make that happen?

# King of Swords – Quarks and Quirks

**Stripped Down Overview:** Unlike the rash Knight of Swords that would pull out a shiv without forethought, the King of Swords takes a considered view before wielding scalpel, pen or gavel. Astrophysicists, surgeons and mathematicians, these Kings hang out in the intellectual stratosphere, often teetering on the bleeding edge of science. Many hold multiple advanced degrees as evidenced by the string of alphabet soup trailing their names. Valuing numbers, data and facts, many atheists populate their ilk. Thus, they often spurn notions of faith, magic and whimsy, earning them descriptors like "cold", "unfeeling" or "dour". Those who know them, however, report streaks of humor—dry wit, punny jokes and droll wordplay—but usually only their own kind "gets" them. Although they appear unsentimental in the face of crises, they're usually the first to offer clear-headed counsel—helping friends and colleagues cut a path through the dense fog of emotionalism, irrationality and catastrophic thinking. What these ones lack in bedside manner they more than make up for in competence. And if the King of Swords can't fix it, he'll know the perfect specialist who *can*.

**Keywords:** Orchestrating Strategy; Deciding Judgment; Legislating Division; Ordering Analysis; External Mastery of Communication; Controlling Thoughts; Devising Restrictions; Arranging Curriculum; Guiding Resolutions; Coordinating Information; Regulating Intellectual Property; Managing Anxieties; Leading Objectives; Dictating Words; Engineering Decisions; Organizing Intelligence; Governing Discrimination; Monitoring Messages

**Personifications and Embodiments:** Mr. Spock; Big Brother; Data (*Star Trek: TNG*); Carl Sagan; NSA; Albert Einstein; Neil DeGrasse Tyson; ACLU; Psychiatrists; The Unabomber; FCC; Christopher Hitchens; Pythagorus; Bill Nye (The Science Guy); Stephen Hawking; Dr. Seth Hazlitt (*Murder, She Wrote*); *The Absent-Minded Professor*

**Quote:** *Scientists are peeping toms at the keyhole of eternity.* – Arthur Koestler

**Nickname:** Scientific Simon

**Way to His Heart:** Stimulating Conversation; Intellectual Pursuits

**Challenge:** Aloofness

**Gift:** Specialization

**Occupations/Vocations:** Psychiatrist; Publisher; Scientist; Library of Congress Staff; CDC Administrator; Textbook Author; Museum Curator; Code Breaker; Speech Writer; Policy Maker; IP Lawyer; Atheist Apologist

**Disney Totem:** King Triton (*The Little Mermaid*)

**Animal Symbol:** Kestrel

**Flower Essences:** Vine (Bach); Hibbertia (Australian Bush); Red Lily (Australian Bush)

**Crystal/Stone:** Snowflake Obsidian – Encourages spontaneous thinking and materialization of ideas. Promotes spiritual awakening. Warms up the hands and feet. Dispels fear and emotional blockages. Supports critical evaluation of theories. Helps organize information.

**Aromatherapy:** Cedarwood

**Body Parts/Systems and Health Issues:** Parkinson's Disease; Palsy

**Mystical Messenger** – Saint Jerome

**Sabian Symbol:** Pisces 13 – A sword, used in many battles, is now in a museum.

**Writing Prompt:** A long-held scientific belief is disproven, shaking the masses.

**Affirmation:** I take charge of what needs to be analyzed and communicated.

**Strengthsfinder 2.0:** Analytical; Futuristic

**Cattell's 16PF:** Reasoning

**Enneagram:** Type 1; Type 5; Type 6 (Counterphobic)

**ANSIR:** Sage; Sentinel; Healer; Philosopher

**MBTI/Keirsey:** INTP – "The Diagnostician"

- **Beneficial Traits**
  - ⚔ Whizzes at solving puzzles, spotting patterns and cracking codes
  - ⚔ Uncanny ability to identify faulty logic and clarify fuzzy reasoning
  - ⚔ Dares to question scientific and societal "rules"; takes us "beyond"
  - ⚔ Eschews popularity and security in favor of pioneering theories

- **Detrimental Traits**
  - ⚔ Tendency towards cynicism and hyper-skepticism
  - ⚔ May get involved in dangerous or violent social rebellion
  - ⚔ Overestimation of personal importance; assumes indispensability
  - ⚔ Often absent-minded, scatterbrained, disorganized and messy

## Naked Advice for the King of Swords

*Career:* Do you find knowledge exhilarating? Get your rocks off by the radical recombination of items and ideas? Favor analysis and detailed understanding of events, processes and systems? Look for opportunities utilizing one or more of these areas for ultimate job satisfaction. You'd do well as a president, director, researcher, head librarian, diagnostician, inventor, think-tank participant, theoretical scientist, publisher, legal scholar or biographer (especially political or military history). The more you're able to work alone, the better—because we both know your people skills leave much to be desired. Thus, leave human resources, sales and publicity to those with more social finesse.

*Romance:* Although this King may appear emotionally distant or even somber, his detached exterior usually reflects a preoccupied mind. Riddles, project snafus, professional conundrums—he's more at home in the airy world of mental mazes than watery emotions (look to the Cups Court Cards for that). The way to this one's heart is via intellectual repartee, information exchange and interest in his pet hobby or area of expertise. To mask any feelings of uncertainty, incompetence or ignorance, he may become intense, secretive or subversive—so don't take his bluntness personally (unless it is). If your idea of romance includes arm-in-arm attendance of social events, tango dancing or cuddling naked on a bearskin rug in front of a roaring fireplace, look elsewhere. But a firm grasp on the intricacies of the Kama Sutra? You might have something there...

*Parenting*: Whenever discussions with your child seems like practice for the debate team—or figuring out what she means (or needs) resembles a chess game—realize that you're dealing with a sharp mind in a youngster's body. Stubbornness and a no-nonsense attitude makes these ones appear like mini-adults, but don't let this guise fool you: inside, they're craving the solidity, boundaries and supportiveness of caring parents. She feels things just as deeply as the next kid—perhaps more so—which is why she hides behind mental armor or buries her nose in books. Stay available and nearby, for when you least expect it, she'll let you know what she thinks or wants—especially if you remain open and objective.

*Spirituality:* Trying to make sense of your life much like you'd solve a mathematical equation, crack an algorithm or decode the *Voynich Manuscript*? Good luck with *that*. Instead of trying to hack someone else's esoteric codex or convoluted symbol set, create your own system for personal meaning and growth. Because of your knack for breaking down complex wholes into conceptual parts and smaller units, you may miss the forest for the trees—but if anyone understands that a mighty oak lives inside an acorn or a world inside a cell, it's *you*. In fact, it's actually an *angel* in the details—so look for messages in the minutiae.

**Recommended Resources:** *Cosmos* (TV Show Hosted by Carl Sagan); *A Beautiful Mind* (Movie); *The Gross Clinic* by Thomas Eakins

**King of Swords Card Layout:** *Cuts Like a Knife* Spread

1. If I were a doctor, what would be my specialty?
1a. Why?
2. If my life were a diseased body, what would need to be cut out?
2a. Why?
2b. How can I contribute to its healing?
3. What needs diagnosing in my life right now?
4. What is the prescription?
5. How do I prevent a recurrence of this malady?

# King of Coins – The Midas Touch

**Stripped Down Overview:** Bling, *cha-ching,* million dolla partays don't mean a thang... Welcome to the status-conscious world of moguls, industrialists, barons and financiers. These movers and shakers thrive on building better mousetraps and amassing wealth. They believe winning is everything and assume everyone has a price. The dude who created Monopoly (as well as those who enjoy playing that boring-ass game)? Total personification of the King of Coins, where buying railroads and collecting red plastic hotels serve as practice for the real-life pursuit of symbols of wealth, power and prestige. These ones lose and gain *millions* in mere hours, usually because of the stock market, but sometimes as a result of scandal, tragedy or risky gambles. They don't fear loss or financial setbacks, always presuming "there's more where that came from" — and they're right, because the "more" streams almost magically from their Midas touch. Immaculately dressed with every hair (or comb-over) in place, they tend to be uncompromising and uncooperative when defending their gaping vision of greatness. When ready to buy, they analyze cost and rarity. When assessing potential associations, they evaluate net worth, annual income and influence. Ironically, this King can be found on *both* sides of the environmental coin: on one hand, they're responsible for logging, mining, fracking and otherwise raping verdant hills to make way for strip malls, parking lots and condos. On the flip side, they're the philanthropists funding green initiatives, sponsoring renewable energy or donating land for community recreation.

**Keywords:** Controlling Money; Distributing Wealth; Allocating Food; Governing Health; External Mastery of Finances; Deciding on Assets; Selling Possessions; Developing Land; Dictating Fashion; Partitioning Property; Administrating a Foundation; Designating Responsibility; Managing Investments; Engineering Crops; Determining Funds; Expert on Luxury; Leading Material Acquisition; Strategizing Earnings; Overseeing Budgets; Organizing Merchandise; Conquering Environmental Resources

**Personifications and Embodiments:** Capitalists; Donald Trump; Harry Selfridge; Jay Gatsby; Martha Stewart; King Midas; Suze Orman; *Lifestyles of the Rich and Famous*; Leland Horne (*Twin Peaks*); USDA; FDA; Land Developers; Real Estate Magnates; Wall Street; Coal Barons; Steel Industrialists; Treasurers; Frackers; Stock Brokers; Banking; Big Business; Oil Industry; Luxury Goods; Franchise Owners; Moguls; White Collar Crime; Glamor; Expensive "Toys"; *Monopoly*; The Hiltons; Resorts; Gated Communities; Joe Hardy; The Capitol (*Hunger Games* trilogy)

**Quote:** *The desire for success lubricates secret prostitutions in the soul.* – Norman Mailer

**Nickname:** Tycoon Tony

**Way to His Heart:** Fine Food, Material Luxury and Symbols of Wealth

**Challenge:** Acquisition

**Gift:** Midas Touch

**Occupations/Vocations:** Music Producer; Marketing Director; Banker; Professional Sports Team Owner; Billionaire; Hotelier; Luxury Goods Retailer

**Disney Totem:** Eli "Big Daddy" LaBouff (*The Princess and the Frog*)

**Animal Symbol:** Beaver

**Flower Essences:** Vine (Bach); Bluebell (Australian Bush)

**Crystal/Stone:** Tektite – Helps relieve obsession with money or possessions. Aids in recognition that one is a spiritual being in a material body. Helps let go of the fear of the future.

**Aromatherapy:** Black Pepper

**Body Parts/Systems and Health Issues:** High Cholesterol

**Mystical Messenger** – Kubera

**Sabian Symbol:** Aquarius 16 – A big businessman at his desk.

**Writing Prompt:** A billionaire reality TV host becomes POTUS.

**Affirmation:** What I touch turns to "gold".

**Strengthsfinder 2.0:** Achiever; Significance

**Cattell's 16PF:** Privateness

**Enneagram:** Type 3; Type 7w8; Type 8

**ANSIR:** Visionary; Idealist

**MBTI/Keirsey:** ESTJ – "The Aristocrat"

- **Beneficial Traits**
  - ⋏ Financial whiz; knack for making and multiplying money
  - ⋏ Workaholics that plan, execute and achieve
  - ⋏ Knows how to build a better "mousetrap" — then sells it
  - ⋏ Paragons of taste; attuned nose for quality and rarity

- **Detrimental Traits**
  - ⋏ Materialistic and acquisitive; exploits natural resources
  - ⋏ Stubborn and inflexible; thinks they're always right
  - ⋏ Obsessed with status symbols and attaining/maintaining prestige
  - ⋏ Easily agitated when they don't get what they want; demanding

## Naked Advice for the King of Coins

*Career:* As a kid, you were the one setting up a lemonade stand or impromptu neighborhood carwash. Not only did you make passers-by feel like they *had* to have what you were offering, they joyfully tipped you extra for your efforts! Even if you're a college dropout (or never bothered with higher education), you have the uncanny ability to turn straw into spun gold faster than you can say *Rumpelstiltskin*. From your perfectionist perch, everything you survey can be improved—and with your endless checklists, you'll know how to make anything brighter, shinier, faster, sleeker...*better*. Your quick thinking puts you way ahead of most competitors, but because you're a sore loser (and not into small talk), you'll have many more admirers (and envious enemies) than loyal friends. No matter: you prefer arms-length interaction with successful colleagues and influential connections, anyway. Continue to improve everything and everyone you see, for it's *your* standards that the media upholds and proliferates.

*Romance:* Unless you're certifiably gorgeous—preferably with a country club membership of your own—the King of Coins isn't likely to give you the time of day. He considers mates extensions of both his upper crust lifestyle *and* his enormous ego, so he expects well-heeled, camera-ready arm candy. If he has his druthers, intelligence and sharp repartee would also be part of his ideal plaything package—but if he can't have that, then looks and poise will be enough. If you ever get to marriage, you will not pass "Go" until you sign his ironclad prenup agreement. Mistresses galore and one-night flings will keep him company on the road as you hold down the gilt fort, so assume "open relationship" when you say, "I do". *He'll* say, "It doesn't mean anything"—and he's probably telling you the truth—but you'll need to decide if silver spoons, bottles of Cristal and decadent chandeliers trump marital fidelity. Oh, and should you lose your figure or looks thanks to childbearing, disease or age, he'll likely trade you in for a Queen of Cups trophy wife—despite giving him your best years and efforts.

*Parenting:* Your kids will never want for *anything*. In fact, don't be surprised if you get Ivy League college sweatshirts as baby shower gifts. The latest fashions, electronic gadgets and front-seat home team tickets will cushion little Ashton and Ashleigh against the grit of the "masses" and the sweat of (*shudder*) chores. And you'll have a maid, nanny, personal chef, gardener and chauffeur—so expect an easy-peasy ride when it comes to the material side of parenting—but don't expect Rich Daddy to be home much, since career achievement remains his priority. If the kiddos survive an absentee father who tries to buy love, at least expect nepotism to secure a good position in one of his companies. However, if his insidious meticulousness bleeds into family identity, the progeny may suffer "*I am my things*" neurosis at best and eating disorders at worst.

*Spirituality:* With your insane expectations and nosebleed standards, you carry a secret that few discover: you're a gazillion times harder on yourself than others. Rarely do you look in the mirror and find the perfect specimen of humanity you strive to be. You look for answers in Self-Help books and magazines, but your voracious reading gives you more fodder for your self-improvement flow charts and lengthens your already miles-long punctilious yardstick. You tend to shun displays of emotion, religiosity or spiritual devotion (although you'll donate to organizations that further your preferences), preferring the G-O-D spelled M-O-I. To touch something deeper within, ask yourself, "What will I have—what will I *be*—if the back accounts, buildings, businesses, cars and clothes evaporate?"

**Recommended Resources:** *Mr. Selfridge* Season 1 (TV Show); "Of Late I Think of Cliffordville" (*Twilight Zone*); *Henry VIII* by Hans Holbein

**King of Coins Card Layout:** *What's It Worth?* Spread

1. What material thing is worth the most to me?
1b. Why?
2. What emotional condition is worth the most to me?
2b. Why?
3. What mental state/ability is worth the most to me?
3b. Why?
4. What spiritual state is worth the most to me?
4b. Why?
5. Which area needs less focus?
6. Which area needs more focus?
7. What do I need to improve my sense of worthiness/ feelings of self-worth?

## King of Cups – A Touch of Class

**Stripped Down Overview:** Museum curators, wine connoisseurs, orchestra conductors, theater directors, conservatory professors, inspired restaurateurs—the King of Cups watches over the realms of art, aesthetics, imagination and culture. Gravitating towards what is beautiful, benevolent and transcendent, these gentle leaders point out the luminosity within poetry, story, painting, architecture, song, scripture and childhood—enriching schools, churches, lecture halls, documentaries and public television with incandescent insights. Some specialize in love and romance, demonstrating their expertise as relationship therapists, Rumi scholars or ACIM gurus. However, when tending to shun or shame what's crude, coarse or common, they may have their noses so high in the sky that rainstorms threaten death by drowning.

**Keywords:** External Mastery of Aesthetics; Controlling Mood; Guiding Empathy; Organizing Preferences; Orchestrating Sharing; Strategizing Compassion; Authority on Relationships; Supervising Healing; Governing Emotions; Monitoring Values;

Managing Flow; Administrating Culture; Protecting Imagination; Leading Forgiveness

**Personifications and Embodiments:** Joseph Campbell; Patch Adams; Fred Rogers; David Attenborough; Dr. Wayne Dyer; Santa Claus; Bob Ross; Captain Kangaroo; *Reading Rainbow* (LeVar Burton); Sister Wendy; Dr. John Gray; Dr. Robert Greenberg; Pope Benedict; Christmas Spirit; Dr. Sharon Latchaw Hirsh; I Corinthians 13; Oscar Wilde; Aestheticism; Garrison Keillor

**Quote:** *The artist has a special task and duty; the task of reminding men of their humanity and the promise of their creativity.* – Lewis Mumford

**Nickname:** Sophisticated Stanislaw

**Way to His Heart:** Gentleness, Soulfulness, Beauty, Aesthetics and Tolerance

**Challenge:** Snobbery

**Gift:** Refinement

**Occupations/Vocations:** Guidance Counselor; Pre-School Teacher; Facilitator; Art Instructor; Professional Storyteller; Children's Librarian; Theater Director

**Disney Totem:** Mr. Ray (*Finding Nemo*)

**Animal Symbol:** Snail Kite

**Flower Essences:** Beech (Bach); Mustard (Bach); Water Violet (Bach)

**Crystal/Stone:** Copper – Promotes a sense of aesthetics, harmony and love for all beings. Encourages the appreciation of beauty. Lends playful creativity. Encourages a sense of fairness and equality.

**Aromatherapy:** Chamomile German

**Body Parts/Systems and Health Issues:** Blood and Platelet Transfusions; Blood Tests

**Mystical Messenger** – Orpheus

**Sabian Symbol:** Cancer 26 – Guests are reading in the library of a luxurious home.

**Writing Prompt:** A grown woman changed by the life of Mr. Rogers.

**Affirmation:** Wherever I go, I bring cultured and compassionate leadership.

**Strengthsfinder 2.0:** Developer; Individualization

**Cattell's 16PF:** Sensitivity

**Enneagram:** Type 9; Type 2w3

**ANSIR:** Sage; Healer; Kinsmen; Empath

**MBTI/Keirsey:** INFJ – "The Healer"

- **Beneficial Traits**
    - Rarest type among humanity; most likely to be psychic
    - Extraordinary gift for healing emotional scars and soul

wounds

- ⋏ Upholds what is beautiful, gentle, hopeful, childlike and benevolent
- ⋏ Inclusive; celebrates differences and promotes understanding

- **Detrimental Traits**
  - ⋏ Often prone to sadness and depression; may cope with alcohol
  - ⋏ Abhors conflict; internalizes criticism—until a "blow up"
  - ⋏ Withholds parts of themselves from others; secretive and private
  - ⋏ Sweeps problems under the rug; refuses to acknowledge or tackle

## Naked Advice for the King of Cups

*Career:* To uplift, beautify, mend and heal—these are the vocational mandates of this King. Any career overseeing the emotional and spiritual well-being of others—or expanding cultural literacy, emotional intelligence and artistic pursuits— would be a great fit for your big heart and generous nature. Art therapist, child psychologist, pre-school teacher, educational storyteller, pastor, marriage counselor, social worker, elementary school principal, energy healer, church instrumentalist, sacred music composer, comedic physician—the world needs more individuals interested in alleviating suffering, bringing smiles, inciting laughter and sharing gifts. Will you take up the mantle?

*Romance:* Ever hear a guy called "too nice" by a gal—as if this condition were some foul curse? *Those* types crave bad boys (and bad treatment)—which leaves these rare gems wide open for those who can, and will, appreciate them. Warm, cultured and classy, this is the gent you'd be proud to take home to Mama—and have on your arm wearing a tux or tailored suit. Attentive, captivating and worldly, he's able to make you feel like you're the only one in the room—or the universe. He's so adept at anticipating your wants and nurturing your needs, you may fall for him if you have "father issues"—so beware of substituting "Dan" for "Dad" (always a bad idea). Another word of caution: a sensitive disposition sometimes comes with a price, including bouts of sadness or depression. If he seems to always have a drink in hand (or a liquor cabinet stocked out the wazoo), he may self-medicate his melancholia with booze.

*Parenting*: The ultimate father figure, this King displays emotional maturity and deep sensitivity for all under his care. Quick to smile and laugh—and slow to reprimand or correct—he imparts valuable life lessons and empathy through telling "when I was your age" stories, as well as anecdotes from film, folklore and fables. By relaying universal wisdom found in poetry, myth and song, he provides comfort to everyone within earshot. Young and old alike feel seen, heard and understood when graced with his timely tales, even when he's addressing a crowd. For any children under your charge, consider a similar approach right now. If you feel inadequate to the task, or these traits aren't among your caretaking skill set, locate someone who exhibits these qualities to help you out.

*Spirituality:* Your wide-open heart often hurts when faced with humanity's cruelty. Intercessory prayer is one antidote for the world's suffering. Another is displaying and supporting beauty in all its forms. After you're done praying for others, release their care to the Divine—and focus on what is lovely, gentle and good. In the wake of your own wounds and hurts, you've exchanged splendor for ashes; don't underestimate the power of your personal transformation, especially when you share your story with others.

**Recommended Resources:** *Mr. Rogers' Neighborhood* (TV Show); *Attenborough's Life Stories (DVD); Reading* by Alex Grey

**King of Cups Card Layout:** *Spreadin' the Love* Spread

1. What do I need to learn most about love?
2. How can I best teach love?
3. Who/what needs love right now?
4. What act of love can I do next?

# THE MINOR ARCANA

# WANDS

## Ace of Wands – Spark of Purpose, Juice of Life

**Stripped Down Overview:** In July 2013, Heineken staged an Airport Departure Roulette Stunt at JFK airport. Without knowing the final destination first, travelers were dared to ditch their plans, commit to going to the country that popped up on the marquee, and then "spin the wheel" to see where they were headed. (Travelers were reimbursed $2000 and a two-night hotel stay.) This stunt perfectly displays the energy of the Ace of Wands: an unexpected opportunity that invites you to make a snap decision involving change of direction, radical self-assertion or the sudden pursuit of a passion. There's no guarantee how long the "magic portal" will stay open; in many cases, mere minutes or seconds. The temporary nature of such "open doors" infuses these turning points with urgency and excitement. As a result, it's possible that you could "lose your head" by stepping through. It's *equally* possible that you'll emerge from the other side invigorated, transformed or, at the very least, own a fantastic tale to tell the grandkids.

**Keywords:** Sudden Motivation; Personal Affirmation; *Yes!*; Lust for Life; Window of Opportunity; Increased Vitality; Surge of Virility; Go for It; Force; Renewed Purpose; Invitation to Participate

**Personifications and Embodiments:** Thumbs Up; Lit Match; Temporary Wormhole; Special Alignment; Take the Baton and Run; Unpredictable Portal

**Quote:** *Life is no "brief candle" to me. It is a sort of splendid torch*

*which I have got hold of for the moment, and I want to make it burn as brightly as possible before handing it on to future generations. –* George Bernard Shaw

**Challenge:** Action

**Gift:** Excitement

**Occupations/Vocations:** Proctologist; Orchestra Conductor; Track and Field Relay Race Runner; Torch Bearer

**Disney Totem:** Dave Stutler (*The Sorcerer's Apprentice*)

**Animal Symbol:** Firefly

**Flower Essence:** Wild Oat (Bach)

**Crystal/Stone:** Colored Jasper – Supports creative realization of one's ideas. Boosts creative power. Promotes passion.

**Aromatherapy:** Hinoki

**Body Parts/Systems and Health Issues:** Erectile Dysfunction; Testicles

**Mystical Messenger** – Prometheus

**Sabian Symbol:** Capricorn 21 – A relay race.

**Writing Prompt:** At a relay race, a runner attempts to grab the baton—but it's not what he expects.

**Affirmation:** I respond to sparks of inspiration.

## Naked Advice for the Ace of Wands

*Career:* One definition of luck is preparation meeting opportunity. Preparation without opportunity is a waiting game. Fortunately, it's easier than ever to "pick yourself" and *create* opportunity. However, opportunity without preparation means getting your foot in the door (or window)—but not having the skills or character to sustain progress or fulfill expectations. Yet, some people have latent talents that only manifest when a time-sensitive door opens (or, during desperate times). Think of a magic portal appearing out of nowhere. Unpredictable, thrilling and promising, a surge of possibility runs through you. *"What if?"* races through your mind. *"Should I? Or not?"* you wonder. Hesitate too long and the portal disappears. There are always glimmering gateways popping up in your world. All is not lost if you miss a door—but no chance for reinvention or new purpose repeats itself in the exact same way. When the time comes... what will you choose?

*Romance:* Time to jump on the stick! All of the Wands cards sizzle with sexual tension and energy. The Ace is a full-blown erection, ready and willing to rocket to orgasmic bliss. *But*—this is an *Ace*. A starter. A seed. A potential. Can he go all the way? Or will he "blast off" after a mere 10 seconds? Turn into a limp noodle in two minutes? This card doesn't guarantee stamina or long-haul staying power—in sex *or* romance. Whether this lit match sets off a tinderbox or stick of dynamite depends on its surroundings. If your partner is having trouble getting the one-eyed snake to hiss and bite, investigate psychological reasons first: How is his self-esteem? Are things too routine and bland? Has criticism eaten away at his confidence? Then, ask yourself some questions: How can you surprise him? Shake things up? Give him a boost of appreciation and admiration? One thing's for sure: you're off to a good start...but it's too early to tell if you'll get a *ka*-BOOM—or a *ka*-PUT.

**Parenting**: When it comes to "windows of opportunities" with kids, it's usually spelled I-N-C-O-N-V-E-N-I-E-N-C-E for parents. Jason sprouts an interest in piano, Jared demonstrates a sudden talent for dance, Joshua appears to have the feet (and fervor) for soccer, Jacob wants to enter the Spelling Bee, Justin feels like he's *really* Jessica (desiring to wear heels and cosmetics)—newfound desires and realizations in children can really put a monkey wrench (or dent) in the wallet, expectations, assumptions—even the hopes or dreams—of a parent. But it's *our* job to provide the atmosphere and encouragement for kids to flourish and become their "Best Self"—whatever that may look like. Surprising? Scary? Disruptive? Typically, all of the above. But it's time to say *"yes!"*, reassure the hell out of 'em and see what they do. Going forward may lead to nothing or everything—but it's empowering for them to know they at least have a choice.

**Spirituality:** When life surprises you with an opportunity for reinvention, renewal and rock-hard erections—you take it, right? Or, maybe you play it safe (suit of Coins, anyone?)—hopin' and a wishin' something magnificent will erupt on the scene. Thing is, life is *always* offering up these singular batons, inviting you to feel more, do more—*be* more. More of what? Why, *yourself!* Numero Uno. After all, there's only one you! So instead of shrinking from the limitless outline of your "biggerness", why not ride the surge of vital life-force energy to the max? What have you got to lose? (An opportunity for pushing your potential past your wildest fantasies, that's what.) The good news is the Universe never runs out of those *bursting-branches-from-the-sky* to toss your way. The bad news? No one can force you to grab and run. The answer is either *yes* or *no*...because "maybe" is always too late.

**Recommended Resources:** *Yes Man* (Movie); *Sliders* (TV Series)

**Ace of Wands Card Layout:** *Opportunity Knockin'* Spread

1.  What opportunity is right in front of me?
2.  Likely outcome if I jump on it:
3.  Likely outcome if I don't:
4.  What's the next big opportunity heading my way?
5.  Sign that it's almost here:
6.  Benefit if I take the opportunity?
6a. Benefit if I don't?
7.  Drawback if I take the opportunity?
7a. Drawback if I don't?
8.  What knock do I need to *stop* answering?
9.  What opportunity can I make for someone *else*?

# 2 of Wands – What's Next?

**Stripped Down Overview:** Many Tarotists get confused about the 2 and 3 of Wands and it's no wonder: in the RWS traditions, both cards show a cloaked man standing on a parapet overlooking a body of water with mountains in the background, holding an upright stave, with other budding staves around him. But there is a difference between them: the guy in the 2 holds a globe in one hand and a stave in the other. The second stave is bolted to a stone block. He looks rigid, tense. We can see part of his face. In the 3, the figure has his back to us, and his stance appears relaxed. One hand grasps a stave, but all three batons appear fixed in the ground, looking a natural part of the landscape. My take? The guy in the 2 is an ambitious, impetuous, impatient rookie— out to conquer the world with his obnoxious "creative genius" and entrepreneurial flair (if you think this sounds like the stage that might sit between the Page and Knight of Wands, you'd be correct). He has potential, but he's probably making mistakes in his haste (not to mention butting heads with any partners, advisors or investors). But the guy in the 3? Commercial and creative endeavors are "old hat" to him: he's been here before, he knows what he's doing—and now he patiently waits for his ship to come in.

**Keywords:** Clash of Wills; Disagreement; Identity Crisis; Creative Tension; "Take the Bull by the Horns"; Territorial; Impatience; Frustration; Attempting to Get a Project Off the Ground; Needing the Benefit of Experience; Trying to Regain Control; Wrestling with Unforeseen Events; Making Grandiose Plans; Refusing to Be Held Back; Bold Entrepreneurial Move; Desiring Domination; Ignoring Advice; Floundering; Trying to Impress; Challenging Someone; Gridlock

**Personifications and Embodiments:** Pushing to Get to the Head of the Line; Wesley Crusher (*Star Trek: The Next Generation*); Quarterback Looking for an Open Receiver; Ski Jumper About to Exit the Gate; Bull Rider

**Quote:** *Before you begin a thing, remind yourself that difficulties and delays quite impossible to foresee are ahead. If you could see them clearly, naturally you could do a great deal to get rid of them but you can't. You can only see one thing clearly and that is your goal. Form a mental vision of that and cling to it through thick and thin.* – Kathleen Norris

**Challenge:** Hesitation

**Gift:** Vision

**Occupations/Vocations:** Fashion Designer; Cross-Country Skier; Meteorologist; Career Counselor

**Disney Totem:** Nemo (*Finding Nemo*)

**Animal Symbol:** Grasshopper

**Flower Essences:** Impatiens (Bach); Silver Princess (Australian Bush); Kangaroo Paw (Australian Bush); Larch (Bush)

**Crystal/Stone:** Stillbite – Prompts following one's ideas and ambitions. Promotes a calm, relaxed and confident state of mind.

**Aromatherapy:** Dill

**Body Parts/Systems and Health Issues:** Lungs; Bronchitis; Pneumonia; Asthma

**Mystical Messenger** – Grid

**Sabian Symbol:** Aries 21 – A boxer is entering the ring.

**Writing Prompt:** The Long Man of Wilmington comes alive.

**Affirmation:** Armed with common sense and a plan, I boldly walk through open doors.

## Naked Advice for the 2 of Wands

*Career:* When two passionate, inventive people meet, there's the possibility of a personality clash or one trying to "outdo" the other. But another direction—a fruitful one—is putting egos to the side and focusing on the task at hand, which expands the ideas and talents of *both* people. If you draw the 2 of Wands for a vocation or career question, it's advising you to look past any external trait that may irritate or provoke you—high-octane enthusiasm, quirky presentation or loquaciousness—towards the inner gems that can accent your *own* gifts. How might you work well with this person? What do you have in common? What fresh perspective might she bring? How can your differences be harnessed for a project or applied to a problem? When you approach a co-worker or potential collaborator with curiosity instead of suspicion, openness rather than defensiveness, such pairings often end up as a dynamic catalyst for brilliant solutions, fresh ideas and bold creativity.

*Romance:* Some miss out on a wonderful mate because of casting the romantic net out there in the stratosphere. The "order" put in to the Universe? Tall. Handsome. Rich. Dark brown hair and eyes. Six pack. Funny. Smart. Sharp dresser. No facial hair. You see where this is going, right? Standards set so freakin' high, that almost no one could reach them. This ideal is projected "out there", somewhere in "the world" — probably far away — until fate just happens to bring him to your front door. Um... *no.* I don't care *what* Rhonda Byrne and company said in *The Secret* movie: the Universe ain't your genie. Yeah, "luck" favors the prepared — but not with Jedi mind tricks or fairytale pining. Nothing wrong with having high standards where it matters (i.e., character, demeanor, values), but if you keep assuming that a special someone is just floating around like a spacewalker on a tether — somewhere far, far away — you'll miss the wonderful person right under your nose (or in your neighborhood or in the pews of your church or in the aisles of your favorite grocery store or among the stacks of the local library or within your High School yearbook...)

*Parenting:* At some point, you'll butt heads with one (or all) of the kids. It may be mild (depending on the closeness of, and respect within, the relationship), but it can also be quite explosive — especially when two strong, stubborn personalities are at loggerheads. You may feel such conflict weakens your position as a parent and so in the attempt to regain control, you push back harder (and yell louder). In case you didn't get the memo, *it's not working*. In fact, arguing is making things worse. Rather than approach the disagreement head-on, tackle it from the side: determine why your kid wants what he wants. Figure out why *you* want to prevent it. Make a list of reasons. Better yet, ask *him* to make his own list. Now, rather than repeatedly shouting *"No!"* at him, invite him to the dining room for a civil conference—lists in hand. Share your reasons. Listen to his. Who's making the most sense? If it's you (don't assume it will *be* you, either!), offer alternatives that will still accomplish one or more reasons on his list. He's probably feeling a bit of an identity crisis (is he still a kid? A teen? A half-man?)...longing to spread his wings and fly into the world.

*Spirituality:* Your spiritual life isn't for public consumption. And if you're making it so, it's time to look closely at what you're doing—and why you're doing it. The *Snowland Deck* version of this card depicts a mountain valley during autumn breeding season, two male bighorn sheep butting heads as a female looks on. As a part of the mating ritual, charging males clash together at speeds of 40 miles per hour, with the resulting sound of crashing horns heard up to a mile away. *Yikes!* So what does this have to do with your spiritual path? When this card comes up, it's time to examine your relationship with "the world"—and why you may be choosing to take certain classes, attend particular workshops or endeavoring to get a "special" certification (especially if you're blabbing about it on social media). What do you feel "they" have that you don't? What are you gaining by aligning yourself with a particular teacher or group? How do you hope the world sees you by your affiliation? Most importantly, *whose* attention are you trying to get...and *why*?

**Recommended Resources:** *The Boys: The Sherman Brothers' Story*

(Movie); *Tucker* (Movie)

**2 of Wands Card Layout:** *Head-to-Head* Spread

1. How do I feel about going toe-to-toe with someone?
2. In what area (or with whom) am I locked into a battle of wills?
3. What type of personality clash is happening right now?
4. Who is challenging me?
5. What type of confrontation may be brewing?
6. Who am I trying to impress?
6a. Why?
7. Who is trying to impress me?
7a. Why?

# 3 of Wands – Waiting for Your Ship to Come In

**Stripped Down Overview:** You've enacted your plan, sown good seeds and healthy plants are sprouting. How *exciting*! If you've created something that the public will view, read, listen to, play with or consume, *now's* the time to let them know about it! Some folks assume that a product or service must be 100 percent ready to go before telling friends, family or even the world. Not so! In fact, if you wait until then, you're missing out on stoking the anticipation of fans and potential clients (not to mention lucrative pre-orders and offering early bird specials). Another aspect to the 3 of Wands is supportive partnerships and encouragement. If pals are saying, *"You've got something there!"* or *"I know you can do this!"* —believe them! And keep your ears open for practical advice offered by experienced friends, peers or colleagues: their past successes will help magnify *yours*, so eschew any skepticism or stubbornness. Follow their guidance, model their example and allow them to network on your behalf. A bountiful harvest is heading your way—thanks, in large part, to your foresight, smart planning and calculated risks.

**Keywords:** Extension; Operating Under Your Own Power; Intuitive Foresight for Business or Art; Amalgamation of Resources; Expecting Fruition; Enlargement; Marketing Your Strengths; Creative Collaboration; Enterprise; Expanding Influence; Free Agent; Heightened Senses; Awaiting Results; Alert to Opportunities for Advancement; Trade and Commerce; Publicity; Social Media Efforts; Doing Your Own Thing; Feedback; Humble Yet Confident; Backup

**Personifications and Embodiments:** 78 Tarot Artists Assembled (Group Art Projects); Twitter; Instagram; Indie Artists; Self-Publishing Efforts; "I'm Right Where I Need to Be."

**Quote:** *The greatest loss of time is delay and expectation, which depend upon the future. We let go the present, which we have in our power, and look forward to that which depends upon chance, and so relinquish a certainty for an uncertainty.* – Seneca

**Challenge:** Exposure

**Gift:** Amplification

**Occupations/Vocations:** Shipping Magnate; Trader; Marina Owner; Watchman; Ship Restorer; Sailor; Dock Worker; Security Guard; Customs Official

**Disney Totem:** John Smith (*Pocahontas*)

**Animal Symbol:** Seagull

**Flower Essences:** Jacaranda (Australian Bush); Turkey Bush (Australian Bush)

**Crystal/Stone:** Red Calcite – Supports willpower in waiting for results of efforts.

Initiates the competent and successful materialization of ideas. Helps overcome listlessness.

**Aromatherapy:** Wintergreen

**Body Parts/Systems and Health Issues:** Osteoporosis; Bone Disease

**Mystical Messenger** – Martin Caballero

**Sabian Symbol:** Cancer 22 – A young woman awaiting a sailboat.

**Writing Prompt:** A rock star, alone on an island, plugs in his guitar amplifier.

**Affirmation:** I expand my influence.

## Naked Advice for the 3 of Wands

*Career:* Word of mouth is powerful. In fact, according to researcher and Professor Dr. Jonah Berger, word of mouth is the primary factor behind 20-50 percent of all purchasing decisions. A 5-star review on Amazon.com leads to approximately 20 more books sold (compared to a 1-star review). First-time customer raves about an awesome restaurant lead to almost $200 increase in sales. Why is word of mouth more effective than traditional advertising? According to Berger, it's because we trust the recommendations of our friends and family (after all, they have our best interests at heart)—and also because word of mouth is naturally targeted (for example, a pal who knows we love mysteries will recommend a great new whodunit…but he *won't* tell us about a newly discovered burger joint he enjoys if we happen to be vegan). So how to generate more face-to-face recommendations—or enthusiastic, honest online *you-gotta-get-this!* suggestions? Give people something to talk about...and make it easy for them to share your "story".

*Romance:* This card reveals that a love interest has shown more sides to him—and you like what you see! When we're used to someone's behavior, and he's only shown us a few facets of his personality, it can be disconcerting when different sides emerge. But as Walt Whitman said, *"Do I contradict myself? Very well then I contradict myself (I am large, I contain multitudes)."* After all, a multi-dimensional person will likely provide thoughtful conversations, interesting perspectives and (cross your fingers) unusual date nights. As long as he's consistently virtuous, you needn't worry. When the 3 of Wands appears, it's also possible that you've loved someone, so you've "set her free"—or that she's away on an extended trip, a tour of duty or studying abroad. Take heart, and comfort yourself with what you built together: she'll be home before you know it!

*Parenting*: You need to stop being so nervous about your kid's education! If you homeschool, this card indicates that you've given your child a wonderful foundation not only in the facts-and-figures department, but also (and more importantly) in the area of critical thinking. You've taught her how to envision something and make it happen (or, at least, theorize what will occur!)—and she's going to apply that in the form of solid decision making (yes, including what to major in and where to attend college!). If your child's education is in the hands of others, trust that she's being equipped to navigate her potential field *and* life itself. After evaluating afforded opportunities, the quality of her instruction and the educational resources she's using, you can rest easy knowing that your little chick will fly far and high when it comes time to leave the nest. After all, she's equipped with strong wings and clear vision—not to mention a quiet confidence that you and her mentors helped to cultivate.

*Spirituality:* Do you have someone in your life that gives you sound spiritual direction that's so astute—so *appropriate*—you could *swear* it comes straight from God's mouth? And yet, you seem to "forget" it minutes later? Or you disregard it altogether? It's not that you don't respect or trust the person, mind you. Rather, it's the *familiarity.* Somehow, our humanness seems to make us tone-deaf to the wise counsel of those closest to us. (I'm preachin' to the choir here: my husband gives me amazing advice. Seriously, it's like I have a live-in guru. Make that *two*: our son gives me jaw-dropping "out-of-the-mouth-of-babes" guidance, too!) The 3 of Wands is urging you to listen closely to those you hold nearest and dearest: what is the last thing they told you? What bit of instruction did they share (after you asked)? Did you listen? Heed their advice? I didn't think so. Take out a pen and start to journal what you hear coming out of your loved ones' mouths (or texts). Pretend that each is an angel, giving you divine messages on a daily basis. Write it down, no matter how innocuous. Do this for a few days. Then think back: what happened to you this week? How might their pronouncements offer a solution to a dilemma? A sage observation that gives you much-needed encouragement on your path? A juicy tidbit you can sink your existential teeth into?

**Recommended Resources:** *How Ideas Spread* (The Great Courses) by Professor Jonah Berger; *Creative You: Using Your Personality Type to Thrive* by David B. Goldstein and Otto Kroeger; *Fascinate: Your 7 Triggers to Persuasion and Captivation* by Sally Hogshead

**3 of Wands Card Layout:** *Feedback Loop* Spread

1. In what area do I need to "go indie" (or be more

independent)?

2. How will this benefit me?

3. What kind of advice do I need to hear right now that's connected to this pursuit?

3. What type of person will be most likely to share such advice with me?

4. What kind of feedback have I already been getting (but may not be "hearing")?

5. Why is this feedback so important?

6. How/Where/When will my "ship" come in?

7. *(If You're An Entrepreneur)* How might I expand my influence?

8. *(If You're An Entrepreneur)* What type of publicity do I need?

9. *(If You're An Entrepreneur)* How can I provide something that people talk about?

## 4 of Wands – It Takes a Village

**Stripped Down Overview:** Religious commemorations, rites of passage, ethnic celebrations, country fairs, block parties, open-air concerts, community meetings, festivals—anytime or anywhere groups of people gather for a shared purpose or celebration, we're seeing the realm of the 4 of Wands card. While the 3 of Cups features a couple of friends, usually hanging out informally or just to drink themselves silly, this card has a wider reach—and often occurs on a regular basis (often yearly). Some gatherings are held under a cultural umbrella, with folks often sharing the same ethnicity (Italian Heritage Day, Cinco de Mayo or Chinese New Year celebrations, for example), while others are dedicated to a central cause, with participants reflecting diverse backgrounds (Women's March, Burning Man or SxSW). In all cases, the groups gathered are organized and have the common purpose of promoting unity, celebrating a milestone, accomplishing a goal, mass entertainment, thematic education, highlighting a widespread problem or honoring a person/event/ heritage.

**Keywords:** Community; Rites of Passage; Finished Project; Where You Grew Up; Holidays; Town Meetings; Neighborhood; Formative Years; Gatherings; Festivals; Assembly; Federation; Solidarity; Unity; Outdoor Entertainment; Conventions

**Personifications and Embodiments:** Women's March of January 2017; Graduation Party; Cinco de Mayo; Mardis Gras; Carnivale; Company Picnic; *Race for the Cure*; Woodstock; Coachella; Burning Man; Lollapalooza; Chinese New Year; Superbowl Half-Time Show; Open-Air Events; Circumcision; Quincenara; Bar/Bat Mitzvah; Baby Showers; Barn Raisings; Street Fairs; Block Parties; Community Bingo; Carnivals; Stadium Concerts; Pageants; World Fairs

**Quote:** *We may have all come on different ships, but we're in the same boat now.* – Martin Luther King, Jr.

**Challenge:** Commotion

**Gift:** Kinship

**Occupations/Vocations:** Event Planner; Florist; Marching Band Conductor; Caterer; Tent Manufacturer; *Chuppah* Maker

**Disney Totem:** Christopher Robin (*The Many Adventures of Winnie the Pooh*)

**Animal Symbol:** Prairie Dog

**Flower Essence:** Red Chestnut (Bach)

**Crystal/Stone:** Ruin Marble – Promotes the sense of community, teamwork and consensus. Fortifies faithfulness and unity. Supports the idea "it takes a village".

**Aromatherapy:** Tonka Bean

**Body Parts/Systems and Health Issues:** Carbon Monoxide Poisoning; Toxic Gases Released From Fires; Burns

**Mystical Messenger** – The Horae

**Sabian Symbol:** Scorpio 3 – Neighbors help in a house-raising party in a small village.

**Writing Prompt:** Amnesia sweeps a crowd.

**Affirmation:** I celebrate causes and occasions that matter to me.

## Naked Advice for the 4 of Wands

*Career:* Assuming pay and benefits are good, throwing an office party is a great way to boost morale. Have cubicle-decorating contests with fab prizes. Create fun, offbeat awards like "Cheeriest Disposition", "Office MacGyver", "Best Packed Lunches" or "Most Colorful Clothing". Host crazy in-office games like Boiled-Egg-on-the-Spoon Race (even better if you can play outside!). Definitely toot the company horn if sales and customer satisfaction are through the roof, but take care to honor the individuals who make it happen with special recognition. If you're a solopreneuer, consider attending a convention dedicated to your craft or business—especially if it's held in a luxurious destination or with enticing entertainment on the schedule. If you feel like you're surrounded by too much noise, distraction and/or congestion (even if you work from home), consider relocating or moving to a quieter location—preferably where you're surrounded by trees, hills and nature sounds rather than concrete, metal and wailing sirens.

*Romance:* If you're in a serious, fulfilling relationship, now's the time to introduce her to the parents! And the rest of the family! And if your beloved is well-received, consider having a lovely outdoor wedding as soon as the weather is nice, too. Even if your family (or hers) isn't thrilled (or worse, they're just rude idiots), commemorate your love with those who are happy for you—even if it's "just" neighbors, friends or co-workers. Personally, I don't believe that "blood is thicker than water"—but that a *chosen* "family" can be even stronger than one connected via DNA. And if you have some unusual ideas for a wedding or reception? Go for it! (You'll regret it if you don't.) Unity, merriment and pleasure are the order of the day, so whatever group celebration you cook up for your love, do it with originality, enthusiasm and style.

*Parenting:* My mom is one of 13 siblings. My dad's mom was one of ten siblings. One of my favorite things to do as a youth was attend a family reunion. Each side celebrated quite differently: my mom's side met at her brother's house, and he "dug a pit" in his backyard every year and began roasting a pig and chickens early in the morning. Relatives came from all around, bringing side dishes, salads and desserts to share. Alcohol flowed freely, as did clanging horseshoes (a favorite outdoor game) and funny remembrances. My mom's siblings had children of their own—anywhere from 2–5 per family (yes, I have tons of cousins!), and we celebrated well into the night. Reunions on my dad's side were more organized and subdued: there were games for children, games for adults, giveaways and auctions—all held at a local park that featured swings, jungle gyms, a huge slide, a swimming pool and plenty of room to play and run. Not a drop of alcohol to be seen. Now that my aunts and uncles are getting older, reunions aren't as frequent. It would appear that my cousins—now in their 40s and 50s—aren't as keen to keep up the family traditions, especially in the age of Facebook, where "keeping in touch" can happen daily, or in an instant. This makes me a bit sad, and I'm thinking of hosting one this year—coinciding with our son's High School graduation. I've said all this because the 4 of Wands is advising you to keep family traditions alive—and to prioritize celebrating your kid's milestones. Something special can happen when flesh-and-blood folks get together, face to face, to commemorate a child's achievements or a family event (especially if you have the balls to enforce a "no texting" rule—which I hope you do).

*Spirituality:* When you work hard for something—especially over a lengthy period of time—your energy may be sapped without your realizing it. Running on adrenaline and fumes, you've pushed to finish that creative project or accomplish that important goal—and it's done. Uncorked wine bottles or champagne toasts may be the next logical step—and you'd *love* to celebrate—but *first*, you need to regain your emotional center, replenish precious resources, hug your family (and pets!), ground your energy and square away any lingering details. Loved ones may expect you to celebrate right away (after all, they're happy for you!), but they may not realize how "finishing" can feel more like deflation rather than elation. Not to mention that, at this point, you just want to lie around in pajamas for a week, eat ice cream in bed and binge-watch your favorite TV show (that you've been missing out on). Take as long as you want and need. Family and friends will understand. Postpone the blow-out party (complete with a DJ) everyone wants to throw for you so you can refresh your spirit and reconnect with the Divine in stillness. When you're rested and ready, let your pals honor you (and your accomplishment): let your hair down, drink like a fish and boogie all night long!

**Recommended Resources:** *Christmas with the Kranks* (Movie); *The Music Man* (Movie); *Sunday Afternoon on La Grande Jatte* by Georges Seurat; *Industrial Landscape* by L.S. Lowry; *Peasant Wedding Feast* by Pieter Bruegel

**4 of Wands Card Layout:** *Four Pillars of Community* Spread

1. *Pillar One*: What is the greater community that I'm an integral part of?
2. *Pillar Two*: What is the importance of this community?
3. *Pillar Three*: What is my role in this community?
4. *Pillar Four*: How can I bless or help this community?

# 5 of Wands – It's All Fun and Games Until...

**Stripped Down Overview:** *Thwack! Pow! Oof! Biff!* Just like the faux fights on the live action Batman TV show (circa 1960s), the 5 of Wands isn't quite sure if it wants a *real* brawl—or if parading around with tights, tunic and twirling twigs is all the conflict it can handle. From testosterone-soaked soap operas called "pro wrestling" to mock jousts at Ren Faires, flag football among 40-something IT guys to impromptu dance-offs, there's a flux of uncertainty with this card. It seeks to test and engage, but lacks the aggressive stamina or seriousness of, say, the Knight of Wands. Some people just get a high from the thrill of a contest— debate teams, pillow fights, duels with foam swords—or, on a more public stage, *American Gladiators*, *Dancing with the Stars* or air-guitar competitions. Sibling rivalry, good-natured teasing, escalating pranks—it's all fun and games until someone loses an eye or gets offended. Then, we may side step into the more violent and nasty territory of the 5 of Swords. Imagine, if you will, a cosmic washing machine—agitating the water, swirling the clothes, loosening the dirt—everyday shake-ups that disrupt the status quo, foments stagnant energy, changes routines and keeps life interesting.

**Keywords:** Contests; Fighting Paper Tigers; Jockeying for Position; Team Sports; Disorganization; Contradiction; Differences; Tests; Hassle; Trivialities; Competition; Caught off Guard; Disputes; Sham Fight; Teasing; Cross Purposes; Intense Discussions; Wrangling; Dress Rehearsal; Bickering; War Games; Unstable Alliances; Exuberant Play; Outdoor Exercise; Shift of Power

**Personifications and Embodiments:** Paintball; Debate Teams; *Cards Against Humanity*; WWE; Football; Soccer; Basketball; Hockey; Food Fight

**Quote:** *Most sorts of diversion in men, children, and other animals, are an imitation of fighting.* – Jonathan Swift

**Challenge:** Futility

**Gift:** Reinvigoration

**Occupations/Vocations:** Improvisational Theater Troupe; Lacrosse Player; Jouster; Battle Re-enactor

**Disney Totem:** Kay (*The Sword in the Stone*)

**Animal Symbol:** Kangaroo

**Flower Essence:** Kangaroo Paw (Australian Bush)

**Crystal/Stone:** Limonite (Clay Ironstone) – Helps convert selfishness to a sense of community. Strengthens under extreme strain. Aids in standing firm in the face of conflict, yet resist the urge to fight back or lash out.

**Aromatherapy:** Aniseed

**Body Parts/Systems and Health Issues:** Bruises; Sprains; Hematoma

**Mystical Messenger** – Huehuecoyotl

**Sabian Symbol:** Scorpio 30 – Children in Halloween costumes indulging in various pranks.

**Writing Prompt:** Four out of five youth wield a stick. The fifth? Something *else.*

**Affirmation:** I allow myself boisterous, uninhibited self-expression.

## Naked Advice for the 5 of Wands

*Career:* Now is the time to up your game and distinguish yourself from the pack. Jockeying for position, power plays, fake-outs, misdirection, heated contests—if a promotion or position is up for grabs, you'll face all this...and stiff competition. Shine up your resume with awards, achievements, volunteerism, special skills (that you may take for granted) and ongoing education. Such polishing could make a difference when several qualified candidates are vying for the same job. If you thrive on competition, tests and vocational challenges, this is a fortuitous card: it favors those who can keep their heads during upheaval, ambiguity and interoffice conflicts. Stick to your gut, play by the rules, pull out all the stops and maintain good sportsmanship. If you can manage all that, you'll remain standing when the dust settles—probably promoted, and still friends with everyone—invigorated by this latest test of mettle. If you work for yourself, employ methods that make you stand out from the crowd. You can do what others are doing (as long as it's smarter, bolder and better)—but it would be more beneficial if you were the only "orange" on the palette, rather than the bright tangerine among pumpkin, carrot, cantaloupe and peach.

*Romance:* If you're looking for a hot date or committed mate, pick someone that can "hang" with you (and your lively interests). If you enjoy heart-in-your-throat roller coasters, playing softball, attending team sport events and spontaneous games of pick-up basketball—well, a lethargic couch potato, peace-loving artist or quiet-night-at-home introvert may not nudge your passion needle (even a little). Don't be afraid to ask a stranger for a date, pay for that cute guy's latte or invite a friendly career competitor to a hockey game. A lot can happen in the swirling, unpredictable energy of this card—including a bona fide love match. The key is to look for someone who works as hard—and *plays* as hard—as you do...with a spine strong (and flexible) enough to take a joke, or loss, in good-humored stride.

*Parenting:* "God, Mom, get off my *back!*" What parents see as regular doses of well-meaning advice, kids hear as the *"wah, wah, wah, wah"* of Charlie Brown's teacher. Nagging, bitching, nitpicking—your words feel like famished, fanged finches pecking at every square inch of exposed flesh. Am I exaggerating? Maybe just a bit, but kids tend to be hypersensitive about mistakes (real or imagined) and forgetful omissions. When coals of shame are heaped upon their heads, they burn with embarrassment. Instead of having your parental record stuck on *"how many times do I have to tell you..."*, deliver your expectations clearly and concisely (in writing, if need be). Choose your battles wisely (i.e., the truly important things) and you may find a significant reduction in endless bickering, silent treatments and avoidance. Hey, you just might end up with a kid that actually *wants* to talk to you!

*Spirituality:* The word "Israel" means *"wrestling with God"*. The 5 of Wands reflects the same energy: some of us—whether because of disposition, path or calling—frequently "get on the mat" with the Divine. The whole *"work out your own salvation with fear and trembling; for it is God who works in you both to will and to do for His good pleasure"* (Philippians 2: 12-13) sentiment encapsulates this God-as-opponent dynamic. There are times on our spiritual path that we must "have it out" with the Divine—yell, pout, blame, cuss—in order to clear out cobwebs of confusion, untie the frustrating knots of unanswered prayer and hammer out our coexistence with unanswerable questions. Go ahead; God can take your pile drivers. Seriously. After all, if the Divine doesn't have big enough shoulders (and heart) to take it...who *can*?

**Recommended Resources:** *Stomp!* (Percussion Show); *Basketball* by Normal Rockwell; *Saturday's Heroes* by Normal Rockwell

**5 of Wands Card Layout:** *Pick Up Sticks* Spread

1. What "stick" should I pick up?
2. What "stick" should I *not* grab?
3. What "stick" should I dodge?
4. What "stick" is heading for my head?
5. What "stick" will defend/protect me?
6. What "stick" should I hit with?
7. What "stick" could trip me up?
8. What "stick" will win it for me?

## 6 of Wands – Flavor of the Day

**Stripped Down Overview:** Whether it's Kanye insisting disabled concertgoers stand (to the point of marshalling security to enforce his decree), Muhammad Ali boasting he's "the greatest" or Trump blustering about his *yuge* financial accomplishments, the 6 of Wands spans the first-class ass, cheering fans and awards of all kinds. From blue ribbons at the county fair to shiny gold Oscars, Teen Choice Awards to Best in Show, having your pie, book, movie or dog get a trophy swells breasts, heads and (usually) wallets. The crowd goes wild, the media calls, orders pour in and *everyone* claims to be your BFF (even the D-lister too snobby to blurb your now-award-winning creation). There was a time when medals were few and far between—and richly deserved by talented individuals. Nowadays? Gold stars for first graders for having their shoes tied, certificates of achievement for not punching anyone, satiny ribbons for spelling your name right, buttons with number one blazoned on them just for breathing…cray cray! Hell, some "societies", "coalitions" or "associations" bestow dubious back-door "awards" on friends, fuck buddies or even themselves (never-you-mind their lack of experience, originality or excellence!). Here's the thing about fame and public approval: the unwashed masses *love* to elevate their darlings on pedestals—only to gleefully topple and trample them for the most petty of reasons. Just ask Jesus: one day, he's riding high (well, as high as you can ride on a donkey) to shouts of *"Hosanna!"*…only to have the same crowd demand his brutal death via ignominious crucifixion shortly thereafter.

**Keywords:** Victory; Public Acclaim; Awards; Conquest; Triumph, Approval; Winning; Popularity; Reward; Promotion

**Personifications and Embodiments:** Winner's Circle; Gold Medal; First Place; Blue Ribbon; Coronations; Parades; Olympics

Award Ceremonies; Grammys; Tonys; Oscars; Emmys; Golden Globes; Celebrated Hero/Heroine; Olympics; Champions; Employee of the Year; Miss Universe; Best in Show; Superbowl; World Series; Stanley Cup; World Cup

**Quote:** *Do not trust the cheering, for those persons would shout as much if you or I were going to be hanged.* – Oliver Cromwell

**Challenge:** Hubris

**Gift:** Recognition

**Occupations/Vocations:** Trophy Maker; Accomplished Jockey; Big Game Hunter; Award-Winning Entertainer

**Disney Totem:** Simba (*The Lion King*)

**Animal Symbol:** Moose

**Flower Essences:** Elm (Bach); Heather (Bach)

**Crystal/Stone:** Yellow Topaz – Helps one acknowledge and celebrate achievements. Promotes self-assurance and awareness of one's importance.

**Aromatherapy:** Bay Laurel

**Body Parts/Systems and Health Issues:** Hemorrhoids; Anus; Rectal Disorders; Varicose Veins

**Mystical Messenger** – Nike

**Sabian Symbol:** Gemini 30 – A parade of bathing beauties before large beach crowds.

**Writing Prompt:** On a new TV game show, the winner takes all. I mean, *all*.

**Affirmation:** Every victory deserves celebration—even small ones.

## Naked Advice for 6 of Wands

*Career:* Champ or chump is in the eye of the beholder. Yeah, this is simplistic, but it's true: some awards are utter bullshit and others a product of "right time, right place"—more random that most would like to admit. But if you've strove for excellence, always going above and beyond what's requested or required, you're chances are pretty damn good of getting a promotion at best or an award of some type at worst (because, let's face it, unless an "award" pads your bank account, sends you to Hawaii or gives you a few weeks off with pay—it's practically useless). Speaking of taking a trip, say *"Yes!"* to any opportunities to travel for work, even if it appears inconvenient or unappealing. You never know what extra benefits, promotions or even raises will occur because of your willingness and performance.

*Romance:* Time to throw off any hints of shyness or tendencies to wallflower! Instead, imagine yourself going up to that cutie in the bookstore and *asking him out*. Yes, *you*! You must *envision* yourself as a dating success in order to snag attention. Believe me: how *you* see yourself (and talk about/to yourself) makes a difference in how *others* respond to you. If you don't focus on your good qualities and accentuate the positive, how do you expect potential mates to do so? If it will help, confer with a color consultant, get a new hairstyle, dare to wear fabulous clothes (that, normally, you'd be too scared to try), visit a cosmetics counter and ask for a makeover (and invest in some good makeup), hire a life coach to help you with confidence or assertiveness—whatever it takes to get your from shrinking violet to sexy honeysuckle, chickie. Already married? Same advice applies! You've already landed a wonderful mate (YAY!), so now it's just a matter of amping up the romance and spicing up the sex life. You've *got* this!

**Parenting**: Moms and dads rarely see themselves as "winners" in the parenting game, largely because no one was kind enough (or smart enough) to compile an owner's manual at birth. *Boo! Hiss!* So we stumble along, referencing *other* sources to help us not fuck our kids up—Dr. Spock (no, not the *Star Trek* guy), parenting magazines, friends with kids, our religion, our intuition, our parents (only if we're desperate)—*gah!* So many opportunities to screw up! But not for you. No, if you've drawn the 6 of Wands card and your question involves dealing with your kids, pat yourself on the back. In fact, keep doing what you're doing, because your reliability and predictability likely contributes to your mad parenting skillz and any props you get from the offspring (or even onlookers). Expect out-of-the-blue comments like *"Mom, I love you"* or *"Dad, you're really cool"* (which, now that I've tipped you off, won't really be out-of-the-blue, but you'll still be surprised when you hear them...promise!).

**Spirituality:** Your soul, the eternal part of you that incarnated for specific lessons and experiences, has its own agenda—and it may not include mass acceptance, public acknowledgement or awards in the material world. The spirit realm's measuring stick is *nothing* like that of the Earth's; in fact, what is lauded, promoted and rewarded here doesn't even register on the heavenly Success-o-Meter. The New Testament goes so far to call such things "wood, hay and straw"—things easily burned up (I Corinthians 3:12-16). So before you get *too* discouraged when people overlook your achievements, pass by your offerings or ignore your unique brilliance, think about what's truly "gold, silver and precious stones"—those significant actions and shared occurrences that are eternal, where neither moth nor rust nor public opinion can destroy. After all, you didn't come here to win a popularity contest, my friend.

**Recommended Resources:** "We Are the Champions" (Song); *Akeelah and the Bee* (Movie)

**6 of Wands Card Layout:** *Success? I'll Give You Success!* Spread

1. How do I define success?
2. How does my *soul* define success?
3. What is a major sign my soul is fulfilling its purpose?
4. How will I know when I'm striving for the wrong (*for me*) thing?
5. What do I need to know about public opinion?
6. What do I need to remember when my achievements are ignored?
7. In what area am I unequivocally a "spiritual champion"?

## 7 of Wands – D-E-F-E-N-S-E...*Gooooo* Defense!

**Stripped Down Overview:** Look. At. *You!* Worked your ass off, completing myriad successful projects, huh? And just happen to own that rare mix of talent and confidence. *Woohoo!* But...now you're attracting wannabes *itching* to knock you off that prized stallion from the 6 of Wands. *Wooboo!* Maybe you've caught some Knight of Wands zeal, determined to right some wrong by taking on the establishment, the community, Twitter—the *entire world*! Or perhaps you've taken an unpopular position—and the pushback has begun. Welcome to the world of the "Higher Ups": Higher up on the totem pole, corporate ladder, sales roster, sports stats, movie billing, draft list—or those with impressive records, impeccable ethics, (very) public moral indignation or consistently stellar creative output. You may as well have a sign glued to your forehead that says, *"Hit me with your best shot!"* (Hey, that was a great 80s song, come to think of it! *"Fire awayyyyy..."*)

**Keywords:** Defending Your Position; Witch Hunts; Proving Yourself; Standing Your Ground; Relishing a Challenge; Deviation from the Norm; Refusing to "Stoop Low"; Fending Off; Moral High Ground; Rabid Enemies; Battling Objections; Rejecting the Status Quo; Deflecting Harassment; Taking the High Road Against Mistreatment; Maintaining Your Footing; Unyielding; Mutiny; Vantage Point

**Personifications and Embodiments:** People Running Their Mouths; Taking on the Bullies; DaPL Protestors; Lying in Front of Bulldozers to Prevent Deforestation; Human Chains; Swordsman on a Hill; "Hold Down the Fort"

**Quote:** *I do not regret one professional enemy I have made. Any actor who doesn't dare make an enemy should get out of the business.* – Bette Davis

**Challenge:** Elevation

**Gift:** Standpoint

**Occupations/Vocations:** Pest Exterminator; Body Guard; Bouncer; Dojo Sensei

**Disney Totem:** Robinson Family (*Swiss Family Robinson*)

**Animal Symbol:** Badger

**Flower Essence:** Philotheca (Australian Bush)

**Crystal/Stone:** Staurolite Garnet Schist – Fortification. Encourages holding one's ground. Aids in coping with strain. Grants composure. Enables handling of what is necessary and completing what's required.

**Aromatherapy:** Arbovitae

**Body Parts/Systems and Health Issues:** Adrenal Glands

**Mystical Messenger** – Shango

**Sabian Symbol:** Aquarius 17 – A watchdog standing guard protecting his master and his possessions.

**Writing Prompt:** A crowd goes after a decorated soldier.

**Affirmation:** I will defend what matters to me.

## Naked Advice for the 7 of Wands

*Career:* You've exceeded the company sales goal for six straight months, snagging an Employee of the Year Award. Or launch an online business that takes the Self-Help market by storm. Or win a scholarship to art school because of your poster design. Or maybe write 1,000 plus reviews with tens of thousands of "helpful" votes, earning you the coveted Hall of Fame Reviewer designation at Amazon.com. Think you're going to get pats on the back and hearty congrats? Perhaps from family and close friends. But the public at large? Peers? Colleagues? Don't bank on it: The more you outshine your competitors, create original content, land the big deals or dare to be different—the bigger the bullseye on your back. Insecure and feeling small, jealous others will attempt to knock you off the pedestal—either with a full-on frontal attack, or by disseminating slander in the shadows (these types are usually denizens of 5 of Swords Land). It puts you in a Catch-22, though, because to answer their lies dignifies the mud-slinging—and draws unwanted attention. But to let them attempt to chisel away at your reputation and tarnish your accomplishments is unacceptable, as well. What a *shitty* position to be in! Vocational success and standing out in a crowd comes with a price when the 7 of Wands comes up. Are you ready?

*Romance:* I really think you need to explore the whole dominance/submission thing in the bedroom. No, seriously. (Ha!) Well, I'm only *half* joking: playing around with role reversals can be a fun way to not only enhance your sexual endeavors, but also expand your personality—and how you see the world. Stand strong in your sexuality. Experiment with D/s playacting. Examine who takes on the dominant role in your romantic relationship—and who tends to be submissive. Think about how those approaches are working (or not), and bring your partner on board to discuss (including whether he likes to be on top...or not).

*Parenting*: Teaching your kids to stand up for themselves—let alone what they believe in, or on behalf of marginalized others—is tricky. On one hand, if you tell him to keep his head down, don't make waves or ignore bullies—then you send the signal that it's OK to be a pushover (and perhaps destine him to a lifetime of cowering, not to mention becoming part of a larger problem). On the other, if you encourage her strong convictions—telling her to fight for what matters to her—she'll likely invite more scrutiny or opposition. When to keep silent? When to speak up? When to stand your ground? When to let it slide? Encouraging the kiddos to choose their battles wisely is imperative. The thing is, when the 7 of Wands shows up, those skirmishes have *already* arrived outside their front door. How you, as a parent—an adult—have handled similar clashes up until now will likely speak the loudest to them, though...*despite* what you say.

*Spirituality:* OK, out of this entire book, you who draw this card when inquiring about your spiritual growth will be getting the *most* direct advice from Spirit, I reckon. See, I was all ready to write about "narrow is the way" and breathing rarified air when committed to ruthless self-awareness (and the type of "enemies" that your path will tend to attract). So I got my old salmon pink NKJV off the shelf—I'm lucky if I do so once a year—to look up the *exact* reference of Jesus' comment. (I used to be a Pentecostal minister, mind you, so I still keep the Good Book in my library—especially for its mystical wisdom.) My Bible *flipped open* to Isaiah 54:17. This passage is not only highlighted in neon yellow—but the first sentence *is underlined in red*. Holy synchronicity, Batman! Talk about a double-strength Jehovah Signal glowing in the air! Oh, I guess I should share it here with you: *"No weapon formed against you shall prosper. And every tongue which rises against you in judgment you shall condemn..."*

**Recommended Resources:** *Pacific Rim* (Movie); "Vital Signs" by Rush

**7 of Wands Card Layout:** *Go Ahead...Make My Day* Spread

1. What is the strength of my current vantage point?
2. What is its weakness?
3. What do I need to know about my "enemies" (external or internal)?
4. How can I best combat them?
5. What is my "secret weapon"?
6. What will "victory" look like?
7. How can I best ensure it?

## 8 of Wands – Faster Than a Speeding Bullet

**Stripped Down Overview:** *Incoming!* Whether via a flood of phone calls, an avalanche of emails or a flurry of zooming golf balls headed straight for your noggin, the 8 of Wands careens on the scene with sudden, forceful speed. Especially welcome after periods of stagnation or during discouraging plateaus, this card screams "move, move, *move!*" This energy plows through mountains, unleashes dammed streams and ignites turbo jets. Such sudden thrust, rapid acceleration and unhindered progression can be disorienting for the unprepared — leading to missed opportunities and plenty of dust eating. To use a running metaphor, this card is a sprinter, capitalizing on bursts of energy and limited propulsion. To use a car metaphor, the 8 of Wands is a dragster — burning through fuel faster than Satan scarfing up damned souls for breakfast.

**Keywords:** High Speed Messages; Speedy Delivery; Quick Action; Urgency; Transmission; Swift Communication; Fast Reply; Notification; Internet; Texting; Phone Calls; Internet; Digital Transfer; Intuitive Download; Long Distance Connection; Air Travel; Rapid Transit

**Personifications and Embodiments:** Mr. McFeely (*Mr. Rogers' Neighborhood*); Airplanes; Trains; Javelin; Jets; Air Force; The Roadrunner; Speedy Gonzalez; Autobahn; Pony Express; Sprints; Blast Off!; Skype; WiFi; Flash Drives; Shorthand; Speedways; Grand Prix; Flying Arrow; Kentucky Derby; Newsflash; Morse Code

**Quote:** *Fast is fine, but accuracy is everything.* – Wyatt Earp

**Challenge:** Stopping

**Gift:** Velocity

**Occupations/Vocations:** Computer Programmer; Mail Carrier;

FedEx or UPS; Airplane Pilot; Printer; Stenographer; Javelin Thrower; Archer; Baseball Pitcher

**Disney Totem:** Dash (*The Incredibles*)

**Animal Symbol:** Cheetah

**Flower Essences:** Bauhinia (Australian Bush); Paw Paw (Australian Bush)

**Crystal/Stone:** Tiger's Eye – Sharpens the senses and helps maintain a big-picture view when things are happening fast. Aids with overwhelming external influences. Ameliorates stress arising from a deluge of messages or opportunities. Encourages detachment.

**Aromatherapy:** Eucalyptus Citriodora

**Body Parts/Systems and Health Issues:** Angina; Heart Palpitations

**Mystical Messenger** – Saint Expeditus

**Sabian Symbol:** Pisces 9 – The race begins: intent on outdistancing his rivals, a jockey spurs his horse to great speed.

**Writing Prompt:** A woman strikes when the iron's hot...but it's a *curling* iron.

**Affirmation:** I move swiftly.

## Naked Advice for the 8 of Wands

*Career:* I don't know about you, but I *love* getting flashes of inspiration and running with an idea. Tons of energy in the beginning, I accomplish more in the first few hours following a sudden brainstorm than I do in a week or more. And that can be a problem. After the caffeine wears off and the basic foundation lies waiting for further construction—I tend to flatline. I chalk this up to being an ENFP (specifically, the "P"—which makes for great starters...but not-so-good finishers). If you're the type to exit the gate gangbusters but lose steam halfway through the race, this is "that" card. A leopard can't lose its spots, so what to do? Two choices: Call on The Emperor to crack the whip or perhaps the 8 of Coins for butt-in-chair discipline. Either as a partner, coach or cheerleading friend—those who embody these energies can truly help you! The other choice is to use your startup speed to do just *that*: launch start-ups or help others get started on *their* dream project. Win/win either way! Just remember to see your speed as a gift, not as a liability.

**Romance:** If the Ace of Wands is a penis, then the 8 of Wands is ejaculation. It's time to reach out and touch someone—and your encounter will be fast and furious. This is a card of one-night stands and quickies—not luxurious *luuurve*-making. If your partner is inexperienced, expect premature climax (*oops*). Is it possible that this card could herald long-term romance and monogamous stability? Unlikely—although there is a slim possibility that a brief, chance encounter or speed dating could evolve into something greater...but only if coupled with The Lovers (commitment) or the 2 of Cups (deep, if not long-lasting, intimacy). 8 of Wands + 2 of Cups + Lovers? You're looking at a fast friendship turning into romance and resulting in marriage... likely within weeks or months. Hey, it can happen! When I met my husband, we became fast friends—and wed less than 6 weeks later (we've been happily married for 20 years).

**Parenting:** OK, 'rents, time to take the kiddos on a mind-altering trip! No, not 'shrooms or pink elephant quests—but rather a journey to expand perspectives. Pick a destination, extricate your kids from their comfort zones, expose them to culture and stand back to watch what happens. Historic locales, stunning architecture, transcendent art, magnificent music—transport them to a time and place where color, sound or form changed the world. Spontaneous travel to interesting destinations will enlarge a child's vision, as well as broaden her idea of what is possible for her own life. The trick is to move fast so excuses, protests or whining can't shut down spur-of-the-moment visits to Diverse City.

*Spirituality:* Bursts of intuitive information beg to be captured. If you don't, they wink out like fireflies refusing to share their glow. Inspired ideas and sparks of passion won't last long. In fact, if you keep refusing to acknowledge them—let alone bring them into the material world—they'll stop flying by you. Visionary flickers favor the receptive. They'll only knock so many times before moving on to someone else who will willingly catch their glimmer. If you're waiting for a sign, this is it. Now, set your ear to the wind, open your eyes and prepare to follow the Muse's transitory twinkle.

**Recommended Resources:** *Turbo* (Movie); "The Comet" (Sculpture) by Maurice Guiraud-Riviere; "Flight of Birds" (Lithograph for the "Daily Herald", 1919) by Edward McKnight Kauffer; *Vacation Boy Riding a Goose* by Normal Rockwell; *No Swimming* by Normal Rockwell

**8 of Wands Card Layout:** *Leaving on a Jet Plane* Spread

1. *Weather*: What mood surrounds me?
2. *Plane*: How's my overall condition?
3. *Left Wing*: What's a stabilizing influence?

4. *Right Wing*: What's another stabilizing influence?
5. *Fuel*: What's my power source?
6. *Thrust*: What will propel me to move quickly?
7. *Lift*: What will support me?
8. *Altitude*: How can I fly higher?
9: *Ground*: What am I leaving behind?
10. *Air*: What will I see better from a higher perspective?
11. *Traffic Control*: What's my best source of guidance?
12: *Parachute (Open Only in an Emergency)*: What indicates a "bail out"?

## 9 of Wands – Broken, But Not Defeated

**Stripped Down Overview:** How many gamers out there...raise your hand! You, too? *YAY!* Since the early 80s, I've been playing video games (*Pong* on a black and white TV in my parent's bedroom, no less). Atari, Sega Genesis, PlayStation...I've had to slow down the last decade, though, because of severe arm/hand pain from chronic tendonitis. But when I'm on the computer, in between projects (or, sometimes, procrastinating amid them), I'll play a few casual desktop games like *Plants vs. Zombies* or *Zuma's Revenge*. On both of those games, there is a Boss to defeat: gamers know full well what *those* are. But for the luddites among you, a Boss is a final opponent to overcome — either at each level, or at the very end of the game. In *PvZ*, it's a showdown on the roof: Dr. Zomboss, a mad scientist zombie controlling a huge *mechanical* zombie. With your weaponized plants, you gotta give it all you got to not only defeat him...but the bad boys he sends your way (like the Zombini that paves ice — or Gargantuar, who's tough to neutralize). The 9 of Wands is sorta like a Boss Level in life: you've had the shit kicked out of you a few times, learned to strategize pretty well, tired as hell — but you will *not* give up until that fucker is defeated! Yeah, you may be down to your last life — or your power bar is down to the quarter level — but you dig in your heels, marshal your strength, breathe deeply…and give it all you got.

**Keywords:** Fortitude; Endurance; Perseverance; Last Stretch; Stamina; Final Push; Survival; Grueling Circumstances; Marathon; Going the Distance; Fighting for Life; Harsh Environment; Wounding; Battle Weary; Self-Neglect; Setback; Refusing to Give Up; Waiting for Allies; Stay Watchful; Anticipating Reserves; Hindrance; Barriers; Interference; Sticking It Out

**Personifications and Embodiments:** School of Hard Knocks; Fortresses; Barbed Wire Fences; Jack Youngblood; "Iron Horse" Lou Gehrig; Great Wall of China; Castles Surrounded by Moats; Rocky Balboa; Red Alert; Lock the Door; "It's a Nail Biter!"; Feeling Your Age; When It Rains, It Pours; Final Moments of a Close Football Game; Wounded Soldiers That Go Back Into the Fray; Murphy's Law

**Quote:** *Victory or defeat are largely out of my control, but putting up a good fight… putting up the kind of fight that makes the earth shake and the gods blush… this I can do.* – Daniele Bolelli

**Challenge:** Demoralization

**Gift:** Resilience

**Occupations/Vocations:** Physical Therapist; Triage Nurse; Retired Veteran; Medical Supply Worker; Palace Guard

**Disney Totem:** Woody (*Toy Story 2*)

**Animal Symbol:** Polar Bear

**Flower Essences:** Macrocarpa (Australian Bush); Oak (Bach);

Elm (Bach)

**Crystal/Stone:** Brecciated Jasper – Helps to stand up again and again after defeats. Makes one ready for conflict. Promotes resolution and makes up for harm. Rejuvenates and revitalizes.

**Aromatherapy:** Elemi

**Body Parts/Systems and Health Issues:** Concussion; Head Trauma

**Mystical Messenger** – Airmid

**Sabian Symbol:** Scorpio 5 – A massive, unchanging rocky shore resists the pounding of the sea.

**Writing Prompt:** A guard decides not to protect his charge.

**Affirmation:** I endure.

## Naked Advice for the 9 of Wands

*Career:* Time to take the Civil Service Test to get a government job (because your plonkin' factory moved to Mexico and you need a better paying line of work). Or pass your finals to graduate college. Or get your CDL license. Or pass the boards or the bar. Or finish your dissertation to finally get that Ph.D. Or audition in the final callback. Or complete the last phase of an important job interview. Or apply for a coveted, competitive scholarship or fellowship. In other words, *this is it*. You've worked hard towards something that will better your chances for advancement, growth, exposure, bigger wages, better benefits — or all of the above. Now's *not* the time to coast or to assume you have it in the bag: if anything, double your efforts to make the best impression possible and sail through tests with high marks.

*Romance:* Have you been flogged by a debilitating disease, chronic illness or devastating accident—while your partner remained steadfast and supportive? Or maybe you've put in long hours, for years, putting your spouse through college? Perhaps it's your *marriage* that's taken a beating via vocational struggles or outside interference? Even in the best of circumstances— including a happy marriage—certain challenges can eat away at strong foundations, much like termite to wood or acid to metal. *"Us against the world"* may have kept you strong for this long, but now you're tired. So. Very. *Tired.* Feeling like a veteran of the psychic wars, a part of you just wants to lie down and sleep for a few days. Or weeks. But *another* part of you—the scrappy fighter—says, "Oh yeah? I'll show you. *We'll* show you!" Unfortunately, you're not at the end of your battle just yet. But if you keep those steel balls to the wall, chances are quite good you'll overcome what's looming before you *and* your sweetheart.

*Parenting*: *"Weebles wobble but they won't fall down!"* If you were born before 1975, you probably remember this commercial jingle. The toys were cute, egg-shaped people and creatures that wobbled when pushed, always returning to their upright position. If you happen to have some in your attic, go get them! They'll serve as a wonderful object lesson for the kids: when life (or some poke-silly idiot) keeps jabbing at you, bounce right back to where you were. Ah, if only it were that easy to ensure Preston or Priscilla becomes hardy and irrepressible in the face of adversity! Do your best to encourage them to *keep on keepin' on*. Provide them with kid-friendly biographies about ordinary folks who overcame great odds, then went on to make something of themselves because they never gave up. Remind them of the freedoms and privileges they have because someone (or many) took a stand and fought for them. Examples of resilience are literally everywhere: sports figures, military heroes, those who clawed their way out of poverty to achieve enormous success and champions of social justice. Or what about those with "disabilities", like brilliant astrophysicist Stephen Hawking, inspirational speaker Helen Keller or President Franklin D. Roosevelt, who have impacted humanity with their *extraordinary* abilities?

*Spirituality:* I'm sure you heard the phrase, *"What doesn't kill me makes me stronger"*. And for many spiritual warriors, this is true. But why? *How?* I think the answer may be found in one of my favorite scriptures:

> *But we have this treasure in earthen vessels, that the excellent of the power may be of God, and not of us. We are hard-pressed on every side, yet not crushed: we are perplexed, but not in despair; persecuted, but nor forsaken; struck down, but not destroyed... Therefore, we do not lose heart. Even though our outward man is perishing, yet the inward man is being renewed day by day. For our light affliction, which is but for a moment, is far more exceeding and eternal weight of glory; while we do not look at the things which are seen, but at the things which are not seen. For the things which are seen are temporary, but the things which are not seen are eternal".* (2 Corinthians 4:7-9; 16-18)

Those of us who consciously choose a spiritual path—a *mindful* path—cling to something that isn't seen with physical eyes. It may be a sacred text. A steadfast belief in humanism. A meditation practice. A religious system. A deity or pantheon. The Universe. Guides. Ancestors. Nature spirits. Gaia. The 9 of Wands encourages you to stand fast in whatever brings you strength, calm and peace of mind—your shelter in the storm, your oasis in the sweltering desert or your mighty fortress that protects a world-weary heart.

**Recommended Resources:** *The Way Back* (Movie); "Stronger" by Kelly Clarkson; "Rise" by Katy Perry; "Fight Song" by Rachel Platten; "Titanium" David Guetta

**9 of Wands Card Layout:** *The University of Adversity* Spread

1. When adversity hits, what is my go-to response?
2. What is beneficial about this response?
3. What is detrimental about this response?
4. How do I best deal with adversity right now?
5. What lessons have I learned from adversity?
6. What psychic wound might I be experiencing?
7. How do I dress/address this wound?
8. How can I heal this wound—once and for all?
9. What will fortify me against future adversity?
10. Final advice

# 10 of Wands – So Many Burdens, So Little Time

**Stripped Down Overview:** While the battered-and-bruised 9 of Wands may have some fight left—and the strength to clinch or maintain some type of triumph—the 10 of Wands is pretty much down for the count. It's the wife and mother with a jam-packed calendar...who says "yes" to everything asked of her. It's the guy who works overtime—*all* the time—even though he makes a comfortable living. It's the kid who not only does her homework—but also her best friend's and the next-door neighbor's (essay questions and book reports, no less!). It's the creative entrepreneur so passionate and confident—he commits to not one, but *three* art showings in a month. It's the writer who submits several book proposals at a time—then scrambles to get them done when they're all accepted. All the 10s are "over" something: with the 10 of Swords, it's overkill. With the 10 of Cups, it's overjoyed. With the 10 of Coins, it's overabundance. With the 10 of Wands—well, it's over*extension*, over-*commitment*, over*expansion*...and over*whelm*. It's keeping your head above water—as your legs begin to cramp. It's climbing a mountain of paperwork—while another truckload gets dumped on you. It's being able to get up in the morning—but not without the help of caffeine at best or mystery pills at worst. It's running at the park before dawn and running errands and running a household and running the kids to practice and *runningtheelderlyladynextdoortoherdoctorappointment*...*OMFG*, you realize. *I can't say "no". To anything!* Hopefully this realization comes to you during "just" mental exhaustion or extreme physical weariness—rather than, say, a nervous breakdown or heart attack.

**Keywords:** Burden; Needing Relief; Stressed; Excess Weight; Maxed Out; Pending Collapse; Heaviness; Overloaded; Burnout; Stockpiling; Inconvenience; Boiling Point; Mounting Pressure; Dangerous Workaholism; Taking On Too Much; Can't Handle Anymore; Breaking Under Pressure; Cracking Under Strain; Overextension; Biting Off More Than You Can Chew

**Personifications and Embodiments:** Overwhelmed Bellboy; Pack Animal; Overstuffed Suitcase; Overflowing Shopping Cart; Hands Full

**Quote:** *People become attached to their burdens sometimes more than the burdens are attached to them.* – George Bernard Shaw

**Challenge:** Exhaustion

**Gift:** Munificence

**Occupations/Vocations:** Heavy Laborer; Lumberjack; Truck Loader; Furniture Deliverer; Piano Mover; Roofer

**Disney Totem:** Mack (*Cars*)

**Animal Symbol:** Camel

**Flower Essences:** Centaury (Bach); Macrocarpa (Australian Bush); Sweet Chestnut (Bach); Olive (Bach)

**Crystal/Stone:** Cappuccino Jasper – Helps with tackling a huge pile of work by sensibly apportioning one's energy. Bestows stability and inner calm. Fortifies the stomach and intestine. Aids in elimination.

**Aromatherapy:** Tangerine

**Body Parts/Systems and Health Issues:** Sciatica; Torn/Pulled Back Muscles

**Mystical Messenger** – Ganesh

**Sabian Symbol:** Taurus 13 – A porter carrying a mountain of heavy baggage.

**Writing Prompt:** What happens when Atlas drops the world?

**Affirmation:** I know, and respect, my limitations.

## Naked Advice for the 10 of Wands

*Career: Whoa!* Too fast, too much, too soon! Your enthusiastic go-getter approach is admirable, but if you're a solopreneur or start-up, you're accumulating too much debt, overhead and/or inventory. Scale back and reassess before it all blows up in your face. And what about *you*, cubicled job hog? Are you scarfing up assignments, clients or overtime—at the expense of your colleagues? Good *grief*. Your obsessive pursuit of achievement, status and recognition is about to boil over and burn your crotch. Don't be the overripe pimple on the company's ass, because it's only a matter of time before someone pops you.

*Romance:* Sometimes, marriage requires sacrifice. Perhaps our spouse is getting older—and health issues start coming fast and furious. Shuttling to doctor's appointments. Filling prescriptions—and making sure they're taken properly. Massaging muscles. Changing dressings. Making meals. Providing a listening ear when the pain inches towards unbearable. Giving gentle hugs and words of comfort. Just *being* there. It's your privilege—and joy—to take care of the one who took such great care of *you* when you most needed it. It is easy? Not usually. But there's something poignant and fulfilling about getting outside ourselves, taking on the "burden" of caretaker, and ministering to the needs of our beloved. *You've got this.* And help *is* available if only you'll ask for it—or agree to the already-offered assistance.

*Parenting*: Have you seen the amount of homework kids have these days? Jesus on a *bike*. While some of us may wax nostalgic about the "carefree" days of youth, our progeny is anything *but*: five or more hours of assignments a *night*, not to mention the extra time spent with extracurricular activities, is the rule rather than the exception. Kids wilt under these type of demands. It's nearly *impossible* to retain what's taught in class or covered in homework when lacking solid sleep. In fact, the medical profession recommends *at least* ten hours of sleep for youth under 18. And if they don't get it? They "borrow" from the next night (which is probably just as paltry as the night before). Their growing brains need this much rest to function properly. You can see why so many kids amble around like zombies! (Apart from the whole *heads-down-texting* abomination, that is.) Do what you can to lighten the load (even if it requires talking to teachers—or taking the issue to the school board).

*Spirituality:* What *is* it with some people? They take advantage of your generous spirit and big heart, dumping their drama on you like a demon-possessed garbage truck. *"Oh, I just called to see how you were"*, they begin...but within 60 seconds, they're bitching about Frank, or whining about their sore toe, or complaining about the weather, or bellyaching that the manicurist raised her prices—*geez Louise!* Yeah, the New Testament may say, *"Bear one another's burdens, and so fulfill the law of Christ"* (Galatians 6:2)—but this passage ain't talking about putting up with shit like idle words, petty annoyances, venomous gossip or first-world complaints. You're a Light Worker...not a diaper! Let this be your mantra, honey: *Not my circus...not my monkeys.*

**Recommended Resources:** *Vendedora de Flores* by Diego Rivera; *Jamal Al Mahamel II* by Suleiman Mansour; *Lorenzo's Oil* (Movie); *Led Zeppelin IV* Cover Art

**10 of Wands Card Layout:** *Ten Heavy Sticks* Spread

1. How am I burdened physically?
2. How am I burdened financially?
2. How am I burdened mentally?
3. How am I burdened emotionally?
4. How am I burdened spiritually?
5. How does the world burden me?
6. How does the media burden me?
7. How does my vocation/calling/job burden me?
8. How does my ego and ambition burden me?
9. How does my "wants" burden me?
10. How does my lack burden me?
11: What will lighten the load? *All of it.*

# SWORDS

## Ace of Swords – To the Point

**Stripped Down Overview:** While the maxim "might makes right" is doubtful, it's true that the pen can be mightier than the sword—especially when words are clear, sharp and brief. Communication has always been a two-edged sword, because it takes two to tangle: Speakers have listeners. Writers have readers. In between that space stretches a possible canyon of assumption, preconception, bias, misunderstanding and confusion—which then leads to aroused feelings and more words. The Ace of Swords cuts through all this bullshit, stating the obvious, brandishing the "truth", piercing groupthink and delivering the "facts". It reduces doubletalk to singular lucidity, and pares propaganda down to size. This card also proves that you don't need The Tower to experience reality for what it is— but you *do* have to be brave and proactive to embrace (or use) the blade.

**Keywords:** Sharp Clarity; Piercing Insight; Lofty Idea; Single Minded; Razor Wit; Bursting Bubbles; Distinct Speech

**Personifications and Embodiments:** Sword; Knife; Razor; Scalpel; Lance

**Quote:** *Be who you are and say what you feel, because those who mind don't matter and those who matter don't mind.* – Theodor Geisel (Dr. Seuss)

**Challenge:** Precision

**Gift:** Clarity

**Occupations/Vocations:** Soldier; General; Fencer; Knife Maker; Sword Swallower; Bloodletter; Barber

**Disney Totem:** Wart/Young King Arthur (*The Sword and the Stone*)

**Animal Symbol:** Swordfish

**Flower Essence:** Bauhinia (Australian Bush)

**Crystal/Stone:** Apophyllite (Clear) – Stone of truth that encourages introspection and clear sight. Helps overcome psychological blocks. Calms a hyperactive mind. Promotes "one thought at a time". Cuts through confusion and BS. Supports frank communication.

**Aromatherapy:** White Birch (*Betula Alba*)

**Body Parts/Systems and Health Issues:** Surgery

**Mystical Messenger** – Joan of Arc

**Sabian Symbol:** Pisces 13 – A sword, used in many battles, is now in a museum.

**Writing Prompt:** A warrior wields not a sword, but a feather.

**Affirmation:** I communicate simply and concisely.

## Naked Advice for the Ace of Swords

*Career:* A new idea slices through your consciousness. Aces are mere portals, though, opening and closing at a rapid rate. If you don't grab the handle, speak your mind, submit your initiative or send that communiqué, an opportunity will be lost. If your workplace is in disarray—with co-workers or employees acting like bewildered zombies trying to solve a Rubik's cube—it's time to implement simple, succinct guidelines or strategies so they know what end is up. Don't be afraid to communicate directly and boldly, for Fate favors the ballsy.

**Romance:** It's time to stop stringing her along: say what you mean, mean what you say, and let the other person decide to stay or go. No more hedging bets, no more hem hawing, no more playing with feelings. See, it's *this* kind of mixed signals mindfuck that creates repeat clients for psychics and Tarot readers: not knowing what the other person *really* thinks—which engenders uncertainty, nervousness and panic. In an ideal world, individuals would act and speak transparently—*every* time—but thanks to shaky self-esteem, fear of rejection and perceived societal taboos, we get repeated rounds of "Relationship Games People Play". (And trust me: your best friend, your mother and your Tarot reader are *really* tired of this perpetually muddled drama...)

**Parenting:** Rare is the parent that appreciates when a child points out unreasonableness, inconsistency or the logic flaws embedded within the dreaded *"because I said so"*. (I have echoes of smacked cheeks—both ends—as proof.) It may be especially infuriating if you're the type that keeps your trap shut in the face of pretense, contradiction or unfairness. This is why kids, like the character in "The Emperor's New Clothes", piss people off (or embarrass the hell out of them): they point out to sheeple, shyster tailors and King alike: *"There are no fancy clothes. The Emperor is naked!"* Oh, life would be *so* much easier to allow the Emperor to traipse around buck nekkid, the crowd nodding and grinning as His Majesty's fashion designers try to sell everyone a bag of textile goods... But kids have a special Spidey sense—a BS detector that, unfortunately, is often beat, shamed or conditioned out of them by the time they hit 21. Consider yourself lucky if you have a perceptive child in your orbit that will give you the gift of honesty...because you're unlikely to get this kind of medicine from other adults.

*Spirituality:* Before you get offended by a teacher, book, radio guest, sound bite or accidental mystic (or, immediately thereafter), don't lash out, vent or write a post about it (tempting as it may be). Instead, stay quiet and allow truth to pierce down to the bone. Any time we have a vigorous reaction to words on paper or broadcasted through the air, they're touching something in us—usually an unhealed wound, a judgment or a shadow projection. This kind of pain is good, because it has the potential to cut away soul cancers like hatred, envy, greed and ingratitude. Stay with the discomfort just like you stay with cutting an onion until it's all chopped up and ready for use: tears may flow, many layers to go, but once you're done, so is the woe.

**Recommended Resources:** *The Art of Thinking Clearly* by Rolf Dobelli; "The Emperor's New Clothes" (Fairytale); *The Invention of Lying* (Movie)

**Ace of Swords Card Layout:** *Sharp Tongue* Spread

1. How do I muddle attempts at communication?
2. Why is this?
3. How can I be more clear?
4. What area of my life could use some sharp, pointed words?
5. How can I be more open to this type of relating?
6. Who do I need to be more direct with?

## 2 of Swords – Fence Sitting

**Stripped Down Overview:** Denial's not a river in Egypt, but rather the refusal to see things as they are. When clarity's Ace of Swords appears and cuts deep, a choice must be made: expose the wound to truth's medicine—or hurry to cover it with the dirty rags of defiance. This is the choice point of the 2 of Swords: burying your head in the sand, or holding it up high so you can face the music (not matter how difficult or dissonant it may be). Unlike The Lovers card where choices are clear—and with far-reaching ramifications—the 2 of Swords is the "little things": those ignored incidents, explained-away lipstick smears, rationalized excuses and dismissed hunches. A battle between intuition vs. emotion, logic vs. security, certainty vs. shame, facts vs. fear of fallout—it's really a *damned if you do, damned if you don't* type of situation. On the other side of the blindfold, one question remains: can you live with yourself after discarding veracity, and by continuing to tolerate lies, discomfort and embarrassment? (*Tip:* There will be no forward movement until confrontation or coming clean.)

**Keywords:** Avoidance; Willful Blindness; Vacillation; Indecisive; Refusing to Choose; Going Back and Forth; Two-Faced; Cognitive Dissonance; Paradox; Speaking with "Forked Tongue"; Agreeing to Disagree; Tension Between Facts and Feelings; Repudiating Proof; Blurred Distinctions; Contradiction; Double Minded; Procrastination; Dispassionate Debate; Mistaken Identity; Two Sides

**Personifications and Embodiments:** BTK's Wife; Blindfolds

**Quote:** *If you choose not to decide you still have made a choice.* – Neil Peart

**Challenge:** Acknowledgement

**Gift:** Pressure

**Occupations/Vocations:** Hair Dresser; Hibachi Chef; Draftsman; Ninja; Teacher for the Blind

**Disney Totem:** Susan Evers and Sharon McKendrick (*The Parent Trap*)

**Animal Symbol:** Zebra

**Flower Essences:** Cerato (Bach); Paw Paw (Australian Bush)

**Crystal/Stone:** Clear Quartz – Encourages seeing things for what they really are.
Supports neutrality. Strengthens personal point of view. Improves memory. Increases perception and awareness.

**Aromatherapy:** Benzoin

**Body Parts/Systems and Health Issues:** Eye Disorders; Blindness; Tension Headaches

**Mystical Messenger** – Saint Thomas

**Sabian Symbol:** Sagittarius 3 – Two men playing chess.

**Writing Prompt:** Holding two swords, but using a blindfold as a weapon.

**Affirmation:** I see clearly and choose wisely.

## Naked Advice for the 2 of Swords

*Career:* It's a crying shame, but almost *no one* likes a whistleblower. Never mind that they expose corporate malfeasance or political corruption—most people consider such types "tattletales" or "snitches". Sure, some, like Erin Brockovich, gain heroine status. Others, like Julian Assange, must live in exile. Yeah, you have a right to be nervous reading this, because you're going to come across some piece of information, some tawdry evidence, some fudged figures, some *not quite right* evidence that points to "Oh *shit*" dealings. NOT an easy place to be. I do not envy you, my friend. But when the time comes and the facts slide across your desk or scroll in front of your eyes, you'll need to weigh the greater good with personal security. Is it *your* responsibility to expose? What will you gain? What might you lose? You may not be able to tell if it's truly "worth it" until after the fact, so the best you can do is research history and the fate of informants to determine if you want to be a character in *that* kind of drama.

*Romance:* Analyzing a relationship to death is a sure way to kill it: *"What did he mean by that?" "Does he really love me?" "What is he thinking about?" "Does he think I'm desirable?"* —if you really want to know the answers to such questions, *don't* ask your best girlfriend, your mom or (*for God's sake!*) a Tarot reader…ask your significant other. If you're not willing to communicate, then don't ruminate. Overthinking complicates and confuses *everything*, but with relationships, the scrutiny also entangles and strangles. If you have enough common ground to not only stand together comfortably but also build a fulfilling life, then focus on those shared values. If you suspect something is *seriously* wrong—and your gut is throwing red flags faster than a masturbating teen with only a minute to live—then do something about it. *Now.* Between the rigid stance of being "right"—and peace at any price—there is wisdom.

*Parenting*: In this age of helicoptering and snowplowing, every decision a parent faces feels like a life-and-death one. Apart from medical situations like selecting a competent doctor, deciding on grave treatments or the conundrum "to vaxx or not to vaxx", 99 percent of parental choices will not make-or-break our kids. They just *won't*. You need to relax, take a deep breath and realize that it's the "on average" of a child's experience that contributes most to his overall well-being. Do you give him positive regard? Provide a stable home? Engage in respectful dialogue with your partner (or ex)? Have food on the table? Use your words to encourage and soothe? If you checked "all of the above", pat yourself on the back and keep up the good work! Don't sweat the small stuff or major in the minors, because such needless tension only *creates* problems...not solves them.

*Spirituality:* Beyond conscious thinking is the moon—the realm of dreams, imagination and the deep subconscious. Logic serves a purpose...and keeps us from flaking out. But when it comes to our spiritual path, faith is the bigger slice of the pie. We underestimate ourselves and the infinite wisdom inside. When the blind lead the blind, they may fall into a ditch—but only in the concrete world of facts and reason. In otherworldly realms, allowing fantasy to sweep us up can lead to real-world breakthroughs and personal growth—not to mention sacred illumination. Trade the trench for a cradle of kaleidoscopic whimsy (because the difference is really all in your mind).

**Recommended Resources:** *Undecided* by Normal Rockwell; *Tarot in Reverse* by Janet Boyer (Chapter on the 2 of Swords, Reversed).

**2 of Swords Card Layout:** *Road Not Taken* Spread

1. *Left Path*: What do I need to know about this choice?
2. *Left Path*: How will this road affect me emotionally?

3. *Left Path*: How will this road affect me materially?

4. *Left Path*: How will this road affect my family/close relationships?

5. *Left Path:* How will this road affect my career/vocation?

6. *Left Path:* How will this road affect my overall well-being?

7. *Right Path*: What do I need to know about this choice?

8. *Right Path:* How will this road affect me emotionally?

9. *Right Path:* How will this road affect me materially?

10. *Right Path:* How will this road affect my family/close relationships?

11. *Right Path:* How will this road affect my career/vocation?

12. *Right Path:* How will this road affect my overall well-being?

13. What happens if I don't take the Left Path?

14. What happens if I don't take the Right Path?

## 3 of Swords – Shot Through the Heart

**Stripped Down Overview:** Unfriended. Unfollowed. Uncircled. Unfanned. Blocked. It sucks from strangers, but doubly so from someone you *thought* was a true blue friend. Sure, we say it doesn't matter, but truth be told, it can hurt like hell—especially when you find out the reasons were petty, immature or based on falsehoods. Being a lone wolf by choice is one thing; forced into aloneness, marginalized in a corner, is quite another. This insidious energy of division, rejection, betrayal and exclusion poisons trust, breeds paranoia and puts the heart on lockdown. One consequence of our modern microwave society is that people are used and then tossed aside with the speed and frequency of convenience store condoms. Much better to have a few rock-solid peeps in your coterie than scads of hangers-on that can turn into a Brutus faster than you can say *et tu*? True devotion, commitment and care are rare; don't take it for granted if you have it. No one likes to see the 3 of Swords turn up in a reading because, no matter how you slice it, anguish is involved. Because it's a 3, though, you may very well birth liberating healing amidst a veil of tears. If you're a member of a close-knit group or family—a Three Musketeers clan, as it were—you'll have shoulders to cry on, hands to hold and spirits to pray for you in your time of need. No, it won't make up for the perfidy or loss, but your current bond will become stronger for it. If no one's in your physical corner, try to take solace that millions are suffering much like you are—and that consciousness, not time, will heal all wounds...including yours.

**Keywords:** Rejection; Exclusion; Outcast; Heartbreak; Lamentation; Rupture; Grief; Banishment; Severance; Blackball; Blacklist; Scapegoat; Mourning; Dejection; Suffering; Weeping; Woundedness; Alienation; Depression

**Personifications and Embodiments:** Pariahs; Golgotha; *Via Dolorosa*; McCarthyism; The Red Scare; Lepers; Lone Wolf; Love Triangle; Divorce; House Committee on Un-American Activities (HUAC)

**Quote:** *Most things break, including hearts. The lessons of life amount not to wisdom, but to scar tissue and callus* – Wallace Stegner

**Challenge:** Pain

**Gift:** Catharsis

**Occupations/Vocations:** Cardiac Specialist; Heart Surgeon; Butcher; Grief Counselor

**Disney Totem:** Widow Tweed (*The Fox and the Hound*)

**Animal Symbol:** Swallow

**Flower Essences:** Willow (Bach); Illawarra Flame Tree (Australian Bush); Sturt Desert Rose (Australian Bush)

**Crystal/Stone:** Rhodonite – Alleviates emotional injuries. Strengthens the heart. Promotes forgiveness. Encourages mutual trust. Excellent for wound healing.

**Aromatherapy:** Birch (*Betula Lenta*)

**Body Parts/Systems and Health Issues:** Arteriosclerosis; Heart Attack or Failure

**Mystical Messenger** – Saint Dwyn

**Sabian Symbol:** Taurus 5 – A youthful widow, fresh and soul-cleansed from grief, kneels at an open grave to receive the secret of eternal life.

**Writing Prompt:** A woman walks around with three swords sticking out of her chest—but they can't be removed…and if you touch them, something happens.

**Affirmation:** This, too, will pass—but I must actively look towards healing the pain.

## Naked Advice for the 3 of Swords

*Career:* You've worked decades for a non-union company—and they decide that you're making too much money (and can be replaced by three temp slackers for the same wage)—so you must be "let go". Or, you sink most of your life savings into a friend's new restaurant—only to realize that while he can cook, he sucks at management and human resources…and goes bankrupt within two years. What about having a shiny college degree—you were Valedictorian, for God's sake!—but you can't find a job in your field within your hometown...so you must consider aiming for employment you're overqualified for, or one that moves you away from family, friends and familiar surroundings. And don't get me started about a workplace romance gone sour... Seriously, keep your eyes on your own paper, and not on any tail. When this card comes up for a career reading, your parachute is decidedly black—with a few rips in the fabric—so don't get your hopes up for the perfect job, a promotion or a pay raise. In fact, if you're still employed within a month, thank your lucky stars that you dodged a career bullet!

*Romance:* OK, this doesn't bode well. Whether dealing with a love triangle, liar or cheater, your heart will be pierced with arrows of treachery. It may be after you find your best friend in bed with your husband. Or, after twenty years of marriage and four kids, wifey declares she's gay, runs off with your secretary, and leaves you holding the marital bag as you crumple, gobsmacked, by her sudden revelation and exit. Sometimes, the 3 of Swords points to the overwhelming news that a loved one has been diagnosed with a god-awful disease—that may be incurable. The Tower card deals with the moment the blow strikes, the secret divulged or the betrayal discovered. The aftermath, though— that's the bleeding, hurting 3 of Swords. Elizabeth Kubler Ross formulated the 5 Stages of Grief: Denial, Anger, Bargaining (with God), Depression and Acceptance (DABDA). Sometimes, the grief-stricken may toggle through all five within any 24-hour period. Although the 5 Stages of Grief is usually connected with dying and death, we may grieve loss of companionship and the end of a relationship, too. Try to be gentle with yourself, allowing for the time and space to heal. Lean on those who care about you. Attend support groups. And please realize that self-recriminations such as *"I should have seen it coming"*, *"How can I be so stupid?"* or *"If only the doctor was seen earlier..."* is like trying to lock the barn door after the horses get out. Adding to your suffering through self-blame and second-guessing is cruel. Ask, instead, "How can I make the *best* of this situation?—as well as *"How can I be kind to myself today?"*

***Parenting***: When Sarita is rejected by her first crush—or Simon is repeatedly picked last for team sports during recess—it's tempting to use your 20/20 parental vision and wave off such "small potatoes" pain. Yeah, you've got bigger fish to fry—working as a single mom, dealing with a spiteful ex, lacking sleep because of the neighbor's barking dogs (and that damn do-nothing, worthless-piece-of-shit zoning officer)—what's some squashed hopes for puppy love or not being selected for kickball, right? *Whoa there, Nelly:* if you're dismissive of your child's destroyed heart or treat kiddo's repeated rejection as "just part of growing up", not only are you being an asswipe of a parent, but you're teaching your child to swallow grief, stuff down emotions and ignore pain. OK, that may have worked during 1970s High School football, but such lessons that lead to low EQ, low empathy and low self-esteem are a really bad idea in this world of mindless aggression and knee-jerk violence. Help save your kid years of feeling rejected and invisible—not to mention future therapy—by taking a few minutes to listen, to understand and to sympathize.

***Spirituality:*** *"Blessed are those who mourn, for they shall be comforted."* Spoken by Jesus from the Sermon on the Mount, this line from The Beatitudes (Latin: *beautitudo*, meaning blessedness) seems a bit presumptive: you mean, if I mourn, I'll get automatically comforted? Well…yes and no. It depends on your ego and your willingness to hang onto pain for some type of pay-off. In this particular verse, the Greek word for blessed is *makarios*, from the root *mak*, *"indicating large or of long duration. The word is an adjective suggesting happy, supremely blessed, a condition in which* *congratulations are in order"* (notation from the NKJV *Spirit-Filled Life Bible*). There's something liberating—even refreshing—about allowing yourself to be cracked open by sorrow (*see The Devil*). Not self-pity—that's the 5 of Cups—but truly experiencing grief and rejection from your toes to your scalp. It breaks you (*see The Tower*), but also allows something beautiful to come forth. Such a process requires a sense of surrender—of entitled ego, of trying to protect yourself from the hurt, of attempting to avoid the stark, dark truth of what happened. The mystery of this experience and the strength and resilience—yes, even deep joy—it affords can't be properly addressed here. From someone who's been broken many times and put together again (*we can rebuild her, we have the technology—better, stronger, faster…*), trust me: you *can* rise from the ashes, eventually finding love, beauty and meaning. Hang in there, for your "redemption" draws nigh!

**Recommended Resources:** *Weeping Woman* by Pablo Picasso; *Authentic Happiness: Using the New Positive Psychology to Realize Your Potential for Lasting Fulfillment* by Martin Seligman, Ph.D.; *The Woman's Book of Confidence: Meditations for Strength and Inspiration* by Sue Patton Thoele; *The Five Ways We Grieve* by Susan A. Berger

**3 of Swords Card Layout:** *Sucky Swords in the Heart* Spread

1. *Sword 1* – Why does this hurt so damn much?
2. *Sword 2* – What would I do to this person if I could get away with it?
3. *Sword 3* – How do I deal with the pain without killing someone (including myself)?
4. *Heart* – What does my heart need most right now?

# 4 of Swords – Time Out!

**Stripped Down Overview:** In a world that values busyness, speed and measurable productivity, stopping and stillness seems anathema. While this may be fine for the Energizer bunny, appliances and anything with a plug, the human body needs periods of rest for optimal functioning and performance. In fact, your physical vehicle heals and repairs itself during sleep—with even the most knotty problem appearing manageable after a good nap. However, even during physical rest, your mind may remain a whirlwind of activity. This is where meditation and tracking your thoughts come in. The mental hamster wheel can prove just as strenuous and exhausting as physical activity. Round and round on well-worn ruts, our unsupervised, habitual thoughts undermine our attempts at reaching clarity, peace of mind and overall well-being. The only way out is through, which means taking an inventory of your daily thoughts, attitudes and assumptions (journal them), determining the gap between your expectations and reality (journal them) and formulating an organized plan for simple, clean, peaceful approaches to recurring situations (journal them, too). Oh, did I mention journaling? A pen and paper can be your best friend for organizing thoughts and cleaning your mental windshield of splattered intellectual bug guts.

**Keywords:** Rest; Retreat; Sabbatical; Recuperation; Healing; Placid; Meditation; Repose; Quietude; Calm; Contemplation; Stillness; Ordering Mental Habits; On the Mend; Convalescence; Putting Things Into Perspective; Relief from Strife; Organizing Thought

**Personifications and Embodiments:** Pause Button; Retirement; Yoga; Hospital Bed

**Quote:** *Where the heart lies, let the brain lie also.* – Robert Browning

**Challenge:** Stillness

**Gift:** Respite

**Occupations/Vocations:** Casket Manufacturer; Mausoleum Owner; Armor Maker; Rest Home Staff; Biofeedback Technician

**Disney Totem:** Princess Aurora (*Sleeping Beauty*)

**Animal Symbol:** Sloth

**Flower Essences:** Wild Rose (Bach); Boronia (Australian Bush)

**Crystal/Stone:** Smoky Quartz – Aids in relaxation and stress reduction brought on by mental busyness. Alleviates headaches and tension in the neck, shoulder and back muscles. Strengthens nerves. Enhances rational, realistic thought processes.

**Aromatherapy:** Angelica Seed

**Body Parts/Systems and Health Issues:** Fainting; Coma; Catalepsy

**Mystical Messenger** – Saint Odile

**Sabian Symbol:** Pisces 13 – A sword, used in many battles, is now in a museum.

**Writing Prompt:** Someone is in the knight's tomb—but it's not the dead soldier.

**Affirmation:** I withdraw from distractions to clear my mind and calm my body.

## Naked Advice for the 4 of Swords

*Career:* Ever watch a TV show or movie featuring an executive barking to his secretary *"Cancel all my appointments today!"* or *"Hold all calls!"*? That's the energy of this card: a deliberate withdrawal from the world—not to gain insights, wisdom or self-knowledge (as with The Hermit)—but in order to stop the barrage of interruptions, irritating thoughts and demands for immediate decisions. It's the "pause" button on the DVD or MP3 player...but applied to your life, instead. No, you may not be able to literally stop your life for a few minutes (or days)— wouldn't *that* be nice!—but you *can* make a concerted effort to put everything on hold for a while. Ninety-nine percent of your emails are not emergencies—and could be answered tomorrow or even next week. Ninety-nine percent of your clients don't expect you to get back to them within sixty seconds of receiving their voicemail. And for God's sake, ninety-nine percent of Facebook posts or PMs from friends are mere gossip or mundane BS—not requiring an immediate thumb's up or reply, either. So consider the 4 of Swords your "Breather" card. It gives you permission to take a power nap, put on earbuds to listen to a five-minute meditation or do a few yoga poses before appointments. When you get home from the office or finish your work, continue creating the atmosphere of a mini-retreat.

*Romance:* Every once in a while, it's healthy to conduct a "State of the Union" address where you and your partner sit down and square away any grievances, issues or concerns. It may not seem romantic, but the Swords suit is anything *but* lovey dovey. Yet, dealing with challenges, airing complaints and asking for help contributes just as much to a balanced relationship as kisses and hugs. Notice the "asking for help" part. This is particularly difficult for both sexes because men assume they can handle everything and (most) women don't want to be a burden. If you draw this card, it's possible that your mate requires some good, old-fashioned comfort: a pot of homemade chicken soup, a hot cup of tea, a shoulder massage or an uninterrupted nap. It's also possible that he may need an appointment with an allergist, eye doctor (new glasses, anyone?) or chiropractor. Don't be afraid to gently suggest a visit to a health care professional—including the offer to drive to the appointment—then provide some loving post-care ministrations.

*Parenting*: In some ways, this card reflects the energy of summer vacation (well, for the kids, anyway): a cessation from structured learning, school routines, homework and tests. When the 4 of Swords comes up, your child desperately needs a rest from academic pressures. Mental decompression and relaxation is in order. Permit your child to sleep a lot, read tons or binge watch cartoons or family-friendly movies. If your child's a high achiever (especially firstborns and onlys) steer her away from college prep courses during the summer: she needs to integrate what she's *already* learned. If your kid is involved with sports and recently experienced an injury, consider "benching" him (even if his coach *won't*). Be particularly cautious and proactive about protecting the head area—or getting second opinions on concussions, back sprains, neck pain or head trauma.

*Spirituality:* Sit your ass down and give it a rest. No, really. It's time to recuperate and recover. Your body needs to mend and heal itself, even if only on a cellular or vibrational level. You may be tempted to argue *"But..."*, but as I said, the only "butt" you need to concern yourself with is the one smashed against a recliner or the bed's headboard. Don't fight it. Settle into your body (and fluffy cushions), gather your energy, shut off all electronic devices and surrender to the moment. Drop your guard, let go and take the Nestea plunge into peaceful "not doing". If your monkey mind still clangs those irritating cymbals, imagine each cacophonous note (i.e., troubling thought or concern) frozen into a cartoon strip. Mentally "cut" it out with imaginary scissors and allow a gentle breeze to blow them away for another day. Keep doing this until you reach a calm, meditative state. Breathe deeply. In and out. Slowly. Rest totally, for this mental and physical retreat is about quality, not quantity. Release all attachments. Abide in stillness.

**Recommended Resources:** *Quiet: The Power of Introverts in a World That Can't Stop Talking* by Susan Cain; *Mindfulness for Every Day* by Yvette Jane; *Girl Sick in Bed* by Normal Rockwell; *Bunny Buddhism* by Krista Lester

**4 of Swords Card Layout:** *Pause Button* Spread

1. What needs "pausing" right now?
1a. How can I best bring that about?
2. What will *not* pause right now (even though I may want it to)?
2a. How can I best deal with it?
3. What needs pausing physically?
4. What needs pausing mentally?
5. What needs pausing emotionally?
6. What needs pausing spiritually?
7. What's "on pause" that's ripe to resume?

## 5 of Swords – Seamy, Sleazy, Slimy

**Stripped Down Overview:** It's always someone *else's* fault, problem or responsibility. Oh, you know the type: on the playground, it's the girl with the sidewalk chalk who—when others don't play hopscotch the way *she* wants—defaces the squares, puts all the chalk in her pocket and strolls away. Or, more insidiously, she's the one that whispers insults as she saunters by—or tucks nasty, anonymous notes in the textbook of her nemesis. One day, though, her foe gets tired of her passive-aggressive bullshit and punches her in the face. "*Ow!*" she howls, like a hairy banshee undergoing electrolysis. "She *hurt* me! She's a *bully!*" Marshalling sympathizers against this "violent" enemy, she grins when no one is looking...knowing damn well the venomous seeds she's sown will likely never be connected to her karmic harvest. When such girls grow up, they continue to act as though their shit don't stink, often maintaining a Teflon reputation matching their slick, lip-glossed smiles and tarantula eyelashes. "Who, *me?*" her gaze implies. "Why, *I'd* never do such a thing!" But behind the monitor, she's the one telling her Facebook friends who they're allowed to associate with...*or else.* What fuels such immature petulance? Envy? Low self-esteem? The need for ego strokes? Unfortunately, such emotional and psychological cripples may go on to play much more dangerous—even criminal—games. Cyber-hacking, stalking, libel, impersonation, road rage—their cowardly stunts find them hiding behind steel chassis, malignant susurrations, unsigned emails and false names. The scourge of humanity, we can only hope that evolution weeds out such takers, players and oxygen wasters.

**Keywords:** Disdain; One-Upmanship; Cruel Words; Provocation; Ridicule; Plagiarism; Mind Games; Humiliation; Treachery; Preying on the Vulnerable, Schadenfreude; Passive-Aggression; Gloating; Degradation; Stigmatize; Slander; Ill-Gotten Gain; Gaslighting

**Personifications and Embodiments:** Online Trolls; Energy Vampires; Stalkers; Terrorists; ISIS; Hackers; Idea Thieves; Anonymous Guerilla Reviewers; Nelly Oleson (*Little House on the Prairie*); Liars; Christian Day

**Quote:** *Failure is the condiment that gives success its flavor.* – Truman Capote

**Challenge:** Integrity

**Gift:** Toughening

**Occupations/Vocations:** "Cooler" (Gambling); Card Shark; Multi-Lever Marketer; Loan Shark; Mob Goons

**Disney Totem:** Chick Hicks (*Cars*)

**Animal Symbol:** Vulture

**Flower Essences:** Dagger Hakea (Australian Bush); Slender Rice Flower (Australian Bush)

**Crystal/Stone:** Mahogany Obsidian – Dispels dismay caused by insults, disparaging comments and false accusations. Brings power, initiative and new drive.

**Aromatherapy:** Clove (Bud)

**Body Parts/Systems and Health Issues:** Ingested Poison

**Mystical Messenger** – Ate

**Sabian Symbol:** Libra 19 – A gang of robbers in hiding.

**Writing Prompt:** An unfair fight takes an unexpected turn.

**Affirmation:** I stay authentic and honorable despite what others do.

## Naked Advice for the 5 of Swords

*Career:* A missing stapler, misplaced orders, re-arranged paperclips, enigmatic Post-Its—someone's screwing between the ears. Is it a co-worker? A boss? An unstable client? A vendor? Or...*you*? There's not a whole lot you can do if you're the one being played. After all, these games are mental in nature. Sure, there's emotional fallout from the stories you weave about such machinations, but unless the attempts to keep you off-balance are criminal, telling others about them (except your partner or best friend) will make *you* look like the crazy one. Unfair? You bet. The 5 of Swords reeks of unfairness. What you *can* do is refuse to let it get to you—and act like it's never happened. Another way this card manifests is deliberate exclusion. Even if you're the most talented one in the bunch, he'll gather a "special" team without your knowledge. When launch day comes (much to your utter surprise), you'll hear, *"Oh, we couldn't fit you on the team. All the slots were filled."* Utter BS, of course, but what do you expect from a castrated coward? If your workplace is home-based, with suspected colleagues (and taunts) online, avoid them like the plague. Refuse to take the incendiary bait. Block them all, if you must. Peace of mind is much more valuable than attempted retribution or seeking vindication. Now, what if *you're* the one yanking chains? Take some serious stock about the *who* and *why* of your actions. If you're not careful, a smarter, quicker and more lethal contender will cut you down faster than you can cry *"Uncle!"*.

*Romance:* Some people are so damn miserable that they can't bear to see love and harmony between partners. Their envy and hatred solidify into "swords" of foul communications, including spiteful tale bearing, innuendo and character assassination. Knowing she can't undermine such a cemented, peaceful bond, the loser attempts to chip away at the only thing the happy couple can't fully control: their reputation. Damnable no matter the origin, such repugnant efforts are especially sick when coming from relatives, in-laws, co-workers, fellow congregation members or supposed "friends". Just as you would hope no one would believe such rumors about *your* relationship, take what you hear about other partnerships with a huge grain of NaCl. In fact, ignore it altogether (or, better yet, stop the rumormonger in her tracks). As pathetic as the "if I can't be happy, then *no one* should be happy!" mindset is, such wretchedness will always plague humanity—as will those who seek to separate, sully and slander the joyful pairings they resent.

*Parenting*: It's heartbreaking to find out a child is being humiliated, teased and bullied. Ideally, childhood's a time for play, discovery and exploration. Abuse of any kind—whether from parent, neighbor, teacher or classmate—not only devastates the psyche, erodes confidence and wounds emotions, but also negatively impacts cognitive development. That's right: studies show that continual exposure to arguments, harassment and even spanking stunts mental growth. When such volatility and unpredictability surrounds a child like an icy, churning sea—at a time when he's already vulnerable and unsure—the winds of violence shred the sails of self-esteem. Such instability needs some semblance of constancy, so take measured, decisive steps to add solidity, security and consistency to your child's life. If need be, and possible, extract him out of the tumultuous environment. An "inconvenience" today can save years of therapy tomorrow...

*Spirituality:* Any perceived advancement, favor or praise following the vicious stomp of boots or stilettos is fleeting, hollow and illusory. It can be discouraging to watch others cut corners, rip off ideas, produce derivative works or pander to the lowest common denominator—especially when they're heralded as the best thing since sliced bread. How frustrating to walk in integrity and authenticity—to birth original ideas from the sweat of your brow—only to be ignored or marginalized. I'd love to tell you that, one day, your imaginative brilliance will be revealed for all to see. That the throngs will realize the Emperor has no clothes. That honesty, sincerity and enthusiasm triumphs in the end. Unfortunately, in this temporal, dualistic world, the "winners" (re)write history—obliterating the contributions of the "defeated" (look up Hypatia to see what I mean). So, do good for good's sake, make art for art's sake, create meaning outside of kudos or criticism—and maybe, just maybe, the Akashic Records will crack open on the other side, illuminating your efforts and virtues.

**Recommended Resources:** *So You've Been Publicly Shamed* by Jon Ronson; *The Dugout* by Normal Rockwell; *The Celestine Prophecy* by James Redfield; *Carrie* by Stephen King; "Little Yellow Book" (SpongeBob SquarePants); *Gaslight* (Movie); *Utterly Wicked: Curses, Hexes & Other Unsavory Notions* by Dorothy Morrison; *Psychic Self-Defense* by Dion Fortune; *Defense Against the Dark* by Emily Carlin; *The Practical Psychic Self-Defense Handbook* by Robert Bruce; *Dear Bully*; *Star Trek: The Next Generation* "Skin of Evil"

**5 of Swords Card Layout:** *Energy Vampire* Spread

1. Where do I lack power/energy?
2. How have I tried to take it/suck it from others?
3. What is the root of the emptiness that I'm trying to fill?
4. How do I generate my *own* power?
5. What will help me resist taking from others?
6. How can I become more honorable in my interactions?

# 6 of Swords – Moving On

**Stripped Down Overview:** *Enough is enough! This is the straw that broke the camel's back! I'm FED UP! I can't take any more. I've had it up to HERE! That's it. It's over.* Often spoken in frustration or anger, these phrases can serve as implied threats, but when such words are truly (*finally!*) meant, it's the point of no return. Suitcases are packed. Homes are fled. New phone numbers are acquired. One-way tickets are bought. Locks are changed. Credit cards are cancelled. Divorce proceedings are started. Papers for sole custody are filed. Pushed once too much (or too far), this card doesn't just cry *"foul!"* —it screams "It all stops. Here. *Now.*" This is not an instinctual "running for your life" escape, but a firm decision to move forward after *way* too much shit has transpired.

**Keywords:** Emerging from Difficulties; Fleeing to Safety; Heading Towards Sanctuary; Seeking Asylum; Securing a Passport; Path to Legalization; Escaping Trouble; Release from Torment; End in Sight; Emigration; Journey Towards Healing; Travel by Water; Avoiding Negativity; Pursuing Calm Over Drama

**Personifications and Embodiments:** *Bridge Over Troubled Waters*; Refugees; Immigrants; Runaways

**Quote:** *The farther behind I leave the past, the closer I am to forging my own character.* – Isabelle Eberhardt

**Challenge:** Acquiescence

**Gift:** Evolution

**Occupations/Vocations:** Boat Captain; Witness Relocation Agent; Ferryman; Gondola Pilot

**Disney Totem:** Elsa (*Frozen*)

**Animal Symbol:** Antelope

**Flower Essences:** Red Grevillea (Australian Bush); Bottlebrush (Australian Bush)

**Crystal/Stone:** Tiger Iron – Boosts *chi* (life force). Helps carry out solutions quickly and resolutely. Helps to overcome difficulties. Promotes invigoration.

**Aromatherapy:** Melaleuca

**Body Parts/Systems and Health Issues:** Contaminated Water Supply; Legionnaires' Disease

**Mystical Messenger** – Saint Elmo

**Sabian Symbol:** Libra 10 – A canoe is approaching safety through dangerous waters.

**Writing Prompt:** Charon makes a wrong turn on the way to the Underworld.

**Affirmation:** I leave negativity in the past and journey towards healing.

## Naked Advice for the 6 of Swords

*Career:* In the Thoth tradition, this card is dubbed "Science", perhaps because of its astrological correlation of Mercury (information) in Aquarius (reason). Scientists must sift and sort through data, form a theory, then test their preliminary conclusions—all while staying both observant and open-minded to conflicting statistics. Whether you work at a logic-heavy profession or not, the 6 of Swords encourages you to gather details without assumption or judgment—and play the waiting game while the pieces of the puzzle begin to drop into place. There's a chance, though, that there *isn't* a puzzle at all (i.e., some behind-the-scenes agenda or malevolent force)—so don't go charging ahead like someone-in-the-know. Rather, sit back, watch, withhold any opinions—and do your job. Act when you have the facts, moving towards what is helpful and beneficial to you, your co-workers/family and your company/career.

*Romance:* It may be time to "wash that man right out of your hair", especially if he's an asshole—or to ditch that lying drama-Queen of a girlfriend. If you've drawn this card, you've not only considered it, you're already halfway out the door. Good for you! It's not only important to navigate away from this type of unpleasantness, but to *actively choose* more constructive, positive and beneficial relationships from here on out. You'll likely have a dossier of red flags by now, so be sure to use this intel when evaluating future partners. Better to recognize turbulent waters at the onset, opting for a plane ticket or a train trip over a ride in the S.S. Crazy Canoe.

*Parenting:* Time to expose your kids to the joy of science! Rent or buy some wondrous David Attenborough nature documentaries from BBC Video to give them an appreciation of the intricacies of animal behavior and survival. Buy them a solar printing kit or perhaps a chemistry set. Find out their favorite movies or TV shows, then check to see if there's some type of science connection you can use to ~~bait~~ interest your kids (e.g., if they love *Sherlock*, acquire forensic equipment geared towards the smaller set or any DVD series from The Great Courses featuring forensic anthropologist Dr. Elizabeth A. Murray). Not only will you learn a thing or two about the awesomeness of science (you *do* plan to hover around the tykes, right?), but you'll also benefit from the bonding time (covalent or otherwise).

*Spirituality:* For your spiritual and mental well-being, it's time to actively shun negative people and messages. Sure, some may accuse you of being a Star-like Pollyanna, but who cares? It's your life (and sanity) that's at stake. There's no shame in refusing to stream world news or check on what's trending on social media. Hell, even getting rid of regular TV broadcasting altogether would be a stellar move (we've done the latter for almost a decade—and have been so much better off for it!). And unfriending (or even blocking) idiots on Facebook that dare share pics of the bodies of battered animals or stories of horrific child abuse? You *totally* need to do this. Contrary to what drama-addicts say, this is not "burying your head in the sand" (after all, how much can you *really* do to stave off the destruction that humans do to the planet and each other?), but rather, the choice to raise your own vibration towards peace and joy. You'll be surprised at how inspiration, creativity, optimism and even magnanimity increase when you unplug from the fear-based matrix. Remember: *as within, so without.*

**Recommended Resources:** *The Sound of Music* (Movie); *Brooklyn* (Movie)

**6 of Swords Card Layout:** *Crazymaking (and Recovery)* Spread

1. *First Sword*: What do I get out of entertaining or tolerating drama?
2. *Second Sword*: How am I most likely to *start* drama?
3. *Third Sword*: Why is this? (Mitigating Factor)
4. *Fourth Sword*: What is a benefit of putting crazymaking behind me?
5. *Fifth Sword*: How can I best move forward with a positive

mindset?

6. *Sixth Sword*: Piece of logic or reason that will help me stay away from crazy.

## 7 of Swords – The Game's Afoot

**Stripped Down Overview:** Often dubbed "The Thief", the 7 of Swords tends to get a bad rap among Tarotists—and I aim to correct this cynical view. First off, we don't *know* that the figure in the Rider-Waite-Smith is pilfering those swords. He may look smug because he's *actually* taking back what the enemy had stolen from him (and his clan). Or, hell, he may just be playing an ancient version of the shaving-cream-in-the-sleeper's-hand prank—whisking away his brother's swords from a neighboring tent! Besides, if we saddle this card with merely a "thief" interpretation, that doesn't leave much room for further meaning now, does it? So let's break it down by examining numerology coupled with the suit of Swords. In her book *Numerology for Baby Names*, author Phyllis Vega notes that keywords associated with the number 7 include (among others): *mystical, crafty, imaginative, silent, independent, probing, philosophical, wise, secretive, intellectual, creative, solitary, contemplative, wise, refined, spiritual, creative and intuitive.* And yes, also *moody, withdrawn, impractical, aloof* and *phobic.* (Is it me, or does this sound *a lot* like Benedict Cumberbatch's version of Sherlock Holmes?) Now, blend those traits with those of airy Swords—intellect, communication, information, beliefs, assumptions, judgments, facts, data, opinions and discrimination. *Ahhhh*, this looks like so much more than just a "thief", right? (Admittedly, this number/ suit stew could indicate that, too.) But mostly, this is a card of sly curiosity—the willingness to follow the trail wherever it leads *and* having the intellectual capability and resources to uncover a solution or solve a mystery…existential, mundane *or* criminal.

**Keywords:** Strategizing; Stealth; Logistics; Maneuvering; Wily; Playing "Cat and Mouse"; Trying to Find Answers; Cunning; Navigation; Getting to the Bottom of Something; Plotting a Course; Intrigue; Conspiracy; Planning; Paranoia; Wariness; Covering Your Tracks

**Personifications and Embodiments:** Heist Movies; *Myst* (Video Game); Wile E. Coyote; Treasure Maps; Freddie Lounds (*Hannibal*); Scavenger Hunts; Sherlock Holmes; Solving Puzzles; Strategy Games; Reconnaissance; Investigation; Detective Stories; Trivial Pursuit; *Marvel's Agents of S.H.I.E.L.D.*; Hercule Poirot; *Father Dowling Mysteries*; *Star Trek: The Next Generation*

**Quote:** *I make all my decisions on intuition. I throw a spear into darkness. That is intuition. Then I must send an army into the darkness to find the spear. That is intellect.* – Ingmar Bergman

**Challenge:** Mistrust

**Gift:** Detection

**Occupations/Vocations:** Spy; Hostage Negotiator; PETA or Greenpeace Activist; Disarmament Advocate; Intellectual Properties Lawyer

**Disney Totem:** Sam Flynn (*Tron*)

**Animal Symbol:** Magpie

**Flower Essences:** Willow (Bach); Paw Paw (Australia)

**Crystal/Stone:** Spotted Lapis (Lapis Lazuli Calcite) – Enhances sense of personal responsibility, powers of discernment and acute intelligence. Helps a person gain control over his/her life.

Promotes genuineness. Encourages emotional openness.

**Aromatherapy:** Sandalwood

**Body Parts/Systems and Health Issues:** Scratches; Abrasions

**Mystical Messenger** – Jesus Malverde

**Sabian Symbol:** Capricorn 30 – Directors of a large firm meet in a secret conference.

**Writing Prompt:** A girl steals light sabers.

**Affirmation:** I am capable of navigating tricky circumstances.

## Naked Advice for the 7 of Swords

*Career:* Make damn sure everything you do at your job is aboveboard, honest, kind and ethical. Seriously. Now is not the time to cut corners, spread rumors, hurl insults or swipe from the till (as if *any* time is a good time for those behaviors!). Live as though your cubicle is bugged, your smart phone is tapped and your computer monitored. *Every. Single. Keystroke.* Not to encourage the spirit of paranoia, mind you...that would suck. It's just that this card hints at someone being out to get you – or wanting to take advantage of a situation. *Wait:* this isn't describing *you*, is it? *Warning:* you may very well get away with your machinations. Even profit from them. You'll rationalize your decision, too. I can hear the excuses bouncing around in your head all the way from here. *Justified*, you think. *Deserving.* Remember this: when you carry around the swords of bitter self-righteousness in your grasping arms – or try to take on the role of karma police – you're holding them *by the blades.* The phrase "bloody hell" will take on new meaning for you, mark my words.

*Romance:* Your boyfriend is acting sneaky. There's just something...*off* about his behavior. Is he cheating? Planning a surprise birthday party? Anticipating test results from the doctor (that he didn't tell you about)? Intercepting nasty texts from his ex that he doesn't want to bother you with? Concealing bad news? Anticipating a good report (but he doesn't want to jump the gun)? As with all Swords cards, communication is a central component: the lack of, hiding of, miscommunication of—you get the drift. Remember the ol' saying *Assume = making an "ass" out of "u" and "me"*? The phrase holds true here: confront your partner (gently, but clearly) about his behavior. It may truly be "nothing" as he says—as in, nothing that's directly related to your relationship—but airing your concerns will, at least, help ease your mind and pave the way for more honest, open communication. Still playing the field? Make sure you practice safe sex because, in this case, both sperm and STDs can be sneaky buggers...and completely change your life if you're not careful. If it were me, I'd choose abstinence for the foreseeable future when this card comes up in a relationship or romance reading.

*Parenting:* Time to be sneaky, folks. Sorry, ACLU, but when underage kids are in the house, they give up most of their rights. "But *privacy!*" you squeal. Yeah, well, too many kids are left alone in their bedrooms, stockpiling automatic weapons, heroin or naked selfies. And then, in the aftermath of their poor (and sometimes, deadly) decisions, family members and neighbors walk around like clueless zombies: "But, we didn't *know*" or "How could this have *possibly* happened?" or "They were such a *good* family". Here's how you *know*: go into their bedroom and search *everything*, including backpacks and closets. Don't leave any digital stone unturned, either (including web surfing history). If they find out, they'll get over it.

*Spirituality:* Have you ever been so enraptured by a cloud

formation or a sunset or a wild animal standing in the grass or gently falling show that you just stared in awe? No camera or phone in hand to share on social media—just you and the beauty you beheld? On the Kabbbalistic Tree of Life, the 7s—including the 7 of Swords—lies within the sphere of Netzach (Victory), which is linked to the planet Venus. Having a "Vision of Beauty Triumphant" (the spiritual experience of this sphere) is to feel profound wonder, especially when faced with nature's immensity and exquisiteness. Morning dew drops on red roses, intricate webs spun by tiny spiders, roaring waterfalls, delicate pink paws of a kitten, double rainbows—no analysis, no comparison, no judgments: we just feel, deeply, a sense of connection, of Oneness, with all that is. And sometimes, afterwards, out of stillness, a stirring of emotions propels us to create—perhaps, inspired by the Creator/Creatix of everything—and we pick up paintbrush, musical instrument, pen or clay...hoping to capture, and convey, the splendor just experienced. It's time to get back "there"—like a child who colored, sang or danced with abandon—no grades, no timelines, no evaluation...just you and self-expression in the wild moment of the everlasting Now.

**Recommended Resources:** *The Bletchley Circle* (TV Show); *Sherlock* (TV Show); *Murdoch Mysteries* (TV Show); *Boy with Dog in Picnic Basket* by Normal Rockwell; *Sherlock Holmes Tarot* by John Matthews and Wil Kinghan; *Think Like a Freak* by Steven D. Levitt and Stephen J. Dubner

**7 of Swords Card Layout:** *Seven Deadly Sins (That Lead to Others)* Spread

1. **Pride** – How am I arrogant or feel a need to be "better than"?
1a. – How to "outsmart" Pride
2. **Avarice** – How am I greedy?

2a. – How to "outwit" Avarice

3. **Lust** – What do I ache for?

3a. – How to "outmaneuver" Lust

4. **Anger** – What am I irate about (or pisses me off)?

4a. – How to "defuse" Anger

5. **Gluttony** – What can't I get enough of (or indulge excessively in)?

5a. – How to "outfox" Gluttony

6. **Envy** – Who (or what) am I jealous of—or feeling spiteful towards?

6a. – How to "triumph over" Envy

7. **Sloth** – How am I lazy, idle, indifferent or apathetic?

7a. – How to "get the better of" Sloth

## 8 of Swords – Trapped in an Unlocked Cage

**Stripped Down Overview:** In the late 1960s, Dr. Martin Seligman—the father of Positive Psychology—conducted some fascinating experiments involving dogs, cages, food and aversive stimuli. He found that random shocks—*a damned-if-you-do-damned-if-you-don't* situation—resulted in something he called "learned helplessness". Discovered quite by accident, and in opposition to what behaviorist B.F. Skinner predicted, the dogs that received unpredictable shocks did not try to escape. Instead, they just lay down and whined because of the lack of control—replicating clinical depression in humans. Further research, however, explained why, when facing the same negative event, some people succumbed to depression and learned helplessness while others did not: explanatory style. That is, how an individual explains what happened to them—the private "story" he tells about the situation—affects the likelihood of both learned helplessness and depression. The crux of this disempowering explanation of reality? The "Three Ps": Permanence, Personal and Pervasive. Thinking of a negative event as permanent is to conclude that it will never, ever change. Assuming a deleterious situation is personal causes a person to think *"it's all my fault"*. And believing "I'm a screw up" falls under pervasive—an all-encompassing, seemingly inescapable inference. *This* is the domain of the 8 of Swords: assuming lack of control, cynicism, refusal to reach for betterment and playing the victim. I'm not talking about those who suffer a lack of serotonin retention or other physical reason for depression, mind you. Blaming those dealing with mental illness for their own state is an act of assholery. I'm talking about—and this *card* is talking about—those who repeatedly tell themselves a disempowering story when faced with any and all setbacks. Those who erect an invisible cage made with impenetrable bars of blame and negative self-talk. The *good* news is learned helplessness can be reversed. The *bad* news is that it takes a major overhaul of beliefs and mental constructs to do so—sometimes involving Cognitive Behavioral Therapy.

**Keywords:** Learned Helplessness; Woundology; Boxed In; Feeling Powerless; Victim Mindset; Blaming; Fear of Personal Responsibility; Trapped by Patterns of Poor Decision Making; Immobility; Self-Sabotage; Preconceptions; Restriction

**Personifications and Embodiments:** Writer's Block; Straitjacket

**Quote:** *Life is thick sown with thorns, and I know no other remedy than to pass quickly through them. The longer we dwell on our misfortunes, the greater is their power to harm us.* – Voltaire

**Challenge:** Resistance

**Gift:** Escape

**Occupations/Vocations:** Escape Artist; Eye Surgeon; Seamstress; Tailor

**Disney Totem:** Rapunzel (*Tangled*)

**Animal Symbol:** Unicorn

**Flower Essences:** Crowea (Australian Bush); Dog Rose (Australian Bush); Red Grevillea (Australian Bush)

**Crystal/Stone:** Violet Fluorite – Liberation. Encourages self-determination. Brings emotional stability and inner peace. Helps with learning and concentration.

**Aromatherapy:** Bergamot

**Body Parts/Systems and Health Issues:** Arthritis; Stiffness; Joints

**Mystical Messenger** – Saint Aubin

**Sabian Symbol:** Gemini 12 – A black slave girl demands her rights of her mistress.

**Writing Prompt:** A woman allows herself to be tied up—because she knows something her captor does *not.*

**Affirmation:** I am free to think, believe and act as I please.

## Naked Advice for the 8 of Swords

*Career:* Your employer doesn't owe you "the perfect job". That's your responsibility. *"Be the change you see in the world"* isn't just a cute bumper sticker incorrectly attributed to Gandhi. No, *you* create the type of environment you want to experience in the workplace. Stop blaming and complaining. Wish your workplace was livelier? Add some spice by talking to co-workers, telling jokes or decorating your cubicle. Desire to collaborate? Talk to your manager and colleagues about working on team projects. Want a raise? Ask for it! See ways to cut waste, boost morale or increase profits? Do what you can—then offer suggestions to your supervisor. (Note: this isn't ass kissing. This is taking responsibility for your job satisfaction.) If you're really *that* miserable—and have tried multiple ways to make things better— then have the balls to quit (contrary to what you've been told, the devil you *don't* know is much better than the one you *do*). Either make a difference in your career path...or make excuses. Which one will it be?

**Romance:** If your date or partner attempts to "shut you up" in any way, run for the hills. Do not pass "Go". Do not collect any benefits (or rue what you'll be missing if you leave). Trying to shut down your self-expression, governed by the Throat Chakra, is not cool. In fact, it can paralyze. Ways of trying to keep you quiet or docile can manifest as shaming your behavior (*Why do you laugh so much in public?*), deliberate embarrassment (*My wife's boobs sag so much, she could sweep the floor with 'em!*) or interfering with your decisions (*I called the satellite company to change your subscription back to what it was. You didn't need all those channels.*). The worst case scenario, of course, is to hear an actual *Shut up!* (often coupled with name calling). If you allow this type of treatment to go on, you'll begin to expect it...and believe you deserve it. You will shrink. Your soul will wither. And someone *else* will start calling the shots, dictating your every move and telling you what to think. And if that person leaves? You'll just find a substitute who'll do the same. Take heart: your path doesn't *have* to end up this way. At the first sign of someone trying to control how you think, what you say and what you do—just *run*. Better to be alone and free than in a relationship rife with restriction.

*Parenting*: Assuming that *"your hands are tied"* is the worst attitude to adopt right now. You may think *"they never listen, anyway"* or *"what's the use in trying?"*, but those excuses for inaction are a recipe for disaster. Put on your big girl pants, determine the problem, come up with a detailed plan...then implement *every* step. You have choices. *Make* some. Look, if you *don't*, society or bad influences will do it *for* you. Don't forget to extend the same courtesy to your kids while still holding your ground: give *them* as many choices as they can handle. Decisions as seemingly inconsequential as what to have for breakfast (*cereal or scrambled eggs?*), what to wear (*red T-shirt or black sweater?*) or what movie to watch during family night (*action or CGI cartoons?*) can have an enormously beneficial effect on their psychological health. If, however, they seem to be personalizing and internalizing recent disappointments or perceived failures—to the point of losing interest in their friends, hobbies and previously enjoyed activities—consider consulting a child psychologist before full-blown depression sets in.

*Spirituality:* It's one thing to surrender to the Divine, hoping for the best but trusting that all will be well no matter *what* happens— and believing for a stupendous miracle, instant debt relief, healing from a fatal disease or winning the 50 million dollar Power Ball... while doing nothing practical about it. Assuming that God pulls strings, loads the dice or grants superpowers according to mere "faith", repeated positive affirmations, reading a sacred text for hours a day or sending scads of money to your favorite *"name-it-and-claim-it"* televangelist is refusing to take responsibility for your own life. Sure, those things can help you on your journey (well, not the latter), but they do *not*—and *will* not—guarantee that you'll get what you're after. In fact, you'll likely get a shitload of disillusionment, frustration and anger for your trouble. Take off your blinders, give God the week off and take practical steps towards your dream or goal. Want to be healed? Go to a doctor.

Research remedies. Ask for a second opinion. Want to make money? Get a job. Invest in continuing education. Be willing to work at something "beneath" you. Want a soul mate? Go out and meet people. Practice the art of conversation. Risk asking a stranger for a date. Visit the places that attract your type of partner. *"God helps those who help themselves"* may not be in the Bible (although it's often misquoted as such), but the Divine can't meet you halfway if you're not even walking on the road.

**Recommended Resources:** *Learned Optimism* by Dr. Martin Seligman; *The Optimistic Child* by Dr. Martin Seligman; *Women Who Think Too Much* by Dr. Susan Nolen-Hoeksema; *The Truman Show* (Movie); "Caged Bird" by Maya Angelou; *The Van Gogh Blues* by Eric Masiel; *Writing Past Dark* by Bonnie Friedman

**8 of Swords Card Layout:** *Taking Back My Power* Spread

1. What part of my life do I think I can't change?
1a. How can I affect change in this area after all?
2. What part of my life do I feel is "all my fault"?
2a. How is that area actually beyond my control?
3. What part of my life do I assume will always be as it is?
3a. How can I best prepare for when it's *not*?
4. What am I afraid to say?
4a. How do I say it?
5. What am I afraid to do?
5a. How do I do it?
6. What am I afraid to embody?
6a. How can I rock it?

## 9 of Swords – Nervous Wreck

**Stripped Down Overview:** When the boogeyman's under the bed, your pounding heart full of dread, it's the 9 of Swords clattering in your closet. The stuff of nightmares, unfounded fears and nervous anticipation, this card points to what goes bump in the night—including the mental ricochet of worst-case scenarios. Also the realm of infernal panic attacks, pervasive anxiety, phobias and manic thoughts, this tormentor afflicts *everyone* at some point. Medical tests, wrong numbers, unexplained noises, upcoming exams, delayed homecomings—our minds accelerate to future *what ifs*, while our extremities tingle with the flight-or-fight response. The good news is there's no boggart in your bureau, stalker on your stairs, tumor in your titty or loved one tangled amid twisted metal. The *bad* news is that you need to address the root of these prevalent cognitive afflictions—before they eat your sanity for lunch.

**Keywords:** Anxiety; Nightmares; Fears; Worry; Phobias; Insomnia; Headaches; Catastrophic Thinking; Hysteria; Guilt; Mental Torment; Nervousness; Self-Criticism; "Butterflies", Dread, Migraines; Stage Fright

**Personifications and Embodiments:** PTSD; Horror Stories; Slasher Movies; Monsters; Boogeymen; Panic Attacks; Ghosts; Poltergeists; Ouija Boards; Haunted Houses; Scary Pranks; Creature Under the Bed; Boggart

**Quote:** *We consume our tomorrows by fretting about our yesterdays.* – Persius

**Challenge:** Perspective

**Gift:** Actuality

**Occupations/Vocations:** Quilt Maker; Mattress Manufacturer; Bedding Seller; Coffee Buyer

**Disney Totem:** Piglet (*The Many Adventures of Winnie the Pooh*)

**Animal Symbol:** Coyote

**Flower Essences:** Aspen (Bach); White Chestnut (Bach); Dog Rose (Australian Bush)

**Crystal/Stone:** Chrysoprase – Promotes trust and a sense of safety. Helps with heartache, jealousy and nightmares. Shields from negative energy and psychic attack. Aids in solving relationship problems.

**Aromatherapy:** Lavender

**Body Parts/Systems and Health Issues:** Anxiety; Insomnia; Panic Attacks; PTSD; Depression

**Mystical Messenger** – Boyuto

**Sabian Symbol:** Leo 1 – A man is under emotional stress and blood rushes to his head.

**Writing Prompt:** A boy expects the very worst...but gets the very best.

**Affirmation:** I focus on best-case scenarios.

## Naked Advice for the 9 of Swords

*Career:* A co-worker ignores your greeting, the boss looks at you sideways, a colleague hasn't returned your email, a client behaves extra weird—and you could *swear* you just saw the delivery guy stick out his tongue as you signed for a package. Before you start fabricating outlandish stories involving conspiracies, workplace politics and your imminent firing, take a deep breath. Then another. Hard as it may seem to believe, it's not all about *you*. You rarely cross other people's minds, because they're too busy obsessing about their *own* shit. So relax, don't read into facial expressions, assume the best (or, at the very least, neutrality) — and get on with the job at hand.

*Romance:* Instead of plucking petals while playing *She loves me...she loves me not,* consider sending an actual bouquet to your paramour. Don't wait for her to spell it out (in Copperplate Gothic) with squid ink, on rare, gently weathered ecru parchment. If you want (need?) to know how she *really* feels, then pick up the damn phone and call her already! Don't guess, don't assume, and don't wait. Otherwise, you'll be making your own bed of romantic nails — and wake up with a backside full of unnecessary puncture wounds. (And no, she is *not* cheating. But if you keep acting like she *is* — you might drive her into the arms of another with your paranoia, suspicions and innuendo.)

*Parenting:* Just like adults, kids can get themselves in a tizzy worrying about potentials. Will I pass tomorrow's test? Will someone sit with me at lunch in the cafeteria? Are people laughing at me? How will I get all this homework done? Will I be safe at school? What if my best friend suddenly drops me for someone new? The good news about this card is that your child's heightened concerns are unfounded and unwarranted (if they were, you'd have the 5 of Swords — not the 9 of Swords). The tricky thing about negative anticipation, though, is that sustained anxiety stresses the body in very real ways. Just as visualization is a powerful attractor, so is worry. Thus, over time, we could be looking at a self-fulfilling prophecy at best or a spiral down to depression at worst. Kids lack mature foresight or the wisdom 20/20 hindsight, so they assume things will *never* get better — or that they're doomed to a life of uncertainty and unease. As with most Tarot cards, communication is paramount when dealing with the kiddos. Share stories from your youth about *what if?* situations that threatened your well-being—yet never materialized. Avoid saying, *"It's all in your head"* (which rings of patronizing dismissiveness), but *do* share (and show) how we humans can be our own worst enemies when we live in an *imagined* future—rather than a *more-than-OK* now.

*Spirituality:* If your religion involves dread of any kind—fear or threat of divine retribution, eternal damnation, religious disapproval, excommunication or shunning—it's time to ask yourself how much freedom your spiritual path affords. What's the point of your journey, anyway? Love? Joy? Acceptance? Meaning? Finding your place and purpose in this world? If you feel stuck, confined or confused, follow the thread back to your answers to those questions. You'll either find a knotty ball of yarn worth tossing out (or giving the cat to play with)—or a cohesive granny square reminding you of why you began this spiritual journey in the first place.

**Recommended Resources:** *Learning to Breathe* by Priscilla Warner; *The Scream* by Edvard Munch; *Study After Velazquez's Portrait of Pope Innocent X* by Francis Bacon; *The Conjuring* (Movie); *Haunted Objects* by Stacey Graham; *Twisted Tarot Tales Deck* by James Battersby and Christine Aguiar

**9 of Swords Card Layout:** *Monster under the Bed* Spread

1. What's *really* under the bed? (What you're "lying on" by avoidance)
2. What's your blanket made of? (A source of comfort right now)
3. What's outside the window? (A new perspective or view for switching focus)

4. How do I turn on the light in the dark? (Internal resource or strength to draw on)
5. Light's on! (Reality or truth that dispels the "monster")
6. How do I monster-proof my bedroom? (Tool, talisman or approach to prevent or ameliorate the tendency to worry)

## 10 of Swords – No Way But Up

**Stripped Down Overview:** Personally, I think Swords cards are the most fascinating and underappreciated of all the suits—usually receiving just a few negative or scary keywords each. When we look deeper, though, we find a rich depository of insight covering a huge chunk of life—yes, including challenges and rough patches—that encompasses the complex workings occurring between our ears. The nature of language, communication, customs, laws and beliefs all stem from words—agreed upon or argued over—which form the basis of civilization. Dreaming doesn't separate us from animals (anyone who's had a cat or dog for a pet has seen them "chase" while sleeping), but the attempt to *understand* those dreams *does*. Which brings me to the 10 of Swords: In the RWS tradition, there's a prone individual with ten swords sticking out of his back. It seems like a straightforward (though violent) image, pointing towards being "stabbed in the back" (*et tu, Brute?*). The figure likely dead. But unlike oracle cards, the Tarot never wastes images on a meaning so simplistic, so...*obvious*. Look closer at the RWS version. The right hand forms a *mudra* (yoga for the hands, as it were)—the Surya Mudra, to be exact. Also known as the Sun Mudra (*Prithvi Shammak*), this hand position increases fire (*agni*) in the body, which would elevate body temperature and raise blood pressure. Something a man lying on the ground with ten swords in his back would need, right? (By the way, anyone else think "acupuncture" when seeing the RWS version of this card?) The Surya Mudra also decreases the Earth element (attachments to the material world?) *and* increases vision (clarity?). And it just so happens that the Sun is rising in many versions of this card, too. So out of a card that appears to simply mean "betrayal" or "violent attack", we are now led to look at the Sun for comfort, hope, healing and answers. We are down, but not out. Excessive words, opinions and data may have overwhelmed us—the overkill causing partial paralysis—but we still can move our right ("rational, conscious, logical, virile") hand, a symbol of the "corporeal manifestation of the inner state of the human being" as well as "protection, authority, power and strength" (Cirlot, 131).

**Keywords:** Overkill; Hitting Bottom; System Overload; Bewilderment; End of Conflict; New Day Dawning; Humility; Mental Subjugation; Brainwashing; Neutralized Threat; Information Glut; Neurological Breakdown; Worst is Over; Back from the Brink; Thriving After Massive Injury or Abuse

**Personifications and Embodiments:** Good Friday; Concussions; Busy Signal; The "Humble Bumble" After Tooth Extraction (*Rudolph the Red-Nosed Reindeer*); Noisy Crowds; Hectic Switchboards; Entering Rehab; Power Outage; Buzzer Sounding; Clock Strikes Midnight; Light at the End of the Tunnel; Escaping a Cult

**Quote:** *I was set free, because my greatest fear had already been realized...I had an old typewriter and a big idea. And so rock bottom became the solid foundation on which I rebuilt my life.* – J. K. Rowling

**Challenge:** Will

**Gift:** Humbleness

**Occupations/Vocations:** Acupuncturist; Chiropractor; Addiction

Specialist; Detox Therapist

**Disney Totem:** Doris (*Meet the Robinsons*)

**Animal Symbol:** Starfish

**Flower Essences:** Rock Rose (Bach); Waratah (Australian Bush); Grey Spider Flower (Australian Bush)

**Crystal/Stone:** Gneiss – Helps recognize unhelpful tendencies, habits and thought processes. Promotes endurance until transformation sets in. Aids in facing unpleasant situations, dealing with upheaval and making transitions.

**Aromatherapy:** Myrrh

**Body Parts/Systems and Health Issues:** Numbness; Paralysis; Aneurism; Stroke; Meridians

**Mystical Messenger** – Saint Acacius

**Sabian Symbol:** Capricorn 22 – A general accepting defeat gracefully.

**Writing Prompt:** Swords that give life, not take it.

**Affirmation:** I can only go up from here...and I will.

## Naked Advice for the 10 of Swords

*Career:* The memory of a difficult, perhaps even traumatic, vocational experience immobilizes, as the sting of fear or humiliation prevents you from striving for advancement, asking for a raise, aiming for an award or attempting to expand your influence. You future isn't set in stone, determined solely by your past choices—unless you believe it is. Because then, your assumption becomes an insurmountable boulder of intimidation and self-sabotage. In numerology, the Tens, when reduced (10 = 1+0), equal the vibration of One—The Magician. Like the Mage, you are aware of the tools at your disposal. However, *unlike* the talented Wizard, you have the benefit of hard-won experience (and battles) under your ourorboric belt—allowing for spiraling upward towards a wiser and, arguably, more adept, manipulator. Need to make a precise cut? Reach for the scalpel... not the machete.

*Romance:* To a hammer, everything looks like a nail. If you've been pounced on one too many times in the romance department, it's no *wonder* you view dates or mate with underlying suspicion and trepidation. Thing is, no relationship benefits from doubt and apprehension, especially ones that appear promising and (dare you hope?) fulfilling. You need to extricate and examine all the mental swords impaled in your psyche, neutralizing them with dispassionate analysis and common sense. You'll also need to arm yourself with a good dose of optimism and self-confidence. If you need to seek counseling to get there, *do it*. The investment in your mental health—and the potential undoing of the psychological damage your harrowing experiences or personal stories has inflicted—will repay you with sanity in spades.

*Parenting:* Sometimes, neurological, psychological or immunological problems remain hidden from view—except to the one dealing with them. There's even a term to describe those suffering with an "invisible illness": *spoonies*. Fortunately, pediatricians now use an informal scale to help identify depressive tendencies (but you have to take the kids to the doctor on a regular basis to benefit from early detection). Please understand, I'm not sharing this to frighten you—but to give you a head's up just in case your child is suffering with malaise, confusion, undetectable seizures, repetitive habits, learning challenges or generalized anxiety (frequent stomach aches could hint to the latter). Keep an eye on the kiddos, especially if they attend public school (where busy or clueless teachers are unable to notice these often subtle behaviors). If involved in athletics, make sure their heads are well protected to prevent injury (and if the coach isn't ensuring safety in this area, raise your voice—or yank your child out of the program—until he *does*).

*Spirituality*: In his book *Step-by-Step Tarot*, Terry Donaldson notes about this card: *The more you hang on to any rigid notion of who you are and how you should be treated the more difficult you will find this period*. In the episode "Sisters" from Season Five of the TV show *Once Upon a Time*, Cora (the Queen of Hearts) completes her unfinished business in the Underworld by restoring the memories of her daughters Zelena (Wicked Witch of Oz) and Regina (the former Evil Queen of the Enchanted Forest)—showing them that they once cared for each other very much. This reconciliation spurs Cora's revelation that it's time for her to face her fate: resigned, she walks the stone ledge perched above roiling lava. Should she stroll over the edge, it's off to a worse place. But to her surprise and delight, her reconciliatory act has redeemed her: she walks the span of the ledge...which transforms into a bridge leading to a bright white light (a better place). Sometimes, our opinion of ourselves—especially in light of past mistakes—can lead us to believe that we are beyond redemption (it doesn't help if you have 5 of Swords nasties heaping that kind of shit on you, either). We judge ourselves so harshly, assuming that our missteps have ruined our chances for happiness or success. While it may be that certain opportunities appear lost or destroyed, there comes a time when we must believe it was all part of a Grand Plan we scripted (or, at the very least, the human acknowledgement that it is what it is—we can't change it—and when we know better, we *do* better). Look to the Sun, and let its warmth heal, its light reveal and its rays revitalize.

**Recommended Resources:** *Leah Remini: Scientology and the Aftermath* (TV); *A Child Called "It"* by David Pelzer

**10 of Swords Card Layout:** *Druid Triad* Spread

1. What is the spiritual instruction for me when I encounter worldly misfortune?
2. What is the spiritual instruction for me when I encounter bodily illness?
3. What is the spiritual instruction for me when I encounter unmerited hatred?

# COINS

## Ace of Coins – Pennies from Heaven

**Stripped Down Overview:** Ever walk down the street when a glint on the ground catches your eye? Why, it's a shiny dime! *Woohoo!* Or, ever come across an unscratched lottery ticket blowing on the sidewalk? Or perhaps stumbled on an online discount code that saved you, like, $50 or more? Or what about this: convinced you're dying of cancer or advanced heart disease, you go to the ER, get a slew of tests…and, lo and behold, you're actually *perfectly fine*! (Gotta watch that stress, tho, bub.) And your wretched, tight-fisted boss—for inexplicable, miraculous reasons—gives everyone in the shop a $100 bonus for Christmas. And get this: your cousin, who has a timeshare in Fiji, *"can't make it this year…would you like to go, all expenses paid"*? Oh, the surprise! The relief! The *gratitude*. That's what I'm talking about, Holmes: A peculiar yet welcome invitation to increased material and physical abundance.

**Keywords:** Material Gift; Unexpected Windfall; Starting Over; First Home; New Way of Eating; Chance for Better Health; Opportunity to Make Money; Invitation to Prosperity; Sanctuary; Opening for Responsibility; Entry-Level Position; Seed Fund; Available Property; Environmental Well-Being; Applying for a Grant or a Scholarship; Internship; Embodiment; Refuge; Solidity; Becoming Tangible; Bonus

**Personifications and Embodiments:** Lump of Clay; Egg; Spa Day; Lottery Ticket; An Acorn; "First Dollar"; Seedling; Getting a New Haircut; Manicure/Pedicure; A Makeover; Found Object; Brand New Item (Gifted or Purchased); Coupons; Discount Codes; Promotional Gifts; Golden Rock at Shwe Pyi Daw

**Quote:** *You may send poetry to the rich; to poor men give substantial presents.* – Marcus Aurelius

**Challenge:** Refusal

**Gift:** Manifestation

**Occupations/Vocations:** Concierge; Dish Washer; Lottery Ticket Vendor; Investor; Plate Manufacturer; Numismatist; Archway Mason

**Disney Totem:** Winnie the Pooh (*Winnie the Pooh and the Honey Tree*)

**Animal Symbol:** Coral

**Flower Essence:** Wild Potato (Australian Bush)

**Crystal/Stone:** Petrified Wood – Brings stability. Enhances rootedness in the Self. Promotes a "both feet on the ground" state. Helps with excess weight caused by ungroundedness. Encourages embracing the here and now.

**Aromatherapy:** Chamomile Roman

**Body Parts/Systems and Health Issues:** Lumps; Bumps; Moles; Warts; Cysts

**Mystical Messenger** – Eirene

**Sabian Symbol:** Taurus 3 – Natural steps up to a lawn blooming with clover.

**Writing Prompt:** Eggs are currency.

**Affirmation:** I dwell in abundance, health and comfort.

## Naked Advice for the Ace of Coins

*Career:* Sometimes, raises and vocational windfalls seem to come out of the blue. You can't force it to happen, or even lay the foundation to prepare the soil. It just *is*. Surprising, welcome and—sometimes—game changing, these extras may arrive just in the nick of time. From an unexpected smoked turkey for Thanksgiving to a $2000 Christmas bonus—or a job opening in the Florida branch to a newly created position that you'd be perfect for (and are offered...*would you be interested?*), these unforeseen boons feel like the gods are smiling down on you. (Since it rains on the just and the unjust, it stands to reason that the sun also shines on both—so don't go patting yourself on the back, thinking you "deserve" it. Just sayin'.) Oh, and if the boys at the factory or the girls at the office ask if you want to chip in for a Powerball ticket...*do it!* You may not be able to plan for Aces, but when an opportunity for increase shows up, you'd be silly to turn it down.

*Romance:* It's important for you to have your *own* space—preferably, a home. With your name on the deed. You feel the urge to lay down roots, possibly fueled by ripening eggs or maturing spermies. No, you're not getting any younger. And yes, deciding to own a home will ground you—as would starting a family. The proverbial door is definitely open to you. Thing is, there's no guarantee what's on the other side. Some couples start in vitro fertilization—and end up on a reality show for having their own baseball team. Some start late in the game—and birth a child with a genetic disorder. Others fail to conceive despite their best efforts (literally or metaphorically). Whether blessing or bane, it all depends on your world view, values and personal philosophy. And buying a house? Could turn into a money pit.

Or the home of your dreams. Or mine subsidence could finally claim your residence. We just don't *know*. It's a cliché to say that it's the *journey* that counts, not the destination...but in this case, it's true. If you're a Stoic or optimist, you'll be fine no matter what. After all, Eden can be regained through an act of material grace (or, just as easily lost by bad attitudes or unrealistic expectations).

*Parenting*: A memory burned into my consciousness: I was in third grade. In the library. Reading a book. By myself. Mrs. Gray, the librarian—an old, crusty, serious woman with hard brown eyes and a perpetual frown on her face—walked over to me. *"My, my, my! Seems like you're turning over a new leaf!"* And she smiled at me. To this day, I'm not sure what my "old leaf" was (talkativeness? Wisecracks?), or why she felt the need to praise me—but I'll never forget it. It's just one of those frozen-in-time moments that bubbles up every once in a while. Like now. So, this tells me I have a message for you and your youngerlings: When the Ace of Coins comes up, be ready for someone (or some*thing*) to "turn over a new leaf". It may be a 180 in attention span, studies or interests. Or a clean bill of health. Or a sudden interest in books, nature, finances or physicality. The time is ripe and the seed is there. Nothing you can do to foster it or prevent it. Get ready.

*Spirituality:* Manifestation and even the Law of Attraction can be tricky things, in my opinion. I've seen good people (read: *saintly*) believe for food, money and even healing—and it doesn't come (even after praying for hours a day, meditating on scripture, trusting Jesus or "casting spells"). As popular as *The Secret* and related books have become, they're really just get-rich-quick schemes pandering to humanity's First Chakra materialism. Sure, there's some truth in attracting what you're vibrating—what you focus on does get bigger—but the keys are feeling states such as joy and gratitude. And for some people, they just won't vibrate happiness or thankfulness until they get what they want (*more, more, more!*). Which is a bit of a Catch-22, don't you think? Well, for them, it *is*. In the Old Testament, when the Jews were in the wilderness, God sent manna (heavenly bread, it's believed) *every* day...ensuring they wouldn't die from starvation. Funny thing, though: they couldn't collect it for the next day, let alone stockpile it. It would just disappear. There's a valuable lesson in this: we have what we need just for today. *Just for today.* Let that be your mantra. Who knows? Your proverbial breadbasket might catch some heavenly dough in that present-moment state of trust.

**Recommended Resource:** *Above Lake Superior* by Lawren Harris

**Ace of Coins Card Layout:** *Coin, Bulb and Bread* Spread

1. *Coin:* What material boon might I grant to someone?
2. *Bulb*: What beneficial thing was planted in my life?
3. *Bread:* What will sustain me today?

## 2 of Coins – An Octopus with Hives

**Stripped Down Overview:** Have you ever bent over backwards for someone, only to get it up the ass (with no lubricant)? Juggling day-to-day activities, you try to please everyone—but it just ain't happening. Robbing Peter to pay Paul, allocating a lump of money for rent while cobwebs form in your pantry, enduring a busted head gasket while car-pooling—it's enough to make a grown woman cry. But what choice do you have? Either pick up the pieces of broken dishes, vacuum the cat litter that Whiskers kicked three feet from the box, run lunch money to little Lucinda...or lay down and give up. You've come too far for that, though, right? Simplify if you can, delegate if you must—

but create a pocket of downtime in your overbooked schedule to catch your breath...because the neighbor kid is about to throw a baseball through your already-cracked window.

**Keywords:** Multi-tasking; Balancing the Checkbook; Improvisation; Shuffling Responsibilities; Moonlighting; Adaptation; Covering Your Bases; Shift Work; Coping with Alterations; Thinking on Your Feet; Trading; Bartering; Juggling Appointments; Swapping; Trading Scheduled Days; Substitutions; Spread Too Thin; Toggling Between Activities; Trying to Make Ends Meet; Parceling Out Attention

**Personifications and Embodiments:** Juggler; Harried Mother; Full Schedule; Busy Waitress; Inexperienced Substitute Teacher; Overwhelmed Fry Cook

**Quote:** *Imagine life as a game in which you are juggling some five balls in the air. You name them—work, family, health, friends, and spirit, and you're keeping all of these in the air. You will understand that work is a rubber ball. If you drop it, it will bounce back. But the other four balls—family, health, friends, and spirit—are made of glass. If you drop one of these, they will be irrevocably scuffed, marked, nicked, damaged, or even shattered. They will never be the same.* – Brian Dyson

**Challenge:** Harmony

**Gift:** Flexibility

**Occupations/Vocations:** Cirque de Soleil Performer; Accordion Player

**Disney Totem:** Tuck and Roll (*A Bug's Life*)

**Animal Symbol:** Bee

**Flower Essences:** Hornbeam (Bach); Peach-Flowered Tea-Tree (Australian Bush)

**Crystal/Stone:** Onyx Marble (Aragonite Calcite) – Promotes rhythmic development and flexibility. Encourages harmonious interchange between rest and activity. Makes one feel freer. Enhances sensitivity

**Aromatherapy:** Rosemary

**Body Parts/Systems and Health Issues:** Repetitive Strain Injury; Tendinitis; Carpal Tunnel Syndrome

**Mystical Messenger** – Julian the Hospitaller

**Sabian Symbol:** Aries 7 – A man successfully expressing himself in two worlds at once.

**Writing Prompt:** A ball juggles some humans.

**Affirmation:** I ably handle all tasks and appointments.

## Naked Advice for the 2 of Coins

*Career:* It's a mistake to focus on your weaknesses, trying to improve or fix them. If you hate public speaking, don't seek out jobs requiring it. If you suck at math, don't torture yourself by handling financial records. Instead, play up to your strengths. Pursue projects and positions that allow you to flex your naturally strong vocational muscles—endeavors that you could do "blindfolded" or "in your sleep". Compensate for weak spots by delegating to others—or volunteer to switch assignments for a better fit. There's a time and place to challenge yourself, expand your skill-set and take on less-than-desirable tasks. This isn't one of them.

*Romance:* Cooking, cleaning, errand running, trying to make ends meet—who has time for romance, right? If your fella's a real catch, he'll understand. And who said romance can't be mixed with everyday duties? Take him grocery shopping—and pinch his butt when no one's looking. Sneak in a few kisses while waiting for the kids to get out of ballet class. Flash a boob while he's fixing the sink. I'm telling ya, the hottest nights burn from the kindling of stolen moments! Hell, by the next evening, you may end up pounding more than tough meat on your kitchen counter...

*Parenting*: Time to stop playing parental hot potato: you can't keep spreading yourself thinner than Angelina Jolie's forearm. Explain to your children that you only have so much time, energy and money. They cannot have five extracurricular activities each. No, they get to pick *two*. No one benefits from frenzied appointments sustained over months at a time. Something (and someone) usually suffers. It may be sleep, quality time with the family, schoolwork or even physical health (not to mention your bank account). Learning to prioritize desires and choose wisely are worthwhile lessons in themselves. No one can be all things to all people—and we surely can't do every single thing we want to in life, even (and especially) as adults. Better he learns this lesson before his first semester in college, when his sense of invincibility and entitlement convinces him that he can maintain eighteen credits, a full-time job, a girlfriend, a first-string football position and drumming in a garage band semester after semester.

*Spirituality:* Approaching your spiritual life with a sense of play would do you much good. Imagine that life is a game, not an arduous journey, a hostile schoolroom or an exercise in self-abasement. What if, instead, our greatest revelations and meaningful moments come via recreation? Maybe it's time to switch out the Good Book for a coloring book, a rosary for a jump rope or mala beads for a bag of marbles. Experiment with what is possible. Try manipulating the quantum field and playing with intentions. Be curious about spontaneous miracles, the nature of light and the notion of manifestation. Explore parallel lives, past lives or even future lives. Redefine reality—and make your spiritual investigations the best circus in town.

**Recommended Resources:** "Lucy the Helpful Mother" (*Here's Lucy*); "Job Switching" (*I Love Lucy*)

**2 of Coins Card Layout:** *Jongleur* Spread

1.  What is in the air now? (Unsettled/Undetermined)
2.  What needs grabbing next? (Immediate/Important)
3.  What needs dropping? (Unimportant)
4.  What will help my grip? (Ability/Competence)
5.  What makes things too slippery? (Hindrances)
6.  Break Time (Consciously Pick a "Respite" Card for Focus)

## 3 of Coins – Measure Twice, Cut Once

**Stripped Down Overview:** If all else fails, read the directions. Or consult the manual. Or look at the friggin' diagram. Whether assembling a bike on Christmas day, installing new software on a computer or heading on a road trip with a specific destination in mind—know what the hell you're doing *beforehand*! Nothing wastes more time than rushing headlong into a project without considering the overall shape, function or *point* of it all. What precedes *informs* what is present now. In fact, in many cases, it's the foundation for what you see before you. At this stage, it's better to have *more* parts, input and tools at your disposal than a dearth. Whatever situation you find yourself in, it's best to live by the map...and die by the map.

**Keywords:** Following a Plan; Reading the Directions; Consulting a Map; Taking Advice from a Third Party; Seeking a Professional Opinion; Building on a Foundation; Freelance Work; Subcontracting; Sum Greater Than Its Parts; Consultation; Elevating Quality; Raising the Bar; Checklists; Business Plan; Personal Best; Teamwork; Protocols

**Personifications and Embodiments:** Blueprints; Maps; Diagrams; Human Pyramids; Balancing Stones; Art Using Natural Materials; Taxidermy; Woven Fabric; Archways; Instructions; Programs; Restaurant Kitchens; Apprentices; Textbooks; Keystones

**Quote:** *Without craftsmanship, inspiration is a mere reed shaken in the wind.* – Johannes Brahms

**Challenge:** Compromise

**Gift:** Design

**Occupations/Vocations:** Architect; Stone Mason; Brick Layer; Construction Worker; Interior Designer; Commissioned Artist; Remodeler; Draftsman; Mural Painter

**Disney Totem:** The Kids from *High School Musical*

**Animal Symbol:** Ant

**Flower Essence:** Turkey Bush (Australian Bush)

**Crystal/Stone:** Dalmatian Stone (Aplite) – Prompts one to plan carefully and reflect on every phase of development. Aids in carrying out plans with vigor. Has a fortifying, restorative and harmonizing effect.

**Aromatherapy:** Litsea Cubeba

**Body Parts/Systems and Health Issues:** "Sick Building" Syndrome; Asbestos Hazard; Mold or Dust Allergy

**Mystical Messenger** – Arachne

**Sabian Symbol:** Sagittarius 27 – The sculptor's vision is slowly but surely taking form.

**Writing Prompt:** A trio is hired to do a job, but only one knows the real objective.

**Affirmation:** Necessary tools nearby, I thoroughly understand the task at hand.

## Naked Advice for the 3 of Coins

*Career:* When mediocre results are lauded, half-assed efforts are rewarded or derivative works are popular, you may be tempted to call in a lackluster performance. Don't. Do. It. Yes, the troglodytic hoi polloi resemble voracious goats gnawing rubber tires or scarfing down tin cans. But don't pander to those pedestrian puddin' heads! Instead, value personal effort and excellence, knowing you did your very best—or even stretched beyond what you assumed were the limits of your capabilities. Others may never recognize or prize what you've accomplished, but you'll sleep well knowing that *you* know—and that you refused to reduce to the lowest common denominator. Besides, every "great" stands on the shoulders of those who came before, and your courageous efforts may very well form the scaffolding for a truly enduring contribution.

*Romance:* When it comes to relationship troubles, it's mind-boggling how many run to a friend, minister or psychic for advice instead of—you know—actually talking to their partner! Sure, there's a time to consult a priest or psychologist, but only after raw, respectful face-time has been attempted several times. Just like the old adage "too many cooks spoil the broth", so it is when conferring with umpteen outside sources—especially at the exclusion of engaging with your mate. Sit down, determine what you need in a relationship and share your findings with your partner. Ask him to do the same. Do you share similar priorities and desires? If so, how might you work to achieve them separately? Together? Put your pride aside and allow your partner to offer advice or help to get you back on track. Take care to sift the wheat of your personal values from the chaff of unrealistic ideals or, more insidious, the standards pushed by glossy magazines, fairytales or romance novels.

*Parenting:* When the 3 of Coins shows up, issues involving competence are popping up—either yours *or* your child's. Are you missing a few tools in your parenting toolbox? Don't deny or bury; instead, read some articles or books that address your (real or perceived) deficiencies. Even support groups can help bolster your parental game plan. Sometimes, realizing you're not alone in your trials to build a solid family provides the missing piece/peace! Also, take care to evaluate which "tool" you grab by default when communicating with your kid—*especially* in the areas of discipline, correction and rules. If your verbal pliers aren't doing the trick, consider a tape measure, level or piece of sandpaper to get your desired result.

*Spirituality:* Creative people often experience a peculiar kind of torment: what is the *purpose* of my art? Do I create for myself... or others? What is the meaning of life? Can I make a living from my creativity? How does that even *work* if I'm trying to focus on self-expression? How much discomfort or hurt is acceptable when pursuing a creative life? Is the pain coming from outside...or within? Is it really *worth* it? These are knotty existential questions that plug up our lower chakras. The 5th Chakra (Throat Chakra) wants to run wild with the 6th Chakra's visions, but we loop around to preoccupation with acceptance, validation, influence and material concerns (Chakras 1–3). There are no easy, definitive answers here. We must force life (and our art) to *mean*—and we are the ones that supply the "whys" and "what fors". Find your own personal reasons for being and creating, and let *that* be your map in unfamiliar territory.

**Recommended Resources:** *Listful Thinking* by Paula Rizzo; *Time* by Andy Goldsworthy; *The Creative Thinker's Toolkit* (The Great Courses) by Professor Gerard Puccio; *Life Purpose Boot Camp* by Eric Maisel

**3 of Coins Card Layout:** *Value of My Work* Spread

1. What do I need to know about my work?
2. Who might I consult for advice or wisdom?
3. What does the "Creative Me" need to know?
4. What do I need to know most about the practical aspects?
5. What is the spiritual dimension of my work?
6. How will I know when I've reached "The End" of a project/career?

# 4 of Coins – Scrooge You!

**Stripped Down Overview:** Tightwad. Penny-pincher. Cheapskate.

Skinflint. Money-grubber. Welcome to the constricted, rigid world of the miser—the one who never lets his family turn up the thermostat past 62 F in winter (*that's what sweatshirts are for!*) or turns down the hot water heater to tepid temperatures...all to save a few cents. I'm not talking about someone who's *actually* deprived, mind you—or a conservation-minded individual that wisely washes and re-uses plastic storage bags. No, I'm referring to someone who is poor-*minded*—so afraid of using up resources or running out of money, she curbs her quality of life (and that of those who live with her). *"A penny saved is a penny earned"* reflects the prudent side of the 4 of Coins (and, let's face it, some of you *desperately* need to rein in your spending!) but most times, this card implies stagnation—a Dead Sea of ratty couches on porches, treadless tires piled in the yard and stacks of old magazines obstructing your doorways.

**Keywords:** Stinginess; Hoarding; Financial Control; Scarcity Mindset; Withholding; Greed; Preservation; Miserly; Fear of Lack; Refusing to Share; Saving; Obsessed with Security; Owned by "Things"; Trapped by Gain; Stifled by Money; Stockpiling; Safeguarding; Paralyzed by Accumulation; Keeping; Isolated by Wealth; Conserving; Storing; Cash Only

**Personifications and Embodiments:** King Midas; Dollars Clenched in a Fist; Safes; Fire Box; Safe Deposit Box; Security System

**Quote:** *Everything that can be counted does not necessarily count; everything that counts cannot necessarily be counted.* – Albert Einstein

**Challenge:** Spending

**Gift:** Saving

**Occupations/Vocations:** Retirement/Long Term Investment Specialist; Accountant; Rarities Collector; Conservationist; Safety Deposit Box Teller

**Disney Totem:** Ebenezer Scrooge (*A Christmas Carol*)

**Animal Symbol:** Chipmunk

**Flower Essences:** Dog Rose (Australian Bush); Bauhinia (Australian Bush); Bluebell (Australian Bush)

**Crystal/Stone:** Yellow Chalcedony – Encourages contentment with very little. Promotes modesty. Aids in the discovery of simple solutions. Promotes stability in thought and action. Enhances joy.

**Aromatherapy:** Cardamom

**Body Parts/Systems and Health Issues:** Constipation; Uremia

**Mystical Messenger** – Sylvanus

**Sabian Symbol:** Aquarius 28 – A tree felled and sawed to ensure a supply of wood for the winter.

**Writing Prompt:** A re-telling of *A Christmas Carol*—where Tiny Tim is the villain.

**Affirmation:** My saving and spending is balanced, appropriate and fulfilling.

## Naked Advice for the 4 of Coins

*Career:* There is *more* than enough to go around. Seriously.

Any time you start to act like you have to "own" the corner of your market or niche—to the point that you're tracking every move, blog post or tweet made by your "rivals" with worried obsession—it's time to sit yo ass down and get some perspective. No author appeals to all readers. No Tarot reader appeals to all potential clients. No deck creator appeals to all oracle users. Got that? You weren't made to be "all things to all people", so attempting it is madness—especially when you try to poach customers, dis colleagues or ruin reputations in the process. After you get your ego in check, learn to play nice and share: share the glory, share credit, share your ideas, share time-saving tips, share good books, share via affiliate links, share stellar blog posts, share your admiration for those in your field, share via giveaways, share your encouragement... Get the point? When this card comes up for career concerns, it almost always points to ass cheeks clenched so tight you're practically turned inside-out. It's painful. It causes tension. It's based in fear of lack. So. *Stop*. It. Financial constipation will poison your whole system (and vocational prospects) if you *don't*.

*Romance:* How we treat what we own can impact our relationships—sometimes, in imperceptible, yet energetically significant, ways. For example, is your house more of a museum than a place to crash and relax? Are your cherry-wood side tables polished to a gleam and your kitchen floor clean enough to eat off? Is your couch and upholstered chairs uncomfortable to sit on—but, *damn!*, they sure do look pretty! Could it be that you never take out the "good" dinnerware or utensils for dining, let alone the crystal glasses your great-grandmother gave you? Let me ask you this: when will an occasion be "momentous" enough for you to bring out the fine china? Your death? Well, shit, you can't enjoy them *then*, now, *can* you? It's time to oil the wheels of usage in your house. Why? Because you come across uptight and anal. People are afraid to visit your house because they know they have to take off their shoes and mind any crumbs that may fall from the plate. And if they have small children? Oh hell *no*; they aren't going to risk the tykes breaking your Precious Moments collection or Capodimonte lamps! So...can you see how such attitudes may subtract enjoyment from your romantic relationships? Or, if you're unattached but seeking partnership, how ultra-preservation tendencies may repel, rather than attract, a mate? It's time to evaluate your relationship to "stuff"— because stuff like that can ruin a relationship.

**Parenting**: Check out this fascinating quote by Dovid Krafchow from his book *Kabbalistic Tarot*, specifically about the number Four: *Every baby comes into this world with a closed fist as if to say, "This world is mine", and leaves this world with an open hand as if to say, "Take it".* ::Cue the Bill and Ted *Whoa!*:: Thanks to ubiquitous toy and electronics advertising, kids are indoctrinated to *want, want, want* and *buy, buy, buy.* You can absolutely choose to pull the plug on TV programming to limit this insidious message that will follow them the rest of their lives and guide many of their adult choices (*yes*, it's possible—and *yes*, it does help). But most of you won't do that, so this means you'll have to do the hard work of actually sitting down with your children at a young age and explain to them—every few months, ideally—the whole supply-and-demand cycle...including *who* benefits from families purchasing thousands of dollars of junk that rarely gets used. When kids understand—I mean, *really* get it—that advertisers (and the companies that employ them) don't have their best interests at heart, realization may finally dawn...and they can make informed, conscious buying decisions when they get older (and better grasp now why you're saying "*No!*" to their pleas for the newest, hottest item hitting the shelves). Of course, you'll have to lead by example! *Ha!* Yeah, adulting sucks sometimes—but raising mindful kids that won't grow up to be hoarders or mindless consumers will be well worth it. (And here you thought I was going to tell you to teach your kids to share for this card! Well...do *that*, too.)

*Spirituality:* Before you buy another Tarot deck, altar set, spell kit or bag of crystals, ask yourself this: Have I *truly* learned from, used and integrated what I *already* have? With the dawn of Instagram—and the glut of oracular artistry—images of perfectly arranged cards, stones, candles and sage bundles enticingly scroll past our eyes at lightning speed. Facebook groups dedicated to Tarot, Lenormand or other decks also showcase Card-of-the-Day pulls and layouts from its members. Whether through peer pressure or just a conditioned magpie response, many are caught in the *"gotta-buy-that-deck!"* frenzy. And hey, I'm not above this: I used to own over 250 Tarot books (could only stomach a handful) and around 170 Tarot decks. And I'm *still* an enabler, recommending cool decks I find on Etsy or via a crowdfunded campaign to my pals on social media. But, a few years back, I came to the realization that not only wasn't I *using* any of those decks—but I hadn't really gone deep with the ones I *already* had. What a disservice to the artist and creator of the Tarot deck! What a disservice to *myself*. So I began selling off or gifting most of my Tarot stuff—and I'm down to around 50 decks and 135 books. I can feel a definite difference energetically. My relationship to Tarot has also deepened. And, I'm comforted by the fact that the decks and books I've given away or sold are in the hands of appreciative new owners. When you draw this card in relation to your spiritual path, it's time to examine how, and why, you feel a strong need to acquire—and hoard—mystical tools. Do you *really* need another deck? Or might your funds be better used elsewhere?

**Recommended Resources:** "Krabs a la Mode" (SpongeBob SquarePants Season 5); *The Stingiest Man in Town* (TV Show); *Kitab al-Bukhala'* (Book of Misers) by Al-Jahiz; *Ego is the Enemy* by Ryan Holiday

**4 of Coins Card Layout:** *4 Coins of Lack* Spread

1. *Coin One*: What am I afraid of losing in the material/ financial realm?
2. *Coin Two*: What am I afraid of losing in the reputation/ fame/success realm?
3. *Coin Three*: What am I afraid of losing in the emotional/ relationship realm?
4. *Coin Four*: What am I afraid of losing in the life purpose/ personal meaning realm?
5. *Eternal Coin*: Reminder of infinite abundance.

# 5 of Coins – Shit Out of Luck

**Stripped Down Overview:** This is a difficult chapter for me to write, quite frankly: it reminds me too much of my marriage to my first husband, John—a kind, simple, altruistic minister who looked like Rob Lowe and played the trumpet like Doc Severinsen. A health-freak who lifted weights, with eight percent body fat. We met when I was 15 and he was 18; half Italian and half Polish, he left the Catholic Church (much to his parents' chagrin), got "saved" and began attending my Assemblies of God church. Soon after I laid eyes on him, I told the girls in my youth group, *"Don't even think of looking at him. He's mine. I'm going to marry him someday."* And I did in 1989—when I was almost 19, and while we both attended Valley Forge Christian College. In 1995, John contracted leukemia. It was bad...*very* bad. The hematologist said she's never seen a white count that high (300K plus). Two days after diagnosis, when he was transferred to a cancer center in Pittsburgh, he collapsed in the shower—and busted out his front teeth and smashed some bones in his mouth. For an accomplished trumpet player, this is akin to a concert pianist getting their hands mangled in a machine. I stayed in the hospital room with him for six weeks as he received chemo.

No longer pastoring, we were in dire straits…and had to go on food stamps and government disability. "Christian" friends, who *we* were there for in their time of need, abandoned us. (What do you say to a man who preached faith healing, but is suffering with a dreaded disease?) When he got out of the hospital, before reconstructive surgery on his mouth, he looked a mess: bald, gaunt, pale, toothless. When we went to the grocery store, employees looked at us with disdain—as if we had some disgusting contagious disease (the shame of paying with food stamps made it doubly embarrassing). Long story short, John died a little over a year after diagnosis…two months before his 29th birthday. I watched him writhe, naked, as he suffocated to death in the hospital. So. My little story—shitty as it is—perfectly encapsulates the energy of the 5 of Coins on oh-so-many levels: it is poverty. Disease. Hunger. Homelessness. Treated like a subhuman. Viewed as a spiritual pariah. Feeling like you've been abandoned by the Universe. *"There but for the grace of God, go I"*, folks. Seriously. No one is untouchable when it comes to hardships like this.

**Keywords:** Poverty; Material Instability; Deprivation; Prohibitive Expenses; Disease; Destitution; On the Skids; Inadequate Clothing; Sub-Par Housing; Lacking Heat; Misfortune; Hunger; Sick and Uninsured or Underinsured; Scarcity; Needing Medication; Infection; Homelessness; Low Self-Worth

**Personifications and Embodiments:** Slums; Ghettos; Amnesty International; Doctors without Borders; Feed the Children; Domestic Shelter

**Quote:** *When a person is down in the world, an ounce of help is better than a pound of preaching.* – Edward Bulwer-Lytton

**Challenge:** Discomfort

**Gift:** Hope

**Occupations/Vocations:** Medical Supply Proprietor; Homeless Shelter Worker; Stained Glass Artisan

**Disney Totem:** Oliver (*Oliver and Company*)

**Animal Totem:** Rat

**Flower Essences:** Southern Cross (Australian Bush); Tall Yellow Top (Australian Bush)

**Crystal/Stone:** Red Aventurine Quartz – Helps make one hearty, hopeful and courageous. Aids in expressing needs. Encourages generosity. Promotes understanding and curiosity towards fellow humans.

**Aromatherapy:** Nutmeg

**Body Parts/Systems and Health Issues:** Malnutrition; Mineral Deficiency; Pica

**Mystical Messenger** – Margaret of Castello

**Sabian Symbol:** Leo 25 – A large camel crossing a vast and forbidding desert.

**Writing Prompt:** The Biblical figure Job gets revenge on his "comforters".

**Affirmation:** As long as I have breath, there is hope.

# Naked Advice for the 5 of Coins

*Career:* Although the 5 of Coins paints a dismal picture, much like Scrooge's Ghost of Christmas Future, it may only show what *could* be. Yes, it could indicate job loss and the unemployment line—or a significant reduction in income. It could even indicate a severe work-related injury. So what can you do? Try some preventative measures: make sure you wear safety goggles, cutting gloves, hardhat and steel-toed boots. Stay away from risky speculations, deals that sound too good to be true or heavy investments that could go south. Don't collaborate or partner up with someone that gives you pause. Take practical steps to increase your marketability (e.g., get additional certifications, education or experience). If there's a chance you could be laid off or fired, have a detailed back-up plan. Secure excellent insurance—homeowners, health, car and life. While no amount of preparation can ward off *every* eventuality, at least you can rest easier knowing you've covered your material bases (and maybe that's all this card needed you to do).

*Romance:* Even the most healthy, loving, mutually satisfying relationships suffer strain under circumstances like grueling vocations, low wages, neighborhood crime, disabled children, chronic pain or persistent illness. And truth be told, it can be difficult to resist being envious of others who seem to have it easier than you—especially if they appear to flaunt their good fortune all over Facebook, in church or while visiting relatives. Why you? *Why us?*, you may ask. Well, why *not* you? What makes you and your beloved so special? Couples suffer every day, all around the world—and most have it a *helluva* lot worse than you do. I say this not to be cold-hearted, but to give you a reality check: sometimes, suffering results more from how we *interpret* what's happening to us more than what is *actually* happening to us. When we assume we're "protected" somehow—

our lives stitched together with golden threads of entitlement and privilege—the greater the sense of betrayal, anger, shame and demoralization we tend to feel when our material life is squeezed, crushed or vaporized. Count your blessings—in fact, actively *look* for them—every single day. Try to find reasons to laugh (seriously, life on Earth *is* absurd). Chuck your bruised ego and exchange it for a humble heart. Find beauty. Hold on tight to your beloved and affirm together *it will get better*.

*Parenting*: In the RWS version of the 5 of Coins, the lame figure on crutches wears a bell around his neck, an indication that he has leprosy—a visible symbol that broadcasts "stay away or I may infect you". For whatever reason—a tragic incident, difficult upbringing, past-life echo, physical challenge, cruelty, disadvantage—some children feel branded, even *defined*, by what they went through (or are going through). It's tough enough to convince *adults* that they aren't their bank balance, clothes, house or appearance...let alone kids. And the fact that nine-, ten- and eleven-year-olds are hanging themselves in closets reflects the sad truth that they assume "it" will never get better. That they lack any redeeming qualities. That their worth isn't tied to external, material states. You're going to have to look to either spiritual or philosophical texts—perhaps even lessons from nature—to show them the beauty of inner qualities and the greater value of strength of character. If need be, get them to a qualified therapist specializing in treating youth. There's a house of worship featured in many versions of this card, but the destitute pair appear to be walking right past it—oblivious to the notion that help and refuge *is* available...and that they are worthy of standing shoulder-to-shoulder with the rest of humanity.

*Spirituality:* Humans are such silly creatures: so terrified of suffering, we attempt to control fate or prevent hardship by working out, taking vitamins, eating organic, going vegan, eschewing sugar, practicing meditation or doing yoga. Spiritually, we memorize scriptures, chant, pray, attempt to balance our chakras, cast protection spells, interact with crystals or wear "healing" amulets. We may even try to "be holy" according to our religion, following commandments, going to confession, making penance, performing charitable acts and sowing seeds of "good karma". *Good luck with all that.* My first husband, whom I told you about, was (on top of being super health-conscious) a *faith healer.* Seriously, he had *the gift of healing.* And never said an unkind word about, or to, *anyone.* Never smoked or drank. Didn't even cuss! Seriously, you couldn't *find* a better poster boy for clean living and righteous behavior. The point? When you get this card, don't think that you're *better* than others. More *evolved.* Protected from misfortune by your Law of Attraction vision boards or a colorful array of Post-Its featuring Bible verses or pastel-bathed oracle cards (*gilt-edged, no less!*) promising abundance, healing and Divine favor. If you shun those of "lower vibration" (i.e., the sick, the poor, the discouraged, the friendless, the meat-eaters—or those who have nothing to offer you in terms of advancing your wants), you'll want to have a ruthless check-in with your Soul...because you may find that your "perfect" facade is really just a *"white-washed tomb, full of dead-men's bones"* (as Jesus put it).

**Recommended Resources:** "Rose-Colored Stained Glass Windows" by Petra; *Winter's Bone* (Movie); *The Beggar Children* by Gustave Dore; *Journey of Souls* by Dr. Michael Newton; *Why Bad Things Happen to Good People* by Dr. James Dobson; *Courageous Souls: Do We Plan Our Life Challenges Before Birth?* by Robert Schwartz

**5 of Coins Card Layout:** *Stained Glass Windows* Spread

1. What "stain" do I most perceive in others?
2. How do I judge them for this "stain"?
3. How is their "stain" an integral (or beautiful) part of the human mosaic?
4. What "stain" in myself do I view with rose-colored glasses?
5. What does it *really* look like?
6. Secret door to the Cathedral of Inclusion:

# 6 of Coins – Give and Take

**Stripped Down Overview:** Granting a loan, tipping a waitress, dropping a fiver in the offering plate, applying for credit, exchanging chicken eggs for raw honey—whether bartering, borrowing and lending, the 6 of Coins is all about giving and receiving. Any time favors, money, services or goods change hands in equitable fashion, smooth transactions and satisfied participants are guaranteed. Sometimes, there's an imbalance with such exchanges—minimal ROI, usury, mooching, items not as described or shoddy workmanship. At least we have the review sites and social media to turn to when we're shafted! Even raising money or donating services for good causes fall under this card: kids going door-to-door to raise money for field trips, husband selling raffle tickets at work to help the VFD, businesses donating goodie baskets to a baseball team's Chinese auction, beauticians giving free makeovers to cancer patients—regardless of motive, such actions tend to beget feel-good emotions and satisfaction that one has *done her part*. Unfortunately, some want *more*...disdainful of what's received, while others expect a hand-out rather than a hand-up.

**Keywords:** Charity; Exchange of Goods; Welfare; Bartering;

Contribution; Handout; Giving; Receiving; Government Assistance; Donation; Borrowing; Lending; Credit; Financial Aid; Grants; Non-Profits; Stewardship; Fair Trade; Paycheck; Gains; Renting; Leasing; Symbiosis; Tips; Global Service; Material Influence; Wage; Pension; Patronage; Restitution

**Personifications and Embodiments:** Salvation Army; Goodwill; Blood Drives; Social Programs; WIC; Subsidies; Patreon; Co-Ops; eBay; PayPal, IndieGoGo; Kickstarter; Fundraising; GoFundMe; American Express; Mastercard; Department of Health and Human Services; Bail-Outs

**Quote:** *Sometimes our light goes out but is blown again into flame by an encounter with another human being. Each of us owes deepest thanks to those who have rekindled this inner light.* – Albert Schweitzer

**Challenge:** Worthiness

**Gift:** Generosity

**Occupations/Vocations:** Case Worker; Stock Broker; Financial Comptroller; Philanthropist; Loan Officer; Community Action Staff; Soup Kitchen Attendant

**Disney Totem:** Robin Hood (*Robin Hood*)

**Animal Symbol:** Dog

**Flower Essence:** Bluebell (Australian Bush)

**Crystal/Stone:** Pink Topaz – Promotes readiness to help others as well as self-love. Encourages strong social commitment and benevolence.

**Aromatherapy:** Hyacinth

**Body Parts/Systems and Health Issues:** Food Poisoning (Listeria, E. coli, Botulism, Salmonella, etc.)

**Mystical Messenger** – Saint Yves

**Sabian Symbol:** Pisces 5 – A church bazaar.

**Writing Prompt:** In the future, citizens are required to give as much as they take.

**Affirmation:** I can afford to be generous.

## Naked Advice for the 6 of Coins

*Career:* If you need an angel investor, financial backer, one-time gift or temporary benefactor, this card bodes well for you! As long as your credit rating and reputation are good, loans are likely to sail through without a hitch. If you're a solopreneur or head a non-profit, look for imaginative ways to raise awareness and money: crowdfunding, unusual fundraisers, publicity stunts (safe and legal!) or outrageous gimmicks. Too docile or shy for such exploits? Investigate little-known grants for apply for, as well as small biz incentives or loans offered by your local government. Avail yourself to the local Chamber of Commerce and press the flesh with like-minded proprietors: their wisdom, advice and connections will have you taking smartcuts to success. Also consider leveraging your talents and enthusiasm into board member positions with your local library, arts council or department of parks and recreation—any organization that's actually "giving back" to your neighborhood and making it a better place for everyone.

*Romance:* What is the sound of one hand clapping? Never mind, here's a better question: What is the color of one heart loving? There's a disparity in the Force when it comes to romantic relationships—and it's up to *you* to determine what it is. Who's keeping track of how many times *"I love you"* is said in a day? Who's tallying mistakes, omissions and absences? Who's withholding time, conversation or sex? Who's making the effort—and who's phoning in their role? Who fishes for compliments—and who can't be bothered to give them? In short, one-sided relationships *suck*. You can only get away with the excuse *"that's just how he is"* until your anger, disappointment and frustration begin seeping out in a lava of discontent—a mere precursor to the *"thar she blows!"* looming on the horizon.

*Parenting:* Worried about where the money's going to come from for your child's school supplies, extracurricular activities, educational hobbies or college tuition? This card encourages you to search high and low for help, because aid is available. Whether via government funding (set aside your pride), scholarships, community outreaches, yard sales, work study opportunities or used bookstores, hidden treasures await you and your progeny. Also, think about your neighbors, acquaintances and those you see frequently—as well as those who may be in a position to assist (e.g., a former teacher, principal, coach, scout leader, minister, professor, local politician, business owner, etc.). While you're at it, look for ways to aid another child or family in the same way you require: not only will you be sowing good Karma, but you'll teach your child the valuable lesson that resources are best spread around and shared...and that giving/receiving are two sides of the same abundance coin.

*Spirituality:* When we live according to the Threefold Law of Return—or consciously sow seeds of kindness, peace and love— we often expect the harvest to resemble our investment. Alas, this isn't how energy works. Material generosity may reap romantic harmony. Prayers of peace may result in the perfect job opportunity. Healing intentions may bring in a pair of jeans on sale. Refusing to participate in gossip just may reap the reversal of heart disease. Never measure what you've given to what you're getting—or already have. Gratitude, and trust in perfect, glorious karma, should underscore your spiritual practice right now.

**Recommended Resources:** *Pay It Forward* (Movie); *Leverage* (TV Series); *Helping Hands* by Gilbert and George; *Never Let Me Go* (Movie); *The Island* (Movie)

**6 of Coins Card Layout:** *Giving, Receiving, Accepting, Refusing* Spread

1. What am I giving right now?
2. What can I afford to give?
3. What can I *not* afford to give?
4. What am I receiving right now?
5. What do I need to receive?
6. What do I need to refuse?
7. Where is there an imbalance of power?
8. What will bring balance to the situation?

## 7 of Coins – Time for Inspection

**Stripped Down Overview:** Don't sneeze at that uncommon cold, spurn the suggestion of diet modification, shun a full medical exam at the doctor or laugh at the idea of an apple a day: the 7 of Coins encourages you to evaluate the physical realm, noting what's working...and what's *not*. This card also points to inspecting *any* aspect of the material plane for the purpose of improving, upgrading or scrapping: property, house, crops, investments, vehicles, furniture, clothes, decorations, flowerbeds, recipes, exteriors, hairstyle—you get the picture. What's in dire need of a tune-up? What's clogging up the flow of abundance (or your arteries)? What weeds are crowding out perfectly good vegetation? What might you plant, uproot, harvest—or raze altogether? And for God's sake, how many fucking shoes do you *need*, anyway?

**Keywords:** Inspection of Possessions; Taking Inventory; Diagnosis; Check-Ups; Forecasting; Debating on Whether to Continue Current Trajectory; Evaluating Livestock, Garden or Crops; Monitoring Weather; Assessing Monetary Value; Surveying Land; Pondering Return on Investment; Appraisals; Considering Where You've Been and Where You're Going; Prediction

**Personifications and Embodiments:** Farmer's Almanac; Weather Channel; Calibration; Testing Soil, Water or Atmosphere; EPA; Surveyors; Auditors; Evaluators; Early Detection Devices; Diagnostic Machines; Cleaning Out Closets; Decluttering; Tune-Ups; Home Inspection; Insurance; Spring Cleaning

**Quote:** *Life is a grindstone; whether it grinds us down or polishes us up depends on us.* – Thomas L. Holdcraft

**Challenge:** Neglect

**Gift:** Examination

**Occupations/Vocations:** Gardener; Insurance Adjuster; Car Inspector; Landscaper

**Disney Totem:** Rabbit (*The Many Adventures of Winnie the Pooh*)

**Animal Symbol:** Meerkat

**Flower Essence:** Gentian (Bach)

**Crystal/Stone:** Iron Nickel Meteorite – Aids in crosschecking personal intentions and aims. Renews outdated structures. Helps accept new ways of doing things. Promotes the questioning of existing values. Encourages materializing spontaneous impulses. Regulates muscle tension.

**Aromatherapy:** Lemongrass

**Body Parts/Systems and Health Issues:** Pesticides; Benzene Exposure; Soil Contamination

**Mystical Messenger** – Alicanto

**Sabian Symbol:** Scorpio 25 – An X-Ray helps with the diagnosis.

**Writing Prompt:** During a routine car inspection, a mechanic finds something that shouldn't be under the hood.

**Affirmation:** I take time to check in with my body, home and environment.

## Naked Advice for 7 of Coins

*Career:* Don't even think of cheating on your income taxes, pilfering office supplies or wasting company time by screwing around online, because you'll likely be caught red-handed for thefts big or small. While you're busy being an Honest Abe, also take stock of your current career or educational path. It's never too late for course correction—or for getting off the plane. If you can't see yourself doing what you're doing ten years hence, for any reason, consider stepping off that treadmill you mistook for a fast lane or highway to fulfillment.

*Romance:* It may seem unromantic to have a hard think about what you want in a partner or relationship, but it's important to write down those desired traits or states—and place your proverbial order with the Universe's Department of Love, Sex and Marriage. Think of it this way: if you aim at nothing, you'll hit it every time. The first step of manifestation is getting clear on what you want so that you can recognize it when you see it—and likewise steer clear of what *doesn't* fit the bill.

*Parenting:* Compensating for our own past inability to make the grade, chase a dream or achieve a goal by pushing our kids to "be more" puts unnecessary and undeserved pressure on them. Sure, we wish the very best for our children—and there's nothing wrong with having some expectations—but make sure they're adjustable ones that account for disposition, personality, innate talents and preferences. When it comes to steering the guidance boat, let their natural strengths take the helm. One day, they'll likely thank you for not wrecking their lives on the rocky shores of your dashed expectations and unfulfilled hopes.

*Spirituality:* Counting the cost—of an investment, decision or action—isn't always easy, especially since there's never any guarantee of a desirable or wished for outcome. As Roberts Burns wisely observed, *"The best laid schemes o' mice an' men, gang aft a-gley."* (Or, to put it in modern English, *"The best laid plans of mice and men often go astray."*) 'Twould be a pity to be halfway through life, only to realize you've been acting in the starring role of someone else's movie. Go within, find your own North Star and commit to authentic, self-defined fulfillment as the director of your *cinéma vérité.*

**Recommended Resources:** *We Bought a Zoo* (Movie); *Robots* (Movie)

**7 of Coins Card Layout:** *Life Audit* Spread

1. What physical/material aspect of my life needs evaluating?
2. What emotional aspect of my life needs assessing?
3. What attitude, assumption or belief needs reviewing?
4. What time/energy investment needs examining?
5. Which area of life requires more patience?
6. Which area of life requires more hope or faith?
7. Final advice/blessing.

# 8 of Coins – Do It Again. And Again.

**Stripped Down Overview:** In the movie *The Karate Kid*, martial arts expert Mr. Miyagi instructed his young protégé to do menial tasks such as waxing the car (*"wax on, wax off"*). Ticked off that his mentor wasn't teaching him to fight, but assigning him tedious cleaning jobs and repetitive tasks, the kid threw a tantrum. But what the master knew (that his student didn't...until later) was that these seemingly monotonous jobs were teaching muscle memory—and the basic foundational moves of karate. Or let's consider a prima ballerina: she doesn't secure her position and dazzle crowds by sheer luck or even raw talent: behind each exquisite performance lies repetitious barre exercises, grueling pointe work and thousands upon thousands of arabesques, pirouettes, entrechats, fouettés and jetés. And this, my friends, is the core of the 8 of Coins: grunt work and routine. Focus, sustained concentration, dedication and practice—these lead to mastery. Want to become an expert? There are no shortcuts. Sure, some may learn and progress faster, but unless you're, say, a piano prodigy by the age of five—you gotta put in the time and effort to become adept.

**Keywords:** Occupation; Perfected Procedure; Formula; Step-by-Step; Practice; Patient Application; Reproduction; One Thing at a Time; Training; Craftsmanship; Constructive Habits; Reliable Employment; Uniformity; Detailed Preparation; Simulation; Chipping Away at an Intimidating Goal; Absorption in a Task; Rehearsal; Repetition

**Personifications and Embodiments:** Piano Scales; Repetitive Exercises; Factories; Assembly Lines; Stencils; Sketching; Paint-by-Numbers; Engraving

**Quote:** *Habit is a cable; we weave a thread of it each day, and at last we cannot break it.* – Horace Mann

**Challenge:** Banality

**Gift:** Proficiency

**Occupations/Vocations:** Factory Worker; Craftsman; Engraver; Carpenter; Precision Machine Operator; Mass Manufacturer

**Disney Totem:** The Seven Dwarves (*Snow White*)

**Animal Symbol:** Spider

**Flower Essence:** Hornbeam (Bach)

**Crystal/Stone:** Black Spinel – Supports perseverance while fulfilling duties. Promotes disciplined, structured thinking. Focuses willpower on constructive approaches. Encourages modesty.

**Aromatherapy:** White Fir

**Body Parts/Systems and Health Issues:** Abnormal Cell Growth; Cancer

**Mystical Messenger** – Saint Eligius

**Sabian Symbol:** Scorpio 9 – A dentist hard at work.

**Writing Prompt:** A factory that manufactures custom pets.

**Affirmation:** I discover what works—and do it often.

## Naked Advice for the 8 of Coins

*Career:* In her excellent book for writers *Bird by Bird: Some Instructions on Writing and Life,* author Anne Lamott tells the story of her older brother who, when he was ten, had a report to write. The topic was birds, and the teacher gave the students three months to finish. Except that her brother waited until the *day before the report was due* to begin. Panicked and overwhelmed, he sat at the kitchen table—surrounded by unopened books on birds, reams of paper and pencils. Their dad put his arm around the son's shoulders and said, *"Bird by bird, buddy. Just take it bird by bird."* As a writer, I can't tell you how many times this story has encouraged me over the years. In fact, as I was writing this mammoth book, the excruciating, crushing enormity of my ambition felt like trying to level a mountain with a butter knife and trowel. I'd tell myself, *"Card by card, Janet. Just take it card by card."* Like a spider returns to spin the same web design even after wind or human tears it down, so we go back to our task—again and again—to do what we do best. Is it always easy? *Hell no!* Sometimes boring? *Hell yes!* But this is what expertise looks like, and arises from: sitting our ass down, practicing our craft and relentlessly pursuing mastery. It's showing up, refusing to "call it in" and doing the job...all because our integrity demands it.

*Romance:* Rome wasn't built in a day, and neither are solid, fulfilling relationships. You're making steady progress, so keep applying what you know, and have learned, about romantic satisfaction. However, now's not the time to go on cruise control: just like a healthy garden needs attention and nourishment, so, too, does your partnership or method for attracting a mate. It's important not to focus on what *seems* to work for your neighbors or colleagues, because you're only glimpsing the public facet of their relationship—not necessarily what goes on behind closed doors. Avail yourself to books, podcasts or blogs about romance and attraction, especially if they resonate, because learning additional ways to develop stronger bonds can enhance what you already have. If you're Facebook relationship status says "It's complicated", it's time to make it more straightforward and simplistic (if only in your head).

*Parenting*: If you have a son, nephew, grandson, little brother—or have babysat young boys—you probably know *Thomas the Tank Engine* and crew like the back of your hands. Sir Topham Hatt, the Controller of the railway system on the Island of Sodor, encourages and praises the trains when they are *"responsible, reliable and really useful"*. When the 8 of Coins chugs into your reading, it's time to evaluate what it means to be those three "R"s—and teach it to the younger set in both word and deed. Consistent practice and dogged dependability will outshine raw talent (and privilege) most times, so assign tasks of incremental difficulty to give kiddos a sense of confidence and accomplishment. How they perform the "little" things when young (e.g., homework and chores) can translate to how they go on to approach adult responsibilities. Likewise, show them how building upon past efforts can transform into a large creation—so provide jigsaw puzzles, Legos or Erector sets, crocheting supplies, quilting paraphernalia or paint-by-number kits for them to use.

*Spirituality:* With the assembly line, Henry Ford changed manufacturing history. Before his ingenious idea, many people would converge, all working together to complete one car (much like the 3 of Coins approach). But with an assembly line, stationed workers waited for the partially assembled car to reach them via conveyer belt. Each person performed one job...and one job *only*. Presently, assembly lines are still used, but robotic automation has largely taken over for humans. Sometimes, our spiritual practice is best approached by sections or compartments, especially if we yearn to see growth. For me, I use the Four Elements approach: if I'm too much in my head with thoughts, ideas and creative plans (Air)—with an abundance of passion, curiosity and energy (Fire)—I know from experience that I need grounding with nature, food and sensuality (Earth), as well as emotional connection, self-care, family time and long, hot baths (Water). Determine what's lacking, then take small steps to incorporate them into your routine. When you address your spiritual "pie" one slice at a time, you'll (eventually) feel more balanced and whole.

**Recommended Resources:** *New Yankee Workshop* (TV Show); "Working Man" by Rush; *Rachael Ray's 30 Minute Meals* (TV Show); *The Weaver* by Vincent van Gogh; *Ghostly Gourds* by Normal Rockwell; *I've Been Working on the Railroad* (Song)

**8 of Coins Card Layout:** *Personal Stamp* Spread

1. What is a defining hallmark of my work?
2. What has led to this trademark?
3. What can I do to enhance it even further?
4. What is likely to cause procrastination or decreased resolve?
5. How can I best prevent or cope with such a scenario?
6. Who or what needs my personal stamp most right now?

7. How can I bring my special touch to this situation?

8: Final Advice

## 9 of Coins – This is the *Life!*

**Stripped Down Overview:** I've noticed that this card *rarely* comes up in readings or within Tarot group discussions. Why? Because not many live *within* this realm of personal satisfaction, fulfillment of basic needs, savoring rewards from past efforts, enjoying the Arts or taking pleasure in the "finer" things in life. Nay, most people are either wanting or suffering—never content with *what is*, wishing things would be different, looking for something better, passively hoping that Fortuna's Wheel begins an upswing or whining about their lot in life. The 9 of Coins? The antithesis of all this dissatisfaction. Does a person have to be rich to experience this card? Absolutely not! Granted, it's easier to value and create art with a full belly and adequate shelter. And it's possible to adore luxury items without envy or yearning, even if it may be next to impossible to actually *own* them (this is known as "good taste"). And it is *equally* doable to appreciate your station in life, even if it doesn't match the world's idea of prosperity (because success is self-defined). By now, you've probably realized that this woman (it could be a man, but it's usually a woman) must have done a good bit of internal work to be so comfortable and satisfied with her status. She often *has*, dedicating her life to pursuing a treasure that doesn't rust, burn or wear out. But there are a few unusual folks who appear to be hardwired like this, almost like Athena springing fully-formed and armored from Zeus's brow. So *this* is why it's unlikely you'll see this card on a regular basis—but if the 9 of Coins *does* make its way out of your deck and into a reading, consider either yourself, or your client, *very* blessed.

**Keywords:** Autonomy; Luxury; Enjoying Abundance;

Refinement; Knowing Your Worth; Certainty; Wanting What You Have; Independent Means; Self-Defined Success; Savoring; Comfortable in Your Own Skin; Elegance; Good Health; Sovereignty; Valued; Supreme Satisfaction; Earned Rewards; Leisure; Discretion; Elite; At Peace with What Is; One with Nature; Ego in Check; Soaring Human Spirit; Opulence; At-One-Ment; Unbowed by Passions; Self-Acceptance; Financial Settlement; Bills Paid; Debt-Free

**Personifications and Embodiments:** Madame Rennard aka Lady Mae Loxley (*Mr. Selfridge* Season 4); Kitty Edwards (*Mr. Selfridge* Season 4); **Dr. Julia Ogden (*Murdoch Mysteries*)**; Rich Fabrics; Fabergé Eggs; Income from Royalties; "Living on Interest"; Self-Made Woman; "Kept" Woman

**Quote:** *He enjoys true leisure who has time to improve his soul's estate.* – Henry David Thoreau

**Challenge:** Privilege

**Gift:** Freedom

**Occupations/Vocations:** Animal/Wildlife Rehabilitator; Falconer; Aviary Attendant; Heiress

**Disney Totem:** Madame Adelaide Bonfamille (*The Aristocats*)

**Animal Symbol:** Peacock

**Flower Essence:** Five Corners (Australian Bush)

**Crystal/Stone:** Rainbow Fluorite – Stone of the freethinking spirit. Promotes inventiveness and flexibility. Aids in freedom of choice. Brings variety and emotional liveliness.

**Aromatherapy:** Rose Otto

**Body Parts/Systems and Health Issues:** Hay Fever; Tree Allergies; Rhinitis; Sinus Infection

**Mystical Messenger** – Marie Laveau

**Sabian Symbol:** Gemini 3 – The charming court life at The Garden of the Tuileries in Paris.

**Writing Prompt:** A man needs a certain woman who needs *nothing*.

**Affirmation:** I have what I want, and want what I have.

## Naked Advice for the 9 of Coins

*Career:* You *finally* get paid for work done—and perhaps even receive that (much delayed) recognition for your past amazeballs efforts. You may even obtain a financial settlement, endowment or fellowship that allows you to pursue your dreams. In fact, you're so comfortable at this point, you'll be able to turn *down* work—only taking on projects that truly intrigue and inspire you. Your finances and career are solid: everything from here on in is just window dressing. Thus, you may choose to upgrade or beautify your workspace as you coast along. Or, you may decide to take time off to renovate your home (*New kitchen! In-ground pool! Gorgeous landscaping!*)—or simply take a sabbatical to paint landscapes, read the classics (that you never got around to) or bird-watch in your backyard.

*Romance:* Quite simply, this is a woman who likes her own company. She doesn't *need* you, so if she *wants* you, consider yourself lucky. It's not that she considers romantic partners playthings (although I suppose that's possible); no, in most cases, she's just so used to being self-sufficient and relatively isolated that she doesn't have a longing to be attached. The best way to approach such a person is to be a self-reliant, self-made "wo/man of the world", because "demanding" and "possessive" aren't in her vocabulary—and won't be tolerated in others. However, in *Tarot for Grownups* (also published by Dodona Books), Amythyst Raine paints a slightly different picture of this woman, noting, "*I don't care how comfortable it is, who in the hell wants to be caged—even if it is gilded.*" She then shares a story of a medical doctor's wife who came to her for a reading: well groomed, nicely dressed and not in want of anything materially—except for her freedom. Turns out that her now-ex dumped her for a younger model, but while married, she was forced to abandon a budding career as a sculptor and, instead, run a health food store as unpaid hired help. Raine considers this a type of abuse and encourages readers to not judge from appearances because that gilded cage "*may be an absolute frickin' nightmare if you're on the inside looking out*". While this hasn't been my experience with the 9 of Coins, I bow to my colleague's years of Tarot reading experience—because it may be the interpretation *you* need when this card comes up.

*Parenting*: Not only is it unusual for the 9 of Coins to show up in a reading, it's *especially* so when it pertains to kids. Why? Because unless you have a child prodigy or super-young entrepreneur with independent means, most kids haven't the life experience yet for this leisurely state (unless, of course, she has a great head on her shoulders...and is seeking parental emancipation). One of the Keywords for this card is *Earned Rewards*—especially the enjoyment that comes from them. So if kiddo receives some tangible swag for a major accomplishment, let her relish the booty: doing so won't spoil her or lead her to believe that future income or accolades will come just as easily. Instead, it will teach her that hard work *can* yield eventual pleasure—

and that confident self-reliance will pave the way. (P.S. If your progeny has the grades and gumption to aim for the Ivy League or some other top college...tell her to *go for it!*, because this is an auspicious card for the best schools.)

*Spirituality:* You've come to realize that the most powerful and satisfying spiritual experiences aren't found in a conference hundreds of miles away or a retreat thousands of miles away or in the presence of expensive Himalayan salt lamps, authentic Tibetan singing bowls, chunks of rare crystals or specially-charged accoutrements. Rather, a supreme sense of well-being arises from within, resulting in a greater appreciation of nature, animals and your surroundings. In fact, you feel the Divine broadcasting messages through pets, trees, clouds, gardens and wildlife on a regular basis—as well as when you use your hands to cradle, nurture or create. Any religious or esoteric training you've had comes full circle: complete illumination from these studies dawns on you...and stays.

**Recommended Resources:** *Lilacs* by Alex Grey; "Self-Reliance" by Ralph Waldo Emerson; *Mr. Selfridge* (Season 4); Vogue Cover March 15, 1927 by Georges Lepope

**9 of Coins Card Layout:** *Life of Leisure* Spread

1. What will it take to experience internal contentment?
2. What will it take to achieve self-reliance?
3. What will it take to obtain financial prosperity?
4. What will it take to fully appreciate the Arts?
5. What will it take to embody good health?
6. What will it take to enjoy material comforts?
7. What will it take to live a life of leisure?

# 10 of Coins – Family Trees, Genes and Money

**Stripped Down Overview:** Lower the disco ball, channel Wolfman Jack and cue up the vinyl with Sister Sledge's "We Are Family", because the 10 of Coins puts the "fun" in dys*function*. Blood that's thicker than water courses through this card's veins, infusing its energy with matters of heritage, ancestry and heirlooms. From brooches to silverware, patchwork quilts to DNA, property to manors, debt to feuds, "things" get passed down and around when this card turns up. Family may fight like hell on their own turf, but woe is the outsider that targets kin and kith! As soon as the bull's-eye or crosshair falls on a relative's ass, *"the enemy of kinfolk is an enemy of mine"*. Flying a flag featuring the family crest, displaying the ancestral coat of arms, prancing about in the clan's tartans, bragging about bloodlines going back to Adam himself—"proof" and pride of pedigree are parcel part of tribal loyalty. Scads of money tend to paper this card, too, with a wealthy King of Coins multiplying the family holdings while presiding over his dynastic brood (sometimes, with bought titles like "Duke" or "Earl").

**Keywords:** Extended Family; Lineage; Pedigree; Ancestors; Wealth; "Old Money"; Legacy; Inheritance; Tribalism; Heredity; Bequests; Family Estate; Relatives; Nepotism; DNA; Family Tree; Congenital; Herd Mentality; Roots; Genealogy

**Personifications and Embodiments:** *Dynasty; Falcon Crest; The Waltons*; Hatfields and McCoys; Montagues and Capulets; Family Feuds; Mormons; Tribal Factions; Erinyes

**Quote:** *If you cannot get rid of the family skeleton, you may as well make it dance.* – George Bernard Shaw

**Challenge:** Enmeshment

**Gift:** Connection

**Occupations/Vocations:** Genealogist; Antiques Dealer; Family Therapist

**Disney Totem:** Django (*Ratatouille*)

**Animal Symbol:** Gorilla

**Flower Essence:** Dagger Hakea (Australian Bush)

**Crystal/Stone:** Bloodstone

**Aromatherapy:** Storax

**Body Parts/Systems and Health Issues:** Hereditary Disease; Genetic Disorders; Congenital Disorders

**Mystical Messenger** – Agathos

**Sabian Symbol:** Virgo 14 – Finely lettered names and mysterious lines are seen; it is a family tree.

**Writing Prompt:** A member of a wealthy family hatches a plot.

**Affirmation:** I assert my individuality while embracing my tribe.

## Naked Advice for the 10 of Coins

*Career:* You may experience outside pressure to take over the family business, enter the same career as Granddaddy or follow in the vocational footsteps of Auntie—but it's up to *you* if you're going to be a lemming or break from the fold. When it comes to job or college, family name, reputation and/or money could help slide your foot in the door, but that kind of influence isn't guaranteed to keep you inside the building. If you're in a position to hire, take on an apprentice, mentor or give a financial "hand up"—look to your gene pool *first*.

*Romance:* I'm going to assume that kissing cousins and the risk of four-eared children are out of the question, so let's consider casting your romantic net outside the family tree. Your father's co-worker, brother's roommate, uncle's neighbor, mom's hairdresser—hit up *la familia* for introductions, blind dates or "chance" meetings. Be bold in asking relatives to dish on potential matches and trust their recommendations. After all, they know you best.

*Parenting:* Whether you intend to or not, your "hand me downs" may be more than worn corduroys, faded KISS shirts or your older children's cast offs. What will be your legacy, likely manifested through your kids' attitudes, choices and worldview? Parents pass on more than genes and jeans, so take time to examine how your beliefs, words and actions might be setting up a bequest you'll be proud of...or come to regret.

*Spirituality:* At core, you are not a congenital illness, an inherited set of traits or a rattling pile of closeted skeletons. Yes, we are products of our upbringing—but we are not beholden to it. Embrace the gifts of your heritage (even the ones that came in yucky packaging), but cast off any projections or expectations that don't fit your wild, fabulous, unique soul. Surrender any blame or resentment connected to kin so your spirit may soar past their mistakes—and fly into your self-created destiny.

**Recommended Resources:** *Dallas* (TV show); *Freedom from Want* by Normal Rockwell

**10 of Coins Card Layout:** *Family, Oh Family!* Spread

1. How do I view my ancestors?
2. What do I need to know about them?
3. How can I best honor (or recover from) my lineage?
4. What is my concept of family?
5. What is my role/contribution to family?
6. Blessing from my family of origin.
7. Blessing I'm passing on.

# CUPS

## Ace of Cups – My Cup Runneth Over

**Stripped Down Overview:** Deeply internal and personal, the Ace of Cups cradles new dreams, fresh emotions, overflowing feelings and chances for love. Expansive, rising and effervescent, most of the sensations associated with this Ace are positive and uplifting—and yet, it's also the card symbolizing having a "good cry". When it comes to emotion, a fine line often separates joy and pain, especially when this card comes up (largely for the sense of relief it brings). Michel de Montaigne once said, *"The most profound joy has more of gravity than of gaiety in it."* Because this is a rather narrow, specific card when it comes to interpretations, it's challenging to write an overview that doesn't repeat the words "joy", "love", "intuition", "feeling" and "compassion"! Just know that good things are likely to come your way when this card pops up in a reading—but you have to remain open in order to benefit.

**Keywords:** Opportunity for a Wholesome Relationship; Pure Love; A Chance to Forgive; Flood of Emotion; Adoration; Expecting Goodness; Healing; Upsurge of Compassion; A New Feeling; Birth; Poignancy; Spiritual Renewal; Beauty; Tender Self-Expression

**Personifications and Embodiments:** Artesian Well; Spring Rain; A Flower's First Bloom; Toasting a Happy Event; Well Wishes; Pregnancy Test Shows +

**Quote:** *Never lose an opportunity of seeing anything that is beautiful, for beauty is God's handwriting—a wayside sacrament. Welcome it in every fair face, in every fair sky, in every fair flower, and thank God for*

*it as a cup of blessing.* – Ralph Waldo Emerson

**Challenge:** Openness

**Gift:** Refreshment

**Occupations/Vocations:** Sommelier; Fountain Designer; Plumber; Pool Supplier; Bird Bath Manufacturer

**Disney Totem:** Mama Odie (*The Princess and the Frog*)

**Animal Symbol:** Blue Whale

**Flower Essence:** Little Flannel Flower (Australian Bush)

**Crystal/Stone:** Rose Crystal – Stimulates the ability to love. Comforts. Affords emotional protection. Enhances warm treatment of self and others. Supports sensitivity.

**Aromatherapy:** Myrtle

**Body Parts/Systems and Health Issues:** Dehydration; Water Retention

**Mystical Messenger** – Castalia

**Sabian Symbol:** Gemini 7 – An old-fashioned well with the purest and coldest of waters.

**Writing Prompt:** A magical cup heals a village.

**Affirmation:** I am open to joy, beauty, love and healing.

## Naked Advice for the Ace of Cups

*Career:* It's unusual when this card comes up in a career reading, but when it does, the Ace of Cups heralds a time of renewal — usually, on the cusp of a joyous surprise. You may find yourself opening to compassion, even towards difficult colleagues or clients. Often inexplicable, these doorways can revive your current trajectory, much like the "Refresh" option on an internet browser or the "Restart" button on your PC — but it all happens internally, from a deep place. Some would call it "spiritual" or "soul level" or even "profoundly intuitive". In some ways, it's the opposite of the River Lethes: instead of forgetting, you remember...*something*. When this remarkable occurrence is work-related, know that **1.** It is rare **2.** It is an invitation **3.** You will spiral "upward" if you act upon it. A cascade effect will result, likely blowing your Heart Chakra wide open.

*Romance:* If you're in the market for the blush of first (or new) love, this Ace is most auspicious. I doubt it's a rekindling of an old flame (look to the 6 of Cups for that), or even the resurrection of an existing relationship (Judgment and 2 of Cups for that scenario), although you *may* plan for a renewal of marriage vows if this card shows up in tandem with The Lovers. No, this is usually *the brand-spanking-new* romance card — the chance meeting in the elevator (that leads to a number exchange), the "missed connections" section of Craig's List (yes, your airplane seat mate *did* notice your smile!) or the new guy in church with the baby blue eyes that keeps flashing you a kind, genuine smile. It's way too early to even *think* about long-term commitment, let alone ask about it in a Tarot reading (I'm looking right at you, reading your mind) — but *do* enjoy the flirting...because it may be all that comes from this coquetry.

*Parenting*: As a homeschooling mom and an avid proponent of educational reform, I'm a strong believer in following interests "just for the love it". Most people who are good at what they do, and enjoy it, have gotten where they're at because of pursuing pure delight. In fact, the word amateur really means "for the love of it" (not necessarily a novice or unpaid worker). When your child expresses irrepressible curiosity—such as a desire to learn an instrument, buy a book on a "frivolous" topic, visit a library or museum, get a set of paints, join a local theater, study "just rocks" or map the stars—encourage and indulge him. Doesn't matter if the pursuit meets any "core curriculum" goals of an institution or moves him closer to a scholarship (in the area of study *you* think best). Most public schools don't even consider "love" for a topic as a prime motivator: instead, they look to grades, threat of punishment or the job market or "future employability". *Yuck!* The ones who will excel in the modern marketplace are the passionate, the focused and the determined...and what better way to be *all* these things than to love what you do?

***Spirituality:*** Ritual purification, funeral rites, hand washing, baptism—hell, even exorcism!—there's no denying the powerful symbolism of water. In *The Woman's Dictionary of Symbols and Sacred Objects*, Barbara G. Walker provides many historical examples:

> *"Water of Life" was once identified with the cosmic womb, "the Deep" of many different creations myths. To Thales of Miletus, water was the* arche, *the First Cause at the beginning of all things. Zosimus said, "Without divine water, nothing exists"...Hindu compendia like the Tantrasara declared that baptism in water was more effective than any mantra or prayer for protection against enemies, catastrophes and evil spirits.*

Your challenge, should you choose to accept it, is to intuit ways that *you* can use water as a part of your personal spiritual practice. Will you add a small cup of distilled or fresh spring water to a tabletop altar, perhaps alongside a picture of your favorite saint or savior? Take cleansing baths to wash off the "bad vibes" (don't forget the Epsom salts)? Scry into a silver bowl to discern deeper truths? Create homemade flower or crystal essences?

**Recommended Resources:** *The Titan's Goblet* by Thomas Cole; "On Joy and Sorrow" by Khalil Gibran; "A Song of Joys" by Walt Whitman; "Ode to Joy" by Beethoven

**Ace of Cups Card Layout:** *Waters of Life* **Spread**

1. What needs purifying in my life?
2. What needs cleansing, blessing and then burying?
3. What needs renewing and refreshing?
5. What needs exorcizing?
6. Where to look next time I need a dose of joy.

# 2 of Cups – Soul Mates

**Stripped Down Overview:** Love at first sight is dubious, but according to Professor Arthur Aron of State University of New York at Stony Brook, two people could experience a relationship "closer than the closest relationships in their lives"...in *less* than one hour. Pairing random heterosexual psychology students (those who disagreed on strongly held beliefs, screened beforehand, were not matched), each couple was brought into the lab, seated at a table across from one another, and then asked to read—and answer—36 questions over a 45-minute period. Each question became increasingly personal, requiring major levels of self-disclosure and exposure, not to mention trust. At the end of the Q and A session, the pair sat quietly, staring into one another's eyes. *Thirty percent* admitted that this new "relationship" was closer than the closest ones they already had. Many pairs in the study stayed close friends afterwards. Six months later, one pair got married—and invited all the study participants to the wedding. Intrigued by Aron's results, writer Mandy Len Catron asked a blind date to do the experiment with her (after they had visited a local museum, they went to a bar to replicate the Q and A—then went outside, on a bridge, to do the whole "look deeply in the eyes" thing). Guess what happened? Yep, they began dating...and fell in love. This, my friends, is the realm of the 2 of Cups: it's not infatuation (Knight of Cups), it's not lust (Devil) and it's *certainly* not an arranged marriage, contracted pairing or coupling based on social or financial advancement (Lovers). It's vulnerability. Honesty. Deep connection. Trust. In other words...*intimacy*.

**Keywords:** Intimacy; Deep Connection; Emotional Bonding; Supreme Closeness; Peace; Relational Fulfillment; Soul Mates; Mutual Admiration; Loving Someone "Warts and All"; Courtship; Simpatico

**Personifications and Embodiments:** Loving Couples; "Bosom Friends"; Anne Shirley and Diana Barry (*Anne of Green Gables*)

**Quote:** *Your task is not to seek for love, but merely to seek and find all the barriers within yourself that you have built against it.* – Rumi

**Challenge:** Separation

**Gift:** Familiarity

**Occupations/Vocations:** Wine Steward; Waiter/Waitress; Marriage Counselor; Honeymoon Resort Specialist

**Disney Totem:** Carl and Ellie Fredericksen (*Up*)

**Animal Symbol:** Leopard Slug

**Flower Essence:** Bush Gardenia (Australian Bush)

**Crystal/Stone:** Star Rose Quartz – Promotes openness, intimacy, helpfulness and romance. Enhances living together in harmony.

**Aromatherapy:** Carnation

**Body Parts/Systems and Health Issues:** Mononucleosis; Herpes Simplex; Canker Sores

**Mystical Messenger** – Mirabai

**Sabian Symbol:** Aquarius 15 – Two lovebirds sitting on a fence and sitting happily.

**Writing Prompt:** Soul Mates in space.

**Affirmation:** I open up and share my heart.

## Naked Advice for the 2 of Cups

*Career:* This may seem an odd card to get in answer to a career question, but it happens! You're being encouraged to share your feelings on a matter—perhaps even your deepest fears about a project or the job itself. By unloading what's going on outside of you with a colleague or manager—getting it out in the open calmly, simply and honestly—a new sense of clarity and closeness will be invited to the scene. It may be that you need to confide what's going on in your vocation with your spouse or a bosom buddy, so that an outside perspective can arise. Look for ways to be authentic and vulnerable in your work to promote more satisfying connections with your clients and colleagues.

If disagreements or conflicts are a concern, look for common ground—and then focus on, and build up, that mutuality.

*Romance:* Aw *hell!* Why in the name of God do you need to consult the Tarot about a relationship when *this* card comes up? You've got it *made,* baby! Well...not *quite.* But you're close! This is the most auspicious card in the deck when it comes to deeply rewarding relationships. But if you're getting the 2 of Cups, even when already in a relationship, it often signals one of two things: First, you're in a solid relationship—but you want to go deeper. In this case, you're being called upon to lay your soul bare and stop holding back...because what's *unsaid* is creating an emotional obstruction (that will only increase over time). The second scenario is that you crave a sense of comfort and closeness—but you're not getting that because your partner can't seem to find extra minutes to spend quality time with you. As a result, you feel pretty low on her priority list. In this case, you must share how you feel and what you want. If you have, and nothing's changed, suggest couple's counseling. If that doesn't work—well, you deserve better. And there is someone out there that will love you exactly for who you are—and give you the affection and respect you deserve. Now what if you're unattached, but you've met someone who seems awesome—or, you haven't met anyone *yet,* but you wonder if you will? Again, we're looking at the best card in the deck for this question—so don't blow it! Remain open, curious, trusting and soft to all who drift into your orbit. (By the way, I've seen this card come up when a straight, married woman is close friends—*simpatico*—with a gay guy. So, it's not *always* a romantic entanglement card but, well, a *soul-mate* one.)

*Parenting:* *Aaaaand* your kid wants to date. *Ack!* The Minor Arcana 2s fall within the Kabbalistic Tree of Life's sephirah *Chokmah*—the realm of pure wisdom. Knowing when to allow your kids to date—and under what circumstances—will take a shitload of common sense and heart knowledge on your part. If you haven't already, now's the time to start talking about "saving yourself" for a good, solid person—as well as what it means to be open, honest and vulnerable with another. The biblical phrase *Don't throw your pearls before swine* would be a nice teaching tool here, but you're going to have to define "swine" wisely (if you categorize porcine individuals according to social status, family income, religion or race—get someone more progressive to advise the kiddos, K?). Now age—that's something different, obvs. IMO, if your kid is under 14 and wants to date, chaperone them. Older than that? I hope to hell you've already schooled them on healthy relationships and what they entail. Also, it's important for the younglings to recognize that naked selfies and social media attention-whoring are NOT equivalent to vulnerability or authenticity (after all, any exhibitionist can rip her clothes off at a moment's notice)—and one of the *last* places you'd want to find a date is via Instagram or Snapchat.

*Spirituality:* Intimacy with the Divine has been a theme among poets like John Donne, Hafiz, Rumi and the author of the *Song of Solomon*. All of them, though, were monotheists. How does one cultivate intimacy with the Divine when pagan? A deep connection could be forged via ritual, contemplation, meditation and/or devotion to a deity, pantheon, ancestors or nature Herself. Spiritual practice can be rigid and structured—or emotional, intuitive and mystical. Atheists aren't left out in the cold, either: they often have a spiritual life as well, but instead of a Divine as Source, they're fueled by an affinity for the earth, science and humanity. Whatever the "Other"—a Deity or a person or even humanity in general—love, self-discovery and growth are often forged in the crucible of relatedness. You're being encouraged to examine how you relate—and the depth of your relationships (human or otherwise). How might you be more open? More vulnerable? More emotionally *honest*?

**Recommended Resources:** *Frank and Ollie* (Movie); *The Fountain* (Movie); *Ocean of Love* by Alex Grey; *The Kiss* by Gustave Klimt; *Personality and Social Psychology Bulletin* Vol. 23, No. 4, 1997 (Study by Professor Arthur Aron) ; New York Times article "Modern Love: To Fall in Love With Anyone, Do This" by Mandy Len Catron (1/11/2015); *The Art of Asking* by Amanda Palmer; *The Singing Butler* by Jack Vettriano

**2 of Cups Card Layout:** *The Cost of Vulnerability* Spread

1. How can I be more vulnerable to others?
2. How do I hold back from those I love?
3. How does holding back from loved ones affect them?
4. How does holding back from loved ones affect *me*?
5. How does holding back affect interactions with the world at large?
6. How is vulnerability beneficial to me?
7. How is vulnerability detrimental to me?
8. How will I gauge if it's worth it?
9. How will I gauge if it's *not*?
10. Final Advice

# 3 of Cups – Party!

**Stripped Down Overview:** Donning low-cut dresses with hems barely below the bush line and four-inch heel *fuck me* shoes (toddling about with the gait of drunken flamingos), the gals get together for a "good time". Blowing off steam, gossiping about neighbors, dishing on the new guy at work, bitching about husbands or flaying interfering in-laws, such gatherings can spiral from frivolous decompression to a toxic scuttlebutt. Rare but glorious to find a group of women celebrating their successes and each other! And the guys? Huddled together at sports bars, the American Legion or VFW, their exchanges range from sullen silence, grunts or obnoxious guffaws. While female convos spread far and wide (like their legs), the fellas stay within a narrow range of sports scores, asshole bosses, dickwad politicians, hunting kills and the T&A that just walked by. Everything's "let down" in the 3 of Cups: our guard, our expectations, our inhibitions. In fact, in the *Snowland Deck*, this card shows three Japanese snow monkeys lounging in warm springs, drinking cocktails, while one of them lets off a fart (as evidenced by the surfacing bubbles behind it). Laughter and gaiety tends to infuse this card, so minds, hearts and mouths tend to be much more open than usual. Thus, an abundance of words (especially fueled by too much *vino*) could flow into a ten-car pile-up of innuendo, insult and hurt feelings.

**Keywords:** Celebration; Partying; *Squee!*; The More the Merrier; Informal Gatherings; Cliques; Gossip Sessions; Support Groups

**Personifications and Embodiments:** TGIF; Clubbing, Happy Dance; Slumber Parties; Bromances; New Year's Eve Revelry; Super Bowl Festivities; Happy Hour; Ladies' Night; Strip Clubs; Circle Jerks; Coffee Klatches

**Quote:** *Friendships begin with liking or gratitude—roots that can be pulled up.* – George Eliot

**Challenge:** Segregation

**Gift:** Gaiety

**Occupations/Vocations:** Vineyard Owner; Wine Maker; Distillery; Brewery; Home Party Consultant *(Tupperware, Avon, Home Interior, Pampered Chef, etc.)*

**Disney Totem:** Thomas O'Malley (*Aristocats*)

**Animal Symbol:** Bonobo (Pygmy Chimpanzee)

**Flower Essence:** Heather (Bach)

**Crystal/Stone:** Lapis Lazuli – Promotes friendship and sociability; Encourages honesty and dignity; Helps one tell, and accept, the truth

**Aromatherapy:** Melissa

**Body Parts/Systems and Health Issues:** Alcoholism

**Mystical Messenger** – Uzume

**Sabian Symbol:** Virgo 27 – Aristocratic elderly ladies drinking afternoon tea in a wealthy home.

**Writing Prompt:** A group of women go out to a popular bar to celebrate...but no one's inside.

**Affirmation:** I allow myself to relax and celebrate with others.

## Naked Advice for the 3 of Cups

*Career:* Work in an office with others? You know how tricky human interactions can be, especially with the dynamics of employer/employee, reward/punishment, inclusion/exclusion, pay inequities and politics. When this card comes up, you'll be tempted to share (vent?) your feelings—especially ones laced with tears. Trust me: the workplace is *not* the place to do so! Lest you be labeled a crybaby at best or unstable at worst, confide in a close friend or mate, instead. Otherwise, you may be causing irreparable damage to your position or reputation. However, if you've had it up to your eyeballs with office bullshit—and are ready for a new job or career—let 'er rip!

*Romance:* Sharing, caring...if polyamory and the idea of "sisterwives" appeals, then this is the card for *you*! Apart from "ethical slutdom", there's a really good chance of meeting someone special at a bar or party, especially if there's large quantities of social lubricants going around. This is a "thinking with the dick" card, though, so birth control is a must if you want to remain childless. The 3 of Cups is also the "just friends" card when it comes to romance, so while he may be into your pants...he's just not that into you when it comes to emotional intimacy or commitment. Beware of orgiastic frat parties (the possibility of unwanted advances multiplies exponentially), as well as ecstatic "too good to be true" emotions (it probably is).

*Parenting:* The 3 of Cups involves "sharing", but because kids and teens have yet to achieve brain/heart/pee-pee alignment (thanks to immaturity and hormones), there may be some *over* sharing going on. Shirtless selfies? Check. Late night chat sessions with bigdick4u? Double check. Divulging personal information to complete strangers (including physical location, blood type and social security number)? I'm tellin' ya...kids can be socially *stoopid*! Pay attention to sudden changes in behavior, especially sleep patterns, eating and moods—because the kiddos may be sharing in ways and times that's robbing them of self-respect and well-being.

*Spirituality:* There's something intoxicating about high-energy worship or lively gatherings centered around praising God, glorifying deities or honoring Nature. Whatever your spiritual path, consider attending a communal meeting convening for the express purpose of upliftment and celebration—including concerts, plays, festivals or candlelight services. If you're stuck at home, search for cyber-gatherings online to fulfill the same expressions and intentions.

**Recommended Resources:** *Poem of the Soul – The Sun Rays* by Louis Janmot; *Nightlife* by Archibald Motley, Jr.; *Mean Girls* (Movie)

**3 of Cups Card Layout:** *Please Share!* Spread

1. What have I been sharing too much of?
2. What have I been holding back?
3. Where is my sharing best received?
4. Who has something to share with me?
5. Who's sharing something I *don't* need?
6. What does the Universe want to share with me?

# 4 of Cups – Ho Hum

**Stripped Down Overview:** Boredom, lack of drive, no ambition, absent motivation—when the 4 of Cups creeps up, it tends to drain the color from our life's portrait. Often without warning, and seemingly no logical cause, thoughts of "Why can't I get my shit together?" permeate these lackluster times. The reasons might be found in the Major Arcana cards—for example, The Moon could indicate female hormones, The Sun male hormones, The Hanged Man puberty issues, and Temperance chemical imbalances—in which case, medical advice could be called for. But sometimes, this crappy malaise might point to existential angst—a spiritual crisis or an inability to create personal meaning. Hell, it may just be a hangover, come to think of it. Whatever the source of this ennui, it's rarely a summer picnic under a shady tree. Barring a need for drugs (legal!) or therapy (persistent disinterest in activities that formerly brought joy could signify depression), remember that this, too, shall pass. Or, put another way, if you thrash in quicksand, you'll only sink faster.

**Keywords:** In a Funk; Ennui; Lack of Interest; Unmotivated; Cynicism; Pessimism; Malaise; Inability to See the Good; Wallflower; Refusing to Participate in Celebration; Emotional Flat Line; Apathy; Closed to Love; Unwilling to Commit; Blind to Goodwill

**Personifications and Embodiments:** Squidward Tentacles; Sighing; Yawning; Bored Teenager (stereotype)

**Quote:** *Common men pass treasures by; they respond to the spectacle of nature as guests at a banquet who are neither hungry nor thirsty.* – Eugene Delacroix

**Challenge:** Boredom

**Gift:** Dissatisfaction

**Occupations/Vocations:** Spoiled Celebutante; Lazy Bum; Hobby Shop Owner; Government Clerk; Supermarket Checkout Lane

**Disney Totem:** Eeyore (*The Many Adventures of Winnie the Pooh*)

**Animal Symbol:** Koala

**Flower Essences:** Hornbeam (Bach); Kapok Bush (Australian Bush)

**Crystal/Stone:** Red Calcite

**Aromatherapy:** Lime

**Body Parts/Systems and Health Issues:** Hearing Problems; Deafness

**Mystical Messenger** – Lethe

**Sabian Symbol:** Aries 27 – Through imagination, a lost opportunity is regained.

**Writing Prompt:** A town where boredom is punishable by death.

**Affirmation:** I actively look for what's good and right with my life.

## Naked Advice for the 4 of Cups

*Career:* Every one of us wears a set of perspective glasses that tints (or taints) what we see. Right now, you're viewing your career path though rather gray lenses. Do you require more challenging work? Need greater mental stimulation? Desire an opportunity to expand (or use) your innate strengths? Want to switch out your soul-sucking job for one holding greater personal meaning? You'll need to ponder these probing questions as you traverse this plateau, especially if you want to reach higher ground.

*Romance:* Have your sights set on a specific target? You might as well drop those romantic arrows, because she can't—or won't— be felled by Cupid's bow. *"He's just not into you"* is more about his emotional unavailability than your desirability, so don't take the disinterest personally. Attempting to push yourself on someone—whether by dressing seductively, talking suggestively or buying drinks at a bar—will be rebuffed, so save yourself the embarrassment by just sitting tight for now. Better to wait to hunt for a date among a thriving herd than to aim for a lame stag.

*Parenting*: Kids can seem like alien creatures, especially when prone to sulking, silence or shrugging. *"What is she thinking?"* and *"Why won't he talk to me?"* are common parental thoughts when this card comes up. After investigating the obvious—bullying at school, lack of challenging curriculum, effects of divorce, depression, poor eating, drugs—and coming up empty-handed, consider that your child just may be a flaming introvert...or processing rapid physical changes and growth. It's possible he's numb from information overload, too, so limit texting, computer use and TV watching—and encourage time in nature or other grounding outlets.

*Spirituality:* *"Look up, for your redemption draws nigh."* (Luke 21:28) In this case, the Biblical verse refers more to recognizing blessings and silver linings than preparing for an apocalyptic rapture. An intentional gratitude practice not only forces you to look for the good in life, but also cultivates a sense of well-being and contentment. Commit to writing down five things you're thankful for or blessed with—every day—to stir up winds of change. You'll be surprised how powerful an attitude of gratitude can be, especially when daily gratefulness blows you right out of the doldrums and into sparkling currents.

**Recommended Resource:** *Melancholia* by Albrecht Durer

**4 of Cups Card Layout:** *Out of the Doldrums* Spread

1. Why am I motionless (or emotionless)?
2. What precipitated this emotional stall?
3. What do I need to do next?
4. What needs removing (or less focus)?
5. What needs adding (or more focus)?
6. Where will the winds of change come from?
7. Unseen blessing that needs embracing.

# 5 of Cups – Boo. Hoo.

**Stripped Down Overview:** Nobody likes as whiner, so this is a troubling card when it comes up: are you being a crybaby? Always complaining about first-world problems like screwed-up manicures, Wal-Mart checkout lines, the price of beef or the flimsy card stock on your latest Tarot deck acquisition? What about posting endless "poor me" statuses on Facebook to get attention and sympathy? Yeah, the 5 of Cups is *that* card. There *is* an exception, though, when this card is NOT about being an all-out attention whore: individuals suffering from chronic health issues who are "sick and tired of being sick and tired". If you fall into this category (shout-out to fellow fibro chums), you are exempt from feeling any guilt for griping. But the rest of you? It's time to grow up, accept delayed gratification, take charge of your life and be accountable for your own well-being. How we deal with dashed expectations determines whether our lives are constricted by stress, irritation and frustration—or expanded by joy, peace and openness.

**Keywords:** Disappointment; Self-Pity; Disillusionment; Weariness; Separation Anxiety; Unstable Emotions; Dashed Expectations; Woebegone; Holding Grudges; Let Down; Always Noticing What's "Missing"; Whining; Down in the Dumps; Complaining; Regret; Glum; Disenchantment; Assuming Others Have it "Better" Than You; Impotence

**Personifications and Embodiments:** Pushovers; Crying Over Spilled Milk; Crocodile Tears; Angelica Pickles; Olive Oyl; Pearl Krabs; Lippy the Lion; C-3PO; George McFly; Jar Jar Binks; Gloomy Gus; Wet Blanket; Killjoy

**Quote:** *Self-pity in its early stages is as snug as a feather mattress. Only when it hardens does it become uncomfortable.* – Maya Angelou

**Challenge:** Wallowing

**Gift:** Contrast

**Occupations/Vocations:** Irrigation Specialist; Canal Worker; Bridge Builder

**Disney Totem:** Mike Yagoobian (*Meet the Robinsons*)

**Animal Symbol:** Loon

**Flower Essences:** Gorse (Bach); Star of Bethlehem (Bach); Boronia (Australian Bush)

**Crystal/Stone:** Tugtuptite – Dissipates feelings of revenge and self-pity. Ends self-doubt and regret. Aids in learning from mistakes. Enhances self-confidence. Helps one stand up for convictions to avoid being a "pushover".

**Aromatherapy:** Linden Blossom

**Body Parts/Systems and Health Issues:** Lupus; Multiple Sclerosis; Chronic Fatigue Syndrome; Fibromyalgia

**Mystical Messenger** – Avalokiteshvara

**Sabian Symbol:** Scorpio 2 – A broken bottle and spilled perfume.

**Writing Prompt:** A woman laments over spilled wine, but finds out it was poison.

**Affirmation:** I check my expectations, gain perspective and stay grateful.

## Naked Advice for the 5 of Cups

*Career:* Although a cliché, *"the grass always seems greener on the other side"* stays in our collective conscious because it's often true: we assume many things about "other" people—including their success, wealth, health, upbringing, environment, relationships or happiness. When feeling like a failure—often because of toxic comparisons—it may become easy to resent the achievements, accolades, authority or approval of colleagues or co-workers. But we never, *ever* know the whole story trailing behind a person and their appearances. He may be taking care of a terminally ill spouse at home. She might be a single mom with Lupus and an autistic son. He could suffer from severe back pain because of a car accident. She may have clawed her way out of poverty, working her ass off to accomplish what she has. He may have refused an inheritance because the conditions would lead him to violate his values and conscience. Even when an individual appears to be a "golden boy" or "favorite gal", we have no idea if they're truly happy, fulfilled, healthy or at peace. But let's say they are: why does their joy, success, influence or prominence have anything to do with *you*? Maybe their pre-incarnation curriculum differs significantly from yours. If you want something, work for it—but if life seems to keep handing you the same cards, ask the Dealer what your primary archetypes and soul lessons are. It would suck if your highest good were to be a Networker, Servant, Wounded Healer, Student, Lover or Hedonist—but you keep envying (and trying to become) a Queen, Teacher, Warrior, Goddess, Mystic or Pioneer.

*Romance:* Bottom line: someone is unfulfilled. Right now, the drawbacks to your relationship outweigh the benefits. You have to determine how serious these "negatives" are, and if the positive tradeoffs are worth it. This may come as a surprise, but leaving dirty socks on the bathroom floor (yes, even when you've told him umpteen times to put them in the laundry basket located three feet away!) doesn't equate to spousal abuse. Forgetting to put down the toilet seat (while a major pain in the ass) isn't grounds for divorce. Falling asleep on the couch after a hard day's work (when he promised to take you to a movie) won't earn you a restraining order. I'm being facetious, but seriously: how many relationships end because of a pile-up of petty, minor stuff that eventually turns into solemn, "major" issues? And does it *really* have to be that way? What are you expecting? Did he agree to it? Are your wants (demands?) realistic? I mean, truly *make-or-break-the-relationship* stuff? Or are you being unreasonable about inconsequential quirks common to almost every coupling? Whining may gain you temporary victories, but if you're not careful, you may wake up one day to find he's packed his things and bought a one-way ticket to Fiji. Here's a quick exercise to help: Imagine that you've just been diagnosed with a terminal illness. You have three months to live. You'll probably be in pain, and maybe even lose your mobility. *Now* how do those grievances look to you? *That's what I thought...*

*Parenting*: I don't think you can teach gratitude in a purely didactic way. Same with behaviors like how to treat women with respect or how to become a life-long reader. I believe these attitudes and practices begin with watching how parents and family members engage with challenges, people and (in the latter example) books on a daily basis (not just on special occasions when someone's "looking"). One of the best ways to teach our kids resilience is to help them manage expectations—and cultivate the skill of looking for other opportunities in the midst of disappointment. You may need to up your game on this, as well as a spirit of thankfulness (i.e., actively looking for what's going right in life). It's a cliché, but the whole "when a door closes, a window opens" mindset does contribute to familial happiness. Every one of us experiences dashed expectations, and yes, it sucks. But did someone die? Do you still have your eyesight? Are you sheltered? Is there food in the fridge? You get my drift.

*Spirituality:* Following a spiritual path may compel you to abstain from certain substances, shun particular behaviors or avoid practices that "everyone" seems to like and do. The feelings of being "left out" or "missing something" may be especially acute when you're young—both chronologically *and* within your faith. However, the reason humans participate in specific religions or creeds is because there is a tradeoff (and payoff): we master base urges, acquire self-discipline, grow in grace, receive comfort, gain wisdom and (hopefully) become better people (however your path defines "better"). Seek solace among others who share your beliefs (even if you're a solitary), or from reading sacred texts that inform and shape your spiritual path.

**Recommended Resources:** Debbie Downer Skits (*Saturday Night Live*); "Whale of a Birthday" (*SpongeBob SquarePants*); "Do You Really Want to Hurt Me" (Culture Club); "I Still Haven't Found What I'm Looking For" (U2); *Reverie* by Dante Gabriel Rossetti

**5 of Cups Card Layout:** *Five Cups* Spread

*Cup 1:* What fills me with disappointment?
*Cup 2:* What fills me with resentment?
*Cup 3.* What fills me with dread?
*Cup 4:* What fills me with joy?
*Cup 5:* What fills me with hope?

# 6 of Cups – Memory Lane

**Stripped Down Overview:** *In my day, we didn't* have *the luxury of indoor plumbing, let alone quilted toilet paper or after-shit spray. No,* *we crapped in the woods, wiped our ass with tree bark...and pinesap covered the smell. And we liked it. We loved it!* OK, so our grandparents didn't regale us with stories quite like this, but most of us have heard tales of *walking eight-tenths of a mile to school, in the snow, uphill both ways,* Mama baking fresh bread from scratch every day or snatching used cigarette butts off the ground to sneak in a smoke (fun times, Gram, fun times). This is the halcyon glow of the 6 of Cups, a card replete with faded photographs, old year books, cassette mix tapes and rotary phones. It's also the card of cuteness overload—sharing adorable animal videos on Facebook and posting baby pics for Throwback Thursday—as well as scouring antique shops for vintage treasures or searching yard sales for kitschy kitchen finds. Memories of bygone days blur at the edges, magically softening (or removing) beatings with leather belts or gleeful taunts of "four eyes". Nostalgia is a mixed bag: on one hand, it can generate feel-good fuzzies that comfort and anesthetize. On the other, it may turn into the La Brea Tar Pits—sticking us to the past and ossifying any chance of appreciating progress or enjoying the present moment. Yes, we must know and understand history lest we repeat it. Yet, driving while your eyes are glued to the rearview mirror can have disastrous consequences...

**Keywords:** Nostalgia; Reminiscing; Wistful Yearning; Blast from the Past; "Good Ol' Days"; Memories; Genealogy; Historical Research; Reflecting on What's Come Before; Dwelling on What's Happened; Faded; Antiquity; Reunion; Remembering; Sentimentality; Retro; Random Acts of Kindness; Grandchildren; Timelessness; Surrogate; Small Gifts; Tokens of Appreciation; Simple Pleasures; Idealizing Youth; Living Vicariously; Sweetness; Cuteness; Homesick

**Personifications and Embodiments:** Gift Exchanges; Photo Albums; Classmates.com; Time Capsules; This Day in History;

Documentaries; Treasures in the Attic; Books from Childhood; Vintage Toys; Boomerang (TV Channel); Cute Cat Videos and Images; The Smithsonian; Museums; Ancestry.com

**Quote:** *Keep some souvenirs of your past, or how will you ever prove it wasn't all a dream?* – Ashleigh Brilliant

**Challenge:** Romanticism

**Gift:** Sentimentality

**Occupations/Vocations:** Ice Cream Truck Driver; Day Care Worker; Babysitter; Street Bouquet Vendor; Event Photographer; Scrapbooker

**Disney Totem:** Carl Fredericksen (*Up*)

**Animal Symbol:** Elephant

**Flower Essences:** Honeysuckle (Bach); Sundew (Australian Bush)

**Crystal/Stone:** Pink Halite (Salt Stone) – Helps free one's attention from the past. Eases burdens. Lightens mood. Promotes a life-affirming outlook.

**Aromatherapy:** Mandarin

**Body Parts/Systems and Health Issues:** Rosacea; Acne; Eczema

**Mystical Messenger** – Therese of Lisieux

**Sabian Symbol:** Sagittarius 1 – Retired army veterans gather to reawaken old memories.

**Writing Prompt:** A grandfather goes back in time to relive a special day.

**Affirmation:** I focus on only good memories.

## Naked Advice for the 6 of Cups

*Career:* When at work or passionately following a vocation, we rarely stop to wonder: *How will I be remembered here? What gifts do I share with my boss, colleagues, customers or clients? What impression do I leave with my words and actions?* Many of us have fond memories of a coach, teacher, Girl Scout leader or guidance counselor that believed in us, encouraged us and prodded us to stretch beyond what we *thought* were our limits. We can do the same for interns, new employees and volunteers circling our orbit. Regardless of your position, you can lead by example— promoting a culture of cooperation, consideration, integrity and respect. If you lacked positive role models growing up, imagine being the mentor you *wish* you had—consciously cultivating and demonstrating admired traits at work and during any commercial transactions. You may even go so far to attempt to make your business or services memorable via feel-good promotions, community outreaches, company field trips, employee picnics, bring your kids (or dogs) to work days, table-top puzzles/games, silly-hat Fridays and so on. Don't underestimate the power of sentimentalism for fostering good will, increasing production, supporting camaraderie and instilling a sense of loyalty.

*Romance:* There's a good chance a "blast from the past" will contact you or cross your path. In fact, *you* may get a hankering to check Classmates.com, Google an ex or search Facebook for an old crush. A thrilling *what if?* zips up your spine as you re-live that hallway kiss, extended footsies session in the library or holding hands under the lunchroom table: *Could it happen again? Can this old flame rekindle?* If you're single, such musings rooted in the past may very well flower into a second-chance relationship. Or, someone that you've "known forever"—a friend, neighbor, sibling of an old school chum—may suddenly look like a candidate for dating. A surprising and unexpected turn of events, for sure, but the 6 of Cups contains a special kind of magic that can whitewash memories, re-frame history and generate portals of reconnection. Don't be afraid to make the first move via a friendly greeting, an invitation to coffee or even a bouquet of wildflowers. Even if nothing serious develops, you've brightened someone's day with simple kindness—and God knows the world can use more of *that*.

***Parenting***: Parenting missives and approaches from "the good old days" may not align with your standards, so don't allow well-meaning relatives or old-school folks to derail your *running-like-a-well-oiled-machine* family. On the other hand, if things are going a bit rough, you'd benefit from considering some retro values that tend to be cast aside these days: Less texting, TV and video games—more outdoor exploration, board games, playing dress-up and tinkering with hands-on toys. And if you long to share childhood memories with the kiddos, don't get discouraged if they've no interest in family trees or tales from the farm (or city streets). Their curiosity about ancestry may not develop until they reach *your* age, but do write down your stories for them to discover one day. One fun way you can instill a sense of the past is creating then burying a time capsule with them, filled with personal notes, observations, predictions, mementos, magazines—as well as wishes and wisdom for their "future self". Dig it up in 20 years to see what's changed—the ultimate trip down memory lane.

***Spirituality:*** According to her seminal book *Sacred Contracts: Awakening Your Divine Potential*, Caroline Myss posits that all humanity shares four survival archetypes that "symbolize our major life challenges and how we choose to survive". Those four primary archetypes are Child, Victim, Prostitute and Saboteur. The 6 of Cups intersects with childhood in many ways, but one of them is often unconscious: the Child Archetype. Whether Orphan, Wounded, Dependent, Abandoned, Eternal, Divine, Nature or Magical, each of us contains an Inner Child that interacts with the world — or, in many cases, *reacts*. The Child is the Guardian of Innocence, and, depending on how our formative years played out, may have made certain vows in order to defend and protect our psyche. Thing is, those forgotten promises may still control how we react in groups, toward authority figures or when we're faced with responsibility. There's a fine line between childlike and childish, non-conformity and bratty behavior. When you draw this card, your Soul is inviting you to take a good, hard look at the vows (and assumptions) you made as a child — and if those promises still run the show on an unconscious level. How do you feel about adulting? As a child, what was your default reaction to stress or rejection? Do you recognize these same default patterns in current interactions? Other questions to ask yourself: Who protects your Inner Child when you're left alone? How might you regain innocence? How have you matured emotionally?

**Recommended Resources:** "The Incredible World of Horace Ford" (*Twilight Zone* Episode); "Directive" by Robert Frost; *Somewhere in Time* (Movie); *Where Are They Now?* (VH1 TV Show); "The Grumpy Old Man" (*SNL* Skit with Dana Carvey); "Ode: Intimations of Immortality" by William Wordsworth

**6 of Cups Card Layout:** *What Child Is This?* Spread

1. What part of my Inner Child was wounded?
2. What part of my Inner Child feels Orphaned or Abandoned?

3. How have I healed (or need to heal) my Inner Child?
4. How do I regain/preserve the core of Innocence?
5. What is the gift of the Magical Child?
6. What is the lesson of the Eternal Child?
7. What is the message from the Divine Child?

## 7 of Cups – So. Many. OPTIONS!

**Stripped Down Overview:** Ever feel like your brain is a computer browser, and you have 1,258 tabs open (because everything is oh-so-*interesting*)? Or did you ever send your hubby to the store for ranch dressing, but he calls back, telling you there are fifty different kinds...*which one did you want*? What about back-to-school shopping? Ever go to buy your kid some jeans, only to discover there's straight leg, slim-fit, relaxed, faded, distressed, button-fly, zipper-fly...? Yeah, gone are the days where you can just buy "regular" jeans. Or "just" ranch dressing (when there was only Hidden Valley). This infinite variety catering to consumer culture serves every niche imaginable—but it can leave most people confused, overwhelmed and frustrated. Many just walk away rather than make a choice. Or, with artistes—painters, writers, composers, sculptors and the like—the kaleidoscopic choices that dance behind our eyes mesmerize and enchant... often to the point of paralysis or even procrastination. On one hand, this polychromatic fly in the one-size-fits-all ointment is a blessing. On the other—especially for those of us who already have a penchant for active imagining and the ability to generate options at the drop of a hat—the 7 of Cups can be our weakness, our bane, our *Kryptonite*.

**Keywords:** Weighing Options; Indecision; Inspiring Visions; Scattered Focus; Brainstorming; Shopping; Clarifying Values; High Cost; Considering the Price; Numerous Choices; Analysis Paralysis; Questioning; Overwhelmed by Variety; Difficult

Selection; Daydreaming

**Personifications and Embodiments:** Question Marks; Castles in the Air; Pie in the Sky; Amazon.com; Candy Store

**Quote:** *Without leaps of imagination, or dreams, we lose the excitement of possibilities. Dreaming, after all, is a form of planning.* – Gloria Steinem

**Challenge:** Selecting

**Gift:** Multiplicity

**Occupations/Vocations:** Pawn Shop Owner; Jewelry Store Owner; Buyer; Dilettante; Personal Shopper; Producer

**Disney Totem:** The Lost Boys (*Peter Pan*)

**Animal Symbol:** Octopus

**Flower Essences:** Scleranthus (Bach); Wild Oat (Bach); Red Lily (Australian Bush); Sundew (Australian Bush)

**Crystal/Stone:** Mookalite (Chert) – Encourages envisioning many possibilities and the ability to choose the appropriate one. Promotes variety. Intensifies emotional experiences.

**Aromatherapy:** Niaouli

**Body Parts/Systems and Health Issues:** Hallucinations; Schizophrenia

**Mystical Messenger** – Pandora

**Sabian Symbol:** Gemini 20 – A cafeteria with an abundance of choices.

**Writing Prompt:** Tribal reactions when loincloths now come in *three* colors.

**Affirmation:** I settle on one or two options. I can get (or do) the others later.

## Naked Advice for the 7 of Cups

*Career:* You're facing a shitload of options, and it doesn't help that you're the type with gazzilions of interests and hobbies. As a result, you're aggravated by the dilemma of following your bliss vs. "making a living". Should you monetize one of your quirky passions? Or get a "real" (mundane) job that may somehow contribute to your ultimate goal? Should one interest be a "purely for fun" experience...or should you dive in deep with the goal of creating a career path? These are NOT easy questions. For some, once money enters into the picture, a hobby loses its appeal. For others, the idea of earning money via enjoyable vocations seems like a dream. Determine your personal values, recognize what engages your attention, evaluate whether you can combine one or more of your passions at work and look for (or create) a job where you have the extra time and money to chase your curiosity. Simply put, you won't be happy if you're not painting with ten color-laden brushes, so don't attempt to draw your life with only a graphite pencil.

*Romance:* When choosing a partner, it used to be easy: select the biggest, hairiest and strongest. Now, armed with (mostly) evolved survival instincts and (at times) sophisticated preferences—not to mention myriad media blasting what's supposed to be "ideal"—figuring out who to date and what makes a good mate can be as confounding as which type of tomatoes to grow in your garden. Especially difficult if you don't even know what makes you happy, let alone the traits of a romantic good fit! The shine of new love wears off pretty quickly, as does the trophy sheen of externals like "pretty", "rich", "talented" or "prominent" — for any of those could tank at any moment via disfigurement, stock market plunge, disease or slander/scandal. Don't chase after tantalizing mirages or promising illusions, which amounts to clutching at smoke. Instead, identify *your* core values and what-I'd-*love*-to-live-with ideals and make *that* your touchstone, your yardstick, your *last-word-on-the-subject*.

*Parenting*: If the 9 of Swords is an overactive imagination gone awry via leaden paranoia, anxiety, suspicion and assuming worst-case-scenarios — the helium 7 of Cups balloons the other way: daydreams that defy physics, economics, physical restrictions, mental ability or disposition. I'm a firm believer that the past does NOT equal the future, that hardships can be transcended and that aiming for the stars should be the rule, not the exception. And yet...when you have a child, certain walls and limitations become evident. What a shitty dilemma for us parents, who would love for our kids to be POTUS, an Olympian or an astronaut per kiddos' dearest fantasies! (Except for the whole "be famous" or rock star delusion. Screw That! More trouble than it's worth.) So what to do? Recognize what they're good at and gently redirect them. Even the most "simple" gifts like sustained focus, attention to details, thoroughness, facility with language or numbers, hand-eye coordination, refined taste and ability to synthesize are vital clues that can lead to fulfilling hobbies, worthwhile extracurricular endeavors or eventual careers. Play to their strengths. Always.

*Spirituality:* With the dawn of the internet, waves of esoteric knowledge crashed upon the shore of the masses. Unfortunately, consumerism threaded its way through alternative spirituality and occult traditions, as well. While "you get what you pay for" may apply to sofas, mattresses and cars, the same doesn't hold true for perennial wisdom. Some teachers charge hundreds or *thousands* of dollars to gain "special" knowledge from them, while a few *too-big-for-their-britches* astrologers and Tarot readers think nothing of charging $500 per 30 minute consultation (do the math—that's over $16 *a minute!*). You know what? That's The Hierophant, for you: setting themselves up as the "only true" portal. Well guess what? There is *so much* knowledge and hard-won wisdom shared on the web—freely and enthusiastically—often in friendly Facebook groups. (My personal favorites? Shonna Hill's *Tarot Nerds*, Paris De Bono's *Tarot Tarot Tarot* and Avril Price's *Exploring Tarot*.) Don't be dazzled by slick websites, pretty colors or celebrity "endorsements" (they're usually penned by friends and family members)—*or* high prices. Expensive doesn't mean quality, depth, accuracy *or* usefulness.

**Recommended Resources:** *The Paradox of Choice: Why More Is Less* by Barry Schwartz; *The Renaissance Soul* by Margaret Lobenstine; *I Could Do Anything If I Only Knew What It Was* by Barbara Sher; *Refuse to Choose!: Use All of Your Interests, Passions, and Hobbies to Create the Life and Career of Your Dreams* by Barabara Sher

**7 of Cups Card Layout:** *7 Cups a Spinning* Spread

1. What feeling/dream is a "castle in the air"?
1a. What is the ladder to reach it? (Or grounding force that says "no go")
2. What do I assume will bring me riches?
3. What do I presume will bring me accolades/fame?
4. What temptation will I face if I chase my dream?
5. How is my sense of Self defined/affected by chasing/achieving my dream?

6. What is the spiritual benefit of pursuing my dream?
7. What menace lurks on the path to going after my fantasy?

## 8 of Cups – Higher Ground

**Stripped Down Overview:** It stands to reason that many of us would rather walk away from a bad situation than stay and suffer (6 of Swords). But there are times when something seems to be working well—and is "successful"—but our Soul is pulling us to ascend. We may feel the urge to leave a solid relationship, a satisfying job or a profitable project—for no other reason that our intuition says, *"It's time to go"*. It's an existential longing to fill the silhouette of our Soul and expand into our full potential here on Earth—which may compel us to walk away from a row of neatly stacked golden chalices. On a more mundane level, the 8 of Cups can indicate a temporary hiatus, a well-earned sabbatical or a much-needed vacation—or even the choice to retire from a great position or relocate from a desirable town.

**Keywords:** Moving Away; Heading to Higher Ground; Leaving What's Familiar; Taking a Trip; Relocation; Vacation; Retirement; Voyage

**Personifications and Embodiments:** Going on a Cruise; Day Spa; Spiritual Pilgrimage; Holistic Retreat

**Quote:** *The great thing in the world is not so much where we stand, as in what direction we are moving.* – Oliver Wendell Holmes

**Challenge:** Uncertainty

**Gift:** Aspiration

**Occupations/Vocations:** Tour Guide; Pilgrimage Leader; Rock

Climber; Hiker

**Disney Totem:** John Carter (*John Carter*)

**Animal Symbol:** Sea Turtle

**Flower Essence:** Silver Princess (Australian Bush)

**Crystal/Stone:** Green Titanite (Sphere) – Encourages following one's own path, despite attractiveness of surrounding options. Promotes personal integrity.

**Aromatherapy:** Hyssop

**Body Parts/Systems and Health Issues:** Teeth (Cavities, Root Canal, Abscess, Dentures, Implants, Braces, etc.)

**Mystical Messenger** – Saint Uncumber

**Sabian Symbol:** Capricorn 27 – A mountain pilgrimage.

**Writing Prompt:** A rich, pampered princess leaves her castle to find her true birthright.

**Affirmation:** I go where my Soul leads me.

## Naked Advice for the 8 of Cups

*Career:* There's no concern or worry about leaving a job or familiar vocation, it just feels...*done.* On the outside, your choice to depart may appear to be a momentous occasion to some—or a foolish decision to others. Know that those well-meaning folks are just operating according to the rational mind or perhaps even a fear-based ego. Regardless, you know it's time to move on—

and nothing but peace and quiet determination fill your heart. You've *no* idea what to expect—and, truth be told, you don't *want* to know (after all, it will be an adventure, right?). In fact, don't be surprised if your new employment or entrepreneurial endeavor has a mystical bent to it—or that you end up in a field that is tangentially related to metaphysics.

*Romance:* Ever know a divorced couple who seems to fit so well together—and they still remain friends? You can't help but wonder (and often are dying to ask one of them) "Why did you separate in the first place? What in the world *happened*?" Sometimes, friendships and romantic partnerships just run their course. There's no malice, no scandal, no conflict—it's just... *over*. Like a beautiful scarlet leaf about to fall off the branch in autumn, it's time for the connection to dissolve. There may be some poignancy involved—a sweet sadness (we're not talking the 3 of Swords here)—but there's also a fulfilled peace and quiet hope pulling the Soul to a new phase of relational experience (which may even be a solitary one). In fact, it wouldn't be unheard of (although not likely) that someone leaves traditional relationships or lifestyles altogether—perhaps choosing to enter a convent, religious order or spiritual discipline that requires celibacy. It's OK...*OK*? Everything will be OK.

*Parenting*: Just because your kid excels in some area—especially extracurricular activities like sports, music, cheerleading, voice or theater—it doesn't mean she has to keep at it...especially if she's expressed that she'd rather do something else. You'd draw a different card if you were being encouraged to pressure her to remain involved (for example, the 8 of Coins or Page of Coins). The 8 of Cups, though, lets you know that her spirit has already experienced what she needed to within a particular activity— but now, it's time to explore something new. It may be that her ideals or values have changed, or that her Soul just knows she's "done". If you're the type that regrets what you didn't get to do as a youth, one who has a tendency to push your child because you want to live (or re-live) vicariously or, worse, want to impress your boss, neighbors, co-workers or community with her talent and awards—then, allowing your child to quit will be a problem. Not for her, mind you, but for *you*. It's your choice: either contribute to her maturity and spiritual growth—or allow your big, fat ego to run (and ruin) the show. And if your progeny is older, he'll likely want to either take a year off after graduation to "see the world", switch majors (much to your chagrin), or even drop out of college to purse a higher purpose.

*Spirituality:* In RWS-style decks, all the golden cups are neatly stacked, symbolizing completed emotional or creative endeavors. There is no "unfinished business" with the 8 of Cups (at least, not where the querent is concerned), but merely a spiritual frustration that prompts the assertion *I know there's more*. This isn't a card of material envy, emotional childishness or materialistic discontent, either (*"I bet the grass is greener on the other side"*), but rather a desire to recover any soul fragments or explore newly activated archetypes—to "be all you can be" as a spirit embodied in human form. You may look for (or even require) a Spiritual Director, ethical guru or reputable teacher to help you along your path (people like Adyashanti, Gangaji and Pema Chodron come to mind). It's also time to reevaluate your values, because they can, and do, change. For example, you may have once valued solitude, security, reputation and achievement—but now, you value socializing, leisure, risk taking and spiritual development. Allow your Soul to shift gears, because you're headed upward towards a fresh perspective.

**Recommended Resource:** "Movin' on Up" (Theme from *The Jeffersons*); *The Monk Who Sold His Ferrari* by Robin Sharma

**8 of Cups Card Layout:** *Growing Up* Spread

1. What am I starting to outgrow?
2. What have I *definitely* outgrown?
3. Where am I headed?
4. What (or who) will help me get there?
5. How will I know when I've arrived?

# 9 of Cups – Too Much is Never Enough

**Stripped Down Overview:** You've seen them at the Chinese restaurant buffet: 700 pound behemoths making multiple trips, plates laden with General Tso's Chicken, Honey Shrimp, Moo Goo Gai Pan, Crab Rangoon, Ma La Beef, Pork Lo Mein, Sushi and Fried Donuts—*each* and *every* time. Where do they put it? Are their tree-trunk legs hollow? Reflective of the American milieu—riddled with sedentary slobs, microwave mindsets, Hummer hogs and a defiant sense of entitlement—the insatiable appetite for *more* gnaws at their bellies, provokes jealous eyes and skyrockets credit card debt. McMansions, $5,000 handbags, $800 haircuts and $400 dinners, the gaping maw of "want" stretches thousands of miles—spanning every socio-economic demographic. It's not about rich or poor, it's about *more*. Externally, this card is about flash, bling, the appearance of perfection and the accoutrements of "wealth". Internally, the 9 of Cups becomes a hungry monster that can't be filled by food, sex, shoes or alcohol. Never content with the way things are or the face they've been given—nips, tucks, implants, bleaching, tanning—life becomes all about improvement or increase, making gratitude an incomprehensible concept to these ones.

**Keywords:** Façade; Consumerism; Gluttony; Indulgence; Concealing Mistakes; Acting Superior; Plastic Surgery; Getting What You Think You Want; Eat, Drink and Be Merry; Desiring

Satisfaction; Craving Fullness; Excess; Conceit; Epicure; Materialism; Demanding Entitlement; Debauchery; Trappings; Hiding Imperfections; Vanity; Satiety

**Personifications and Embodiments:** Photoshop; Anti-Aging Creams; Paula Deen; Cornucopias; Facelifts; Tummy Tucks; "Touch Ups"; Krispy Kreme Cheeseburgers; Buffets; Smorgasbord; Spoiled Brats; Heiresses; Trust Fund Kids; "Born with a Silver Spoon in His Mouth"; Stuffing Your Face; Fixing What's Not Broken; Butter; Liposuction; Airbrushing; Hungry Ghosts (Japanese Mythos)

**Quote:** *A gourmet who thinks of calories is like a tart who looks at her watch.* – James Beard

**Challenge:** Voracity

**Gift:** Sybaritism

**Occupations/Vocations:** – Beer Distributor; Bartender; Barista; Image Consultant; Digital Artist; Gourmand

**Disney Totem:** Auguste Gusteau (*Ratatouille*)

**Animal Symbol:** Bluebird

**Flower Essence:** Wild Potato Bush (Australian Bush)

**Crystal/Stone:** Thulite – Encourages unadulterated sensual pleasure. Helps live out desires, fantasies and needs. Aids in overcoming inhibitions and societal limitations. Stimulates romance and sexuality.

**Aromatherapy:** Cumin

**Body Parts/Systems and Health Issues:** Diabetes; Gout; Pancreas; Gallbladder; Liver

**Mystical Messenger** – Saint Arnold of Metz

**Sabian Symbol:** Cancer 15 – A group of people who have overeaten and enjoyed it.

**Writing Prompt:** A society where altering appearances becomes illegal.

**Affirmation:** I allow myself to enjoy the good things in life.

## Naked Advice for the 9 of Cups

*Career:* Let's face it: sometimes, sprucing up the wardrobe, getting a new haircut or decorating our office space makes us *feel* better. In fact, "looking the part" can encourage *being* the part (but only if you truly have the goods in the first place). Look for ways to bring fun, indulgence and comfort to your work. If you're in charge of the purse strings at your job, don't settle for industrial, bland or cheap: invest in the stylish artwork, the luxurious wood finish, the sleek brushed aluminum, the glass-blown sculpture or the high-end window treatments. Spread the love among employees, bringing in chilled bottles of water or cups of cappuccino. Give your best workers surprise bonuses. Work for yourself? You know what that means! Reward yourself for showing up, day after day, putting in the hours of effort and concentration to better your business and meet the needs of your clients. Or, allow yourself to schedule a few days off, come home from work, put your feet up and polish off an entire bottle of wine (provided you don't have a drinking problem!). Not a drinker? A pint of Ben & Jerry's will do. Treat yourself, especially if you rarely do so.

*Romance:* This is a card reflecting absolute comfort in one's own skin. That is, the freedom to chew with your mouth open, bath, burp or fart in front of your significant other. While some would consider these behaviors rude, others would say it's a "fits like a glove" partnership. It's the energy of comfort food and cozy living—eating pretzels in bed with wifey, binge-watching DVDs with your girlfriend, sleeping in on Saturdays and catching some Hanna-Barbera cartoons with hubby—even going out shopping to buy fluffy throw pillows, downy blankets or an oh-so-soft robe. Making (and eating) meatloaf, mashed potatoes, mac and cheese and apple pie—washed down with beer, wine or pop—also reflect the heavy, drowsy, inviting energy of the 9 of Cups. Don't consider such relaxation a "waste of time" but, rather, an investment for a happy, close and snuggly relationship.

*Parenting*: Right now, it's important to show your child how appearances can be deceiving. Recall books (Oz's "Wizard"), fairytales ("The Ugly Duckling") or movies where the main character presented himself one way—but, in the last half of the story—proved to be something far different (both "positive" and "negative" examples). Subtly bring these stories to your child's attention. Remind her how butterflies come from caterpillars and oak trees from acorns—amazing transformations that would dazzle if we weren't so desensitized to nature's magic. Or, introduce historical and biographical accounts where a person ended up "successful", despite childhood "flaws" or challenges (e.g., Einstein's late speech, Beethoven's deafness, Helen Keller's physical challenges, etc.). When the time comes for him to feel like he's the odd-one out—and when this card comes up, it's probably "that" time—try to help him understand that not everything is as it seems, the grass is rarely greener across the fence and some of the most miserable people on the planet are those who seem to "have it all".

*Spirituality:* Existential hunger is as tricky thing to discern. If we're materially minded, we may think more bargains, increased business, greater influence, better food, improved "branding", prettier makeup, fancier jewelry or a better body will somehow remedy this emptiness. If we tend to look for more ethereal solutions to problems, we may try to fill this void with more decks, more books, more workshops, more crystals or more oracles. Yet, these often don't satisfy, either, when they become forms of spiritual gluttony. The solution? Digest what you've already learned. Go back to your journals and re-read your epiphanies. Ask yourself if you're applying previous advice revealed by divination or a teacher. Analyze if you *truly* followed through with the last bit of guidance Spirit gave you. Most times, you'll discover that you haven't assimilated what you've already generously received—mistaking appetite for lack of absorption.

**Recommended Resources:** *Baker Reading Diet Book* by Normal Rockwell; *A Bar at the Folies-Bergere* by Edouard Manet; *The Young Bacchus* by Caravaggio; "Taco Town" (*Saturday Night Live* Commercial Parody); *The Stepford Wives* (Book or Movie); *It's Not What You're Eating, It's What's Eating You* by Janet Gleeson

**9 of Cups Card Layout:** *What's Eating Me?* Spread

1. What's eating at me?
2. What will best address this hunger?
3. What do I need to abstain/fast from?
4. What do I need to reach for instead?
5. Final advice

## 10 of Cups – Happily Ever After

**Stripped Down Overview:** While most would love to catch a leprechaun and implore him to lead on to the pot o' gold at the end of the rainbow, others would be just as content (or moreso) to find a loving, compatible, long-term mate. A roof over the head would be nice (nothing fancy, just comfortable, dry and clean)—and maybe a few happy, healthy children filling the house with laughter (if the Universe could swing it). Or perhaps a cozy menagerie of pets! Yes, some dogs, a cat, a few chickens... It's an ideal existence for many: an equal partnership with shared values, affection and affirmation freely exchanged. Loving glances and gentle touches, even after 10, 20, 30 or more years of marriage. Beautiful harmony at home, despite facing the occasional material or health challenge. There's a special resilience here, too—a "those guys will be together *forever*" assumption by all who are lucky enough to know them. It's the home all the neighborhood kids want to visit—the "Mr. Rogers" house on the street. All who enter feel peaceful and relaxed... because that's *exactly* the energy that's generated all day, every day. Sound too good to be true? It's not. Blessed are you who have this type of life—or are about to enter one like it.

**Keywords:** Happy Family; Familial Contentment; Close-Knit Relatives; Lasting Contentment; Joyous Anniversary; Homebody; Mature Love; Time-Tested Bonds; My Home Is My Castle; Good Reputation; Homecoming; Supreme Blessings of Hearth and Home; Shared Dreams and Values; Sequestered Ecstasy; Domestic Perfection

**Personifications and Embodiments:** American Dream; White Picket Fence; Paradise

**Quote:** *Not what we have but we enjoy constitutes our abundance.* – John Petit-Senn

**Challenge:** Encroachment

**Gift:** Bliss

**Occupations/Vocations:** Realtor; Adoption Agent; Square Dancer; Peace Maker

**Disney Totem:** Pongo, Perdita and Pups (*101 Dalmatians*)

**Animal Symbol:** Deer

**Flower Essence:** Agrimony (Bach)

**Crystal/Stone:** Ametrine – Promotes cheerfulness and fulfillment, as well as harmony. Synchronizes the nervous system. Encourages creativity and dynamism in the face of challenges.

**Aromatherapy:** Grapefruit

**Body Parts/Systems and Health Issues:** Common Cold; Flu

**Mystical Messenger** – Aeolus

**Sabian Symbol:** Capricorn 8 – Birds in the house singing happily.

**Writing Prompt:** A resort community's catchphrase is "Be happy...or *else*".

**Affirmation:** I am grateful for a happy home life.

## Naked Advice for the 10 of Cups

*Career:* Is it possible for a place of employment to actually be "one happy family"? I'm doubtful, but this card indicates that harmony can, and will, prevail when others are seen as equals—

and an atmosphere of genuine fondness is cultivated and encouraged. Some workplaces already see the value of trust, informality, independent creative groups and lack of traditional hierarchies. Think circle, not pyramid (or worse, *square*). Because it is *you* who has drawn this card, be the sunshine, cupcakes and rainbows in the office. Look for ways to make the dreams of others come true. Find out what colleagues and clients are working towards and help make it happen for them. Not only will you raise the feel-good factor at your place of employment, but you'll also be sowing happy seeds that will sprout for you when you need it most.

*Romance:* If you've been in a happy, long-term marriage, why not have a vow renewal ceremony? Or a large anniversary shindig? Or maybe even a special second honeymoon (or, if you're one of the "poor but happy" couples—totally with you— have a *first* honeymoon...even if it's a local getaway). If you're not yet hitched, but in a steady, pleasant relationship—the 10 of Cups bodes well for your future. Still single? Have hope! It would appear that the cards are in your favor (*har har*...I made a punny); just don't put off living and joy and pursuing your dreams while you wait for that "special someone" (because he'll likely find *you* right when you're doing what you love.

*Parenting*: In RWS-style versions of this card, a couple embraces, facing towards home, while kids play beside them—a rainbow stretched across the sky. When I see a rainbow, one of the first things I think of is the story of Noah from the Old Testament— where ROYGBIV symbolized a promise that God made to humanity. One of the greatest things you can do for your kids (besides the obvious—care, acceptance, respect, kindness, etc.) is the gift of promises kept. Nothing shakes the foundation of a kid's world faster than a parent promising something—and then not following through. Sure, emergencies happen—and maybe one or two times of broken promises could be understood and forgiven over a long period of time. But if you or your spouse are in a habit of making promises to go to the amusement park or ball game or concert or some other prized endeavor—and you consistently cancel (and make lame excuses for not going)— you're setting up your kids to mistrust adults, not to mention the entire concept of "keeping your word". Liars beget liars. And life's already challenging enough for kids without their parents promising rainbows—but giving them rain. Honestly? You're better off not promising *anything* than yanking their chain like this. So you want a happy family? Have all the ingredients? *Great!* Make the words you speak to your kids, and your promises, *mean* something—especially in this world where talk is so cheap.

*Spirituality:* When I was growing up—well, even as an adult, when I was a co-pastor—church was everything. Not only did we attend three times a week, but also made it to every single outing and special service scheduled in the Sunday School bulletin. One of the biggest regrets I have from my Pentecostal days, especially the first few years of marriage to my present husband, is all the time wasted at church (especially since we attended a church one hour's drive from where we live). Yes, you read right: *wasted.* So many hours, weeks and months! Sitting in a *church*! Where others told us who God supposedly was—and what he wanted from us (and what he would do to us if we *didn't* provide it)! Let me tell you something: if you have a lovely marriage or a wonderful boyfriend or a close-knit relationship with your folks or even a super-awesome circle of friends—you would do well to spend Sundays with *them*. Actually experiencing, enjoying, feeling and growing love (which, supposedly, God *is*). Because in the early days of Christianity (just as an example) there *weren't* formal services with a pastor leading the flock or even a designated religious structure to meet at. No, there were believers who got together, fellowshipped, ate meals and celebrated their faith in the homes of individuals. Same with many pagan paths, where spirituality was (and is) intertwined with community and family—not some separate "thing" requiring sacrifices of time or money. So if you want to grow in your faith or your spiritual path, I suggest investing time in those strong bonds you have— and look for the Divine in the eyes of those who love you.

**Recommended Resources:** *Love Circuit* by Alex Grey; *Little House on the Prairie* (TV Show); *Dumont TV Ad* (Happy Family) by Normal Rockwell

**10 of Cups Card Layout:** *ROYGBIV* Spread

1. *Red* – What does "putting down roots" mean to me?
2. *Orange* – How does my creativity affect/influence/impact my family?
3. *Yellow* – How is my self-esteem/confidence affected by close family?
4. *Green* – What contributes to my heart opening/expanding?
5. *Blue* – How can I best communicate love to my family?
6. *Indigo* – What higher vision do I need to hold for my family?
7. *Violet* – What is a Divine lesson taught by my family?

# THE MAJOR ARCANA

# The Fool – Nyuk Nyuk Nyuk

**Stripped Down Overview:** When you idolize Pee Wee Herman, long for Michael Jackson's backyard amusement park or wish for Peter Pan's eternal youth, you be a Fool, fool. Perched on a precipice without a parachute, ignoring the warnings of both dog and man, we can't figure out if you're a wide-eyed adventurer, a reckless risk-taker or stupidity personified. Inside-out clothing, mismatched socks, inappropriate comments, clueless literalism, lack of coordination, disregard for etiquette, loud laughter, walking backwards—and yet, we often see a gleam in the eye. Does this Fool know more than he lets on? Is he encouraging us to take life less seriously—or aiming to expose the foibles of authority figures, silly rules or unseeing herds? That's the fine line with this jester: we can't quite tell if he's mad—or a genius.

**Keywords:** Fresh Start; Leap of Faith; Impetuous; Anticipation; Guileless; Carpe Diem; Oblivious; Folly; Blank Slate; Beginnings; Purity; Frivolity; Insouciance; Gullible

**Personifications and Embodiments:** Peter Pan; Jesters; Clowns; Comedians; Slapstick; Trickster Gods; Harlequins; Amusement Parks; *Puer Eternis*; Vagabond; Robin Williams; Jimmy Fallon; Unabashed Laughter; Practical Jokes; Hoaxes; Bungee Jumping; Whoopee Cushion; Buddy Sorrell (*Dick Van Dyke Show*); Mork (*Mork and Mindy*); Three Stooges; Willy Wonka (Played by Gene Wilder); Mad Hatter; Grover (*Sesame Street*); Roscoe P. Coltrane (*Dukes of Hazzard*); Ernest P. Worrell; Mr. Magoo; Dory (*Finding Nemo*); Mater (*Cars*); Puck (*A Midsummer Night's Dream*); Pinocchio; Don Knotts; Hobos; Simpletons

**Quote:** *Mix a little foolishness with your serious plans. It's lovely to be silly at the right moment.* – Horace

**Challenge:** Naiveté

**Gift:** Innocence

**Occupations/Vocations:** Clown; Political Satirist; Vagabond; Comedian; Vaudeville Performer; Pulmonary Specialist; Hobo; Prankster

**Disney Totem:** Goofy (*A Goofy Movie*)

**Animal Symbol:** Ladybug

**Flower Essences:** Walnut (Bach); Wild Oat (Bach); Kangaroo Paw (Australian Bush)

**Crystal/Stone:** Citrine – Promotes desire for new experiences. Encourages extroversion. Promotes self-assurance. Helps process impressions. Addresses fear of responsibility.

**Aromatherapy:** Juniper

**Body Parts/Systems and Health Issues:** Knee; Leg; Foot

**Mystical Messenger** – Janus

**Sabian Symbol:** Gemini 24 – Carefree children skating on ice.

**Writing Prompt:** A clown with a secret pocket.

**Affirmation:** I embrace laughter and light-hearted living.

## Naked Advice for The Fool

*Career:* Clowns, comedians, wanderers, hobos, harlequins and circus performers—if you can swing any of these (especially on a trapeze!), you've found a (mis)match made in heaven. Staying put isn't your style, so hop on a gypsy caravan, join a band of carnies or give the Big Top a spin. *OK*, this may not be reasonable advice—but not much about The Fool *is*! He is the big-hearted wanderer, with no care in the world. He's sweet, simple Forrest Gump whose incredible luck finds him in pivotal moments in American history. He makes a million dollars, runs across the country and falls in love with the girl next door. No planning, no worries—just trust, innocence and openness. You're being encouraged to take the same approach in your career because, as Forrest says, *"Life is like a box of chocolates. You never know what you're going to get."*

*Romance:* If your idea of a commitment is a one-night-stand, then you're obviously not marriage material. As long as your lovers know your predilection—and you have the sense to use condoms—go forth and continue your *no-strings-attached* slutdom. But if you want a long-term romantic relationship—and you're not the *hopping-from-man-to-man* type—beware entering any serious partnership right now: you don't want to be the fool in this particular dynamic, right?

*Parenting*: Why give a kid a parent when you can give him a friend? Video games, bike rides, concerts, DVD marathons, season tickets—c'mon, it's such a drag to discipline and dish out consequences when you can play instead! Jimmy in trouble again? *"Well, you know how boys are."* Tina terrorizing the playground? *"Kids will be kids."* Pleasure Island parenting might be entertaining at first, but when Tommy's living in your basement at age 35, the luminescence of juvenescence loses its shine.

*Spirituality:* *"Unless you become as a crusty myopic curmudgeon, you'll not see the Kingdom of God"* ... said no mystic *ever*. Fresh eyes popping out of the beginner's mind see possibility and play in every moment. You're being given a gleaming new whiteboard and a set of wipe-off markers. What will you do with them? You have a blank slate to do with as you wish. (If you have whiteboards from the past? They're gone. *Poof.*) How might your spiritual practice look if you woke up every day with this in mind?

***Recommended Resources:*** *Gilligan's Island* (TV Show); "My Hero, Zero" (*School House Rock!* Song); *Willy Wonka and the Chocolate Factory* (Movie); *Family Jewels* (Movie); "Jump" by Van Halen; *Pee Wee's Playhouse* (TV Show); *Portrait of Sakata Hangoro III* by Toshusai Sharaku; *April Fool: Fishing* by Normal Rockwell; *Bill and Ted's Excellent Adventure* (Movie); *Grizzly Man* (Documentary); *The Carol Burnett Show*

**Fool Card Layout:** *Leapin' Lizards* Spread

1. Where do I need a blank slate?
2. What's a key ingredient to playfulness?
3. Where do I take a leap of faith?
4. How am I like The Fool?

# The Magician – The Man Behind the Curtain

**Stripped Down Overview:** Time to strap on your BS detector! Slick Willies, Teflon Dons and smooth operators—if any archetype can sling shit and wallow in mud without getting a spot on him, it's this one. Golden tongues, persuasive arguments, convincing advertising and spin doctoring—all smoke-and-mirrors ploys to sell you *something*. Whoring televangelists, snake-oil dealers, devious politicians, fraudulent faith healers, curse removing psychics, loophole loving lawyers and pandering marketers—hold on to your money, honey, because *"now you see it, now you don't"* may end up referring to your wallet. If The Magician refers to you, though, it's time to put your gift of gab or flair for repackaging to good use via storytelling, networking or reinvention. Just like a stage magician entertains the audience with trick after trick after trick, it's time to pull out all the stops and dazzle the world with your special mojo.

**Keywords:** Focused Will; Skilled Manipulation; Eloquence; Dexterity; Applied Talent; Utilizing Skills; Silver Tongued; Mastery Over the Elements; Using Everything Available; Word Weaving

**Personifications and Embodiments:** Illusionists; Magicians; Frank W. Abagnale; Merlin; Escape Artists; Mercury; Politicians; Salesmen; Mary Poppins; Publicists; Commercials; Ads; Spin Doctors; Satirists; Shock Jocks; Professor Marvel/The Wizard; Professor Hinkle; Marketers; Criss Angel; David Blaine; Panaceas; Double Plus Good; Deal-making; Snake Oil Hawker; Pulling a Rabbit Out of a Hat; "Now You See It, Now You Don't"

**Quote:** *The tongue can paint what the eye cannot see.* – Chinese Proverb

**Challenge:** Manipulation

**Gift:** Communication

**Occupations/Vocations:** Used Car Salesman; Advertising Professional; Pundit; Fiber Optics Engineer; Magical Entertainer; Spellcaster

**Disney Totem:** Dr. Facilier (*The Princess and the Frog*)

**Animal Symbol:** Monkey

**Flower Essences:** Bush Fuchsia (Australian Bush); Turkey Bush (Australian Bush)

**Crystal/Stone:** Poppy Jasper – Stimulates imagination and versatility, thus helping to realize ideas. Gives impetus for variety and new experience.

**Aromatherapy:** Peppermint

**Body Parts/Systems and Health Issues:** Shoulders; Wrists; Fingers

**Mystical Messenger** – Hildegard of Bingen

**Sabian Symbol:** Aries 25 – A double promise reveals its inner and outer meanings.

**Writing Prompt:** A street magician pulls something horrific out of his hat.

**Affirmation:** I play with words and expand my perceptions.

## Naked Advice for The Magician

*Career:* In many versions of The Magician, symbols of all four elements are somewhere near the central figure: a cup, coin, staff and sword. As you probably remember from the introduction, each of them represents four distinct areas of life: the cup connects to the water suit of emotion, dreams and values. The coin relates to all things earthy—stuff that can be inventoried by the five senses. The staff correlates to fiery enthusiasm, passion and vitality—while the airy sword deals with opinions, judgments and logic. Now, think of your skills and talents in each of these four areas. Are you using them at your current workplace? If not, could you consciously incorporate them? If not, perhaps it's time to create a career where you *can* utilize your skills in each of the four realms. If anyone can turn a vocational curve ball into a homerun, it's *you*...so play ball!

*Romance:* Wine, dine, I'll make you mine. Suit up, Don Juan: it's time for the art of seduction. Remember, 90 percent of arousal begins between the ears, so talk a good game and titillate all orifices. Make sure you can deliver, though, lest your lover discover that you can't find the right hole even with a GPS. And if you're on the receiving end of Mr. Magic Fingers? You can bet your ass you'll have a great time in bed with the Maestro—but don't be surprised if he's texting behind your back while you're humpin' along...

*Parenting*: Silly parent, tricks are for kids! If you think you can preach one thing and do the opposite without junior noticing, you're deluding yourself. As if by magic, children manifest the unspoken attitudes and buried beliefs of their parents, so if you don't like what you see in your progeny, clean up *your* headspace instead of trying to fix the mirror. With the dawn of YouTube— and behind-the-scene features on DVDs—kids are more savvy than ever. They can tell you how Criss Angel "levitates", and how green screens render plain walls into skyscrapers, rocky cliffs or tsunamis—or how mo-cap technology transforms an average looking actor into a hairy beast, blue superhero or slimy cave dweller. Likewise, they can connect the dots between what you say and what you do—what they see, and what you say is "true". Time to shake all the Aces out of your sleeve and give your kids a fair deal.

*Spirituality:* In the laboratory of life, experimenting with words and meaning can yield incredible insights. My friend Craig Conley, who wrote the foreword for this book, is someone I consider a modern Magician. I mean, the guy is *awesomesauce*. Not only is he the smartest person I know, he's light years ahead of most people in terms of creativity. (Don't believe me? Go to Amazon.com and put his name in the Search field. His books are just mind-blowing in their inventiveness.) On of those books is *The Young Wizard's Hexopedia: A Guide to Magical Words and Phrases*. I guarantee if you get that book, and experiment with the exercises, you'll be as close to the Magician archetype you could possibly get. Who knows? You may even touch the face of God...or rearrange it altogether in a Cubist image of your liking.

**Recommended Resources:** *Catch Me If You Can* (Movie); *The Pretender* (TV Show); *The Illusionist* (Movie); "The Bard" (Twilight Zone Episode); *Now You See Me* (Movie); *The Prestige* (Movie); "The Wizard" by Black Sabbath; "You Can Do Magic" by America; "She Blinded Me with Science" by Thomas Dolby; "Magic" by Olivia Newton John; "Magic Man" by Heart; "Are You a Hypnotist?" by Flaming Lips; "Night on Bald Mountain" by Modest Mussorgsky

**Magician Card Layout:** *BS and Skillz* Spread

1. Where am I deceiving myself?
2. How do I bullshit others?
3. What talent needs more focus?
4. What skill am I abusing?
5. How can I make magic?

# High Priestess – Nothing to See Here.
# Move Along.

**Stripped Down Overview:** The High Priestess may know the enigmas of the Moon—or even the Universe Itself—but she ain't talkin'. In fact, many don't know Her, let alone approach where She lives. No longer honored or revered, She's couched in spiritual riddles, esoteric texts, parables and even fairytales. Most look to the past when searching for her mystifying scrolls, because hardly anyone creates secrets worth knowing these days. And when She *is* found in forsaken (or forbidden) lore, attempts are made to erase, destroy, co-opt or reinterpret Who and What she embodies. Who is worthy of entering the Holy of Holies? You'll know if, and when, you cross the threshold of the Holy Place—and see shining Shekinah for yourself.

**Keywords:** Internal Guidance; Esoteric Wisdom; Occult; Oracles; Silence; Transcendentalism; Unrevealed Future; Sanctuary; Prophecy; Divination; Accessing Intuition; Hidden Knowledge; Know Thyself; Secrecy; Intuition; Inner Awareness; Virginal; Secrets; Still, Small Voice; Deep Reflection; Celibacy; Asexual; Quiet Demeanor; Consulting Inner Wisdom; Vow of Silence; Mute; Internal Guidance; Protected Wisdom; Direct Knowing; Psychic Ability; Frigidity; Refusal to Speak; Guarded; Contact with the Dead; Purity

**Personifications and Embodiments:** Maria (*Sound of Music*); The Oracle (*The Matrix*); The Guardian (*Aeon Flux*); Jacque Sarnier (*The DaVinci Code*); Galadriel (*Lord of the Rings*); Guinan (*Star Trek: The Next Generation*); Agatha, Dasher and Arthur (Pre-cogs in *Minority Report*); Izzy (*The Fountain*); Apollonia (Catatonic Fortuneteller in *Carnivale*); Alison DuBois (*Medium*); Witch; Virgin Mary; Isis; Wise Woman; Oracle at Delphi; Vestal Virgins;

Papess; Pope Joan; Abbess Manfreda; Mystery Schools; Forgotten Lore; Buried Secrets; Sybilline Scrolls; Sacred Sites; Nun; Crone; Runes; I Ching; Tea Leaf Reading; Library; Bookstores; Grimoires; Secret Societies; Fifth Amendment

**Quote:** *Don't play what's there, play what's not there.* – Miles Davis

**Challenge:** Trust

**Gift:** Knowledge

**Occupations/Vocations:** Fortuneteller; Librarian; Mystic; Seer; Prophetess; Medium; Psychic

**Disney Totem:** Grandmother Willow (*Pocahontas*)

**Animal Symbol:** Clam

**Flower Essences:** Billy Goat Plum (Australian Bush); Flannel Flower (Australian Bush); Wisteria (Australian Bush)

**Crystal/Stone:** Blue-Banded Chalcedony (Chalcedony Agate) – Aids in listening to, and confiding in, others. Promotes understanding. Enhances communication, rhetoric and self-expression.

**Aromatherapy:** Eucalyptus Globulus

**Body Parts/Systems and Health Issues:** Larynx; Laryngitis; Vocal Chords; Pharynx; Thyroid

**Mystical Messenger** – Guglielma

**Sabian Symbol:** Scorpio 20 – A woman drawing aside two dark curtains that closed the entrance to a second pathway.

**Writing Prompt:** Reading a scroll, a girl finds out something she wishes she hadn't.

**Affirmation:** I follow my inner knowing.

## Naked Advice for the High Priestess

*Career:* In a world of Chatty Cathy's, you may be feeling pressured to *talk, talk, talk*. Even online—where you'd assume you can be your introverted, reserved and/or humble self—business folks and solopreneurs are bombarded with advice to tweet ten times a day, post on Facebook five times a day, upload dozens of pictures on Instagram to boost your "brand"—God *Almighty*. I don't know about you, but I'm sick of all this social media whoring. The good news is, when this card come up, you're getting a big thumb's up from the Universe that it's A-OK to stage a (secret) boycott and refuse to play the game. YAY! *But, but…how will clients discover me? My services? My art?* (Yes, I can read your mind.) Look, if you've drawn the Grand Dame of Wisdom and Intuition, you're gonna have to trust yourself—and the Ground of Being behind everything. It's not always easy, and it sometimes feels irresponsible, but your heart's already telling you it's time to jump off the whole publicity treadmill. Besides, it will make you look mysterious—even beguiling. (And you know how *that* can work out for reputation and sales!)

*Romance:* The Waxing, Full and Waning Moons are often associated with the High Priestess, largely because of the headdress she wears in the RWS deck. These three moon stages symbolize the idealized Triple Goddess: Maiden (Waxing), Mother (Full) and Crone (Waning). The Maiden state is when a girl becomes visibly "feminine" (and is still "innocent" or virginal). The Mother represents the full expression of womanhood (either through childbearing or the accumulation of experiences). The Crone indicates "fading" feminine vibrancy (menopause), but nevertheless contains an abundance of wisdom from life's lessons that she may pass on to a new generation. If you've seen the videos of silver-haired older women rocking runways, marathons, dance floors, gymnasiums and concert halls, you know what a load of bullshit all this is—at least, on a literal level. Sometimes, the Crone can outperform, outshine and outlive many a Maiden or Mother—especially if her spirit, mind and outlook is "young". Granted, it's more difficult for a young person to exemplify the Mother or the Crone, because an accumulation of both knowledge (Mother) and wisdom (Crone) usually come from experience. And let's face it, just because you're old doesn't mean you're wise—or embody the Crone archetype. My point? Don't let age or even appearance influence or direct how you feel on an emotional level—let alone dictate how you should present yourself or behave in public. "Age is just a number" may be a cliché, but it's true—and if this card comes up for a romance reading, you're being challenged to reevaluate and redefine what it means to be a vibrant wise woman. Your conclusions held deep in your heart will either accentuate *or* hinder your romantic life.

*Parenting*: Here's a situation where you don't need to dispense any advice to your kids. In fact, saying *nothing* is the way to go. Youth need to gain certain knowledge directly, and nothing you could say would hold sway anyway (say *that* five times fast!). However, this doesn't mean that you can't indulge their budding interest in alternative religions or the occult! In fact, feel free to leave your New Age, Pagan or Mystical texts around the house for them to "pick up"—or even your oracles. Hell, buy him a Tarot deck for his birthday! What better way to delve deep into the Self than to practice accessing intuition and Greater Wisdom, right? If he seems fascinated and uses the cards frequently, buy him a Tarot book or two. Our journey on this Psychic Highway started *someplace*, right? So, when it comes to your kids, why not let the mystical adventure begin with *you*?

*Spirituality:* Occultist P.D. Ouspensky summed up the High Priestess perfectly:

> *This is the Hall of Wisdom. No one can reveal it, no one can hide it. Like a flower it must grow and bloom in your soul. If you would plant the seed of this flower in your soul, learn to discern the real from the false. Listen only to the Voice that is soundless. Look only on that which is invisible, and remember that in you yourself is the Temple and the gate to it, and the mystery, and the initiation.*

This archetype is the interface between you and the Universe: no mediator, no teacher, no hand-holder—just your very Being enveloped by Wisdom, sacred knowledge flowing direct, clear and breathtaking. Listen. Listen more. Let it saturate, captivate. *Listen.*

**Recommended Resource:** *Mysteriosa* by Alex Grey; *The Voynich Manuscript*

**High Priestess Card Layout:** *Gateway to Initiation* Spread

1. *Gnosis*: What do I need to know before approaching the Gate of Wisdom?
2a. *Pillar One* – What does my mind/logic need to accept?
2b. *Pillar Two* – What does my heart/emotions need to accept?
3. *The Veil* – What separates me from Wisdom?
4. *Opening* – What will part the Veil?
5. *Behind the Veil* – What knowledge lies behind the Veil for me?

6. *Initiation* – How will I be introduced to Greater Mysteries?
7. *Silence* – Why is it important for me to keep silent about my experience?

# The Empress – Mamma Mia!

**Stripped Down Overview:** A naked woman squats, reaches down with both hands, and opens up her exaggerated vulva. No, you didn't just walk on the set of a porno flick. (And no, vaginas do *not* have teeth—*the better to eat you with*.) Called *sheila-na-gigs*, such statues and carvings—found all over British and Irish architecture—represent fertility and raw female sexuality. Arguably no other archetype contains more richness, manifestations and conflicted feelings than Mother: she's the first human contact we have, to the point where we depend on her survival for the length of gestation. On one hand, she's nurturing, supportive, protective, fecund and life-giving. On the other, she can be jealous, smothering, withholding, neglectful or abusive. Sometimes, she can be both, depending on her mood (and the actions of her children). No wonder there's so much tension and "mommy issues" in the world! And that's without the whole Electra Complex flavoring this maternal stew. In some myths, the Mother figure oozes sexuality (I mean, *sheila-na-gigs* don't exactly evoke feelings of warm snugglies!). This whole mother/whore dichotomy explains why some teenage boys separate girls into two groups: "those you marry" and "those you screw". Fortunately, with The Empress, you can have *both*... but you may pay the price with years of therapy when you double the archetypal pleasure.

**Keywords:** Matriarch; Divine Feminine; Fertility; Reproduction; Uncontrolled Growth; Mother Archetype; Wildness; Maternal Figure; Generating Activities; Overgrown; Gestation

**Personifications and Embodiments:** *Venus of Willendorf*; Mother Nature; Berchta; Divine Feminine; Lush Gardens; *Vesica Pisces*; Yoni; Pregnant Belly; Breastfeeding; Mandorla; Full Breasts.

Naomi (*Book of Ruth*); Mother Goose; Old Mother Hubbard; Old Woman in the Shoe; Gaia; Kwan Yin; Wicked Step-Mother; Opening Flowers; Venus; Bowls; Circles; Generous Hips; Cups; Grails; Mama Bear; "Octo-Mom"; Michelle Duggar; Mrs. Claus; June Cleaver (*Leave it to Beaver*); Carol Brady (*Brady Bunch*)

**Quote:** *It's amazing how quickly nature consumes human places after we turn our backs on them. Life is a hungry thing.* – Scott Westerfield

**Challenge:** Multiplication

**Gift:** Fruitfulness

**Occupations/Vocations:** Full-time Mom; Homeschooling Parent; Governess; Doula/Midwife; Maternity Shop Owner; Storyteller; Fertility Doctor; Charm School Headmistress; Stage Mother; PTA President

**Disney Character:** Kanga (*Pooh's Heffalump Movie*)

**Animal Totem:** Rabbit

**Flower Essences:** Bottlebrush (Australian Bush); She Oak (Australian Bush)

**Crystal/Stone:** Agate (with Uterus-Shaped Markings) – Aids blossoming, growth and development. Encourages mindful fruitfulness. Instills deep feelings of security, especially when homesick. Supports pregnancy.

**Aromatherapy:** Palmarosa

**Body Parts/Systems and Health Issues:** Pregnancy; Female Reproductive System

**Mystical Messenger** – The Mothers

**Sabian Symbol:** Taurus 11 – A woman sprinkling long rows of flowers.

**Writing Prompt:** A greenhouse owner is not what she seems.

**Affirmation:** I allow myself to blossom to my full potential, wherever I am planted.

## Naked Advice for The Empress

*Career:* Watch out for the casting couch, because you might have to put out in order to keep your job. While the oldest profession still keeps some employed, career prostitution— aka "selling out"—can infect any job. The question is, are you willing to risk vocational STDs, which may render you crazy *and* blind? Creativity should spring forth naturally, not be cattle-prodded into on-demand performance; if your workplace, boss or colleagues are trying to use you for your gifts and talents— while withholding adequate compensation, credit or praise— then go propagate elsewhere. You don't need them and, more importantly, your wildness needs room to flourish, flower and spread for all to see, smell, taste, hear and touch.

*Romance:* Beware the man (or woman) with mommy issues, because you may end up babysitting instead of romancing. Expect to tie shoes, wipe ass and clean up adult-size messes. Be especially cautious around younger men, who tend to look for Mama in older women. If you keep attracting immature, dependent individuals, evaluate what you're projecting: do you try to rescue the strays? Heal the damaged? Transform bad apples into your own sweet brand of *Clafouti aux Pommes*? Answers to these questions yield clues when this card comes up in relationship readings.

*Parenting:* Time to whip out your metaphorical boobs to give your kids some sustenance. Paulie and Patty crave your attention, hoping you'll squeeze in some attentive "we" time. Be generous with the milk of human kindness, for there's no substitute for Mama Juice. If you're childless, this card indicates that you have a strong, protective maternal instinct—and are likely fertile as hell. Pets, neighborhood kids, nephews, nieces—they feel safe with you, which is why you often feel like a Pied Piper around the young and defenseless. Open your heart (and home, if you can), and share that nurturing impulse for their benefit—and *yours.*

*Spirituality:* Who tends the garden of your soul? You do. Close your eyes and check in with your inner world to make sure everything that you need is there. Cultivate and nourish your internal oasis by surrounding yourself with beautiful flowers, robust plants, green vines, trees and fountains—either literally, or in the landscape of your mind. If your inner child lacked good mothering, visualize your younger self in that beautiful, safe garden. Be a mother to her. Ask her how she is—and what she's feeling. She may be shy at first, but she'll warm up to you. Continue your visits and chats; one day, she'll become as old as you are. Then, amazing things will happen.

**Recommended Resource:** *The Mother: Archetypal Image in Fairy Tales* by Sibylle Birkhäuser-Oeri; *A Group Portrait of a Lady and Her Two Children* by Benjamin West; *Marie Antoinette and Her Children* by Louise Elisabeth Vigee-Lebrun; *Mr. Mom* (Movie); *Mrs. Doubtfire* (Movie); *Mommie Dearest* (Movie; Shadow); *A Child Called It* by David Pelzer (Shadow)

**Empress Card Layout :** *Who's Your Mommy?* Spread

1. What needs to be nourished?
2. How am I like a mother?
3. How do I feel about feminine power?
4. How am I like a wife?
5. How am I like a whore?
6. How do I feel about my mother?
7. How am I like my mother?
8. How am I NOT like my mother?
9. Role of the Mother Archetype in life right now.

# The Emperor – The Buck Stops Here

**Stripped Down Overview:** *Dickhead*. From the tax-code toting IRS man to the belt-wielding bully father, the *head-up-his-ass* boss to the super-strict principal (who's decidedly not your "pal"), The Emperor is filled to the brim with testosterone. He's the one rumbling down the road with his *big-as-fuck* truck, an obvious overcompensation for his little *wee wee* and pervasive insecurity (especially when enormous rubber balls dangle from his tailgate). Clipping wings, pruning trees, cropping ears, The Emperor sits upon his throne with stiff neck and stern visage. But if you look closely, notice that his eyes rove from side to side like a Cylon on crack. He'd like you to think that his gaze is fixed— directed by clear analysis, pure heart and *the good of the people*. In actuality, his shifty eyes look for detractors (he'll smash them), sycophants (he'll reward them), unquestioning drones (he'll promote them) and wistful interns (think Monica Lewinsky). He values order to the point of bringing "civilization" to indigenous tribes, teeming rainforests and heathen clans—resulting in erased cultures, devastated flora, burned libraries, trophy tusks and endangered species. The ultimate square, he enjoys erecting fences, drawing boundaries, planning cities and making rules. He lives for uniformity and conformity—standardized tests, SAT scores, ISO, quality control—anything to support, and enforce, the status quo. The Emperor *rarely* takes time to play, but when he does, it's usually war games, golf or armchair quarterbacking. If you remember *anything* about this card, recall the three Cs: coercion, conversion and conquest.

**Keywords:** Authority; Boundaries; Power; Father; Leader of a Country; Rules; God; Measurements; Schedules; Limitation; Civilization; Organization; Government Officials; Dominion; Patriarchy; Yang; Rigidity

**Personifications and Embodiments:** Bureaucracy; Solar Deities; Big Brother (*1984*); Divine Masculine; Monotheism; Jehovah; Allah; Zeus; Ministry of Magic (*Harry Potter* books); President Snow (*Hunger Games* Trilogy); Curfews; The Elders (*The Giver*); Recommended Dosage; Immigration Department; Border Patrol; Food Labels; Daily percent Nutritional Values; Star Fleet (*Star Trek*)

**Quote:** *I am tomorrow, or some future day, what I establish today. I am today what I established yesterday or some previous day.* – James Joyce

**Challenge:** Suppression

**Gift:** Order

**Occupations/Vocations:** Elected Official; Bureaucrat; CEO; President; Dictator; Full-Time Father; Feng Shui Consultant; Organizational/De-cluttering Expert; Ophthalmologist/Optometrist

**Disney Totem:** George Banks (*Mary Poppins*)

**Animal Symbol:** Horse

**Flower Essence:** Red Helmet Orchid (Australian Bush)

**Crystal/Stone:** Fuchsite (Mica) – Promotes a confident appearance. Helps view problems from a distance. Aids in setting boundaries. Encourages big-picture thinking and finding solutions. Provides protection and self-determination.

**Aromatherapy:** Celery Seed

**Body Parts/Systems and Health Issues:** Urinary Tract; Male Reproductive System

**Mystical Messenger** – Bossu

**Sabian Symbol:** Aries 11 – The ruler of one's country.

**Writing Prompt:** An orphan finds out his father is alive.

**Affirmation:** I draw boundaries to protect my personal power.

## Naked Advice for The Emperor

*Career:* Whether you work for yourself or someone else, it's time to get organized. Clean out your desk, throw out the junk, file papers where they belong, banish the dust bunnies, tuck away important receipts in labeled folders and vow to yourself that you'll never, *ever* allow your workspace to get this chaotic again. It's time to be the boss of your own domain, to dominate those areas that you *can* control. True, you may not be able to influence bureaucratic edicts or office rules—let alone ably climb a mountain of red tape—but you *can* determine your outlook, your work ethic and your personal space. De-cluttering drawers and work surfaces can help dispel the *"what the hell was I just doing?"* fog that plagues the disorderly. Who knows? Keeping your workspace (and work habits) organized will lead to a more efficient, productive you—which *may* lead to promotion or career advancement

*Romance:* I once had an acquaintance in her 30s who, frustrated at her lack of connection with men, resorted to creating a "made-to-order" husband. She reasoned that if she'd go to a tailor to get a "perfect fit", why not do the same for a spouse? She wrote down everything she wanted (and didn't want) in a man, including physical appearance, socio-economic status, habits (or lack thereof), values, personality traits and so on. Then, she put in her "order" to the Universe…and let go. Guess what? She landed the man of her dreams that fit every specification on her "order" (I kid you not). Last I heard, she was blissfully married to him (but this was over a decade ago). Personally? I wouldn't trust this method (or I'd be married to an aging heavy-metal rock star millionaire that looked like a member of Motley Crue thanks to my 14-year-old self's "order")—but it worked for my pal. Who knows? Maybe this method will force you to evaluate what you really want and need in a mate. After all, if you shoot at nothing…you'll hit it *every* time.

*Parenting*: Your kid is lost at sea, on a foggy night, without a compass in hand or a lighthouse in sight. *Yikes!* A grim picture, for sure, but such free range shenanigans may be reined in with schedules, curfews, limits and to-do lists. *What?* Did you *really* think the TV, Playstation, Xbox or smartphone would be a good babysitter past, say, age five? The longer the free-for-all ensues, the harder it will be to enforce house rules…but you have to start *somewhere*. Until a child is able to govern himself, he silently (and often subconsciously) craves boundaries and guidance. Imagine yourself drifting in outer space, floating inside a space ship, clueless as to up, down, left or right—with no landmarks—only a vast, black sky strewn with stars. Scary? Confusing? Disorienting? *You bet.* So get your feet on the ground, find out what your child's been doing (or *not* doing) and start mapping out a plan to promote order, accountability and personal responsibility in your house. How *else* will your kid find his own North Star?

*Spirituality:* All-Father, Daddy, Abba—some relate to God as a Divine Patriarch, ready and willing to protect and defend his spiritual progeny. But if you've lived on this Earth more than a few decades, you've probably realized that—despite your offerings, tithes, intense devotion, sincere supplications and zealous apologetics—*shit happens.* Cars break down, faucets leak, friends get sick, neighbors lose their jobs—and loved ones die. Does this mean you are unloved, ignored or kicked to the curb by Spirit? No, it just means it's time to evaluate your view of, and relationship to, God...and why you practice certain rites and rituals.

**Recommended Resources:** "On Thursday, We Leave for Home" (*Twilight Zone* episode); *General George Washington* by Charles Wilson Peale; *John Adams* (Miniseries)

**Emperor Card Layout:** *Order Up!* Spread

1. What mess needs cleaning up?
2. Where do I lack structure (and need it)?
3. How do I put things in order?
4. Where is there a "hole" in my fence?
5. How do I plug the "hole"?
6. How can I create effective boundaries?
7. What do I need to keep out?
8. What do I need to keep in?
9. The Universe is waiting for me to place an order about.

# The Hierophant – Because I Said So

**Stripped Down Overview:** Arguably one of the biggest pains in the ass within the entire Tarot, the *holier-than-thou* Hierophant shames his audience with *shoulds*, *musts* and *always/never* ultimatums—putting the "prick" in "bishopric". Often lording over a church, spiritual group, Tarot organization or elitist subculture, this "man of the cloth" upholds specific traditions, reveres mysterious doctrines, transmits esoteric teachings and polices the moral terrain of his devotees. Specializing in us versus them rituals and customs, he sees only black and white, measures only by right/wrong and rewards only the unquestionably obedient. When suffering from a Messianic Complex (and this narcissistic douche bag usually does), he uses sacred, secret or occult knowledge to puff up his sense of self-importance and shore up his fragile sense of self. Usually hiding behind the words of Jesus, Crowley, Allah, Jehovah or some other revered "expert" as a didactic shield, he couches his insecurity, doubts and megalomania within condescending pronouncements and thinly disguised barbs—often wearing a religious robe, clerical collar or symbolic jewelry while he does it. If/when his illusion of control, assumption of divine authority or sense of special entitlement becomes questioned or threatened, he often resorts to ranting, fire-and-brimstone preaching, intimidation campaigns, slandering from his bully pulpit, defaming rivals on the internet or the outright spiritual abuse of his minions. Relying on co-dependents and sheeple to populate his flock, he preys upon those desperate for a sense of belonging, community or validation. As such, his tactics usually go unquestioned (let alone rebelled against) until someone gets seriously hurt or dies…or his fuzzy income tax math and money laundering flags the attention of the IRS.

**Keywords:** Tradition; Exoteric Religion; Formal Education; Right and Wrong Wrangling; Dogma; Ethical Standards; Social Mores; Morality; Philosophy; Doctrine; Canon; Spiritual Beliefs; Revered Teachings

**Personifications and Embodiments:** The Pope; Pharisees; Mr. Carson (*Downton Abbey*); Tevyev (*Fiddler on the Roof*); Teachers; Ministers; Churches; Synagogues; Esoteric Groups; Covens; Mosques; Organized Religion; Schools; Missionaries; Priests; Ethics Committees; Church Boards; Pastors; Spiritual Directors/ Gurus; Moses; Joseph Smith; Angel Moroni; Victorian Manners; Ramtha; David Koresh; Jim Jones; Trinity Broadcasting Network; *The 700 Club*

**Quote:** *Make your own Bible. Select and collect all the words and sentences that in all your reading have been to you like the blast of triumph.* – Ralph Waldo Emerson

**Challenge:** Absolutism

**Gift:** Guidance

**Occupations/Vocations:** Minister; Educator; Church Administrator; School Superintendent; Abbess; Bishop; Priest; Catechism Instructor; Tribal Storyteller; Sunday School Teacher

**Disney Totem:** Tanana (*Brother Bear*)

**Animal Symbol:** Rhinoceros

**Flower Essences:** Pine (Bach); Sturt Desert Rose (Australian Bush)

**Crystal/Stone:** Granite – Supports tradition. Helps draw strength and stability from one's roots, experiences and cultural origins. Reinforces new ideas to help give them shape and form.

**Aromatherapy:** Douglas Fir

**Body Parts/Systems and Health Issues:** Alopecia

**Mystical Messenger** – Saint Mary MacKillop

**Sabian Symbol:** Aries 10 – A teacher gives new symbolic forms to traditional images.

**Writing Prompt:** Harmful teachings sweep a city.

**Affirmation:** I examine my rituals and traditions, creating new ones when necessary.

## Naked Advice for The Hierophant

*Career:* So you get your paycheck...and realize there's an extra $300 tacked on to your wage. You *know* it has to be a mistake. But *man*...the extra money will *really* come in handy, especially since your clothes dryer is on its last leg. You wait for a week. Then another. *Hey, it's not* my *fault the accounting department is full of incompetents*, you reason. *After all, I work hard...and haven't had a raise in two years!* Or maybe you find a $50 bill on the ground, right outside the boss-from-hell's office. Looking around, making sure the coast is clear, you pocket this "manna from heaven". Is the green *really* divine bread...or are you just a fucking petty thief? The Emperor rules the letter of the law, but The Hierophant governs the spirit of the same. The question is: can you live with yourself, knowing your on-the-job choices?

*Romance:* The influence of The Hierophant is especially tricky for couples: Do we move in together? Fornicate? Use birth control? Abort babies? Partake of fur pie and meat missile? Visit the back door on occasion? Vaccinate our children? These types of issues have been addressed or debated by spiritual groups and denominations—some of them using a sacred text of choice to weigh in on the matter. Those who are deeply religious or heavily influenced by a respected (or feared) teacher bring this rather heavy type of baggage to a relationship. Who determines right and wrong? What if you and your mate have differing religious or moral beliefs when it comes to faith, sex and family? It's of utmost importance to hammer these things out now, rather than waiting until you've signed the lease, prenup or marriage certificate.

*Parenting*: It's been said that kids don't thrive without a sense of boundaries. The Emperor regulates the boundaries of time, place and resources—schedules, homework, curfews, nutritional requirements, bedtime, chores, TV/computer limits, allowances and so on. The Hierophant, however, governs the subjective "I said so" realm—the appropriateness of cursing, what constitutes telling the "truth", church attendance, prayers before meals, holiday celebrations, masturbation, nudity, shaving, bra wearing, etc. What to do amid such complexities? At times like these, it's best to evaluate what attitudes and approaches are, in fact, products of mindlessly ingested teachings from authority figures. Do such beliefs benefit your child? Or are they confusing them at best and hurting them at worst? The intersection of parental love and moral judgments makes for a challenging crossroad—and a wonderful opportunity for growth.

*Spirituality:* Am I doing this ritual correctly? Should I store my Tarot cards in a silk cloth to ward off negative energy? Must I give 10 percent of my income to my church every week? Is it wrong to fantasize about what's under my priest's robes? When we struggle with the appropriateness (or inappropriateness) of *anything,* we enter the cloudy realm of human morality. That's why the pillars behind the Rider-Waite-Smith version of The Hierophant are gray, ya dig? Oh, sure, he *tries* to make black and white pronouncements, decrees and commandments—but he knows damn well that he's proffering a debatable, up-for-grabs bill of spiritual goods. Unlike the laws of math or science, there are no "facts" when it comes to this shifting ball of fog. The answer? Don't look at me. I ain't no Hierophant. (But *you* can be—of your own life.)

**Recommended Resources:** *One Light (Self-Portrait)* by Alex Grey; *Parson Weems' Fable* by Grant Wood; *First in His Class* by Normal Rockwell; *Downton Abbey* (TV Series)

**Hierophant Card Layout:** *A Matter of Conscience* Spread

1. What familial/ethnic/community tradition benefits me most right now?
2. What familial/ethnic/community tradition is deforming/ stunting my growth?
3. What "should" or "must" do I need to toss out for my highest good?
4. What type of guru/spiritual leader is damaging/toxic to my spiritual path?
5. What type of book/teaching do I need most right now?
6. How can I best go about forming my own core beliefs?
7. What does my conscience want me to know at this time?
8. What higher ideal/moral approach would benefit me most right now?

# The Lovers – Sign on the Dotted Line

**Stripped Down Overview:** Taking the plunge, signing on the dotted line, saying, "I do" — The Lovers marks an intense, life-changing choice. As you stand at the crossroads, palms sweaty and heart racing, awareness dawns: your very next step will alter the trajectory of your life. Sound serious? It is. Even in a culture rife with annulments, quickie divorces, bankruptcies and breaches of contract, a solemn partnership or commitment — once entered — transforms almost *everything*. With this card, there's no guarantee of happy endings, healthy babies, thriving businesses or silver anniversaries (let alone golden ones). But unlike the Wheel of Fortune, where chance spins the wheel and fickle fate decides where it stops, The Lovers factors in time spent analyzing the data, weighing pros/cons and applying due diligence — all done *before* approaching that intimidating choice point. That's the difference between, say, The Fool and this card: The former enters agreements willy-nilly — clueless, naïve, inexperienced, untested — while The Lovers knows *exactly* what they're getting into (or, at least, have a pretty damn good idea).

**Keywords:** Contract; Commitment; Marriage; Promises; Devotion; Dedication; Pledge; Vow; Crossroads; Take the Plunge; No Turning Back; Life-Changing Choice; Vice versus Virtue; Election; Formal Partnership; Material Union; Handfasting

**Personifications and Embodiments:** Affidavit; Yin/Yang; Yoni/Lingam; Treaties; Husbands/Wives; Click "Place Your Order"; Notary Seal; "John Hancock"; Official Approval; Wedding Ring; College Enrollment; Name Change; Gender Reassignment; Saying "I Do"; Tying the Knot; Put a Ring on It; "Coming Out"; Voting; Tying/Cutting a Ribbon; Adam and Eve; Prenuptial Agreement

**Quote:** *Man is a knot, a web, a mesh into which relationships are tied.* – Antoine de Saint-Exupery

**Challenge:** Liability

**Gift:** Insurance

**Occupations/Vocations:** Matchmaker; Anti-Trust Official; Wedding Officiant; Notary Public

**Disney Totem:** Princess Aurora and Prince Phillip (*Sleeping Beauty*)

**Animal Symbol:** Gibbon

**Flower Essences:** Bush Gardenia (Australian Bush); Wedding Bush (Australian Bush)

**Crystal/Stone:** Blue Tourmaline (Indigolite) – Promotes faithfulness and ethics. Makes one open and tolerant. Enhances love for truth and responsibility. Dissipates blocked emotion.

**Aromatherapy:** Geranium

**Body Parts/Systems and Health Issues:** Infertility

**Mystical Messenger** – Jonathan ben Uzziel

**Sabian Symbol:** Cancer 24 – A man and two women cast away on a small island.

**Writing Prompt:** An unbreakable contract.

**Affirmation:** I enter serious agreements with clarity and fidelity.

## Naked Advice for The Lovers

*Career:* You've got an important decision to make, bucko. You're facing choices like switching jobs, changing careers, relocating or going back to school. This is not a new revelation, because the enticement of alternative paths, lifestyles and vocations has been beckoning for quite awhile. You may have a bit of research to do, or a few loose ends to tie up, but that inviting (albeit scary) course correction awaits. After all, you've pretty much concluded that *the devil you don't know is preferable to the one you're chained to*. However, if your significant other has accused you of being "married to your work", you might have to choose between the relationship and your job. *Ouch.*

*Romance:* If you're yearning for a proposal or dying to get married, The Lovers is arguably the most auspicious card for this type of thing (especially if The Hierophant and 4 of Wands pops up, too). I trust you've done your homework, though, because this momentous choice will affect your finances (the government loves to punish the married), social status (think your single friends will still hang around once you tie the knot? *Ha!*), and health (studies show that marrieds enjoy better emotional, psychological and physical well-being...unless, of course, you say "I do" to someone with an infected ding dong). STDs aside, you'll be spending a *lot* of time with your betrothed—possibly at places you'd rather not be (the in-laws, doctor's office, baseball games, burger joints, hardware stores) so if you're prepared and thrilled at the prospect of getting hitched...more power to ya!

*Parenting*: The Lovers can apply to several different scenarios in your child's life: either she's trying to come to terms with the idea that you're re-marrying—anguished that she has to leave her friends behind because you're moving—*or* she's wrestling with which college to attend (or major to declare). No matter the situation, you want what's best for your child while still fulfilling your own soul's unique purpose. Applause and confetti if both of your lives dovetail nicely after the "big decision". Groans and sighs if they don't. Life isn't easy, parenting isn't easy, and we wish we could control the whole mess—especially outcomes and universal happiness. Every circumstance has pros and cons, and it's in everyone's best interest to re-frame the current choice in life of the "pros" (i.e., benefits and gains).

*Spirituality:* Everything about this world splits into duality: light/dark, right/wrong, happy/sad, black/white, rich/poor, ugly/beautiful, hot/cold, strong/weak—and on and on and on. We consciously incarnated into this world to experience a dualistic "other" (how *else* would the Divine Fire experience Itself but to descend into darkness as a bunch of mini-flames?), and that's what partaking of the Tree of Knowledge of Good and Evil encompasses. But remember, there's another tree in the Garden: The Tree of Life. This is the realm of at-one-ment, where the integration and acceptance of All That Is resides. (Not "transcendence", as some New Agers would like you to think—or even salvation. Non-dualism isn't floating above the muck and mire: it's realizing that dirt is *exactly* what you're made of—and yet, so much more.) The Lovers card encourages you to resist the temptation to eat the apple of duality and, instead, dine on the fruit of the Tree of Life (oneness)—as well as the Fruit of the Spirit (*love, joy, peace, patience, kindness, goodness, faithfulness, gentleness and self-control*, per Galatians 5:22-23).

**Recommended Resources:** *Man Courting Two Sisters* by Norman Rockwell; *The Marriage License* by Normal Rockwell; "Two Princes" (song); *Romeo and Juliet* (1968 movie); *The Fall* (painting by Hugo van Der Goes)

**Lovers Card Layout:** *Garden of Eden* Spread

1. *Eve* – What does my Anima want me to know?
2. *Adam* – What does my Animus want me to know?
3. *Tree of Knowledge of Good and Evil* – What am I viewing dualistically?
4. *Snake* – What is tempting me to make things black/white, all/nothing?
5. *Tree of Life* – What "fruit" should I incorporate instead?
6. *Archangel Michael* – What level of truth do I need to apply right now?
7. *Paradise* – What's the highest good of all?

# The Chariot – Juggernaut

**Stripped Down Overview:** Despite the black and white creatures often depicted in some versions of this card, there's really no "two ways" about it: an iron will must harness opposing forces to move forward. The charioteer may appear sweaty, edgy and spirited—or, stay cool as a cucumber. Internally, though, the approach remains the same: gritted teeth, steeled spine, eyes ahead and mind made up. Nowadays, we may not lead wagon trains (*westward, ho!*) or lay down tracks for iron horses in hostile territory, but any time we push ourselves to start a new exercise program, tackle a long-term project, run a marathon or complete a degree program, we tap into this same wild-yet-focused energy. Pioneers, astronauts, politicians, prolific artists—outfitted with conviction, armed with determination and adorned with balls of titanium—the spirit of The Chariot can possess any person striving towards a goal or finish line. Often wrangling *some* pair at odds—mind/body, emotion/logic, flesh/spirit, work/family, want/need—it's akin to holding two writhing boa constrictors, hoping they magically turn into thick, sturdy reins to help us steer! But perhaps this is *exactly* what's needed when we apply hard control to a situation: a tension of *several* forces, sometimes contrary, to fuel the engine of tenacity.

**Keywords:** Drive; Barreling Through; Picking Up Steam; Forward Movement; Hard Control; Propulsion; Momentum; Force, Vehicle; Staying on Track; Heroism; Overcoming Obstacles; Will Power; Determination; Developed Ego; Personal Exertion; Harnessing Mind and Body; Dominance; Sustained Effort; Grit

**Personifications and Embodiments:** Marathons; Climbing Mt. Everest; Wagon Trains; Taggart Railroad

**Quote:** *Careers, like rockets, don't always take off on time. The trick is to always keep the engine running.* – Gary Sinise

**Challenge:** Perpetuation

**Gift:** Thrust

**Occupations/Vocations:** Tank Driver; Cabbie; Bull Rider; Cowboy; Chauffeur; Bull Dozer Operator

**Disney Totem:** Dusty Crophopper (*Planes*)

**Animal Symbol:** Shark

**Flower Essences:** Oak (Bach); Silver Princess (Australian Bush)

**Crystal/Stone:** Actinolite – Straightforwardness. Inner Balance. Determination. Boosts Self-Esteem.

**Aromatherapy:** Lemon

**Body Parts/Systems and Health Issues:** Hand/Eye Coordination; Right/Left Brain Challenges; Spatial Relations

**Mystical Messenger** – Boudica

**Sabian Symbol:** Virgo 30 – Having an urgent task to complete, a man doesn't look to any distractions.

**Writing Prompt:** A runaway car…with a mind of its own.

**Affirmation:** I get shit done.

# Naked Advice for The Chariot

*Career:* Trying to manage a team or marshal resources—herding cats as it were—falls under the domain of the 3 of Coins or The Kings (especially Wands and Coins). But what if all the frisky felines are *inside* you—in the form of conflicted interests (2 of Swords), myriad opportunities (7 of Cups), competing loyalties (10 of Coins) or a "grass is greener" notion (5 of Cups)—clawing for your psychological attention? This is the card that declares "no way around, under or over—you gotta go *through* the obstacle". It's the energy of a battering ram, the Iditarod, the Belmont Stakes, a speeding train. There is no request for grants of serenity nor to accept anything, but rather, bearing down, invoking Thor, supplicating Ganesh—and pushing forward towards a goal, promotion, sale or project completion. Thus, now's not the time to coast (4 of Swords), rest on your laurels (6 of Wands), slack (4 of Cups) or complain (5 of Cups): put up... or shut up. The ability to finish what you start—no matter how hard, challenging or painful—separates the men from the boys. So put on your big girl pants, square your shoulders, narrow your eyes, squeeze your sphincter and *get shit done.*

*Romance:* For hundreds of years, Western society (and Puritanical fundamentalism) tried to tell women who "wore the pants" in a family. Angry at patriarchy and insulted by misogyny, feminism rose to correct injustice, combat unfairness and shatter the glass ceiling. Strides were made towards equal treatment and opportunity. In some cases, marital roles turned on their heads (Mr. Mom and working mothers). In others, the need for two parents was dismissed altogether—along with the stigma that remaining single, with or without kids, was a *desirable* option rather than a default relationship setting. In the wake of feminism's fervor (and furor), males became the enemy. Spousal roles, duties and ambitions were thrown into a roiling, confusing soup along with volatile ingredients like religion, principles, spending/saving preferences and conceiving children. Right now, we're at the "phantom diner" phase, evaluating the cultural stew we've created and endorsed—weighing the appeal, taste, cost and nourishment of what our parents and peers had been eating. So if you've drawn The Chariot in response to a romance question, you get another important "card": a relationship evaluation form filled with checklists asking you to rate the restaurant (views on marriage), the atmosphere (comfort zone), the food (personal values), service (what you truly want in a partner) and price (cost of commitment). The Lovers sets you on the path—but it's The Chariot that will drive you where you want to go (hopefully, not to Batshit Crazyville).

*Parenting*: It's so freakin' tempting to write "start carpooling"… and just leave it at that. But that's lazy—and would piss off any reader wanting parenting advice from the Tarot. That said, *start carpooling*. Just kidding! Although The Chariot may indeed indicate vehicles, cars and transportation by land on a literal level, parenting (as you know) is not so straightforward. Kids are not like cars, nor do they come with warranties, guarantees or operating manuals. But this doesn't mean that tossing your hands in the air or ripping your hair out is the answer. No, you have to have a game plan, a set of plays to operate by. Lose a game? Or several? Don't throw out the playbook. Instead, watch how the greats (good parents) conduct themselves on and off field. View in slo-mo, taking notes, and repeat if necessary. Then, get the team ready, enlist cheerleaders (spouse or your parents) and put your game face on. Keep plugging away even in the face of injuries, inclement weather or defeat. Stick with the plan and keep going: now is *not* the time to sit, quit or second-guess.

*Spirituality:* Self-mastery, conscious awareness and a developed ego leads us to apply our will and make decisions. In some cases, the highest good calls us to penetrate matter, forge ahead, tackle obstructions and embrace conflict (Yang). In others, our soul leads us to surrender, yield, disengage or retreat (Yin). Both take courage and strength, especially when we act out of compassion (4th Chakra), right communication (5th Chakra), intuitive guidance (6th Chakra) or divine directive (7th Chakra). Our yardstick is not externally measured, media driven or rooted in reactive patterns or habits. Rather, The Chariot prompts us to open our (third) eye/s, breathe into the zone and do whatever our Higher Self requires in the moment—confident that our drum march is right for us...at that time, and at that place.

**Recommended Resources:** *Atlas Shrugged* (Three-Part Movie); *Ben Hur; In the Car* by Roy Lichtenstein; *Going and Coming* by Normal Rockwell

**Chariot Card Layout:** *Taking the Reins* Spread

1. *Charioteer* – What do I need most right now on my journey?
2. *Rein 1* – What force am I dealing with?
3. *Rein 2* – What's the opposing/challenging force?
4. *Steering* – How do I harness them together?
5. *Roads* – How will the "terrain" be?
6. *Acceleration* – How do I best move forward?
7. *Driving Record* – What past incident will inform/affect my efforts?
8. *Speeding Ticket* – How will I know when to slow down (if ever)?
9. *Bridge Out* – What do I need to avoid?
10. *Shortcut* (Use at Your Own Risk)

# Strength – Courage Doesn't Always Roar

**Stripped Down Overview:** There are two types of strength: the brute force exemplified by power lifters, MMA fighters and Scottish games participants (log throwing, anyone?)—as well as courageous folks who put their life on the line for job, country or values (soldiers, firefighters, Joan of Arc, protestors, et. al.). Then, there is the quiet strength of restraint: the eloquent sage who chooses to hold her tongue in the face of stupidity—or the widow artist with fibromyalgia who, despite debilitating fatigue, approaches her canvas every day, inspired to paint and serve as a witness to nature's splendor. In many ways, Strength is more about the conquering of *ourselves*, and weaknesses, than "power over" another. It's giving in to our "better angels"—overcoming a predatory animal nature within that seeks to win (kill?) at all costs...not because we fear jail time (Justice), but because of a strong character. In the pursuit of "great strength", athletes sometimes take performance-enhancing drugs. Sure, these substances grant an advantage—until the dopers fail a drug test, or their damaged organs begin to shut down. The archetype of the Strength card is utilized more on an *as needed basis*— stemming from an internal well of will—rather than the dogged determination that leaves boxers bloody (9 of Wands), farmers sunburned (Knight of Coins) or mountain climbers going back for more (Knight of Wands). It's an elegant archetypal power so strong, there's no desire to prove, demonstrate or flaunt it...but those blessed to witness this type of strength will likely never forget it.

**Keywords:** Grace under Pressure; Subjugation of Base Instincts; Courage; Finesse; Self-Control; Poise; Confidence; Awareness of Surroundings; Dignity

**Personifications and Embodiments:** Lion Laying Down with the Lamb: Daniel in the Lion's Den (Old Testament); Samson (Old Testament)

**Quote:** *Mastering others is strength; mastering yourself is true power.* – Lao-Tzu

**Challenge:** Hardening

**Gift:** Power

**Occupations/Vocations:** Animal Trainer; Lion Tamer; Strong Man; Pet Groomer; Snake Handler; Otolaryngologist; Gastroenterologist; Zoologist; Veterinarian

**Disney Totem:** Belle (*Beauty and the Beast*)

**Animal Symbol:** Emperor Penguin

**Flower Essence:** Gentian (Bach)

**Crystal/Stone:** Ivorite (Beige Dolomite) – Lends patience and inner contentment. Helps one tackle problems with serenity. Calms and relaxes. Promotes simple, pragmatic thinking.

**Aromatherapy:** Fennel (Sweet)

**Body Parts/Systems and Health Issues:** Animal Attacks; Rabies; Insect Bites; Lyme Disease; Tongue; Mouth; Cleft Palate; Lisps; Sense of Taste

**Mystical Messenger** – Saint Francis of Assisi

**Sabian Symbol:** Aquarius 23 – A big trained bear sitting down and waving all its paws.

**Writing Prompt:** A man-taming lion.

**Affirmation:** I acknowledge, harness and integrate primal instincts.

## Naked Advice for Strength

*Career:* When a colleague irritates us, our initial reaction may to stay as far away as possible. Sometimes, though, this avoidance may escalate into outright disgust or borderline hatred. Before such reactions get out of hand, consider a different approach: how might this person be similar to you? What do you have in common? What strengths do you notice? How might you (*gasp!*) turn this person into an ally? *I know, I know*, but remember: in many a fairytale, the monster or "beast" — when approached with understanding or special knowledge — often turns into a trusted guide. Those who may seem "other" (or even "oh *brother!*"), may hold an integral part to completing a project, navigating a new system or connecting you with better resources. Be a pal and get friendly with the ogre: he may just turn out to be a Shrek to your Donkey.

*Romance:* What are the differences between iron and nylon? After you think of a few, imagine how that may apply to a relationship — including communication, attitude, expectations, scheduling and "house rules" (spoken or implied). *"You draw more bees with honey than vinegar"* may be a cliché, but it's an apt one for this card: tenderness, vulnerability and compromise may seem distasteful if you happen to have an aggressive personality, but you can learn to view those practices as strengths. After all, to open up to another — raw, honest, naked, *hungry* — takes an enormous amount of courage. And don't be afraid to bring this newfound bravery to your sex life: ask for what you want. Show where you like it...and *how* you like it. Embrace soft sensuality and passive enjoyment. Ask your partner what drives them wild—and think of surprising ways to make that happen.

*Parenting*: The poet Dylan Thomas said, *"The force that through the green fuse drives the flower"* —noting that an innate, inevitable natural strength, rather than applied power, unfurls the beauty of nature. Kids are a lot like flowers: each has natural strengths, aptitudes and talents that blossom quite on their own. Some of those may not seem "socially acceptable", depending on their environment. A dad dreams of instilling a love for football and deer hunting in his camo-swaddled baby son—only to realize, over time, that kiddo prefers dancing ballet, watching musicals and wearing pink. Or a rambunctious girl with a high IQ can't keep her mouth shut in public school—so they attempt to label, medicate and (eventually) punish her for her exuberance. *Suckage*. Major suckage. Why can't we just let kids be kids—and turn out they way they were born and meant (provided such behaviors aren't anti-social or criminal, *natch*)? What kind of genius have we stamped out of our future by trying to contain, compartmentalize and "cure" our youth? This is the kind of hard question you're going to have to answer when the Strength card comes up: do you allow your child to flourish as born and meant—or do you prune, isolate or hide the bud for fear of what the rest of the garden will think?

*Spirituality:* To shut the lion's mouth...or open it? In the B.O.T.A. version of Strength, the woman pries open its jaws. In the RWS version, the woman *shuts* its gaping maw. While a seemingly simple image—beauty and beast—this archetype is actually one of *the* most complex: arguably, an entire book could be written just on the psychological aspects of this pattern. It's the stuff of fairytales, myth and religion: riding a beast, befriending a beast, conquering a beast, reveling with a beast, following a beast, hunting a beast, slaying a beast, transforming a beast, turning *into* a beast—you're starting to remember some stories, aren't you? So what is this "beast", anyway? In a nutshell, it's an electric, primal self-generating force. It may lie in the vast collective unconscious that surrounds our little conscious, personal world. But it's just as likely that it lies somewhere within—still on the outskirts of what is "known" to us. I see Strength as the alternative path to The Devil: With The Devil, psychic boundaries are weakened (or dissolved)—and we become slaves to unbridled passion without rational thought. Or, we project our disowned or disliked shadow "parts" outward, in the form of demonization and projection. But with Strength, we recognize our base human instincts and embrace them—resulting in a more integrated Self. We *own* them—even channel those passions—but without bragging about, or threatening others, with them. Which brings us to my initial question: do we open, or shut, the mouth of the beast? Do we articulate the shadow, make friends with it? Or try to clamp down on it, suppress it? What you choose will largely depend on whether you go down the path of Strength...or The Devil.

**Recommended Resources**: "Lacey", Episode in second Season of *Once Upon a Time* (TV Show); "Peaceable Kingdom" (Paintings by Edward Hicks); "Europa and the Bull" (Sculpture) by Carl Milles

**Strength Card Layout:** *Lawd, Give Me Strength!* Spread

1. In what area do I need strength right now?
2. How will this strength take form?
3. How can I best welcome this form of strength?
4. What needs "taming" in the process?
5. What needs space to "roar"?

6. What am I suppressing that I'm oblivious to?
7. How can I "make friends" with (integrate) this hidden aspect?
8. What is the best way for me to define "strength" right now?

# The Hermit – Leave Me Alone

**Stripped Down Overview:** When you want to stay in bed, bury yourself under a stack of blankets and shun humanity until the next Ice Age dawns (when no people are left), congratulations: You've just entered The Hermit zone. The Hermit burns a candle for himself alone, so if you need a light—go buy your own matches. Seriously, what part of "alone time" don't you understand? Why are you still here, looking at me? *Go. Away.*

**Keywords:** Isolation; Withdrawal; Seeking Answers; Going Solo; Seclusion; Privacy; Needing to be Alone

**Personification and Embodiments:** Transcendentalism; Henry David Thoreau; Recluses; Gollum

**Quote:** *God has placed in each soul an apostle to lead upon the illumined path. Yet many seek light from without, unaware that it is within them.* – Kahlil Gibran

**Challenge:** Isolation

**Gift:** Solitude

**Occupations/Vocations:** Statue Maker; Scholar; Forest Ranger; Lighting Specialist; Cave Explorer; Hibernation Expert

**Disney Totem:** Gribble (*Mars Needs Moms*)

**Animal Symbol:** Praying Mantis

**Flower Essences:** Water Violet (Bach); Tall Yellow Top (Australian)

**Crystal/Stone:** Tanzanite – Helps solve questions related to the meaning of life. Aids in coming to terms with oneself. Illuminates spiritual orientation and spiritual calling.

**Aromatherapy:** Narcissus (Absolute)

**Body Parts/Systems and Health Issues:** Rickets; Vitamin D Deficiency; Insufficient UV Rays; Frostbite

**Mystical Messenger** – Seraphim the Wonder Worker

**Sabian Symbol:** Pisces 11 – Men traveling a narrow path, seeking illumination.

**Writing Prompt:** A dare involving solitary confinement.

**Affirmation:** I seek wisdom and insight in solitude.

## Naked Advice for The Hermit

*Career:* In the animated movie *Rudolph the Red-Nosed Reindeer*, Santa was a total dick in the first half of the movie. Like Rudolph's equally dicktastic dad, Donner, Santa considered Rudolph a freak, shaming him into hiding his flaming schnoz. Can you imagine? Poor Rudolph, showing promise at flying— forced to cover his unusual nose and encouraged to stay in his cave. Extrapolating this anecdote to your career trajectory, tell your own North Pole Negative Nellies to *fuck off*. God gave you a unique disposition, unusual talent or flair for the absurd for a reason. One day, it will not only come in handy, but possibly save the day...so turn up that ruby nose to full wattage!

*Romance:* Unless playing with yourself constitutes a good time, get the hell out of bed (or your black-lit basement) and *go meet some people*! A museum, concert, library, church, mall, bookstore…just get out there and mingle already. When it comes to romance—or any endeavor, really—the Universe favors the prepared. So, prepare to meet your match by crawling out of your shell. *Now.*

*Parenting*: Look, wallflowers often turn into brilliant scientists, digital wizards or geektastic gurus. And, yes, sometimes brooding musicians, hackers for Anonymous or even serial killers. But never you mind that! Sometimes, kids have to go within to find themselves. If Mary or Johnny is otherwise happy and healthy, then get off your kid's back about "being social". Let them pursue their solitary interests—reading, coding, fan fic writing, anime drawing, Mine Crafting—so they can build their neural network in peace.

*Spirituality:* Jesus often withdrew from the crowds to commune with his Father. He gave—a *lot*—but knew his strength came from a deep well inside. You're no different. If you keep pouring out without taking time to fill up, you'll go dry. Unplug from formal religion, legalistic dictates and moralistic "shoulds", choosing to drink deeply from Spirit on your own terms, and in your own way—even if it means avoiding groups, passing up the opportunity to join gatherings or entering temporary seclusion.

**Recommended Resources:** *The Stranger in the Woods: The Extraordinary Story of the Last True Hermit* by Michael Finkel; *Crackers in Bed* by Normal Rockwell; *Wanderer Above the Sea of Clouds* by Caspar David Friedrich; *Still Life with Books* by Vincent Van Gogh

**Hermit Card Layout:** *Alone and Lit Up* Spread

1. What do I need to know about solitude?

2. How can I carve out needed alone time?
3. How can I make the most out of this seclusion?
4. What area of my life needs illuminating?
5. How to keep the lantern lit.

# Wheel of Fortune – Spinnin' Round Like a Record, Baby

**Stripped Down Overview:** Jupiter—astrologically associated with the Wheel of Fortune—is the planet of expansion, good fortune, abundance, generosity and breadth of vision. When I think of the symbolic nature of our largest planet, the genial, gigantic, generous and jolly Ghost of Christmas Present from *A Christmas Carol* comes to mind. Interestingly, Dickens' tale takes Scrooge through the past, present and future—showing him the inexorable path his life will take should he continue on the same trajectory. The Wheel of Fortune is all about repeating patterns, as well as the process of sowing and reaping. What may seem like "luck" or "chance" to us is often the visible result of sometimes *invisible* (or behind-the-scenes) actions or attitudes. What may appear as "magic", especially centuries ago, could be obscure or misunderstood technology. Science and Laws of Nature, once known, can be comprehended, mastered and utilized. But what of "laws" we don't yet recognize or grasp? Unseen "forces" we may ascribe to gods, deities or spirits may be yet-to-be-discovered knowledge. And what of Fate? Does "crap happen"—utter randomness in an impersonal universe—or is there a root cause or script behind circumstances? Philosophers, theologians and seekers have been running in mental circles for eons discussing this very conundrum. When reasoning fails, though, sometimes the only thing left to do (if we want to retain our sanity and footing) is to throw up our hands, realize the universality of the human condition and let go (or, as I used to hear at church, *"Let Jesus take the wheel."*). The alternative to surrender is to keep spinning wheels by seeking answers and constancy. Good luck with that, because you'll likely form a rut (which is a grave with the sides knocked out).

**Keywords:** Vicissitude; Rotation; Cycles; Rhythms; Progression; Flux; Déjà Vu; Ups and Downs; Passage of Time; Chance; Luck; Fate; Cause and Effect; Sowing and Reaping; Gambling; Apparent Randomness; Reverberation; Patterns

**Personifications and Embodiments:** Boomerang; Ticking Clock; Ferris Wheel; Carousel; Merry-Go-Round; Roulette Wheel; A Dog Chasing Its Tail; Rise and Fall of Civilizations; Mayan Calendar

**Quote:** *That is the key to history. Terrific energy is expended — civilizations are built up — excellent institutions devised; but each time something goes wrong. Some fatal flaw always brings the selfish and the cruel people to the top and it all slides back into misery and ruin.* – C.S. Lewis

**Challenge:** Fatalism

**Gift:** Churning

**Occupations/Vocations:** Casino Worker; Carousel Operator; Speculative Investor; Professional Poker Player; Bookie; Gambler

**Disney Totem:** The Spinning Arrow (*Pocohantas*)

**Animal Symbol:** Nautilus

**Flower Essences:** Sunshine Wattle (Australian Bush); Chestnut Bud (Bach)

**Crystal/Stone:** Yellow Sapphire – Helps one feel centered. Aids in the recognition of the relativity of "good" and "bad" luck. Promotes meaningful living. Encourages recognition, insight and understanding.

**Aromatherapy:** Amber

**Body Parts/Systems and Health Issues:** Vertigo; Dizziness; Inner Ear; Motion Sickness

**Mystical Messenger** – Saint Cajetan

**Sabian Symbol:** Libra 15 – Circular paths.

**Writing Prompt:** An old man's last merry-go-round ride.

**Affirmation:** I am mindful of cycles and adjust accordingly.

## Naked Advice for the Wheel of Fortune

*Career:* "*Those who don't know history are doomed to repeat it*", a famous quote by George Santayana, indicates that if you can't grasp cause and effect, you'll keep making the same mistakes. Or, as Albert Einstein observed, "*Insanity: doing the same thing over and over again and expecting different results.*" Imagine a large, long circular rubber band placed on a table before you, along with scissors. You pick up the shears and make a cut. Then, you grasp one end of the rubber band and gently pull it upward. Behold...a *spiral!* Circles can only be turned into spirals when a cut is made and an end is lifted. Do you see where this is going? In order to gain a higher perspective—and break out of the rut of repetitive thinking and stale results—you will need to slice into routine, elevate your approach and gain a broader perspective from atop this spiral. However, in order to make an omelet you have to break some eggs...so don't expect everyone to applaud your newfound way of doing and seeing (let alone receive a James Beard award for your breakfast creation).

*Romance:* In the past, our ancestors rubbed garments against stone or washboards to get them clean. Nowadays, most of us toss our clothes and towels into washing machines. The agitation of swirling water and circulating detergent lifts off stains, removes odors and cleanses fabrics. The Wheel is encouraging you to shake things up in your romantic life: if you haven't been attracting dates, change up your approach—including *where* you look for them and *how* you approach them. (Did you just say that you *never* approach anyone? That you wait, passively, for someone to talk to *you*? Well, there ya go. *First* thing to modify, chickie!) If you're already attached, time to go for a drive, get away for a few days and spice up your sex life. Role-playing may be called for here, which can provide endless avenues for exploration and fun. Yes, it may feel risky—*dangerous* even—but that's the point! Nothing ventured, nothing gained. Be bold, take a chance, throw a monkey wrench in the status quo...and romp until you're breathless.

*Parenting*: We are born, we live and we die. Technology seems to have some kids convinced that they'll live forever: if you die in a video game, there are extra lives. If you use *those* up, you can re-start from the beginning or at a checkpoint. Any posts or pics uploaded to the internet seem to live forever (even if your kids wished they *didn't*). This artificial sense of perpetuity can give youth a false sense of security: sure, there's the possibility of second chances and do-overs, but these aren't always possible, especially if others won't reciprocate—or when something irreplaceable is broken, severed or crushed. If a teen dodges a bullet (metaphorical or literal), he may become gun shy, cowering from opportunities. But, almost as likely, he may think he has an armor of special protection—a belief propagated (implicitly or explicitly) within some religions. If you draw the Wheel of Fortune when it comes to matters dealing with children, a reality check may be in order: children need to understand cause and effect—to use critical thinking skills (not often taught in public schools, sadly) for mapping likely scenarios, recognizing that nothing happens in a vacuum and acknowledging interconnectedness.

*Spirituality:* There's an ancient Taoist story that goes something like this: A farmer and his son had a beloved horse that helped their family earn a living. One day, the horse ran away. The neighbors exclaimed, *"Your horse ran away, what terrible luck!"* The farmer replied, *"Maybe so, maybe not. We'll see."* A few days later, the horse returned home, leading a few wild mares back to the farm. The neighbors shouted out, *"Your horse has returned, bringing several horses home with it. What great luck!"* The farmer replied, *"Maybe so, maybe not. We'll see."* Later that week, the farmer's son was trying to break one of the mares and she threw him to the ground, breaking his leg. The villagers cried, *"Your son broke his leg, what terrible luck!"* The farmer replied, *"Maybe so, maybe not. We'll see."* A few weeks later, soldiers from the national army marched through town, drafting all the able-bodied boys. They did not take the farmer's son because he was still recovering from his injury. Friends rejoiced, *"Your boy is spared, what tremendous luck!"* To which the farmer replied, *"Maybe so, maybe not. We'll see."* The point of this parable? In the grand scheme of things—in the massive turning of wheels within wheels—good and bad are relative. Whether something turns out beneficial or harmful is often largely dependent on how we react to it—and the choices we make in the aftermath (including how to frame our "story").

**Recommended Resources:** *Groundhog Day* (Movie); *"What Goes Around...Comes Around"* by Justin Timberlake; *Tooth Fairy* (Movie)

**Wheel of Fortune Card Layout:** *ROTA TARO ORAT TORA* Spread

1. *ROTA*: What is the Wheel of Fortune teaching me right now?
2. *TARO*: What is the Tarot revealing to me right now?
3. *ORAT*: What am I learning about *what* I say and *how* I say it right now?
4. *TORA*: What is the Law of Nature showing me right now?

# Justice – Long, Broken Arm of the Law

**Stripped Down Overview:** Justice and Judgment are often confusing to Tarotists, especially if you throw in the Wheel of Fortune. Then there's The Emperor and Hierophant. So who deals with laws? Rules? Consequences? Court dates? Jail time? Bureaucracy? Government? Karma? Ethics? Morality? Well, you have to read each entry in this book to get my take; if you're reading from front to back, we've already covered The Emperor, The Hierophant and The Wheel. In The Hierophant chapter, I stated, *"The Emperor rules the letter of the law, but The Hierophant governs the spirit of the same."* The boxing ring where these two duke it out? Justice. The roots of legal codes reach downs towards the bedrock of religion; depending on your moral persuasion— i.e., ideas of right and wrong (Hierophant)—you may take issue with how a particular country *translates* their religious decrees into actual laws (Emperor). Even within a particular province or country, some may disagree with laws—as well as their interpretation and enforcement. Thus, the battleground of Justice: this is where laws are discussed, decreed, repealed, appealed and enforced among a group—usually a township, county, state or country. They're "on the books", and subject to argument, objection and sustainment. In some patriarchal, fundamentalist, Middle-Eastern countries, laws are inextricably linked with sacred texts with an *eye for an eye* brand of "justice": you steal, you lose a hand. You cheat on your husband, you get gang-raped. Bring your family "dishonor" as a modern young woman, and your brother gets to strangle you to death with impunity. Even the legal systems of Western countries—which many assert are more civilized, rational and fair—may draw harsh criticisms: what of corrupt cops or courts? Jail time for marijuana possession versus multiple DUIs (any of which could have resulted in the death of motorists)? Or the capriciousness (some would say, *bigotry*) of racial profiling and arrests, not to mention false imprisonments? Granted, some territories appear to uphold equality more than others. In fact, if citizens disagree, they can actually *change* those laws through voting and political pressure. Participation in local government is important because, in essence, *we* make the laws of the land — and they *directly* reflect our sense of parity...or apathy.

**Keywords:** Laws; Trials; Due Process; Honor; Legislature; Arbitration; Fairness; Veracity; Hearings; Weighing a Matter; Neutrality; Legal Matters; Subpoena; Penalty; Impartiality; Fines; Tickets; Testimony; Lawsuit; Warrants; Court Appearance; Sworn Statement; Writs; Objectivity; Court-Martial; Jurisprudence; Equality

**Personifications and Embodiments:** Scales; Lawyers; Policemen; Tribunals; Officers that Enforce Laws; Courtrooms; Judges; Jails; Bailiffs; ACLU; Attorney General; Ma'at

**Quote:** *Laws are like cobwebs, which may catch small flies, but let wasps and hornets break through.* – Jonathan Swift

**Challenge:** Balance

**Gift:** Regulation

**Occupations/Vocations:** Judge Advocate General (JAG); Attorney; Investigative Journalist; Court Reporter; Justice of the Peace

**Disney Totem:** Sheriff (*Cars*)

**Animal Symbol:** Owl

**Flower Essence:** Yellow Cowslip Orchid (Australian Bush)

**Crystal/Stone:** Blue Fluorite – Aids with justice. Ameliorates frustration and disappointment with the legal system. Helps with surrendering rigid ideas and assumptions. Promotes sobriety and quietude.

**Aromatherapy:** Cinnamon

**Body Parts/Systems and Health Issues:** Vertebrae Misalignment; Tilted Pelvis

**Mystical Messenger** – Dike

**Sabian Symbol:** Libra 18 – Two men placed under arrest give an accounting for their acts before the tribunal of society.

**Writing Prompt:** Scales with a mind of its own.

**Affirmation:** I embrace honesty, integrity and truth in all matters.

## Naked Advice for Justice

*Career:* If this card comes up for a work question, I'm sure you know *exactly* what it means: make sure everything you do is aboveboard—nowhere *near* crossing some type of legal boundary. Don't flirt with co-workers (not even a wink). Watch where you put your hands. Watch your mouth (leave the dirty jokes at home lest someone overhears and cries "sexual harassment"). Make sure you know the employee handbook inside and out (because if you're not union, you may be fired for looking at your boss the wrong way). If you're handling money, make sure everything is ship-shape (don't give the IRS *any* reason to audit). If you're a designer, blogger or artist, make sure you buy and/or credit any photos before use (unless you want an intellectual property lawsuit). If you're a Tarot reader, don't overreach your local laws and provide advice for issues you're not qualified for. Bottom line: whether you're employed by others or are your own boss, tow the line like never before. And if you're expecting justice because you've been wronged in the workplace, this card hints at a court case (probably favorable for you). If you're the one screwing over others by illegal acts, expect the same—with a *not-so favorable* outcome (especially if accompanied by the Judgment card).

**Romance:** In the *Snowland Deck*, Justice is portrayed as a cracked statue with human flesh underneath. She holds a balanced scale that has a faceted, jewel-like ruby heart on one side and a six-pointed, diamond-like snowflake on the other. Windswept clouds form a backdrop as a feather falls. Will it land on the scale? Which side? Will it make a difference? Soon, you'll be weighing a very serious matter in the realm of romantic relationships. If you were to project your issue onto this image, what would the snowflake represent? The heart? The feather? The cracked statue? What will "tip" the scales one way or the other? What would make the scales balance out to your satisfaction? Are you able to affect the tipping point—or is it out of your hands? Is this a matter better settled with the heart—or the mind? Objectivity or subjectivity? Logic or compassion? Yes, there are more questions than answers—because when it comes to relationships, *you* are the final arbiter of how to mete out Justice's final decision (or ignore her advice altogether).

**Parenting:** If you're shielding your child from legal consequences, shame on you. If you're doing it as an adult, *double shame*. I know a family of six that lost not one, but *two* children to drug overdoses (the last one just occurred a few weeks ago at this writing). Thing is, the mom hid her son (in his mid-30s) from the cops *multiple* times; they wanted to ask him about his heroin drug dealing (among other legal questions). She did this over and over and over—well over a decade of lies and obstruction. No guarantees, but maybe if she allowed him to pay the price for his "sins" early on, he may not have turned into a serial lawbreaker—or six feet under. Parents, you're not doing your kid a favor by lying to police, destroying evidence, bailing her out of jail or enabling her addiction. Not only that, but bitching about the "stupidity" of parking fees, speeding tickets, misdemeanor fines or paying child support—especially when your kids are young—instills in them the notion that laws are flexible, avoidable and justifiably breakable. Rationalizing bad behavior while demonizing "senseless" laws make for a toxic— and sometimes, deadly—parental mix. (In fact, if I had my way, parents would be required to pass multiple tests to get a license before bringing a baby home. We're required to have one for driving a car; why not for raising a child?)

**Spirituality:** The verdict of the "Court of Public Opinion" may be as painful (or more painful) than any earthly legal process— especially if you know damned well that you, or a loved one, has done nothing wrong. All through sacred texts from various traditions, righteous people have suffered under cruel and fickle laws (like when the Passover crowds yelled for convicted criminal Barabbas to be freed, rather than Jesus). How they thought, acted and spoke during those times not only provide us comfort, but also serve as wise counsel when dealing with legal systems. Obviously, if we can somehow work to change unfair laws, it may very well be our spiritual duty to do so—especially if we feel a strong sense of righteous indignation and a personal calling in the face of them.

**Recommended Resources:** *Matlock* (TV Series); *The Firm* by

John Grisham; *The Pelican Brief* (Movie); *To Kill a Mockingbird* by Harper Lee; *Perry Mason* (TV Series); *The Jury* by Normal Rockwell; *12 Angry Men* (Movie); *The Verdict* (Movie); *Inherit the Wind* (Movie); *People's Court* (TV Show); *Billy Budd: Sailor* by Herman Melville

**Justice Card Layout:** *Snowland Justice* Spread

1. *Scales* – What do I need to know about this injustice/ unfairness/imbalance?
2. *Heart* – What is my heart/feelings telling me?
3. *Clouds* – What is my mind/rational mind telling me?
4. *Snowflake* – How is this situation affecting my sense of Self?
5. *Feather* – What attitude/thought/belief is contributing to my discomfort?
6. *Cracked Statue* – What does this circumstance show me about being human?

# Hanged Man – This is Taking FOREVER

**Stripped Down Overview:** If The Fool to The World were an ordered circle, I'm *convinced* that the Hanged Man would be in between those two cards (rather than, say, Trump 12): After a major completion (The World), there's that lull—that interminable *waiting* that often occurs. What does this ending mean? What next? Why am I not receiving any cosmic downloads on the next step? And before The Fool, who's just stepped from Glory onto this Earth, there's the pre-incarnation (or *in-between* incarnation) realm: Have I learned my last life's lessons? What did I do right? Wrong? Who do I choose for my parents? What curriculum will I script for my *next* life? While The Hanged Man seems like a rather gruesome card, it doesn't indicate literal stringing up (at least, not *these* days): It's the "hang 10" or "big air", except a lot longer (DMV type of *long*). It's delays and postponements—the space between (don't wanna be) here and (wanna be) there. This archetype also plays out when you stand on your head (or use an inversion table): blood rushes to the head and everything seems…*different*. I mean, as a kid, did you ever get on your hands and knees—put your head down—and look through your legs? Then try to walk around? Super cool, right? It's like visiting an alien world! A brand new adventure! All because of inverting our head. Here's a secret: those *pain-in-the-ass* wait times (yes, even when put on hold!) could be an opportunity to slow down, inhale deeply, enjoy the moment, exhale gratitude and ask yourself, "What's *new* about where I'm at right now? How might I see things differently?"

**Keywords:** Suspension; Postponement; Inversion; Hung Up; Sacrifice; Intermission; New Perspective; Waiting; Pause; Standstill; Moratorium; Unusual Perception; Halt; No Progress; Motionless; Fresh Viewpoint; Reversal; Delay; Immobility;

Limbo; Stop; Waiting in the Wings; On Standby

**Personifications and Embodiments:** Jesus; Odin; Holding Pattern; TV Commercials; Tree of Yggdrasil; Expectant Father in Hospital Lounge; Waiting for the Results of a Test, Interview, Audition or Application; Theater Intermissions; Red Light; Stop Sign; Cross; Garrote; Gallows; Bats; Cross (Gymnastic Rings Position); Cryogenics; Stasis Chamber

**Quote:** *It's a good thing to turn your mind upside down now and then, like an hourglass, to let the particles run the other way.* – Christopher Morley

**Challenge:** Patience

**Gift:** Neutrality

**Occupations/Vocations:** Yoga Instructor; Meditation Teacher; Oceanographer; Scaffold Worker; High Rise Window Washer; Peace Corps Volunteer; Executioner

**Disney Totem:** Flash (*Zootopia*)

**Animal Symbol:** Jellyfish

**Flower Essences:** Olive (Bach); Bush Fuchsia (Australian Bush); Isopogon (Australian Bush)

**Crystal/Stone:** Blue Chalcedony – Brings presence of mind. Aids in accepting new situations and perspectives. Helps overcome resistance to *what is*. Bestows inner calm and relaxed attention.

**Aromatherapy:** Ormenis Flower

**Body Parts/Systems and Health Issues:** Neck; Collarbone

**Mystical Messenger** – Gaucho Gil

**Sabian Symbol:** Pisces 6 – Illuminated by a shaft of light, a large cross lies on rocks surrounded by sea and mist.

**Writing Prompt:** A town where upside down is normal.

**Affirmation:** When I have to wait, I use the time constructively.

## Naked Advice for The Hanged Man

*Career:* Ever see the hilarious Geico cavemen commercials? One of my favorites is the caveman at the airport, dressed in his tennis outfit, riding a conveyor belt past a Geico poster that says, "*So easy, even a caveman can do it*" (registering disgust on his sophisticated face). Now, even though the caveman *appears* to be standing still—he's moving forward. In our career, we often take two steps back and one step forward—or feel like we're stuck, immobile, utterly lacking any forward movement. However, when The Hanged Man comes up, he assures us that although we're in the midst of a giant Pause (capital *P*), we're *exactly* where we need to be. In fact, we *are* making progress. Granted, it may seem invisible—silently working alongside the diligence we're investing, within the warm relationships we're forging or around the trust we're building—but advancing we *are*. Use this holding pattern to enjoy what you've accomplished so far and to appreciate how far you've already come. Take this time to catch up on non-essential paperwork, organize your surroundings and see your career with new eyes: you never know what you may discover when you actively experiment with viewing the familiar from a whole new angle.

*Romance:* Don't expect any commitments, proposals or weddings when this card comes up. Everything is literally "up in the air" for you right now. If you're unattached, your romantic life will pretty much stay the same. Either way, don't try to force anything. Don't push, don't chase, don't call, don't text, don't ask, don't fret—just let circumstances run their course. This approach is likely contrary to how you usually handle relationship issues, which is a good thing: the Hanged Man runs counterclockwise— widdershins instead of deosil—forcing you to act, speak and even *think* differently from "normal". This cosmic stoppage will require you to freeze frame your current relationship—or your efforts in obtaining one—then turn it upside down, backwards and on its edge...allowing for time and perspective to deliver an unexpected revelation.

*Parenting*: No two ways about it: children demand time, energy and money—and *lots* of it. When this card comes up in relation to kiddos, the whole notion of sacrifice is at play. Yes, parenting itself (when done right) is sacrificial by nature—but this archetype points to a much larger pattern: how much are you willing to give up for your child's well-being? For his future? And how much is your *kid* willing to give up for the same? I'm reminded of Olympic-grade athletes, who give up their carefree youth (and oftentimes, living in their hometown or with family) in order to pursue excellence—and a shot at the gold. Granted, most families won't be faced with this kind of enormous sacrifice, but giving up *something* is at stake here. It may be traveling an hour, one-way, so your child can attend a free performing arts charter school—or investing in a musical instrument and lessons because he shows promise. Or maybe you need to surrender your preconceived idea of the "right" path for your progeny— allowing her to major in theater and puppetry, even though she comes from a long line of medical doctors.

*Spirituality:* In the Gospels, each provides different versions of Jesus' last words as he died on a cross. Matthew reports that He said, *"My God, my God, why have You forsaken Me?"* (27:46), as does Mark (15:24). Luke states His final words were *"Father, into Your hands I commit My spirit"* (23:46), while John's account states that it was *"It is finished!"* From a mystical standpoint, each of these phrases—the last words of the most famous "hanged man"—can apply to how we feel when this archetype visits our life, as well as our best response during its stay. This is the Dark Night of the Soul, where heaven seems deaf to our cries or demands for answers. No brush of angels' wings, no goose bumps, no stirring of the soul—just...*nothingness*. So we surrender to the Divine—or to *what is*—realizing that praying or yelling ourselves hoarse won't change a damn thing. We stop. We deflate. We throw up our hands. We give up—to something larger than ourselves. Then, eventually, peace descends. We're none the wiser. No reasons or solutions have emerged. We're till in the same spot, going the same speed (0 mph). But we're OK with it all. The fight is over, because we've put away our boxing gloves and committed our spirit, our path, to the Creator. *It is well with my soul.*

**Recommended Resources:** *Waiting for Godot* by Samuel Beckett; *Purple Jesus* by Alex Grey

**Hanged Man Card Layout:** *Please Standby for a Word from our Sponsor* Spread

1. When life slows down, what do I notice most?
2. What area of my life is in a holding pattern?
3. What will I gain if I'm patient?
4. What will I lose if I'm impatient?
5. Where am I getting "hung up"?
6. What differing perspective needs to be considered?

# Death – The End?

**Stripped Down Overview:** Just like the Astrological sign it's associated with (Scorpio) Death—both the card and the actuality—tends to be misunderstood and feared. Intense, mysterious and transformative, we don't know what lies on the other side. But you know what? When the caterpillar uses its spinneret (mouth) to create a silken pad to hang from—then wriggles its way to remove its old skin to reveal the chrysalis— it has no idea that its innards will be liquefied and rearranged into adult external structures (wings, legs, head and antennae). In fact, none of this is observable to onlookers—until hours before the butterfly is ready to emerge, when the chrysalis turns transparent. Then, the butterfly pumps liquids and blood to its extremities to break free from the chrysalis, head first. Using gravity as its ally, the newly winged adult hangs upside down so it's crumpled, wet wings can stretch and harden. Next thing you know, we see the wondrous creature alighting on a flower. Even if it attempted to crawl back into its discarded shell, it can never be a caterpillar again. Death is something we will all experience; in fact, when our parents gave us life, they gave us our death. There are many types of death (besides the obvious), but all involve irrevocable change. And when it's nearing, we usually have some inkling it's coming (unlike The Tower, which gives us no warning). Digging in our heels and resisting what's coming is the *worst* thing we can do—and will likely prolong the process and cause needless suffering. Does this card mean literal death? *Rarely.* But you're being given a head's up so that you can either work *with* the Forces at play (like the butterfly using gravity to make its wings usable so it can fly into its destiny)—or you can try to stop the inevitable.

**Keywords:** Transformation; Metamorphosis; Irrevocable Change;

Transition; Circle of Life; Passing Away; Saying Goodbye; Regeneration; Ending Something; Allowing Something to Die; Becoming New

**Personifications and Embodiments:** Grim Reaper; Ghost of Christmas Future; Dr. Kevorkian; Graveyard; Tombstone; Coffin; Skeleton

**Quote:** *And the day came when the risk it took to remain tight inside the bud was more painful than the risk it took to blossom* – Anais Nin

**Challenge:** Adjustment

**Gift:** Transformation

**Occupations/Vocations:** Mortician; Funeral Director; Life Coach; Osteopath; Hospice Worker; Clock Maker; Cigarette Manufacturer; Arms Dealer

**Disney Totem:** Ray (*The Princess and the Frog*)

**Animal Symbol:** Butterfly

**Flower Essences:** Sweet Chestnut (Bach); Bottlebrush (Australian Bush)

**Crystal/Stone:** Gold Beryl – Helps one to accept the unchangeable and improve upon the changeable. Promotes hope, optimism and joie de vivre.

**Aromatherapy:** Spikenard

**Body Parts/Systems and Health Issues:** X-Rays; MRI; Scans; Fractures

**Mystical Messenger** – El Rey Pascual

**Sabian Symbol:** Aquarius 29 – A butterfly emerging from a chrysalis.

**Writing Prompt:** The Grim Reaper stops for Emily Dickinson—and he gets more than he bargained for.

**Affirmation:** I make transitions with ease.

## Naked Advice for Death

*Career:* In our *Coffee Tarot*, we've renamed the Death card Out of Business. It shows an empty coffee shop with a "For Sale" sign—a rather desolate image (especially if you're jonesin' for some joe). But if you look closely, a flower blooms between the cracks of the cement sidewalk—a symbol of new life. We don't know why the shop had to close. We also don't know what will happen to the café: we can only hope that some other caffeinated entrepreneur catches the vision for a revitalized neighborhood coffee shop. When this card comes up, it asks: What is slowly dying in your career? Your vocational interests? How do you know? What are the signs? If you can answer these right off the bat, it begs the question: why are you *still* doing what you're doing? Why are you still *there*? What do you have to lose by leaving? Staying? *Changing*?

*Romance:* It's time for your relationship (or notions of romance) to evolve...or die. There's really no sugar-coating this card in *this* area: something is decaying, and it either needs to be cut-off or discarded to ensure survival. It may be a *part* of your relationship—a mindset, attitude or behavior pattern—or the relationship *itself*. If you're unattached, it may be your ideas of what a romantic relationship entails. Something is "rotten in Denmark", and you have to confront the skeleton in your relationship closet. If you don't, its ghost may confront you when you least expect it.

*Parenting*: In our *Snowland Deck*, we've renamed the Death card Impermanence. Youth have built a snowman on a rock—complete with a scarf and stone features. As the temperature warms, the snowman melts—but his spirit winks from the clouds, an assurance that he's only changed form. A bluejay flies above the pond, about to eat a bug, while a moose stands in the water drinking—symbolizing the circle of life. The snowman turns to water which runs into the stream which provides nourishment to drinking animals and so on. So it is with our human body: if you believe in an afterlife—or reincarnation—then a melting snowman and the water cycle are a gentle reminder to kids about the death process. If you're an atheist, I guess you could tell your progeny that they'll become worm food one day, helping to feed grass and trees (*eek*). There are many examples of transformation from nature that can help broach the subject of death with youngsters. The modern Western world sterilizes death, shielding children from what should be a normal reality—which not only dehumanizes us, in my opinion, but leaves us ill-prepared for the eventuality for both ourselves and our loved ones.

*Spirituality:* I love this brief poem from Emily Dickinson: "*A death-blow is a life-blow to some Who, till they died, did not alive become; Who, had They lived, had died, but when They died, vitality begun.*" Meditations upon passing and change and renewal and death and birth and cycles are powerful. Most don't attempt such reflections because of the initial anxious feelings that arise. Yet, to push away the reality of finality only makes it push back harder—in the form of unspecified fears and vague dread. When this card comes up in a reading pertaining to your spiritual path, definitely consider if something is fading away from your life—or needs bidding *adieu*. But more likely, you're being invited to contemplate one of the greatest (and least discussed or considered) Mysteries of them all: the process of life and death.

**Recommended Resources:** *Metamorphosis* by Alex Grey; *What Dreams May Come* (Movie); *The Book of Life* (Movie); *Time and Eternity* from *The Collected Poems of Emily Dickinson*; "Elegy Written in a Country Churchyard" by Thomas Gray; "The Science of Death" by Dr. Elizabeth A. Murray (Lecture 19 *of Trails of Evidence: How Forensic Science Works*) via The Great Courses Lecture Series; "Circle of Life" (Song from *The Lion King*); "Don't Fear the Reaper" by Blue Oyster Cult; *The Fly* (Movie)

**Death Card Layout:** *La Muerte* Spread

1. How do I feel about death?
2. What do I need to know about death?
3. What seems to be melting away right now?
4. Who do I need to say "goodbye" to?
5. What do I need to say "goodbye" to?
6. In what area am I resisting change?
7. What is undergoing transformation?
8. Where am I at in the circle of life?

# Temperance – A Little Bit of This,
# A Little Bit of That

**Stripped Down Overview:** What happens when you blend two colors? Or throw on a scarf, shirt and hat that go together fabulously? Or decide to make an impromptu meal of grilled chicken breast nestled on a bed of basil and sliced tomatoes, drizzled with olive oil and balsamic glaze? Or play around with a MagPo set and come up with a brilliant poem? Congratulations: you're dancing with the Temperance archetype. Although many Tarotists associate Temperance with abstention (as in, *please step away from the booze bottle*), I take a different approach. Taking my cue from Iris, the Goddess of the Rainbow often depicted in this image, I view this card as a celebration of diversity; in fact, that's one reason we chose to have the figure in our *Snowland Deck* painted with chocolate skin and wearing rainbow-striped gloves. For me, Temperance is about all the glorious reflections of "differentness" in the world: thousands of types of flowers, insects, trees, fish, mosses and birds—not to mention human body types, skin tones, preferences and hairstyles—that come together to form a harmonious earthly tapestry. It's also a card of blending two or more items to form something unusual, beautiful, delicious, functional—or all of the above.

**Keywords:** Harmonizing; Confluence; Middle Path; Blending; Combination; Fusion; Avoiding Extremes; Alchemy; Mixture; Diversity; Tolerance; Intermingling; Mediation; Inclusion; Moderation; Synthesis; Equilibrium; Cross Pollination; Modification

**Personifications and Embodiments:** Chemistry; Orchestras; Symphonies; Patchwork Quilts; Cooking; Driving within the Lines; The Point (Three Rivers Meet in Pittsburgh, PA); Julia

Child; Blender; Test Tube; Beaker; Irises

**Quote:** *One recognizes one's course by discovering the paths that stray from it.* – Albert Camus

**Challenge:** Acceptance

**Gift:** Range

**Occupations/Vocations:** Mediator; Pharmacist; Diplomat; Tattoo Artist; 12-Step Counselor; Chef; Lab Researcher; Chemist

**Disney Totem:** Remy (*Ratatouille*)

**Animal Symbol:** Griffin

**Flower Essence:** Beech (Bach)

**Crystal/Stone:** Ivory Jasper – Helps to avoid extremes. Brings constant, harmonious flow of power. Eases release of external thoughts. Cleansing.

**Aromatherapy:** Petitgrain

**Body Parts/Systems and Health Issues:** Drug Interaction; Mixing Medicines

**Mystical Messenger** – Cosmos and Damian

**Sabian Symbol:** Leo 18 – A chemist conducts an experiment for his students.

**Writing Prompt:** An alchemist gifted with the ability to separate atoms, components and people.

**Affirmation:** I mix and match to see what will happen.

## Naked Advice for Temperance

*Career:* If you tend to be a black and white thinker, it's time to start incorporating the other colors available on life's palette. Instead of this OR that, consider this AND that. For example, ever hear of "fusion cooking"? Instead of being strictly one ethnic cuisine, it's a blending of favorite or staple foods from various cultures—sometimes, disparate. Years ago, Chef Bobby Flay introduced this way of cooking to viewers on Food Network. Recently, I saw a *not-so-successful* attempt at "fusion": it was a runway fashion show where the models wore designs inspired by "the homeless culture"—complete with drab-colored over-sized trench coats, woolen scarves, baggy layered clothing... and a "trash" bag. ::wince:: Insensitive and ignorant, for sure; I mean, WTF was the designer *thinking*? But don't be skittish because of the potential for a spectacular fail (if your head and heart are in balance, you'll be just fine!). Make some lists: What are some of the jobs you perform at work? What types of hobbies do you enjoy? What are the various talents you have? What areas are you knowledgeable about? What tasks do you *love* doing? Now, draw lines crisscrossing and connecting them. What new approach can you bring to your job? What career change might you pursue based on this exciting *never-thought-of-that-before!* combination?

*Romance:* Finding the right balance for a satisfying relationship can be tricky: there are personality differences for starters. Mix in careers, vocations, daily obligations, chores and shared resources, and the complication increases. Then add in kids, dogs, cats, bills, neighbors (or neighbors named Bill)—*ack!* For some, this may be a recipe for disaster (in that case, you probably need to cozy up to The Hermit). For others, this sounds like the makings of something wonderful—raw ingredients for growth, adventure and joy. But just like a cake recipe would suffer if you add too many eggs—or if you accidentally put salt in your coffee instead of sugar—finding the right quantities is key. The ideal "measurements", if you will, varies from couple to couple. How often to have sex? Who's doing dishes? When does she need advice—or just needs a hug? Should we put a limit on how many times we eat out in a week? Should I take him shopping with me—or is he best left at home? Who's in charge of the financial paperwork? If you can cement many of these practical matters, they become one (or five) less things to debate about. Experiment with adding and removing to find your special relationship blend.

*Parenting*: It can be challenging holding the whole family thing together, even when things are going great. When you find a groove that works for you, it's tempting to stay within that rut; after all, if life is manageable, why in the world would you want to change anything, *right*? Well, staying in our comfort zone (especially amid an often crazy world) seems like a wonderful plan—and it is. But what if you and your children only associate with certain "types" of people? Or mingle within a small circle of friends, perhaps connected via shared activities like Boy/Girl Scouts, church attendance, dance lessons or school functions? Exposing your kids to those who think, act and look differently from them can be an enriching, rewarding experience— promoting appreciation for different cultures, beliefs and inclinations. If you happen to reside in a rural area with sparse populations, watching movies made by, and about, those who seem "different" from you (and your kids) will be beneficial, as would sampling various music productions, literature and art. At first, the experience may seem strange or even uncomfortable, but stay with it for a while—and the kiddos may just discover something life-altering in the process.

*Spirituality:* Online, if you Google "Rainbow Bridge", you'll find a poignant poem about losing a beloved pet—and his transition to the sunny other side. Let this be of comfort to you, should you experience such a passing. Animals may seem so *different* from us (although, anyone with a pet knows otherwise), and yet we share so much more than one would think. For example, in her moving, fascinating book *The Soul of an Octopus: A Surprising Exploration into the Wonder of Consciousness,* author Sy Montgomery shares the story of how she befriended four octopuses with distinct personalities—"gentle Athena, assertive Octavia, curious Kali and joyful Karma"—and how this meeting of two *very* different types of minds yielded profound insights and revelations. And what of seemingly stationary living things like flowers, bushes and trees? In *The Hidden Life of Trees: What They Feel, How They Communicate,* author Peter Wohlleben relates how trees live in families, warn others of danger and even have "friends". (I kid you not: a tree prevents its branches from encroaching upon "friends" beside it, but will allow wild growth to interfere with a non-friend. One tree even grew differently on one side because a "friend" was next to it!) So when Temperance comes up, you're being invited to taste the rainbow—and interact with people and beings that appear "different" from you, but have *oh-so-much* to share if you allow it.

**Recommended Resources:** *Vision Tree* by Alex Grey; *Apothecary* by Normal Rockwell; *The Bridge* by Joseph Stella

**Temperance Card Layout:** *Rainbow Connection* Spread

1. How do I feel about the phrase "in the middle"?
2. What needs moderating in my life?
3. How do I react towards those different from me?
4. Who could use more tolerance right now?
5. How may I be more inclusive?
6. In what ways might I bridge heaven and earth?

# The Devil – Who "Made" You Do It?

**Stripped Down Overview:** Welcome to the repository of everything humanity deems "bad" — the garbage can of "evil" (I use quotation marks because, really, those adjectives are in the eye, rationalization or culture, of the beholder). When The Devil comes up in a reading, many querents shit a brick at its appearance. Some even ask readers to remove this card *before* a reading (as well as Death, The Tower and the 10 of Swords). Rest assured this nasty looking fella has little to do with demonic apparitions or bogeymen under the bed. Rather, this is more like a you're *your own worst enemy* type of card — the energy of giving in to temptation, addiction, co-dependence and self-abasement. And yet, there's *another* side to The Devil: Saturn, the god of restriction (see the tattoo on the beast's right hand in the Rider-Waite-Smith deck?). In many ways, The Devil is the opposite not of The Hierophant (whose blessing this cloven-footed beast often mocks), but The Sun. Where the bright white/yellow Sun embodies illumination, stark truth, lightness, unabashed joy, heat, unashamed nakedness and self-knowledge, The Devil (and thus, Saturn) dwells in ignorance, darkness, coldness, deception, heaviness and denseness. The Sun depicts vibrant children enjoying their incarnation while Saturn was a "child-eating" character (according to Greek mythology). Interestingly, in some classical art (such as the thirteenth-century German woodcut "Children of the Planets"), Saturn carries a *falx*, or pruning hook. In the Bible, God is characterized as a "pruner", as well as a "refiner's fire". From a mystical standpoint, this might suggest that wrestling with one's own "demons" — addictions or a "dark side" — and then integrating any shadow components of our personality (disowned aspects) could very well set us on the path to The Sun. By cutting away "dead wood", new life can grow. By burning up dross, only pure, precious metal is the only thing remaining. Come to think of it, isn't that what the alchemists of old were after: The Philosopher's Stone—the transmutation of lead into gold?

**Keywords:** Ignorance; Shame; Abuse; Temptation; Predation; Cruelty; Lust; Enslavement; Extremism; Oppression; Habits; Addiction; Confronting Your "Demons"; Anarchy; Counterfeits; Self-Destruction; Fear of the Truth; Subservience; Undignified; Repression; Dehumanization; Conditioning; Torture; Bitterness; Personality Fragmentation; Shadow; Perversion; Taboos; Avoidable "Evil"

**Personifications and Embodiments:** Chains; Rehab; AA; Satan; Hitler; Typhon; Baphomet; Aleister Crowley; Beelzebub; Mephistopheles; Cigarettes; Pan; Bacchus; The 27 Club; The Snake and the Forbidden Fruit in the Garden of Eden; *Book of Job*; Pitchfork; Possession

**Quote:** *No man can put a chain about the ankle of his fellow man without at last finding the other end fastened about his own neck.* – Frederick Douglas

**Challenge:** Admission

**Gift:** Testing

**Occupations/Vocations:** S & M Paraphernalia Manufacturer; Drug Dealer; Prostitute; Arsonist; Serial Killer; Slave Trader; Warden; Sex Worker

**Disney Totem:** Maestro Stromboli (*Pinocchio*)

**Animal Symbol:** Anglerfish

**Flower Essences:** Bush Iris (Australian Bush); Mountain Devil (Australian Bush)

**Crystal/Stone:** Antimonite – Helps with addiction. Aids in cessation of negative habits. Promotes overcoming limiting views. Harmonizes personal interests with higher ideals.

**Aromatherapy:** Angelica Root

**Body Parts/Systems and Health Issues:** Drug Addiction (Meth, Heroin, Cocaine, Narcotics)

**Mystical Messenger** – Dionysus

**Sabian Symbol:** Aries 14 – A serpent coiling near a man and a woman.

**Writing Prompt:** The Devil cries.

**Affirmation:** When in doubt, leave it out.

## Naked Advice for The Devil

*Career:* What separates man from beast? Some would say dreaming, others would say laughter. However, the answer is *self-control*. The ability to reason, rationalize and anticipate or visualize consequences of our actions is what keeps most of humanity in check. A *conscience*, in other words. In order to have a conscience (or superego), though, there must be a "threatening" force keeping us from, say, robbing banks or killing idiots. Usually, a conscience stems from either an internal moral compass (gleaned from religion or humanistic common sense)—or a form of self-preservation instincts (who wants to go to jail—or be fried in Ol' Sparky?). When The Devil comes up in a career or vocational reading, it's time to ask *really* hard questions: How far will you go to get what you want? Who might get hurt—and does it even matter to you? Where are you on the constructive vs. destructive continuum? What ramifications will your words or actions have on others or yourself? Does the end justify the means? And, most important, who or what are you trying to "beat"—and how might your considered choices and likely consequences resemble the very thing you're trying to defeat? Remember: when consumed with obsession or hate, we tend to become the very thing we despise.

*Romance:* In the Rider-Waite-Smith tradition, The Lovers card looks suspiciously like The Devil. We have a naked couple in both, as well as a figure hovering over them: in The Lovers, it's an angel—while in The Devil, it's a horned, winged beast that's part animal, part human. The couple in The Lovers appears free (presumably in the Garden of Eden, amidst two trees and a lurking snake), while the couple in The Devil have sprouted tails (the woman, a clump of grapes—the man, a tail set on fire by the beast's torch)—and are both chained to the square stone The Devil sits upon. It's almost as if we're looking at "before and after" pictures of the same couple. So what happened? Hundreds of years and millions of pages have been dedicated to philosophical and theological theories, all centered around the triangle of Human, God and Devil (although each have been given various names). Mankind as battleground or free will choice maker—either way, the results land on one side of the triangle or the other, which brings me to the symbol on the beast's head: an inverted pentagram (which contains *lots* of triangles). Upright, the pentagram symbolizes a whole, healthy human— all elemental energies, and ether/spirit, integrated and accepted. Upside down, though, we have what De Mellet characterizes as "human nature defiled and enslaved" (circa 1781). Again, this card begs difficult questions: What is "natural" for you and your relationship? What are the signs that you're defiling what's good and right for yourself? What is your relationship to pain and pleasure, including the realm of sexuality and intimacy? What is bondage and what is freedom—and are you OK with whatever it is you (and your partner) are doing? After all is said, done and examined, check the answers against your sense of integrity, self-esteem and well-being. If they're intact, *you're* intact...no matter what anyone says.

*Parenting*: Although many a kid has viewed one or both parents as "The Devil" because of imposing restrictions (especially if they're Pages and Knights of either Swords or Wands), such limiting of behavior has saved more lives than spoiled them— especially when it comes to monitoring friends, influences, attitudes and activities. Unfortunately, the public school system (especially in the U.S.) swarms with unsavory conduct, unmonitored behavior and rampant indifference—and that's just the administration and faculty! Drastic intervention may be called for, especially if your kid's disposition and performance has crossed from mildly troublesome to downright worrying: this could include placing your child into a religious or private school (one known for its competence, compassion and results)— or even homeschooling. (Don't feel up to the task? It's easier than you may think. Alternatively, many states have cyberschools for students to work from home via computer.) Rather than think of yourself as the "bad guy", cast yourself as a King of Swords—a surgeon willing to "cut out" disease in order to save the body. Your kid may chafe against the perceived "chains" now—but will come to thank you once they hit adulthood.

*Spirituality:* In The Gospels, Jesus reportedly dealt with literal temptations from the "devil" not once, but *three* times. Every time, he ordered the tempter to *"get behind me, asshole"* (*New Janet Version*). Obviously, the late Nancy Reagan ripped her

"Just Say No" anti-drug campaign right from the J-Man himself, but there's a nugget of truth in doing so: If we resist temptation at the very first offering, we save ourselves psychological, financial, mental and/or physical ruin. Is it easy in some cases? No, but maturing rarely is. In Matthew 21:44, Jesus is quoted as saying, *"And whoever falls on this stone will be broken; but on whomever it falls, it will grind him to powder."* When we know better, we do better. Growth and increased consciousness can be painful—but there's an easy way (well, *easier* way), and a hard way. The "easier" way is to "fall on the rock", choosing to be stripped of our ego and self-delusion. However, if we choose to ignore warning signs, betray our dignity, sabotage our health and destroy our well-being—entering a cycle of self-destructive addiction that spirals outwards towards others—then the *bolt from the blue* of The Tower may very well come in the form of a *boulder* from the blue...crushing us to dust.

**Recommended Resources:** *The Amityville Horror* by Jay Anson; *The Garden of Earthly Delights* (Painting by Hieronymus Bosch); *Historia von Dr. Johann Fausten* (Opera by Alfred Schnittke); "Young Goodman Brown" by Nathaniel Hawthorne; *American Horror Story: Coven* (TV Show); *Hannibal: Season 2* (TV Show); "The Devil Went Down to Georgia" (Song); *Requiem for a Dream* (Movie); *Owning Mahony* (Movie); *The Fall* (Painting by Hugo Van der Goes); "The Devil and Daniel Webster" by Steven Vincent Benet; *666 Park Avenue* by Gabriella Pierce; *Star Trek: The Next Generation* "Symbiosis"

**Devil Card Layout:** *Better the Devil You Know* Spread

1. What temptation is presenting itself to me?
2. What will it "test" in me?
3. What will I gain from resisting?
4. What personal "demon" needs confronting right now?

5. How can I overcome or heal this "demon"?
6. What Shadow am I disowning or projecting onto others?
7. How can I best "own" it and integrate it?
8. My Philosopher's Stone.

# The Tower – All Hell Breaks Loose

**Stripped Down Overview:** Your house burns down. Your partner loses her job. The accountant ran off with your life savings. A Hummer totals your Prius. We're rarely prepared when the lightning shitastic strikes our lives. These bolts don't always arrive on the wings of material destruction, but rather bloom in our psyche like a mushroom cloud, evaporating worn-out beliefs, demolishing shaky structures and re-routing our trajectory. One thing's for sure: when this baby blows, there's no going back to the way things were. The good news is that the destruction of faulty structures you've built—either with material goods, misplaced values or incorrect assumptions— leaves a foundation for you to rebuild upon. Make sure that *bolt from the blue* isn't in vain by accepting its resulting illumination.

**Keywords:** Shock; Collapse; Sudden Illumination; Crisis; Disaster; Release; SNAFU; Sideswiped; Godsmacked; Shit Hitting the Fan; Obliteration of Faulty Beliefs; Leveling of Man-Made Structures

**Personifications and Embodiments:** Tornados; Twin Towers; Father Mychal Judge; Natural Disasters; Lighting Strikes; Demolitions; Dynamite; Dennis the Menace; Tasmanian Devil (Cartoon Character); H-Bomb; The *Titanic;* The *Hindenberg*

**Quote:** *The best lightning rod for your protection is your own spine.* – Ralph Waldo Emerson

**Challenge:** Evaporation

**Gift:** Release

**Occupations/Vocations:** Pyrotechnics Specialist; Stunt Person; Electrician; Demolitionist; Lightning Rod Manufacturer; Telephone Lineman; Crisis Hotline Operator

**Disney Totem:** Wreck-It Ralph (*Wreck-It Ralph*)

**Animal Symbol:** Scorpion

**Flower Essences:** Rock Rose (Bach); Star of Bethlehem (Bach); Fringed Violet (Australian); Waratah (Australian)

**Crystal/Stone:** Fulgurite (Sand Tubes Formed by Lightning Strikes) – Fosters awakening. Eases stress. Provides impetus. Helps pull one out of emotional lows. Promotes agility of action and mental acuity.

**Aromatherapy:** Tarragon

**Body Parts/Systems and Health Issues:** Seizures; Migraines; Epilepsy

**Mystical Messenger** – Saint Barbara

**Sabian Symbol:** Aquarius 2 – An unexpected thunderstorm.

**Writing Prompt:** At a nighttime carnival, an electric pole crashes.

**Affirmation:** I can withstand any shock or surprise.

## Naked Advice for The Tower

*Career:* If you don't get a pink slip first, you may find yourself singing "Take This Job and Shove It" over the company intercom system. Quit now or forever hold your peace, because if you're looking for a permission slip to burn a bridge, this is it.

*Romance:* Your husband asks for a divorce. You catch your boyfriend in bed with the landscaper. Your wife announces she's a lesbian. Cue "The Break Up Song". But if you happen to be single and unattached, Kundalini lightning will rip from your groin to your crown in a flash of mind-blowing sex.

*Parenting:* Expect the unexpected when it comes to your offspring. School expulsion, a report card littered with Ds, truancy—if you've been embroiled in your own earth-shattering dramas, shockwaves will cascade down the DNA ladder. When grownups play the game of upheaval, it's the kids that pay.

*Spirituality:* When a forest fire ravages the land, the intense heat sears open seeds that would otherwise stay sealed and sterile. If there's a silver lining to this shitty cloud, it's the flowers that will rise out of the ashes.

**Recommended Resources:** *Lightworker* by Alex Grey; *Joni* (the life story of quadriplegic artist Joni Erickson Tada); *Inferno* (Movie); "The Wreck of the Edmund Fitzgerald" by Gordon Lightfoot

**Tower Card Layout:** *Smash, Grab and Release* Spread

1. What outmoded belief needs dismantling?
2. What did I gain from my last Tower experience?
3. How am I prepared to handle the unexpected?
4. What needs immediate release?

# The Star – The Bright Side

**Stripped Down Overview:** Holy Stanley Kubrick, it's the Age of Aquarius! After the lid blows off The Tower, a new hope dawns. Napoleon Hill, ETs, technology and *What the Bleep!?* all meet in a swirl of pink fairy dust above humanity's rubble. Unicorns fart rainbows, vegans despise meatans and New Age ninnies think love is the answer to everything—you know, the special Starseeds and metaphysical snowflakes that are too busy meditating within crystal mandalas to get their hands dirty—all the while admonishing us that we *attracted* our sucky reality. These ones want to make sure your astral body is squeaky clean (shaved pits, optional), but can't be bothered if you're vibrating too slowly. At this point, we long for global *kumbiyahs* and smiley faces all around—not to mention full disclosure (*finally!*) and direct alien contact. Yet, a part of us knows that if we're actually *on* a Cosmic Tourist Map, most advanced beings would choose to fly right past us...

**Keywords:** Hope; Awe; Enchantment; Restoration; Evolutionary Advancement; Futurism; Wonderment; Faith; Transcendence; Humanitarianism; Progressiveness; Technology; Utopia; Idealism; Eccentricity; Unconventional; Invention; Expanding Boundaries; Avant-Garde; Atheism; Group Consciousness; Wishes; Morphogenesis; Electricity; Liberalism; Universal Brotherhood; Friendships; Close Encounters; Astronomy; Astrology; Space

**Personifications and Embodiments:** New Age movement; *Star Trek*'s Prime Directive; Genie in a Bottle; UFOs; Sci-Fi; Utopias; Walt Disney World; Make a Wish Foundation; Lunacy; Shapeshifting; Hay House Publishing

**Quote:** *Feeling gratitude and not expressing it is like wrapping a present and not giving it.* – William Arthur Ward

**Challenge:** Magical Thinking

**Gift:** Idealism

**Occupations/Vocations:** Astronaut; Astronomer; Astrologer; Science Fiction Writer; Horticulturist; Museum Guide; SETI Scientist; NASA Employee

**Disney Totem:** Blue Fairy (*Pinocchio*)

**Animal Symbol:** Dolphin

**Flower Essences:** Sundew (Australian Bush); Red Lily (Australian Bush)

**Crystal/Stone:** Green Tourmaline (Verdelite) – Helps one to see the miracles of life. Encourages wonderment. Promotes interest in fellow humans and the world at large. Awakens gratitude.

**Aromatherapy:** Neroli

**Body Parts/Systems and Health Issues:** OCD

**Mystical Messenger** – Saint Evita

**Sabian Symbol:** Leo 7 – The wonder of the constellations of stars in the night sky.

**Writing Prompt:** The constellation Orion goes missing.

**Affirmation:** I view the world with wonderment and awe.

## Naked Advice for The Star

*Career:* Humanitarian endeavors, non-profits, the Peace Corps, scientific progress, genomic breakthroughs and coded utopias: when searching for a way to apply your idealism and explore uncharted frontiers, these realms offer the celestial berries. Also good for you? SETI, MUFON, NASA and other *out-of-this-world* acronyms. You're a wacky and witty creature, so "normal" just won't do for you: get out there, dive into the advancing social stream, hook up with like-minded others and pursue a vocation that others only dream (and talk) about. You may not get applause from the conventional (or your family), but you'll feel good knowing that you're dancing on the bleeding edge of human evolution.

*Romance:* The last thing you want a romantic partner to say to you is *"Dave...I'm afraid"*. While arousal may very well start between the ears, beware of being a mere discombobulated head full of soul-mate notions, past-life connections and twin-flame theories, lest you're left to dance with *yourself* (or your favorite archangel). *Do* share your otherworldly interests and passions—in fact, if you're single, you'll likely find an "out there" partner in those circles—but remember that celestial compatibility will only take you so far (say, the honeymoon stage). After that, you'll have to have something a little more...*earthly* to keep you together.

*Parenting:* With the dawn of the internet, cultural boundaries have softened and, in some ways, disappeared—making for one big global family. If everyone on the 'net behaved themselves and acted like learning from others all around the world was a privilege (it is), human advancement would accelerate. Alas, some have used technology as a breeding ground for baser instincts, allowing lowest common denominators to flourish rather than opening up minds and hearts to world peace and mutual understanding. So what to do? In this case, use your head...not your heart. Draw up a list of rational reasons why associating with people who are respectful, open-minded and courteous will not only help the world, but your kid. Discuss the list. Create a plan for allowing only those types of people in orbit—online and IRL. (Don't worry: adulthood will provide enough opportunities for them to become unsheltered and deal with first-rate assholes.) If your progeny knows how to surround themselves with optimistic and thoughtful people while they're young, it will give their brain and emotions time to grow and expand without the stress of cynicism, negativity and bullying. Tall order? *Yes!* But this is The Star we're talking about...so reach for it.

*Spirituality:* Bright blessings! Love and light! All is one...and it's *all* good! Just. Knock. It. *Off.* Unless you want to be so heavenly minded you're no earthly good, pull chakras 5-7 out of your ass and get to work on making this world a better place. Note the word "work", space cadet: If you're busy building castles in the air without practical scaffolding, then you may very well be part of humanity's problem rather than contributing to a solution. Your platitudes mean nothing if you don't exemplify Universal Brotherhood by how you treat others or speak about them during the daily grind.

**Recommended Resources:** *Arrival* (Movie); *Contact* (Movie); *Starman* (TV Show); *2001: A Space Odyssey* (Movie); *Tomorrowland* (Movie); "What a Wonderful World" by Louis Armstrong

**Star Card Layout:** *I'm a Star* Spread

1. What am I idealizing right now?
2. What area of my life could use some hope or restoration?

3. What do I need to know about my spiritual advancement?
4. Where do I fit into the web of humanity at this time?

# Moon – Tip of the Iceberg

**Stripped Down Overview:** Have you ever gone outside during a full moon? Trees tower with menace, rocks scowl like trolls and bushes look like crouching werewolves ready to rip off your face. And yet, the beautiful milky glow of Luna bewitches and entrances—bathing everything in a soft, reflected light. In the *Coffee Tarot* Majors-only deck, we created two Moon cards (because its archetype prompts so many fascinating images). The first, a special limited-edition bonus card, depicted the nursery rhyme "Hey, Diddle Diddle", but with a twist: instead of the dish running away with the spoon, it absconded with a coffee cup. Fairytales, quirky poems and silly rhymes reside in the realm of The Moon—where things don't quite make sense, and yet, on some level, still resonate. The second, permanent Moon card for our *Coffee Tarot* features a spaceman from JAVA standing on a pockmarked lunar landscape—a huge coffee bean reflected on his helmet's visor. Surrealism, too, lands gently on the gravity-deprived surface: weird juxtapositions, bizarre elements and exaggerated aspects screw with our minds, registering a big ol' *WTF?* from the little gray cells. And our *Snowland Deck?* A luminous full moon shines down on a vast blue ocean, a frosty iceberg standing sentinel over the deep as a mermaid splashes on the edge of the card. According to Freudian and Jungian psychological models, human consciousness looks a lot like the tip of an iceberg, where four-fifths of its mass remains submerged—just like our subconscious fears, suppressed desires and internalized traumas. Forget WYSIWYG: things are rarely what they seem with The Moon, so proceed with caution and common sense.

**Keywords:** Unknown; Hidden; Beneath the Surface; Mystery; Bewitchment; Subconscious; Nighttime Dreams; Symbols;

Archetypes; Illusive; More than Meets the Eye; Intoxication; Unforeseen; Confusion; Complexes; Unexplained; Astral Projection; Psychedelics; Narcotics; Immortality; Distortion; Inconstant; Fantasy; Unfathomable; Moody; Depth Psychology; Strangeness; Obscurities; Signs; Portents; Camouflage; Masks; Subjectivity; Irrational

**Personifications and Embodiments:** Surrealism; The Enchanted Forest; Holograms; Fairytales; "Down the Rabbit Hole"; Labyrinths; Conspiracy Theories; Cover-Ups; Slipstream (Genre); Art of Salvador Dali; Virtual Reality; Mermaids; Undines; Water Creatures; Tides; Phases of the Moon; Menses; Cryptozoology; Werewolves

**Quote:** *Everyone is a moon, and has a dark side which he never shows to anybody.* – Mark Twain

**Challenge:** Confusion

**Gift:** Discovery

**Occupations/Vocations:** VR Game Designer; Gynecologist; Sleep Specialist; Crab Fisherman; Dream Interpreter

**Disney Totem:** Cheshire Cat (*Alice in Wonderland*)

**Animal Symbol:** Dugong

**Flower Essence:** She Oak (Australian Bush)

**Crystal/Stone:** Rainbow Moonstone (White Labrodorite) – Regulates female hormone cycles. Soothes menstrual cramps. Improves sleep and dream recall. Promotes intuitive sensitivity and perception. Boosts alertness and powers of observation.

**Aromatherapy:** Clary Sage

**Body Parts/Systems and Health Issues:** Female Hormonal Imbalance; Ovaries; Uterus; Bipolar; Hypnosis; Mold Allergy

**Mystical Messenger** – Saint Murgan

**Sabian Symbol:** Scorpio 8 – The silvery moon shining across a beautiful gem of a lake.

**Writing Prompt:** It's discovered that the moon surface is a hologram, covering up activity below.

**Affirmation:** I take time to contemplate and decode the symbols that cross my path.

## Naked Advice for The Moon

*Career:* A few years ago, I did an email reading for a gal I'll call Liz. She just finished a contracted job and was looking for new opportunities. After sharing the kind of work she'd be interested in—and the strengths she'd like to utilize—I drew cards for each option. But then, I drew a "Final Advice" card—a position that I almost always include in my client readings (and one that is often the most revealing or helpful). Her Final Advice card? The Moon. I had the immediate sense that there was an opportunity that she hadn't yet seen, was "hidden in plain sight" or was right around the corner—and I shared this with her, encouraging her to keep alert to the unexpected. Within 12 hours, Liz sent me an excited email:

> *You're not going to believe this! I was walking around town yesterday and ran into an old friend I hadn't seen in years. Turns out he owns a tech business—the kind I'm interested in—and he*

*offered me a job right there! If you hadn't stressed the advice of The Moon card, it may not have even occurred to me to share with him about my job search.*

So there you have it, folks: when this card comes up in a career reading, keep your mind wide open, your eyes peeled and your ears tuned like radar—especially to unusual, surprising and *never-thought-of-that-before* situations.

**Romance:** If you're feeling all emotional and teary-eyed, hold it right there: you may be tempted to wail on your partner with accusations like *"You don't love me!"* or *"I know you don't think I'm pretty!"* or *"You're cheating on me with the UPS carrier, aren't you?"* but, before you do, check the calendar: Is it that time of the month? I'm not trying to be insulting, Sister, believe me: I can't tell you the times when a torrential downpour is ready to flow down my cheeks (or has already started) when, asking the Tarot *"What's wrongggggg?"* I pull The Moon card. Or, even more often, when my husband gently answers, *"Honey, it's the first week of the month. It's just hormones."* While it sounds patronizing, it's not. In fact, for me, it's been sanity-saving: as one who's rather uncomfortable with uncontrolled emotions (e.g., sadness)—and who's experienced her share of tragedy and existential angst— it's a *relief* to realize/remember that *"OMG! What a doofus. It's only hormones!"* Then, my Aquarius Moon (see the Spirituality section below) can get to work reining in my emotions before my rational mind starts making wild assumptions as to why I'm feeling the way I do. (And if it's time for your monthly Friend to visit, consider getting your estrogen and progesterone levels checked by a doctor.) If you're a male reading this and your partner is wildly emotional without a specific reason—she answers "I don't know", when asked *"What's wrong, honey?"* — give her all the love, gentleness and non-judgment support you can. (Do *not* ask if it's *that time of the month* unless you have a 2 of

Cups relationship!) And hey, testosterone imbalances can wreak havoc, too, so apply the same care with the guys.

*Parenting*: The very idea of discussing "reality" with a kid is amusing because it's all so *subjective*. Especially during adolescence, where hormones are busy using Ivan or Isabella's brain as a playground, it can be difficult for kids to separate what's "real" or imagined. If you think about it, if it feels "real", it *is*—even if it's not important *or* true. The Moon swirls with fluctuating emotions, making molehills into mountains and ordinary conversations into catastrophes. Instead of *pooh-poohing* feelings or dismissing concerns, allow them to talk about what's going on. Gently ask them *"Is that true?"* when they declare definitive disasters. *"Can you be* sure *it's true?"* If your children are younger, ask them to draw their experience: *If your feelings were an object, what would it be? Or a color? What about a TV show or movie you've seen—or a song you've overheard? Do any of those look, sound or feel similar to what you're going through?* Have a heartfelt dialogue, paying special attention to symbols and descriptors from their expressive art. In times like these, concrete answers aren't as significant as the illuminating discovery process.

*Spirituality:* I don't know about you, but despite my astrological chart being mostly Water (Scorpio x 4, five planets in the 8th House), I have a lot of Air in my disposition. Maybe it's my Aquarius Moon (11th House) and Mars + Uranus in Libra (7th House). This has me leaning heavily on rationality and intellectualism; if someone were to ask me how I feel, I'd probably answer *"I think..."*. When The Moon comes up for spiritual concerns, it may mean you're spending too much time analyzing the Divine, sacred traditions and the root causes for challenges. There's a time and place for scuba-diving the psyche in the attempt to unearth answers to nagging questions. The Moon, though, isn't one of them: instead, you're being invited to dance in the dark, play with symbols, finger-paint with blue pigments, read speculative fiction, stare at surrealistic art, experiment with automatic writing and record your nighttime dreams. When we choose to shut off logic (temporarily), we allow the ebb and flow of intuition to bring valuable keys to surface—unlocking treasures from our subconscious and, indeed, the Universe Itself.

**Recommended Resources:** *Over the Garden Wall* (Mini-Series); *In Search Of* (TV Show); *Ancient Aliens* (TV Show); *X-Files* (TV Show); *Fantasy Island* (TV Show); "The Moon and The Yew Tree" by Sylvia Plath; "Full Moon" by Tu Fu; *Moonshine* by Paul Klee; *Le Chef D'Ouevre Ou Les Mysteres de L'Horizon* by Rene Magritte; *Girl with Shopkeeper* by Norman Rockwell

**Moon Card Layout:** *Moon Songs* Spread

1. *Bark at the Moon* – What's most likely to make me a bit crazy?
2. *Walking on the Moon* – Where do I need some gravity?
3. *Fly Me to the Moon* – Where do I need some lightness of Being?
4. *Old Devil Moon* – What might ensnare on the way?
5. *Moonlight Sonata* – What needs to drift into my life?
6. *Moon River* – What needs to flow out of my life?
7. *Moonage Daydream* – What do I need to keep my "Electric Eye" on?
8. *Shepherd Moons* – What needs to be steered in my life?
9. *Moon over Bourbon Street* – What will intoxicate me?
10. *Moon over Miami* – What will help me heat up my mojo?
11. *Moonlight in Vermont* – What will help me keep cool/chill out?
12. *Sisters of the Moon* – Who will be my ally in exploring The Moon?

# The Sun – Shine On!

**Stripped Down Overview:** There's a curious modern phrase known as *"throwing shade"*. It's a more obvious—usually verbal—version of *"stink eye"*. The roots are the same: jealousy. To *throw shade* at someone is the attempt to overshadow, demean or reduce someone who is "shining". The Sun card reveals many layers to seekers; one happens to be the glowing confidence of being at the top of your game or industry. In fact, of all cards in the Tarot, The Sun is the one most fully embodied, and connected to, *Naked Tarot*: it encourages "stripping down" (who likes to wear clothes when it's hot?), provides illumination, pushes for authenticity (why do you think interrogators use bright lights to coax out the truth?) and promotes playfulness (fun in the Sun!). Can you imagine how the world would look if we all lived this way? As in, the Garden of Eden, before the concept (and mortification) of "sin" set in—*naked and not ashamed*? This card points to the state of utter brilliance and magnificence, a stage of life hallmarked by achievements (especially in the arts), vitality, magnetism, warmth, expansion, fullness, supreme well-being and self-actualization. It is the zenith, the high point in the sky. It is without masks, guile, fear or defense. It is open, liberated, optimistic and contented. If perfection were a card, it would be The Sun.

**Keywords:** Potency; Personal Power; Internal Authority; Performance; Radiance; Fame; Magnificence; Vibrancy; Exposed; Idolize; Displaying Your Talents; Stark; Children; Dazzle; In the Spotlight; Celebrity; Spectacle; Ultimate Congruence; Positive Self-Regard

**Personifications and Embodiments:** Solar Disks; Sunflowers; Icons; Paradise Found; Entertainment Industry; Idols; Sunblock;

Sunglasses; Shade; Parasols; Halos; Fans; Caribbean Islands; Hawaii; Icarus; Wayne Newton; Beyonce

**Quote:** *What is to give light must endure burning.* – Viktor Frankl

**Challenge:** Overexposure

**Gift:** Resplendence

**Occupations/Vocations:** Child Prodigy; Department of Energy; Nuclear Physicist; Solar Panel Manufacturer; Swimsuit Model; Sunscreen Spokesperson

**Disney Totem:** "Zip-a-Dee-Doo-Dah" (*Song of the South*)

**Animal Symbol:** Dragonfly

**Flower Essences:** Heather (Bach); Mulla Mulla (Australian Bush)

**Crystal/Stone:** Sunstone – Aids Seasonal Affective Disorder. Cultivation of personal strengths. Directs focus on the "sunny" side of life. Removes psychic "hooks". Promotes vitality. Increases physical energy. Life affirming.

**Aromatherapy:** Orange

**Body Parts/Systems and Health Issues:** Male Hormones; Sensitivity to the Sun; Sunburn/ Poisoning; SAD

**Mystical Messenger** – Amaterasu

**Sabian Symbol:** Libra 23 – Chanticleer's voice heralds the rising sun with enthusiastic tones.

**Writing Prompt:** Icarus comes back to Earth.

**Affirmation:** I shine brightly.

## Naked Advice for The Sun

*Career:* Now's the time to pull out all the stops—to go big, or go home. Some shirk the mantle of excellence or shy away from reaching their full potential. They're afraid of the "tall poppy" syndrome: when you outshine your peers, stand out, you'll get "mowed down"—knocked back to average, the mediocre, the status quo. I'd like to tell you this mindset is mere superstition or a buried fear of success—but it is not. The herd—groups of any sort (including the workplace)—usually put a bull's-eye on anyone that's better, stronger, smarter or faster. The secure and confident use fellow tall poppies as motivation and inspiration to grow and excel. The rest? Target practice to assuage diseased egos. This card invites you to place fear or jealousy in your back pocket, straighten your tie, smooth back your hair, powder your nose and put your best foot forward. Be the best you. No one else can.

*Romance:* Do you accept your body? Are you comfortable with every curve, wrinkle, discoloration, bulge, dimple or freckle— the size and shape of your boobies or penis? The whole *naked and not ashamed* attitude works beautifully in the bedroom, too: When you fully embrace the wondrous vehicle known as your body, the easier it is to engage in meaningful, fulfilling sexual relations. Instead of focusing on blemishes or *less-than-ideal* (by whose standards, anyway?) physical traits, concentrate on radical self-acceptance which increases sexual confidence— leading to crazy fun and satisfaction in the bedroom. If you're not there yet, talk to your partner to see if he can help you get there. Or, see a sex therapist to put you on the path to unbridled, full-frontal ecstasy. (And pick up a copy of the book *Mars and Venus in the Bedroom*, while you're at it.)

*Parenting*: The opposite of the "stage mother" or "football dad" is the parent who never pushes or nudges a child towards *anything*. The Sun lies between these extremes, encouraging you to introduce your child to a new hobby, extracurricular activity or sport. Pay attention to any interests your child has been exhibiting: Does he mimic celebrities or crack clever jokes? Consider acting classes. Does he mess around on the keyboard? Sign him up for piano lessons. Does he "bend it like Beckham"? Enroll him in soccer. Dancing, painting, woodworking, sculpting, cooking, biking, writing, designing, coding—now's the time to prod your progeny in a new, exciting direction. Attend as many of his functions as you can, be his cheering section and let him know what a fine human being he's turning into. Not only will his confidence and poise likely increase—but you very well may walk him into his destiny.

*Spirituality:* In many ways, the Puritan mindset and ethic are in direct opposition to The Sun: Instead of joy, exuberance, playfulness, lightheartedness, vibrancy, enthusiasm, optimism, abundance, authenticity and nudity, Puritanical practice advocates strenuous labor, seriousness, restraint, suffering, cynicism, poverty, a "righteous" persona and thick, plain clothes covering every bare spot. Despite scriptures like *"the joy of the Lord is my strength"* and *"unless you become as a child you cannot enter the Kingdom of Heaven"*, some get it into their heads that laughter, talent, achievement and recognition aren't "spiritual". What a load of bullshit! In fact, such self-righteous debasement is one of the few things Jesus *ever* condemned. He called the Pharisees "white-washed tombs" that looked clean on the outside, but inside, were *"full of dead men's bones"*. If any spiritual path, group, teaching or leader tries to squash your individuality, knock you down to size, tell you who to associate with (or avoid), silence you or push you into the average box — *run like hell.* Where they live, the Sun *doesn't* shine.

**Recommended Resources:** *The Virtuoso* by Normal Rockwell; *Fame* (TV Show); "Life is a Flower" by Ace of Base; *American Idol* (TV Show); *"Sun" from The Weather Series* by David Hockney; *Chariot of Aurora* (Lacquered Relief Mural with Silver and Gold) by Jean Dunand and Jean Dupas; *America's Got Talent* (TV Show); *La Nouba* by Cirque de Soleil

**Sun Card Layout:** *Tall Poppy* Spread

1. What's your highest form of self-expression?
2. What/who has been an obstacle to this?
3. How can you best defy and overcome this obstacle?
4. What obstacle/insecurity/doubt have you overcome recently?
5. What will best protect your Inner Light and brilliance?
6. Advice for growing as tall as you can.

# Judgment – Payback's a Bitch

**Stripped Down Overview:** For literalist Christians, this card symbolizes the resurrection of humanity where *"the dead in Christ shall rise first"*, then zoom onto eternal life in Paradise (Heaven). In that paradigm, it goes without saying where the "bad people" go. For New Agers, this is the Ascension card: awareness descends through the Crown Chakra, travels down the spine, blasts through that shit pile sitting in the Root Chakra, travels back up, wakening the rest of the energy centers...and we transform into a ball of Light, Love and Lisa Frank rainbows. For Jungians, Judgment represents a piercing wake-up call that rips open the veil of unconsciousness resulting in pure realization, integration of the psyche's four functions (Thinking, Feeling, Intuition, Sensing) and resurrection from the "sleep" of ignorance. Many Pagans connect this card to the Winter Solstice where the Sun is "reborn" every year, symbolizing renewal. For regular folks, this tends to be the *"Karma's gonna bust yo ass"* card, where we hope and pray that mean SOBs, cruel MOFOs and deceitful dicks finally get the deluxe Scorched Earth Treatment at the Cosmic Reaping Spa.

**Keywords:** Hearing a Call; Revelation; Sentencing; Epiphany; Atonement; Karma; Accountability; Consequences; Higher Purpose; Reckoning; Reaping; Past Life Echoes; Reincarnation; Comeuppance; Revelation; "Aha!" Moment; Awakening; Ascension; Triumph of Spirit; Complete Awareness; Conversion; Resurrection; Repentance; Realization

**Personifications and Embodiments:** Last Judgment; Lazarus; St. Paul's Conversion; Buddha's Enlightenment; Archangel Gabriel; St. Peter at the Pearly Gates

**Quote:** *Vocations which we wanted to pursue, and didn't, bleed, like colors, on the whole of our existence.* – Honore de Balzac

**Challenge:** Admission

**Gift:** Redemption

**Occupations/Vocations:** Past-Life Regressionist; Cemetery Worker; Trumpet Soloist; Gravestone Retailer; Red Cross

**Disney Totem:** *Jiminy Cricket* (Pinocchio)

**Animal Symbol:** Phoenix

**Flower Essences:** Spinifex (Australian Bush); Bush Iris (Australian Bush)

**Crystal/Stone:** Strawberry Quartz – Illuminates cause and effect; Shows how personality flaws can give rise to misfortune and failure. Helps ameliorate self-importance.

**Aromatherapy:** Galbanum

**Body Parts/Systems and Health Issues:** STDs; HIV; AIDS

**Mystical Messenger** – Archangel Gabriel

**Sabian Symbol:** Libra 18 – Two men placed under arrest give an accounting for their acts before the tribunal of society.

**Writing Prompt:** A penal colony for Empaths.

**Affirmation:** I recognize and rectify my mistakes.

## Naked Advice for Judgment

*Career:* The attorneys (a married couple) who leave law to take up artisan bread baking, an investment banker who exits Wall Street so she can fly high on the circus trapeze, the Pentecostal pastor who walks away from organized religion to become a New Age writer—drastic job changes can, and do, happen. One day, or over a series of days, these people realized they were in a soul-sucking job, but like a caterpillar bound by silken chains, were unable to use the wings that formed amid the miasma of their discontent. That is, until revelation descended, a clarion call rang out and they decided it was *finally* time to burst out of the cocoon to soar into their destiny. Sometimes, though, such awareness dawns gently but clearly: you wake up one day and realize that a change is needed—perhaps a radical one. It's a knowing, a *calling*...and the journey begins. Whether through a blast or a whisper, an important message has been (or soon will be) echoing between your ears. A new job, career or vocation awaits: what will you do when the time comes to dance with Fate? (Don't expect your newfound waltz to be easy—or for your cosmic tango to receive rave applause from others. When in doubt, allow peace—and relief—to give you confirmation.)

*Romance:* If this card comes up with The Tower and the 3 of Swords, I feel bad for ya. Seriously. By itself, though, it's still a rather sobering card: you will realize or discover something about the nature of love, romantic relationships, a boyfriend/girlfriend or your spouse that will forever change your perspective. In fact, it will be akin to the scene in the *Wizard of Oz* where the film transforms from sepia into glorious Technicolor. No sense in me declaring whether this discovery is "good" or "bad" because, as I discussed in the Reversals section, every card in Tarot (and, really, each situation in life) falls on a continuum—and much of its interpretation and impact depends on the story we're telling ourselves and the cards (or people/situations) surrounding it. *What will be the result? What should I do?*, you wonder. Best answer I can give you is *"it depends"*. Honestly, truly, madly, deeply... *it just depends*. Depends on where you draw the line in the sand, depends on what you're willing to put up with, depends on how much you want to sacrifice, depends on how far you want to grow, depends on what you want to experience in a relationship, depends on your confidence level, depends on your personal spiritual code, depends on your thirst for authenticity... It depends on *you*.

*Parenting*: When I was a kid, parents, teachers, pastors and other authority figures shamed the daylights out of us when it came to "tattling": *Don't be a snitch. Don't go telling on your classmate. Keep your head down and your mouth shut.* So, except for a brave few, we kept quiet. (Ironically, even those in charge often scolded those who told, heaping on further embarrassment—and pretty much cementing we wouldn't cry "foul" even if we eye-witnessed a felony act.) In fact, when I was about 13, a youth leader at church took me to the side and said, *"I hope you don't mind me telling you this—but I was just undressing you with my eyes."* Yeah, *holy shit*, right? My face got hot. I was speechless. Walked away confused as hell. I debated on what to do. It was so freakin' *humiliating*. WTF. So I told my mom. She wanted to keep it quiet. Told me to never, *ever* tell my dad (*He'll never come to church then.* Because, for her, potential "salvation" for him via a church conversion was more important than protecting me...or other girls). I pressed her to tell the pastor. She reluctantly did. The Senior Pastor listened, but I could tell he didn't take me seriously (despite having the youth group President, who believed me, accompany me to the Pastor's luxe office). Nothing was said or done to the youth leader, who continued to "serve" for years (and went on to have sexual dalliances with girls at the Christian school located at the church). My point? Be a "Deep Throat" (Mark Felt). An

Edward Snowden. A Dr. William Thompson. A Bradley/Chelsea Manning. And encourage your kids to do the same. *Transparency shall set you free.*

*Spirituality:* In many decks, the symbolism of the Judgment card features both angels and trumpets. In the RWS, an angel (some say Michael, some say Gabriel) blows a trumpet while the dead resurrect out of coffins. In the *Snowland Deck*, this card is renamed "Calling" and depicts a young member of the heavenly host relaxing on Earth after making a snow angel, trumpet in his lap. In the *Coffee Tarot*, a hand plunges upward from a freshly dug grave, mug in hand, as a flaming angel pours coffee from a carafe bearing a trumpet symbol; appropriately, this card is renamed "Wake Up Call". Sometimes, the Universe tries to get our attention much like a drill sergeant, blaring "Reveille" in our spiritual ear, telling us to wake the fuck up, change our behavior, find our balls, get back to work or make amends for egregious behavior. Other times, the bugle blows a gentle trill, reminding us of where we came from and what our true purpose is this time around. Right now a sound is calling out to your Spirit, telling you to *do the right thing.* There is no external yardstick, barometer or Geiger counter to help you figure this out (so don't bother looking to gurus, ministers or elders for this one). Here's a hint, though: Your path is as unique as a fingerprint or snowflake, as are your soul-specific lessons and personal *can't-get-away-with-anything* set of ethics. You will know what to do. Plug your ears at your own peril.

**Recommended Resources:** *Boy Caught Smoking Pipe* by Normal Rockwell; *Dexter* (TV Series); *Highway to Heaven* (TV Series); *Touched by an Angel* (TV Series); "White Lily" (Episode of *Fringe* TV Show); *Conversion of Saint Paul* by Caravaggio

**Judgment Card Layout:** *All Rise* Spread

1. What part of me is "dead"?
1a. What do I need to know about that aspect?
2. What part of me needs "resurrecting"?
2a. What do I need to know about that aspect?
3. What is Karma dealing me right now?
4. How is it connected to past behavior/choices?
5. What situation needs immediate atonement?
6. What do I need to do next (if anything) to balance remaining Karma?
7. How can I make better choices/lessen my Karma from now on?

# The World – The End. No, *Seriously.*

**Stripped Down Overview:** *Yes!* The End! Can you believe this is the last chapter I wrote for *Naked Tarot*? So not only are you at the end of your reading journey (assuming you started from the beginning of the book) and you've arrived at the last card of the Major Arcana, The World—but I'm now at the end of *my* writing journey. I consider this accomplishment under the aegis of The World because, for me, creativity is an end in itself—something that stands on its own, and to be proud of. Now, for someone who puts more stock in the final product—having the book in hand, seeing it on shelves, hearing the reactions of readers, receiving royalty checks—she may consider *those* milestones The World. The point is, this card signifies "The End"—a glorious culmination of a huge investment of time, thought, sweat and experience. Depending on the question and surrounding cards, The World can indicate world travel, a long voyage or even international issues. Interestingly, this card rarely comes up in readings—perhaps because my clients haven't set/reached any big goals as of late, or aren't in the process of completing a project or waiting for something to be finished. Rather, most are in a process of self-discovery, attempting to understand their life or trying to extricate from a knotty situation.

**Keywords:** Wholeness; Fulfillment; Completion; Ideal Outcome; Culmination; Finished; End of Cycle; Conclusion; Goal Reached; Job Well Done; Global Issues; *Done!*; Long Journey; Finale; World Travel

**Personifications and Embodiments:** When the Ball Drops in Time's Square on New Year's Eve; Last Piece of the Puzzle Put in Place; Tying It Up in a Bow; Hugh Howey Sailing the World on His Boat, "The Wayfarer"; Last World Tour; Final Showing

**Quote:** *This world is a great sculptor's shop. We are the statues and there is a rumor going around the shop that some of us are some day going to come to life.* – C. S. Lewis

**Challenge:** Complacency

**Gift:** Completion

**Occupations/Vocations:** Ambassador; UN representative; Travel Agent; Closer

**Disney Totem:** The Axiom (*Wall\*E*)

**Animal Symbol:** Sand Dollar

**Flower Essences:** Slender Rice Flower (Australian Bush); Tall Yellow Top (Australian Bush)

**Crystal/Stone:** Polychrome Tourmaline – Wholeness. Brings spirit, soul, mind and body into harmonious alignment. Helps one to recognize and control developments.

**Aromatherapy:** Sage

**Body Parts/Systems and Health Issues:** Vaccination Issues; Autism; Epidemics

**Mystical Messenger** – Atlas

**Sabian Symbol:** Pisces 24 – The tiny island seems lost in the broad ocean, but its happy inhabitants have created a world all their own.

**Writing Prompt:** A little boy discovers a ball that looks like the

Earth...but it's not a toy.

**Affirmation:** The end is here...and I'm psyched!

## Naked Advice for The World

*Career:* OMG, finally! Pat yourself on the back for a job well done. Whether you're wrapping up a long-term project, finalizing a big sale, snagging a hefty account, overseeing a consolidation or pulling off a huge event—you're *done*! Breathe a sigh of relief, laugh for joy, cry for joy and celebrate. It may feel like a dream, but it's *not*: it's really over. *Whew!* Hearty congratulations. On a different note, if you're intrigued by relocation—especially abroad—The World is basically handing you a symbolic ticket. *Go for it!* International relations and connections with worldwide colleagues/clients may also begin or increase. Happy travels!

*Romance:* OK, I don't usually advocate internet romance or romantic fishing overseas—but in your case, it's a viable option. More than viable, really. I mean, if you draw The World for a romance reading it could certainly indicate wholeness and happiness (personally, I connect that sentiment with the 2 or 10 of Cups)—but this card more likely refers to casting your net far and wide in the hopes of a love match. The relationship rivers around you are either over-fished or rather polluted, so look far and wide for a suitable partner. Be brave! Be adventurous! Grab the tiger by the tail, and you may find that the world is your love oyster.

*Parenting*: If you're concerned about Junior crossing a proverbial finish line, don't sweat it! He's got it in the bag. If his eyes are roving across borders, support him any way you can: his destiny may lie in far away lands rather than your backyard. Try not to be upset at this revelation! A parent's job is to raise a child in a

·nurturing, stable environment—so we can release them to fly into a world of their own creation. How exciting!

*Spirituality:* Wow. Just *wow*. What ever you're doing, or have done (as the case may be), it has *worked*. Integration, wholeness, fulfillment—you've finally arrived at the point where you know your place and purpose in the Universe. *Woohoo!* Keep up the good work—and continue to shine bright like a fucking diamond.

**Recommended Resources:** *Blue Planet* (DVD); *Person/Planet* by Alex Grey; *CoSM Angel* (Sculpture) by Alex Grey; *Around the World in Eighty Days* by Jules Verne

**World Card Layout:** *Got the Whole World in My Hands* Spread

1. What do I think of when I hear "the world"?
2. How does the world influence me?
3. What do I contribute to the world?
4. What global issues concern me?
5. What is now completed in my life?
6. How do I integrate it now?
7. What do I think of when I hear "The End"?
8. Final blessings

# Six Sample Readings

**Fool Card Layout:** *Leapin' Lizards* **Reading for Rachel**
(Using the *Universal Waite Tarot*):

1. *Where do I need a blank slate?* **Justice** This card suggests that some legal battle or issue needs wiping clean.

2. *What's a key ingredient to playfulness?* **4 of Swords** This card shows a sarcophagus with a knight and often connects to recuperation after illness or injury. If you've experienced a health crisis or illness lately, it may have discouraged you to the point that you've lost some lightheartedness or appreciation of the zany. You'd benefit from reframing the situation, perhaps try some meditation techniques, so that troubling thoughts (especially about any health issues) may be released rather than spun on the hamster wheel of the mind.

3. *Where do I take a leap of faith?* **Page of Pentacles** Often the "student" card, this card indicates that it's time to take a risk in the area of learning and investing in further education, even if on a small scale. This could very well apply to your child.

4. *How am I like The Fool?* **10 of Wands** "Too much is never enough" may as well be the catchphrase for this card. You're not afraid to take on one more client, one more responsibility, one more commitment. You know you can deliver, so you're unafraid and undaunted by taking on as much as you think you can handle. It never occurs to you that something could go "wrong".

*After I sent Rachel the reading, she admitted that a personal issue might go to litigation. She had been experiencing excruciating migraines (sometimes, those swords pointing to various points of the body can indicate literal pain rather than metaphorical mental aggravation), and it turns out that her daughter is flourishing in homeschool (although family members are inexplicably trying to urge her to put her child back into the public school system where she was bullied). And Rachel laughingly admitted that she works a LOT, primarily because she loves helping her author clients use social media sensibly and effectively.*

**Empress Card Layout:** *Who's Your Mommy?* **Reading for Amy**
(Using the *Morgan Greer Tarot*, Amy interpreted her own reading)

1. *What needs nourishing?* **The Emperor** I have always had a strong desire to please and care for the men in my life so this could be as simple as that

2. *How am I like a mother?* **Queen of Swords** I am like a mother in that I am a push over, a softy, as in the roses—but when the boundaries have been pushed too far you will discover I have thorns

3. *How do I feel about feminine power?* **Knight of Wands** For me, power comes from ideas and acting on those ideas, seeing what can be done to improve a situation or to achieve a desired outcome, and having that energy to see it through

4. *How am I like a wife?* **Ace of Pentacles** I am the one in our relationship who grounds us, provides the ideas and inspirations for how to manage our finances and keep ourselves from over-spending

*Amy **reported** that this was a great spread that proved very insightful, and that she'd use it again when reading for someone else.*

**Four of Wands Layout:** *Four Pillars of Community* **Reading for Becca**

*(Using The Green Witch Tarot)*

1. *Pillar One: What is the greater community that I'm an integral part of?* **The Battle Wagon (Chariot)** – Becca is a creative maverick who doesn't feel like she's a part of *any* community. She laughed when she saw The Battle Wagon, because it reflected her feelings that she belongs to an abstract "community at large", composed of artists who get shit done and don't allow anything to get in their way. She's an integral part of those who dare to create and lead the way.

2. *Pillar Two: What is the importance of this community?* **The Moon** – At first, Becca wasn't sure what this could mean. But as she gazed at the image—a figure with a staff standing before a pool of water reflecting the smiling full moon as a fish breaks the surface—she realized that the importance of artists like her was to bring the collective subconscious to the surface...and to highlight things often in the shadows or deemed "mysterious". This creative "community" was important, because it held up a mirror—a reflection—to humanity.

3. *Pillar Three: What is my role in this community?* **5 of Wands** – Becca chuckled again. "Oh, I know what *that* means!" Becca tends to "shake things up" wherever she goes—either with her unusual ideas and projects, or because she bucks the "old guard" and those with their heads buried in status-quo sands. She views such "shake ups" as vital in preventing creative and ideological stagnation. The Trickster part of her personality views this as "fun and games" especially since she holds no malice towards those she may offend.

4. *Pillar Four: How can I bless or help this community?* **6 of Athames (6 of Swords)** – "*Ahhhh...*" Becca sighed, looking at this image thoughtfully. "*This is telling me to steer clear of trouble—to avoid*

*serious conflicts that may hurt someone. I have to be careful not to take the whole 5 of Wands thing too far by venturing into 'personal' territory."*

## Tower Card Layout: *Smash, Grab and Release* Reading for Sue Ellen

*(Using the Snowland Deck):*

1. *What outmoded belief needs dismantling?* **Ace of Mental (Ace of Swords)** Ironically, the Ace Mental card is the "new idea" or "new belief" card. In this position, it's saying that you need to retire the idea that "new ideas" happen to be better, fresher and more desirable than the intellectual and analytical tools you already have. Newer doesn't mean "better".

2. *What did I gain from my last Tower experience?* **8 Emoting (8 of Cups)** You were able to jettison your worries and actually relax because the last Tower experience served as a lid blowing off a boiling pot, bringing with it calm and release.

3. *How am I prepared to handle the unexpected?* **Ace of Energy (Ace of Wands)** You are extremely resourceful when it comes to starting new things, because passion and a sense of purpose fuels you. It's as if you have this "oh well" mindset in the face of the unexpected, and you just get in there, light a torch, use the rubble as stepping stones and then forge ahead on a new endeavor. What a gift!

4. *What needs immediate release?* **Temperance** This card suggests to me that you're trying to be "all things to all people" by demanding excellence of yourself. Like a computer program running in the background (one that's not obvious or on the toolbar/desktop), it's draining you energetically. Release the need to "toe the line" in your endeavors but cutting yourself

some major slack. As the saying goes, "All things in moderation, including moderation".

**The Star Card Layout:** *I'm a Star* **Reading for Jamme**
(*Using the Snowland Deck*):

1. *What am I idealizing right now?* **2 Material (2 of Coins)** – This card shows a white sea lion watching two walruses keeping three balls aloft. The image suggests that you're idealizing group belonging and inclusion (maybe a professional organization?), perhaps assuming that if you were "given the ball", you could (finally) prove your worth.

2. *What area of my life could use some hope or restoration?* **8 Energy (8 of Wands)** – We all like to receive good news, but perhaps you've experienced a deluge of disappointing messages lately. Because of the "swift communication" aspect, this card suggests that you've been discouraged by the misuse of the internet, social media or other electronic transmissions. And, you may even feel like these outlets are more trouble than beneficial.

3. *What do I need to know about my spiritual advancement?* **Director – Material (King of Coins)** – Since you own a restaurant, this "Ebenezer Scrooge enlightened" card tells me that your own spiritual advancement is tied in with how you conduct your business, treat your employees and care for your customers. You're working out your spiritual path most effectively within the minutia of your business.

4. *Where do I fit into the web of humanity at this time?* **Inversion (Hanged Man)** – I can't help but feel this ties into the 2 Material card. The Hanged Man says you do *not* fit (neatly) into the web of humanity; that is, you see things differently from most people. Thus, you're not one to fit into any uniform packages of expectation or convention. This ability to see things from

unusual and fresh angles not only allows you to innovate, but to provide sparkling solutions to everyday problems.

*After I send Jamme the reading, he wrote: This is highly accurate and written as if you were a little bird on my shoulder watching me go about my daily life! I feel dedicated to spiritualizing business by folding the welfare of others within my own. I want to do this more and more! The Hanged Man representing how I fit into the web of humanity as you described it is highly accurate because as a gay guy and as a spiritual person, I've never felt that I fit into the normal human life of eating, drinking, sleeping, working, playing, having sex and then doing it all over again. I have always questioned whatever I do and I feel that doing all of those things I mentioned is the life of an animal. But how are we more than that? As a gay guy, I've always felt that I am an observer of humanity and not as much a participant because I have lived outside of the life of a family and outside of what the expectations of the society are for me.*

# Bibliography

Alexander, Skye. *The Secret Power of Spirit Animals*. Avon, Massachusetts: Adams Media, 2013.

Andrews, Ted. *Animal Speak*. St. Paul, Minnesota: Llewellyn Publications, 1993.

Andrews, Ted. *Simplified Qabala Magic*. St. Paul, Minnesota: Llewellyn, Publications, 2003.

Banzhaf, Hajo. *Tarot and the Journey of the Hero*. York Beach, Maine. Samuel Weiser, Inc., 2000.

Blome, Gotz. *Advanced Bach Flower Therapy: A Scientific Approach to Diagnosis and Treatment*. Rochester, Vermont: Healing Arts Press, 1999.

Boyer, Janet. *Back in Time Tarot*. Charlottesville, Virginia: Hampton Roads Publishing Company, 2008.

Boyer, Janet. *Tarot in Reverse: Making Sense of the Upside Down Cards in a Tarot Spread*. Atglen, Pennsylvania: Schiffer Publishing, 2012.

Burnie, David and Don E. Wilson, Editors-in-Chief. *Animal*. New York, New York: DK Publishing, 2005.

Carr-Gomm, Philip and Stephanie. *The DruidCraft Tarot Companion*. New York, New York: St. Martin's Press, 2004.

Case, Paul Foster. *The Tarot: A Key to the Wisdom of the Ages*. New York, New York: Jeremy Tarcher/Penguin, 2006.

Cirlot, J.E. *A Dictionary of Symbols*. New York, New York: Philosophical Library, Inc., 1962.

Cunningham, Scott. *Cunningham's Encyclopedia of Crystal, Gem and Metal Magic*. St. Paul, Minnesota: Llewellyn Publications, 2003.

Decker, Ronald. *The Esoteric Tarot: Ancient Sources Rediscovered in Hermeticism and Cabala*. Wheaton, Illinois: Quest Books, 2013.

Docters van Leeuwen, Onno and Rob. *The Complete New Tarot*. New York, New York: Sterling Publishing Co. Inc., 2001.

Donaldson, Terry. *Step-by-Step Tarot*. London, England: Thorsons, 1995.

Farmer, Steven D. *Animal Spirit Guides*. Carlsbad, California: Hay house, 2006.

Finander, Lisa. *Disneystrology*. Philadelphia, PA: Quirk Books, 2010.

Gienger, Michael. *Healing Crystals: The A-Z Guide to 555 Gemstones*. Forres, Scotland: Findhorn Press, Ltd., 2014.

Goldstein, David B. and Otto Kroeger. *Creative You: Using Your Personality Type to Thrive*. New York, New York: Atria, 2013.

Grothe, Mardy. *I Never Metaphor I Didn't Like*. New York, New York: HarperCollins, 2008.

Hall, Judy. *Crystal Prescriptions*. Alresford, Hants, UK: O Books, 2006.

Hall, Judy. *Crystal Prescriptions 2*. Alresford, Hants, UK: O Books, 2014.

Hall, Judy. *The Crystal Zodiac*. London, England: Godsfield Press, 2004.

Hayford, Jack W., Gen. Ed. *Spirit-Filled Life Bible (NKJV)*. Nashville, TN: Thomas Nelson Publishers, 1991.

Hederman, Mark Patrick. *Tarot: Talisman or Taboo?*. Dublin, Ireland: Currach Press, 2003.

Hill, Lynda. *360 Degrees of Wisdom: Charting Your Destiny with the Sabian Oracle*. New York, New York: Plume, 2004.

Houtzager, Guus. *The Complete Encyclopedia of Greek Mythology*. Edison, New Jersey: Chartwell Books, Inc., 2003.

Huson, Paul. *Mystical Origins of the Tarot*. Rochester, Vermont: Destiny Books, 2004.

Illes, Judika. *Encyclopedia of Mystics, Saints & Sages*. San Francisco, California: HarperOne, 2011.

Illes, Judika. *Encyclopedia of Spirits*. San Francisco, California: HarperOne, 2009.

Jordan, Michael. *Dictionary of Gods and Goddesses*. New York, New York: Checkmark Books, 2004.

Keirsey, David. *Please Understand Me II*. Del Mar, California: Prometheus Nemesis Book Company, 1998.

Kliegman, Isabel Radow. *Tarot and the Tree of Life: Finding Everyday Wisdom in the Minor Arcana*. Wheaton, Illinois: Quest Books, 1997.

Krafchow, Dovid. *Kabbalistic Tarot: Hebraic Wisdom in the Major and Minor Arcana*. Rochester, Vermont: Inner Traditions, 2005.

Loar, Julie. *Goddesses for Every Day*. Novato, California: New World Library, 2011.

Lilly, Sue and Simon Lilly. *Healing with Crystals and Chakra Energies*. New York, New York: Barnes and Noble Books, 2005.

Matthews, John and Wil Kinghan. *The Sherlock Holmes Tarot Companion*. New York, New York: Sterling Ethos, 2014.

Mercatante, Anthony S. and James R. Dow. *The Facts on File Encyclopedia of World Mythology and Legend (2nd Edition) Volume I A-L*. New York, New York: Facts on File, Inc., 2004.

Mercatante, Anthony S. and James R. Dow. *The Facts on File Encyclopedia of World Mythology and Legend (2nd Edition) Volume II M-Z*. New York, New York: Facts on File, Inc., 2004.

Monaghan, Patricia. *Encyclopedia of Goddesses and Heroines*. Novato, California: New World Library, 2014.

Myss, Caroline. *Sacred Contracts: Awakening Your Divine Potential*. New York, New York: Harmony Books, 2001.

Peschek-Bohmer, Dr. Flora and Gisela Schreiber. *Healing Crystals and Gemstones*. Munich, Germany: W. Ludwig Buchverlag, 2002.

Raine, Amythyst. *Tarot for Grownups*. Alresford, U.K.: Dodona Books, 2013.

Rath, Tom. *Strengthsfinder 2.0*. New York, New York: Gallup Press, 2007.

Reed, Ellen Cannon. *The Witches Qabala: The Pagan Path and the Tree of Life*. York Beach, Maine: Red Wheel/Weiser, LLC, 1997.

Richards, Chip. *The Secret Language of Animals Oracle Cards*. Glen Waverly, Victoria, Australia: Blue Angel Gallery, 2013.

Riso, Don Richard and Russ Hudson. *Discovering Your Personality Type: The Enneagram Questionnaire.* New York, New York: 1995.

Riso, Don Richard and Russ Hudson. *Personality Types: Using the Enneagram for Self-Discovery.* New York, New York: Houghton Mifflin Company, 1996.

Riso, Don Richard and Russ Hudson. *Understanding the Enneagram.* New York, New York: Houghton Mifflin Company, 2000.

Riso, Don Richard and Russ Hudson. *The Wisdom of the Enneagram: The Complete Guide to Psychological and Spiritual Growth for the Nine Personality Types.* New York, New York: Bantam Books, 1999.

Sargent, Carl. *Personality, Divination, and the Tarot.* Rochester, Vermont: Destiny Books, 1988.

Seich, Sandra. *3 Sides of You: Unlocking the Way You Think, Work, and Love.* Huntsville, AL: ANSIR Publishing Corporation, 2000.

Sharp, Damian. *Simple Numerology.* Berkeley, California: Conari Press, 2001.

Todd, Mabel Loomis and T.W. Higginson, Editors. *Collected Poems of Emily Dickinson.* New York, New York: Avenel Books, 1982.

Trobe, Kala. *Magic of Qabalah: Visions of the Tree of Life.* St. Paul, Minnesota: Llewellyn Publications, 2001.

Vennells, David F. *Bach Flower Remedies for Beginners: 38 Essences That Heal from Deep Within.* St. Paul, Minnesota: Llewellyn, 2001.

Vega, Phyllis. *Numerology for Baby Names.* New York, New York: Dell Publishing, 1998.

Walker, Barbara G. *The Woman's Dictionary of Symbols and Sacred Objects.* San Francisco, California: HarperSanFrancisco, 1988.

White, Ian. *Australian Bush Flower Essences.* Scotland, UK: Findhorn Press, 1998.

Woolfolk, Joanna Martine. *The Only Astrology Book You'll Ever*

*Need.* Lanham, Maryland: Madison Books, 2001.

Worwood, Valerie Ann. *Aromatherapy for the Soul: Healing the Spirit with Fragrance and Essential Oils.* Novato, California: New World Library, 1999.

Worwood, Valerie Ann. *The Fragrant Mind: Aromatherapy for Personality, Mind, Mood, and Emotion.* Novato, California: New World Library, 1996.

Dodona Books

# ASTROLOGY, NUMEROLOGY AND GENERAL DIVINATION

The priestesses and priests received the oracles of the Dodona shrine through the rustling leaves of the sacred oak tree. The oracle was an early form of divination, and divination has existed perhaps as long as humankind itself. We use divination to foresee future possibilities, to answer questions about our lives, to explain the unexplainable, for revealing hidden dynamics in ourselves and others, for personal growth and to guide us onto the right pathway through life. Dodona Books offers a broad spectrum of divination systems to suit all, including Astrology, Tarot, Runes, Ogham, Palmistry, Dream Interpretation, Scrying, Dowsing, I Ching, Numerology, Angels and Faeries, Tasseomancy and Introspection.
If you have enjoyed this book, why not tell other readers by posting a review on your preferred book site.

# Recent bestsellers from Dodona Books are:

### Palmistry: From Apprentice to Pro in 24 Hours
The Easiest Palmistry Course Ever Written
Johnny Fincham
Now anyone who wishes to can learn the secrets of Palmistry in this no-nonsense guide.
Paperback: 978-1-84694-047-7 ebook: 978-1-84694-644-8

### Numerology Made Easy
Hilary H. Carter
2012. 666. Sometimes a number speaks a thousand words. This user-friendly guide to numerology teaches you to decode the language of numbers.
Paperback: 978-1-84694-717-9 ebook: 978-1-84694-718-6

### Let the Numbers Guide You
The Spiritual Science of Numerology
Shiv Charan Singh
One of the oldest arts of Divination, Numerology can be found at the core of many religions. This book helps to rediscover the spiritual importance of using numbers.
Paperback: 978-1-90381-664-6

### How to Survive a Pisces
Mary English
From the successful series on the signs of the Zodiac, How to Survive a Pisces helps you avoid common mishaps associated with relationships with a Pisces.
Paperback: 978-1-84694-252-5 ebook: 978-1-84694-658-5

## The Syzygy Oracle

Transformational Tarot and The Tree of Life, The Ego, Essence
and the Evolution of Consciousness
Heather Mendel
In image and word, this primer on Kabbalah, Tarot and
conscious evolution offers daily spiritual practices for
developing trust in our intuitive wisdom.
Paperback: 978-1-78279-160-7 ebook: 978-1-78279-159-1

## How to Read an Egg

Divination for the Easily Bored
Colette Brown
You've tried tarot, ruminated with the runes and are angel-
carded out! Now try the lesser-known forms of Divination.
Paperback: 978-1-78099-839-8 ebook: 978-1-78099-838-1

## When Will You Find Love?

Your Astrological Guide to When, Where and Who You'll Love
Orli Lysen
Why leave love to chance when the planets can show when -
and where - you'll meet 'the one'?
Paperback: 978-1-78099-532-8 ebook: 978-1-78099-533-5

## The Transformational Truth of Tarot

The Fool's Journey
Tiffany Crosara
If you've been in search of a book revealing the deep
transformational power of Tarot for healing, look no further
than The Transformational Truth of Tarot.
Paperback: 978-1-78099-636-3 ebook: 978-1-78099-637-0

Readers of ebooks can buy or view any of these bestsellers by clicking on the live link in the title. Most titles are published in paperback and as an ebook. Paperbacks are available in traditional bookshops. Both print and ebook formats are available online.

Find more titles and sign up to our readers' newsletter at http://www.johnhuntpublishing.com/mind-body-spirit. Follow us on Facebook at https://www.facebook.com/OBooks and Twitter at https://twitter.com/obooks.